TIMES • CHAMBERS

F·I·R·S·T LEARNERS DICTIONARY

SECOND EDITION

Compiler Andrea Ender
Editor Anne Seaton

FEDERAL PUBLICATIONS • CHAMBERS

Preface

This dictionary is intended for schoolchildren in the six- to nine-year-old age group, who are becoming used to being taught in English, and need to consolidate their knowledge of the words they meet in class in a way that will help them, from the start, to use them idiomatically.

The editors have selected a vocabulary of approximately 3000 basic English words, some with associated phrases, and these have been defined in simple language addressed directly to the child. In every case the definitions are followed by one or more examples of usage taking the form of whole sentences. These either reflect or develop the definition, or show some of the typical uses that a child might meet.

The vocabulary used in both definitions and examples is well within the 3000-word scope of the dictionary, and the content of the examples is drawn from the experiences and situations that a young child is likely to be familiar with, whether in everyday life or in story-books.

There are no grammatical labels such as *n* for noun, *adj* for adjective, and so on — these might be intimidating for young children — but where a word is used, say, both as a verb and a noun, the two parts of speech are given separate entries. Parts of irregular verbs have individual entries also, showing which 'root verb' they come from — so that children can easily locate it in the dictionary — and giving brief examples of use.

Many entries are followed by short, simple notes. Some of these help with the spelling of parts of verbs, plurals of nouns, and comparatives and superlatives of adjectives; others tell the children words that mean the same as, or the opposite to, the word they are looking at; others again help with difficult pronunciations.

Finally, the two-colour illustrations provided throughout the text will help children to identify objects and understand concepts defined in the dictionary, and add to their interest and enjoyment as they look through the pages.

This edition first published 1989 by
Federal Publications (S) Pte Ltd
A member of the Times Publishing Group
Times Centre, 1 New Industrial Road, Singapore 536196
by arrangement with W & R Chambers Ltd Edinburge

Reprinted 1990, 1991 (twice), 1992 (twice)
1993 (thrice), 1994, 1995, 1996, 1997

ISBN 981 01 0079 5

Printed by Kin Keong Co Pte Ltd, Singapore.

Using this dictionary

Words in a dictionary are arranged in the same order as the letters of the alphabet. The words beginning with **A** all come before the words beginning with **B**, and the words beginning with the letters **ab** come before the words beginning with the letters **ac**.

You can see here that **ab**sent *comes before* **ac**cept.

absent
away; not present: *Many pupils are* ***absent*** *from school because they are ill.*

- The opposite is **present**.

accept
1 to take something that is given to you: *Please* ***accept*** *this present from us.* **2** to say 'yes' to an invitation: *Mary invited me to her party and I* ***accepted****.*

- The opposite is **refuse**.

Under the word you will find its meaning. The meaning ends with this sign :

Here you can read the meaning of **visible**.

visible
able to be seen: *The moon is not* ***visible*** *tonight, because it is covered by clouds. A ship was* ***visible*** *on the horizon.*

Some words have two short meanings divided by this sign ;

Here you can read two meanings of **stale**.

stale
not fresh; too old to eat: *We took some* ***stale*** *bread to the park to give to the ducks. The orange juice will go* ***stale*** *if you don't keep it in the fridge.*

- The opposite is **fresh**.

Many words have several separate meanings, each with its own number.

Here you see two meanings of **remind**, *marked 1 and 2.*

remind
1 to make you remember something: ***Remind*** *me to ring Alice tomorrow. Mum* ***reminded*** *me that I still hadn't written to Granny* **2** to make you think of someone or something: *Miss Smith always* ***reminds*** *me of my aunt because she looks very like her.*

After the meaning of the word, you will find one or more sentences printed in sloping letters. The word is contained in the sentences and is printed in thick black letters. The sentences tell you more about the word and show you how to use it.

moon
the large shining object that you see in the sky at night, that moves round the earth, and changes shape as the nights pass: *The* ***moon*** *hasn't got any light of its own — it looks bright because the sun is shining on it. Every four weeks there is a full* ***moon****, when the* ***moon*** *looks like a silver ball.*

These sentences tell you more about the word **moon**.

There are very common ways of using some words. The dictionary helps you to learn them.

Here you find **by accident** *under the word* **accident**. *Its meaning is beside it, and then two sentences showing how it is used.*

accident
something bad that happens, when people sometimes get hurt: *The bus crashed into the wall, but no-one was hurt in the* ***accident****.*
by accident by chance; when you don't expect it: *I found this ring* ***by accident*** *when I was looking for something else. I met Kate* ***by accident*** *in the supermarket.*

There are lots of notes in the dictionary that help you to speak and spell words.

With most 'doing' words, called 'verbs', you can add **-ed** and **-ing** without changing the spelling of the word. For example, with **walk**, you say 'he **walked**, he is **walking**, he has **walked**'. This dictionary tells you if a verb changes its spelling.

This note tells you that **lying** *is spelt with* **y**, *not* **ie.**

chat
to talk with someone in an easy, friendly way: *My mother and the lady next door like* ***chatting*** *about their families. In Britain, people* ***chat*** *about the weather a lot.*

- chatted, chatting, has chatted

lie
to tell a lie: *I know you've been* ***lying*** *— please tell me the truth now. The man* ***lied*** *to the police about the robbery.*

- lied, lying, has lied

wade
to walk through deep water: *Peter's ball fell into the river and he* ***waded*** *into the water to fetch it back.*

- waded, wading, has waded

This note tells you that you add a **t** *to* **chat** *before adding* **-ed** *and* **-ing**

This note tells you that **wading** *has no* **e** *in it.*

Some verbs change a lot.

This note shows you that you must say 'he **bought***' not 'he* **buyed***'.*

This note tells you that you must say 'he **swam***', not 'he* **swimmed***'; 'he has* **swum***', not 'he has* **swimmed***', and it also tells you that you add an* **m** *to* **swim** *before adding* **-ing**.

When you look at **bought** in the dictionary, the words see **buy** tell you it belongs to the verb **buy**.

When you look at **swam** and **swum** in the dictionary, the words see **swim** tell you that they belong to the verb **swim**.

buy
to get something by paying for it with money: *I should like to* ***buy*** *a new radio but I don't have enough money. My aunt* ***bought*** *me an interesting book for my birthday. Joe has* ***bought*** *himself a football.*

- The opposite is **sell**.
- bought, buying, has bought

swim
to keep yourself floating in water, and move along using your arms and legs; to move through water the way a fish does: *Can you* ***swim****? I'm going* ***swimming*** *this afternoon. We watched the fish* ***swimming*** *about in the aquarium.*

- swam, swimming, has swum

bought
see **buy**: *Sarah* ***bought*** *some flowers for her granny. Our parents have* ***bought*** *a new car.*

swam
see **swim**: *The boy* ***swam*** *across the river.*

swum
see **swim**: *I've never* ***swum*** *in a river before — is it safe?*

With most words that are names of things, you can add **-s** or **-es** without changing the spelling of the word. For example, you say 'lots of **books**', 'a few **foxes**'. This dictionary tells you some words that change their spelling.

baby

• Two **babies**

*This note tells you to change the **y** in **baby** to **i** before adding **-es**.*

mouse

a small animal with grey or white fur and a long tail: *A **mouse** eats all kinds of seeds and fruit. Some **mice** live in people's houses and some live in fields. A **mouse** squeaks when it is frightened.*

• Lots of **mice**

*This note tells you to say 'lots of **mice**', not 'lots of **mouses**'.*

With most 'describing' words, you can add **-er** and **-est** without changing the spelling of the word.

For example, with **tall,** you say 'Jane is **taller** than Jean, but Janet is the **tallest** of the three'. This dictionary tells you some of the 'describing' words that change their spelling.

fat

large, heavy and round in shape; not slim: *You will get **fat** if you go on eating too much. Mrs Green has the **fattest** cat I've ever seen.*

• The opposite is **thin**.
• fat, fatter, fattest

*This note tells you to add a **t** to **fat** before adding **-er** and **-est**.*

funny

1 amusing; making you laugh: *Peter told us a **funny** story about his puppy. The clown in the circus did a lot of **funny** tricks.* **2** strange: *I heard a **funny** noise coming from the flat above. There is a **funny** smell in the kitchen.*

• funny, funnier, funniest

*This note tells you to change the **y** in funny to **i** before adding **-er** and **-est**.*

With longer 'describing' words you don't add **-er** and **-est**; you have to use **more** and **most**. For example, you say 'An alligator is **enormous**, a hippo is **more enormous**, but an elephant is the **most enormous** of the three'.

When you look at some words, you don't know how to say them. The notes in the dictionary will help you with words that are difficult to say.

plough

a large farming tool that is pulled through the soil to break it up: *In the past, oxen or horses were used for pulling a **plough**, but nowadays most people use tractors.*

• Rhymes with **cow**.

*This note tells you that **plough** rhymes with **cow**. So you say 'plow'.*

bouquet

a nicely arranged bunch of flowers for carrying: *The bride carried a **bouquet** of red roses.*

• Say boo-**kay**.

*This note tells you what **bouquet** should sound like. The part of the word in thick black letters has a longer, stronger sound than the rest of the word.*

Some notes tell you a word that means the opposite to the word you are looking at.

This note tells you that the opposite of ***war*** *is* ***peace****.*

war
fighting between countries: *How long have these two countries been at* ***war****? Many soldiers were killed in the* ***war****.*

- The opposite is **peace**.

Some notes tell you a word that means the same as the word you are looking at.

This note tells you that ***burglar*** *means the same as* ***thief****.*

thief
a person who steals: *The* ***thief*** *stole the man's wallet.* ***Thieves*** *broke into the shop and stole all the precious jewellery.*

- Same as **burglar**.
- Two **thieves**

Some notes belong to only one meaning of a word.

This note tells you that ***hard*** *is the opposite of the first meaning of* ***soft****, and* ***loud*** *is the opposite of the third meaning of* ***soft****.*

soft
1 not hard; not form: *Cotton wool is very* ***soft****. Clay is* ***soft*** *when it's still wet. It's nice to sleep on a* ***soft*** *pillow.* **2** smooth and pleasant to touch: *What lovely* ***soft*** *fur this little kitten has!* **3** not loud: *I can't hear what you're saying when you speak in such a* ***soft*** *voice.*

- Meaning 1: the opposite is **hard**.
- Meaning 3: the opposite is **loud**.

There are lots of words in English that you can join together. For example, you can say **he'll** instead of **he will**.

This note tells you that you can say ***I'm*** *instead of* ***I am*** *and that you say* ***aren't I*** *in questions.*

am
you use **am** with **I**: *I* ***am*** *seven years old. I'****m*** *a good swimmer.* ***Am*** *I good enough to be chosen for the team? I'****m*** *doing my homework.*

- You can shorten **I am** to **I'm**.
- You turn **am not** into **aren't** in questions: ***Aren't*** *I looking smart today?*

Other notes give you other kinds of information.

This note tells you the difference between a ***pony*** *and a* ***foal****.*

pony
a small kind of horse: *Mr Martin has bought a* ***pony*** *for his children to learn to ride on.*

- Lots of **ponies**.
- A pony is a small horse, not a baby horse. A baby horse is a **foal**.

Aa

a or an
1 one: *Jenny has **a** new bicycle.* 2 any; every: *A cat can see in the dark.* 3 for each: *Michael works in the supermarket and earns $6 **an** hour.*

- **an** is used before words that begin with **a**, **e**, **i**, **o**, **u**: **an** animal; **an** elephant; **an** idea; **an** old man; **an** uncle.
- **an** is also used before **h** when you can't hear the **h**: **an** hour; **an** honest girl.
- **a** is used before all other letters: **a** book; **a** house.
- **a** is also used before **u** when it sounds like **you**: **a** useful tool.

a lot of a large number of something; a large amount of something: *What **a lot of** toys you have! John ate **a lot of** ice-cream. I've **a lot of** work to do.*

ability
being able to do something: *Small babies do not have the **ability** to walk.*

Many **abilities**

able
1 having the power to do something: *Will you be **able** to carry that heavy box all by yourself? Is Philip **able** to swim yet? I tried to find out Steven's new address, but I wasn't **able** to.* 2 clever: *Susan is a very **able** pupil.*

about
1 on the subject of: *Tell me **about** your holiday. What is the film **about**?* 2 not exactly, but nearly: *Paul lives **about** two miles from his school. Peter said he would arrive at **about** three o'clock. We're just **about** ready to go out now.* 3 here and there: *Don't leave your clothes lying **about**! The children ran **about** the playground.*

above
higher than something: *When I go swimming, I like to keep my head **above** water. Your nose is **above** your mouth. People look small when seen from **above**.*

The opposite is **below** or **beneath**.

abroad
to another country; in another country: *Last year we went **abroad** for our holidays. Sally's brother has lived **abroad** for many years.*

absence
being away; not being present: *Your teacher has to go away for two weeks, and in her **absence** Mrs Lee will be teaching you.*

absent
away; not present: *Many pupils are **absent** from school because they are ill.*

The opposite is **present**.

accept
1 to take something that is given to you: *Please **accept** this present from us.* 2 to say 'yes' to an invitation: *Mary invited me to her party and I **accepted**.*

The opposite is **refuse**.

accident

something bad that happens, when people sometimes get hurt: *The bus crashed into the wall, but no-one was hurt in the **accident**.*
by accident by chance; when you don't expect it: *I found this ring **by accident** when I was looking for something else. I met Kate **by accident** in the supermarket.*

accompany
to go with someone: *Jenny has to go home because she feels sick — please will you **accompany** her, Lisa?*

accompanied, accompanying, has accompanied

ache
a pain that lasts for a long time: *I've got tooth**ache.** My sister is in bed with a stomach-**ache**.*

ache
to have a pain that lasts for a long time: *My tooth **ached**. John says his head is **aching**.*

- Rhymes with **take**.
- ached, aching, has ached

acrobat
a person who performs difficult gymnastics: *The **acrobat** in the circus walked on his hands and balanced a glass on his head at the same time.*

across
1 from one side of something to the other side of it: *Jenny swam **across** the swimming pool. If the street is busy, don't run **across.** The fallen tree lay **across** the path.* **2** on the other side of something: *Our house is **across** the river.*

act
1 to do something: *Dad had to **act** quickly when he saw the baby crawling on to the road.* **2** to play a part in a film or play: *Nicola **acted** the part of the princess in the play.*

act
1 something that you do: *Running across the road is a foolish **act**.* **2** a performance: *The clown performed a funny **act** on television.*

action
1 a movement that you make: *Lifting your arm is an **action.** Some songs have **actions** as well as words.* **2** something that you do: *The fireman's quick **action** saved the little girl's life.*

actor
a person who acts in a film or play; a man who acts in a film or play: *An **actor** has to learn his words before he can act his part.*

actress
a woman who acts in a film or play: *Sally would like to be a film **actress** when she grows up.*

actual
real: *Everyone calls him Bill, but his **actual** name is William.*

add

1 to put one thing with another: *Jane **added** sugar to her tea.* **2** to find how much numbers make when they are put together: *If you **add** two and two you get four. When you **add** 37 to 50, the total is 87.*

The opposite is **subtract**.

add up to put several numbers together: *I **added up** the cost of each present to find out how much money I had spent.*

addition
the part of arithmetic to do with adding: *I like doing **addition**, but subtraction is harder.*

The opposite is **subtraction**.

address
the number of the house and the name of the street and town where a person lives: *His **address** is 30 Main Street, Edinburgh. Mark wrote the **addresses** of his friends in his **address** book.*

admire
1 to look at something with great delight; to say that you like something very much: *Ann's friends all **admired** her new bicycle. All our neighbours have been **admiring** our new car today.* **2** to like and respect someone or something very much: *I **admire** Helen for being so brave. I **admire** her courage.*

admired, admiring, has admired

adult
a grown-up person: *You may not drive a car until you are an **adult.***

The opposite is a **child**.

advantage
something that is useful; something that helps you: *It is an **advantage** to be able to speak more than one language.*

adventure
something exciting that you do or that happens to you: *I'm reading a book about the **adventures** of three children who got lost in the jungle.*

advertise
to put a notice in a newspaper telling people that you need something, or want to sell something: *Mr Lee's restaurant is* ***advertising*** *for a new waiter. Dad wants to sell our house, so he has* ***advertised*** *it in the newspaper.*

> advertised, advertising, has advertised

advertisement

1 a notice in a newspaper telling people that you want something or have something to sell: *Our father has put an* ***advertisement*** *in the paper because he wants to sell his old car.* **2** a big notice on a wall, or a picture in a magazine, or a very short film on television, that tries to make you buy something: *I saw an* ***advertisement*** *for a new kind of toothpaste on television.*

> Called an **ad** or an **advert** for short.

advice
helpful ideas from someone about what you should do: *Let me give you a piece of* ***advice*** *about how to train for the race. The doctor's* ***advice*** *to the patient was to drink a lot of water.*

advise
to give advice to someone: *The teacher* ***advised*** *her pupils to work harder if they wanted to pass their examinations.*

> advised, advising, has advised

aeroplane
a machine that flies through the air and carries passengers: *Mr Lee went by* ***aeroplane*** *from Singapore to Canberra.* ***Aeroplanes*** *land and take off at airports.*

> Also called a **plane**.

afford
to have enough money to be able to buy something: *My father cannot* ***afford*** *to buy a car. Can you* ***afford*** *a new record-player?*

afraid
frightened: *Are you* ***afraid*** *of snakes? Susan was* ***afraid*** *of jumping into the swimming-pool. Joan was* ***afraid*** *when she heard the thunder.*

after
1 later than something or someone else: *We went shopping* ***after*** *lunch. We arrived at the party* ***after*** *all the other guests.* **2** behind: *Remember to close the gate* ***after*** *you! The pupils entered the classroom, one* ***after*** *another.* **3** trying to catch up with someone or something: *The policeman ran* ***after*** *the thief. Lorna rushed* ***after*** *the ball.*

> Meaning 1: the opposite is **before**.

afternoon
the time between midday and evening: *We start school at 9 o'clock in the morning and go home at 3 o'clock in the* ***afternoon.*** *We're going to the library this* ***afternoon****.*

afterwards
later; after something: *We did our homework first, and went swimming* ***afterwards****.*

again
once more; another time: *Last week, we went swimming on Monday and* ***again*** *on Thursday. I didn't hear what you said — would you say it* ***again****, please?*

against
1 touching something: *The rain splashed* ***against*** *the window.* **2** on the opposite side to someone else: *Every year, two schools play a football match* ***against*** *each other.*

age
the number of years you have lived: *What* ***age*** *are you? My little sister began to walk at the* ***age*** *of one.*

agent
1 a spy: *James Bond is a famous secret* ***agent****.* **2** someone who does some business for you: *The travel* ***agent*** *booked seats on the plane for us.*

ago
at a time in the past: *I visited Malaysia five years* ***ago****. Long* ***ago****, people lived in caves.*

agree
1 to think the same as someone else: *My sister thinks this skirt is too long, and my brother* ***agrees*** *with her. Do you always* ***agree*** *with what your parents say?* **2** to say that you will

do something that you have been asked to do; to say 'yes' to something: *Mark* ***agreed*** *to help us. I* ***agreed*** *to Diana's plan.*

The opposite is **disagree**.

ahead
in front: *Mary was walking too slowly, so Tim went on* ***ahead*** *of her. Go straight* ***ahead,*** *and you will come to the school.*

aim

1 to point a weapon at something or someone: *The thief* ***aimed*** *a gun at the shopkeeper.* **2** to try to do something: *We must* ***aim*** *at finishing this work by next week. We* ***aim*** *to do well in our exams.*

air
1 the thing all around us that we breathe: *Humans cannot live without* ***air***. **2** the space above the ground; the sky: *Peter kicked the football high into the* ***air***.
by air in an aircraft: *We shall travel* ***by air*** *from Singapore to Penang.*

air
1 to let fresh air into the room: *Mike opened all the windows to* ***air*** *the room.* **2** to put something out into the air to get dry or fresh: *Sarah took her clothes out of the case and hung them up to* ***air*** *before she put them in the cupboard.*

air-conditioner
a machine which keeps the air cool and dry in a room or building: *We have to use our* ***air-conditioner*** *in very hot weather.*

aircraft
a machine that can fly: *Aeroplanes and helicopters are two different kinds of* ***aircraft.*** *We flew to Delhi in a large* ***aircraft.*** *Several* ***aircraft*** *were waiting to take off.*

air-hostess
a woman who looks after passengers in an aircraft: *If you want anything to drink, ask the* ***air-hostess.***

airline
a company that owns aircraft on which people travel: *Cathay Pacific, Thai International and MAS are the names of some* ***airlines***.

airliner

a large aircraft that is used for carrying passengers: *This* ***airliner*** *has 200 seats.*

airmail
mail that is sent by aeroplane: *Do you want to send this letter by* ***airmail*** *or surface mail?*

Mail sent by train and ship is called **surface mail**.

airport
the place that aircraft arrive at and depart from: *The plane landed at the* ***airport*** *five minutes late.*

airy
with plenty of fresh air: *Kate has a big* ***airy*** *room with three windows.*

alarm
something that warns people of danger: *When the old man saw the smoke coming from the building, he rang the fire-****alarm*** *and the firemen came and put out the fire.*

alarm clock a clock that makes a loud noise, to wake you up: *I always set my* ***alarm clock*** *for seven o'clock, so that I can get to school on time.*

alarm
to make someone afraid: *The thunder and lightning* ***alarmed*** *the little boy.*

album
a kind of book in which you put stamps or photographs that you have collected: *Granny*

*showed me some old **albums** with pictures of Dad as a small boy.*

alight

to get out of a vehicle: *All the passengers **alighted** from the bus when it reached the city centre.*

The opposite is **board**.

alike
1 like one another; similar: *The twins are very **alike**.* **2** in the same way: *The teacher treated all the pupils **alike**.*

Meaning 1: same as **similar**.

alive
living; not dead: *The cat was hit by a car, but she is still **alive**.*

The opposite is **dead**.

all
1 the whole of something: *Mark and Bill ate **all** the cake and didn't give any of it to us. I have been working **all** day and I'm very tired.* **2** everyone: *Well done! You have **all** passed the exam. **All** the eggs are broken.*

The opposite is **none**.

all at once **1** suddenly: ***All at once** there was a loud bang.* **2** all at the same time: *Don't eat **all** your sweets **at once** or you'll be sick!*
all by yourself without any help: *Did Jane make those paper flowers **all by herself**?*
all over **1** in all parts of: *Mr Jones has friends **all over** the world.* **2** finished: *When the fun was **all over**, the children went home.*
all over again once more; a second time: *Jim made a lot of mistakes in his homework, so he had to do it **all over again**.*
all right **1** not hurt; well; okay: *Andy fell off his bicycle, but he said he was **all right**. You look ill — are you **all right**?* **2** yes: *'Do you want to come to the cinema?' '**All right**.'*

Write **all right**, not **alright**.

alligator

a large reptile very like a crocodile, but with shorter, wider jaws: ***Alligators** live in rivers in America and China.*

allow
to let someone do something: *My parents always **allow** me to stay out late on Saturday evenings. Dropping litter in the street is not **allowed**.*

Same as **permit**.

almost
very nearly: *Sarah is **almost** as tall as I am. Mike is **almost** seven years old. The path was so slippery that I **almost** fell over.*

alone
with no-one else; all by yourself: *'Do you live with your family?' 'No I live **alone**.'*

along
1 from one end of something towards the other end: *Vicky walked **along** the street, looking at all the shops.* **2** moving forward: *We ran **along** together. Joanna was walking **along** beside her mother.* **3** to a place: *'We're all going to Jane's house. Why don't you come **along** too?'*

aloud
loud enough for people to hear; not quietly to yourself: *Please read the letter **aloud** so that we can all hear it.*

alphabet
all the letters of a language arranged in order: *A, B, C are the first three letters of the **alphabet**.*

Say **al**-fa-bet.

already
1 before this time; at an earlier time: *'Would you like something to eat?' 'No, thanks, I've **already** had lunch.' Jane had **already** left when Susan arrived.* **2** sooner than expected: *'Where's Tom?' 'He's gone **already**.' Are you leaving **already**?*

also
as well; too: *David speaks English and he is **also** learning Chinese.*

although
even when; even though: ***Although** Peter said he was sorry for telling a lie, his father was still angry with him.*

altogether
1 completely: *It only rained a little and then stopped **altogether**.* **2** putting everything together: *I got $5 from my parents, $3 from my granny and $2 from my aunt, which makes $10 **altogether**.*

always
1 every day; regularly: *We **always** have lunch at one o'clock.* **2** at all times: ***Always** try to be polite.* **3** again and again: *She is **always** late for school. I am **always** losing my keys.*

am
you use **am** with **I**: *I **am** seven years old. I'**m** a good swimmer. **Am** I good enough to be chosen for the team? I'**m** doing my homework.*

- You can shorten **I am** to **I'm**.
- You turn **am not** into **aren't** in questions: ***Aren't** I looking smart today?*

ambition
1 the wish to be successful, famous, rich or powerful: *When you are young you are full of **ambition**.* **2** something you want to do very much: *Peter says his **ambition** is to become President.*

ambulance
a vehicle that is used for taking sick and injured people to hospital: *When my granny was very ill my mother called for an **ambulance**.*

among
1 in the middle of: *The children played **among** the trees in the park. 'Where is James?' 'He's somewhere **among** the other children.'* **2** giving some to each person: *Share the sweets out **among** you.*

amount
the size, weight or number of something: *There's a small **amount** of ice-cream in the fridge.*

Same as **quantity**.

amuse
1 to make someone laugh: *Sarah's funny story **amused** us all.* **2** to keep someone happy or interested: *We **amused** ourselves by drawing and painting pictures.*

amused, amusing, has amused

an
see **a**: ***An** elephant is very large. Would you like **an** apple?*

anchor

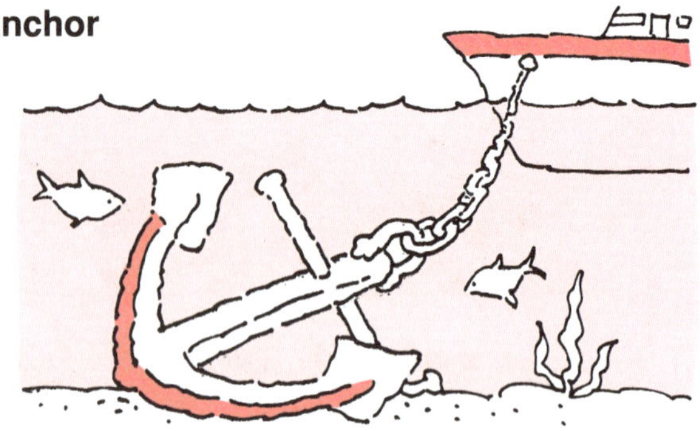

a heavy metal object with pointed hooks on it, that hangs down from a ship on a chain: *An **anchor** is dropped from a ship to the bottom of the sea, to stop the ship from moving.*

ancient
belonging to a time long ago: *In **ancient** times, people wore the skins of animals as clothes.*

- Say **ayn**-shent.
- Same as **old**.
- The opposite is **modern**.

and
1 you use **and** to join words or parts of sentences together: *I opened the door **and** went into the house. A man **and** a woman were standing in the garden.* **2** added to: *Three **and** three makes (or make) six. Two **and** one is (or are) three.*

angelfish

a small fish with a flat, brightly coloured body: *There are lots of beautiful **angelfish** in the aquarium.*

Many **angelfish**

anger
a very strong, violent feeling against someone: *Maggie was full of* ***anger*** *when she saw the man hitting the dog.*

angry
full of anger: *Miss Liu was* ***angry*** *with Joe for shouting in the classroom.*

- angry, angrier, angriest
- Same as **annoyed**.

animal
a living thing that can move about: *Cats, dogs, cows, horses, tigers, snakes and human beings are all* ***animals****.*

ankle

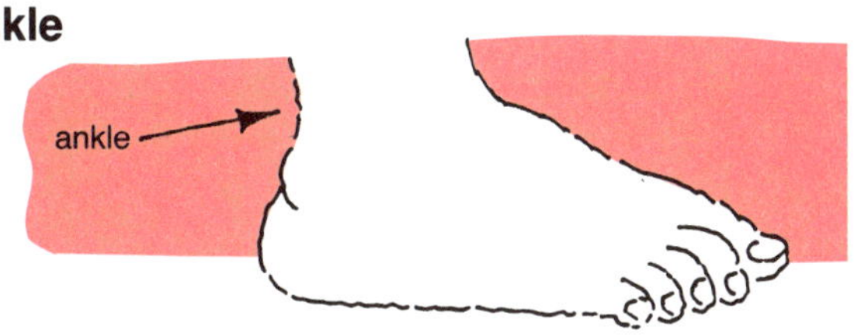

the part of your leg where it is joined to your foot: *Brian fell and hurt his* ***ankle.***

announce
to tell something to a lot of people: *The headmaster* ***announced*** *that there would be a holiday on Monday.*

announced, announcing, has announced

announcement
something which tells you what has happened or what will happen: *Sometimes it is difficult to hear the* ***announcements*** *at the railway station because of all the noise. An* ***announcement*** *was made on television about a change in the programme.*

announcer
a person who introduces programmes on radio or television: *An* ***announcer*** *should have a pleasant voice.*

annoy
to make someone angry: *I am sorry I made a noise — I didn't mean to* ***annoy*** *you. I was* ***annoyed*** *at having to do all the work again.*

another
1 a different one: *I don't like this book — can you lend me* ***another****? We're moving to* ***another*** *house.* **2** one more: *I'd like* ***another*** *of those biscuits. Elizabeth took* ***another*** *sweet.*

answer
1 to say something to someone who has asked you a question or said something to you; to reply: ***Answer*** *politely when the headmistress speaks to you. 'How many players are there in a football team?' asked the teacher. 'Eleven,'* ***answered*** *Jill.* **2** to write a letter to someone who has written to you: *Have you* ***answered*** *your granny's letter yet?*

answer
1 what you say to someone who asks you something or tells you something: *I asked him the time, but I didn't hear his* ***answer.*** *Have you had an* ***answer*** *to your letter yet?* **2** the right reply to a question in a test or puzzle: *The* ***answers*** *to the puzzle are on page 70.*

- Same as a **reply**.
- The opposite is **question**.

ant
a small insect that lives in a very large group: ***Ants*** *have a queen* ***ant*** *— she is very big and lays all the eggs.*

anxious
worried: *Your mother may be* ***anxious*** *about you if you're late getting home from school.*

Say **ang**-shus.

any
1 one; some: *John ate all the sweets, so I didn't get* ***any****. Did you see* ***any*** *good films on television yesterday?* **2** it doesn't matter which one: *Borrow* ***any*** *book you like.* **3** every: ***Any*** *child can tell you that three and three make six.*
any more any longer; ever again: *Grandad is getting old now, so he doesn't go jogging* ***any more****. I won't play with you* ***any more*** *if you don't tell me your secret.*

anybody or **anyone**
any person: *Is* ***anybody*** *there? There wasn't* ***anyone*** *in the house.* ***Anybody*** *could tell you the answer to such an easy question.*

anything
1 something: *Is* ***anything*** *wrong? I couldn't see* ***anything*** *in the dark. Do you want* ***anything*** *to eat?* **2** it doesn't matter what: *Choose* ***anything*** *you want for your birthday.*

anywhere
1 somewhere: *Did you go* ***anywhere*** *nice for your holidays? Thomas couldn't find his watch*

anywhere. **2** it doesn't matter where: *Put the box down **anywhere**.*

apart
1 away from something: *John lives **apart** from his family in his own flat.* **2** away from each other: *The potatoes were planted 20 centimetres **apart**. I pulled the two halves of the shell **apart**.* **3** into pieces: *The baby tore the book **apart**.*
apart from except for: ***Apart from** Josie, the girls are all learning to play the piano.*

apartment
a set of rooms for one family to live in: *There are ten **apartments** in this building.*

Same as a **flat**.

ape
an animal similar to a monkey, but larger and with no tail: *Chimpanzees and gorillas are **apes**.*

apologize
to say that you are sorry about something, especially something bad you have said or done: *Daniel **apologized** to the teacher for shouting at her.*

apologized, apologizing, has apologized

apology
something that you say or write in order to apologize: *You owe your father an **apology** for being rude to him. Mr Jones could not come to the meeting so he sent his **apologies**.*

Many **apologies**

appear
1 to begin to be seen: *The sun is **appearing** over the hill.* **2** to seem: *Mr Zahir **appeared** to be very angry.*

appearance
the way someone or something looks: *You could tell from Mrs Green's **appearance** that she was very rich.*

apple
a round fruit with a red or green skin: ***Apples** grow on trees and have a sweet taste.*

apricot
a small round orange-coloured fruit with a large stone inside: ***Apricots** are similar to peaches but smaller and not as juicy.*

April
the fourth month of the year.

apron
a piece of clothing which you wear to protect the front of your clothes: *Claire put on her **apron** before cooking the dinner.*

aquarium

a large glass container filled with water in which you can keep fish: *In our school we have a big **aquarium** with many different kinds of fish and water plants.*

are
you use **are** with **we**, **you** and **they**: *Jennifer and I **are** free this afternoon, so we'**re** going cycling. How **are** you? Peter and Thomas **are** good friends, but they'**re** always quarrelling.*

You can shorten:
- **you are** to **you're**
- **we are** to **we're**
- **they are** to **they're**

area
1 a place; a part of a town or of a country: *The children who live in this **area** go to St Thomas's School.* **2** how big a flat surface is: *What is the **area** of the classroom floor? The **area** of the floor is 110 square metres.*

aren't
1 short for **are not**: *Why **aren't** you coming with us?* **2** short for **am not** in questions: ***Aren't** I tall? I'm tall, **aren't** I?*

argue
to quarrel; to disagree: *The children were*

arguing *with each other about who had won the game.*

argued, arguing, has argued

argument

a quarrel; disagreeing with someone: *Sarah and Bob are having an* ***argument*** *about whose turn it is to wash the dishes.*

arithmetic

the part of mathematics that has to do with adding, subtracting, multiplying and dividing: *In* ***arithmetic*** *you have to learn addition and subtraction.*

arm

1 the part of the body that goes from your shoulder to your hand: *Mother was holding the baby in her* ***arms****. Lift your left* ***arm****.* **2** the part of a chair that sticks out like an arm: *Helen was sitting on the* ***arm*** *of the chair.*

armchair

a comfortable chair with arms: *Grandfather sat by the fire in an* ***armchair****.*

army

a country's soldiers: *James wants to train as a soldier and join the* ***army****.*

Two **armies**

around

1 in a circle round something: *We sat* ***around*** *the camp fire.* **2** here and there: *Thomas left his toys lying* ***around*** *the room. We wandered* ***around****.* **3** about; not exactly, but nearly: *Tim expects to arrive* ***around*** *10 o'clock.*

arrange

1 to put things in order; to set things out properly: *The teacher was* ***arranging*** *the books on the shelf. Sue* ***arranged*** *the flowers in the vase.* **2** to plan something; to fix a time for something: *The headmaster* ***arranged*** *to see Mary's parents on Thursday. A swimming practice has been* ***arranged*** *for the next week.*

arranged, arranging, has arranged

arrangement

1 the arranging of something; putting something in order: *We all admired Sue's beautiful flower-****arrangement****.* **2** a plan; something you do to prepare for something: *My mother made all the* ***arrangements*** *for my birthday party.*

arrest

to catch someone and take them to a police-station because you think they have done something wrong: *The police* ***arrested*** *the thief just as he was climbing over the wall.*

arrive

to reach a place: *The bus will be* ***arriving*** *in Kuala Lumpur at 11 o'clock. I* ***arrived*** *too late to catch the bus. This parcel has* ***arrived*** *for you.*

- arrived, arriving, has arrived
- Same as **reach**.
- The opposite is **depart**.

arrow

1 a thin, straight stick with a point which is shot from a bow: *Robin Hood and his men used bows and* ***arrows*** *as their weapons.* **2** a sign shaped like an arrow which shows you where something is: *Follow the* ***arrows*** *and you'll find your way out.*

art

painting, drawing and carving: *I would like to study* ***art*** *and become a painter.*

artist

a person who paints or draws or makes statues: *A famous* ***artist*** *was asked to paint a picture of the Prime Minister.*

as

1 when; at the same time: *I met John* ***as*** *I was coming home.* **2** because: ***As*** *Lisa is ill she can't come to the party this afternoon.* **3** in the same way: *Mark tied the bandage round his foot just* ***as*** *the doctor had shown him. Claire was dressed* ***as*** *a nurse.* **4** you use **as** to say two things are the same in some way: *My mother is* ***as*** *tall* ***as*** *my father. A balloon is* ***as*** *light* ***as*** *a feather.*

as a rule usually: ***As a rule****, children start going to school at the age of six.*
as far as up to a place: *I'll walk with you* ***as far as*** *the corner.*
as soon as when: *I'll ring you* ***as soon as*** *I get back home again.*
as soon as possible quickly: *Please write to me* ***as soon as possible****.*
as usual as has happened often before: ***As usual****, Mike forgot to switch off the light when he left the room. This morning my sister was late for breakfast* ***as usual****.*
as well too: *I'll go and visit Granny this afternoon, but I want to go shopping* ***as well****.*

Same as **also**.

as well as and; not only: *I've got a tricycle* ***as well as*** *a bicycle.*

ash
the grey or black dust that is left after something is burnt: *Mr Smith dropped some cigarette* ***ash*** *on to the tablecloth.*

ashamed
feeling shame; sorry because you have done something wrong: *Mark was* ***ashamed*** *of his bad behaviour.*

ask
1 to put a question to someone: *'What time is it?'* ***asked*** *Clare. I* ***asked*** *the teacher about our homework.* **2** to say that you want something: *Have you* ***asked*** *your father for more pocket-money? Jenny* ***asked*** *her brother to help her.* **3** to invite: *Our neighbours* ***asked*** *us to their house for lunch. Susan is* ***asking*** *some friends to tea on Thursday.*

asleep
sleeping: *The children are* ***asleep****. My grandmother fell* ***asleep*** *in her armchair.*

The opposite is **awake**.

assemble
to come together; to gather in one place: *All the pupils* ***assembled*** *in the school hall to hear the headmaster's announcement.*

- assembled, assembling, has assembled
- Same as **gather**.

assembly
a meeting of everybody: *The school meets for morning* ***assembly*** *at 7.30.*

Several **assemblies**

assistant
a person who helps: *The builder sent his* ***assistant*** *to mend the wall. Judy chose some apples at the grocer's and paid the shop-****assistant*** *for them.*

at
you use **at** to show **1** time: *We arrived* ***at*** *three o'clock.* **2** place: *Our neighbours are not* ***at*** *home. My friend lives* ***at*** *174 High Street. My mother is* ***at*** *work.* **3** direction: *Tom looked* ***at*** *me. The teacher shouted* ***at*** *the boys.* **4** whether you do something well or badly: *My sister is very good* ***at*** *English but she is bad* ***at*** *arithmetic.*
at all you use at all with not to make not even stronger: *The headmaster does not want to be disturbed* ***at all*** *today. Simon hasn't any money* ***at all****.*
at first at the beginning: ***At first*** *I didn't know what to do.*
at last in the end; after you have been waiting for something for a long time: *Hello! — There you are* ***at last****! After a long journey they* ***at last*** *reached home.*
at least **1** not less than: *There are* ***at least*** *500 pupils at our school.* **2** you use **at least** when you mention one thing that is good: *This book is boring, but* ***at least*** *it's short.*
at once **1** immediately; without waiting: *When her mother called her she came* ***at once****.* **2** at the same time: *I can't do everything* ***at once****.*
at the moment now: *I am very busy* ***at the moment****.*

ate
see **eat**: *We* ***ate*** *all the ice-cream yesterday, so there is none left for today.*

athlete
a person who is very good at sport: *Twenty* ***athletes*** *took part in the race.*

attach
to fasten; to fix something to something else: *Mary* ***attached*** *the flower to her dress with a pin.*

attack

1 to rush at someone and hurt them: *A man **attacked** the old lady and stole her money.* **2** to damage a place when you are fighting a war: *The army **attacked** the village.*

The opposite is **defend.**

attack

the act of trying to hurt or to damage: *The big dog made an **attack** on the little dog. There were many air **attacks** on this town during the war.*

attempt

a try: *After two **attempts** at climbing the wall I succeeded in getting over it.*

attend

1 to go to something; to be present at something: *Children have to **attend** school until they are sixteen years old. I **attended** a friend's birthday party yesterday.* **2** to listen and watch: *You must **attend** to your teacher. **Attend** to what I'm saying.*

attendant

a person who has the job of looking after something: *The car-park **attendant** showed my father where to park his car.*

attention

listening and watching: *Pay **attention** to what the teacher says! Joe tried to attract my **attention** by waving his handkerchief.*

attract

to make something come nearer: *Butterflies are **attracted** by brightly coloured flowers. A magnet **attracts** iron.*

attractive

1 nice to look at; pretty: *Everybody thinks Julie is an **attractive** girl.* **2** nice: *Do you think Valérie is an **attractive** name?*

audience

a group of people watching or listening to a play, concert, film or someone speaking: *The policeman gave a talk to an **audience** of schoolchildren. There was a large **audience** at the concert last night.*

August

the eighth month of the year.

aunt

the sister of your mother or father; the wife of your uncle: *Your **aunt**'s children are your cousins.*

Rhymes with **plant.**

author

the writer of a book or play: *Robert Louis Stevenson was the **author** of the book 'Treasure Island'.*

automatic

working by itself, instead of a person doing the work: *At home we have an **automatic** washing machine.*

autumn

the season of the year between summer and winter: *In cool parts of the world, the leaves change colour and fall off the trees in **autumn**.*

aviary

a large cage in which birds are kept: *The canaries are kept in an **aviary** in the zoo.*

Several **aviaries**

avoid

to keep away from something: *My father drove carefully to **avoid** the holes in the road. Karen always **avoids** washing the dishes because she's very lazy.*

awake

having woken up; not asleep: *Are the children **awake** already?*

The opposite is **asleep.**

away

1 at a distance: *John lives three miles **away** from the town. Have you been **away** on holiday this year?* **2** with nothing left to see or hear: *All the snow melted **away** in the hot sun. The noise died **away**.*

awful

very bad; terrible: *The weather is **awful** — it has been raining all day. I have an **awful** headache.*

axe

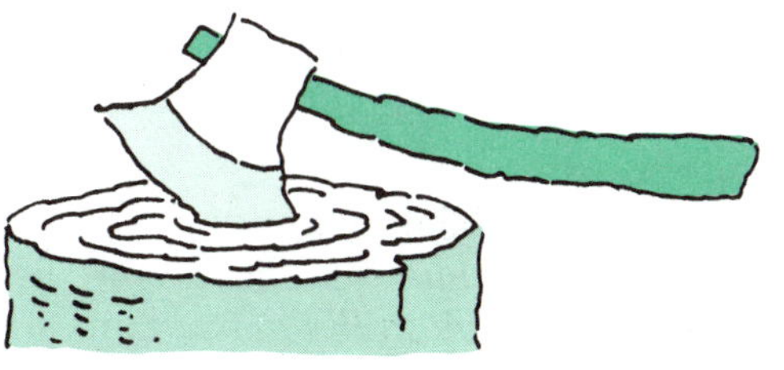

a tool with a handle and a metal blade for cutting down trees and cutting wood into pieces: *George chopped the wood into small pieces with his **axe**.*

Bb

baby
a very young child; a very young animal: ***Babies*** *need a lot of sleep. The* ***baby*** *giraffe was only about one metre tall.*

> Two **babies**

baby-sit
to stay in a house to look after children while their parents are out: *Elizabeth* ***baby-sits*** *for her neighbours every Saturday.*

> baby-sat, baby-sitting, has baby-sat

bachelor
a man who has never been married: *Mr Jones remained a* ***bachelor*** *all his life.*

back
1 the part of you that is behind you when you walk forward; the part of an animal's body which is on top when it stands: *Jenny is lying on her* ***back****. Bob put the saddle on the horse's* ***back****.* **2** the side opposite to, or furthest away from the front: *Julie and I like sitting at the* ***back*** *of the classroom. The price is on the* ***back*** *of the book.* **3** on the opposite side to the front: *When the front door is locked, try the* ***back*** *door.* **4** to the same place or person again: *I went* ***back*** *to the same shop. My friend gave me* ***back*** *my bicycle.* **5** with your back against something: *Granny lay* ***back*** *in the big chair.*

> Meanings 1 — 3: the opposite is **front**.

backbone
the line of joined-up bones going down your back: *Linda hurt her* ***backbone*** *when she slipped and fell in the playground.*

backwards
1 with your back facing in the direction you are moving: *Bill walked* ***backwards*** *across the room.* **2** in the opposite way to the usual way: *Can you say the alphabet* ***backwards****?*

backwards and forwards in one direction and then in the opposite direction: *The tiger walked* ***backwards and forwards*** *in its cage.*

backyard
a garden or small area of ground behind a house: *The children sometimes play football in the* ***backyard****.*

bacon
salty meat from a pig: *Do you like* ***bacon*** *and eggs for breakfast?*

bad
1 not good: *There are good and* ***bad*** *pupils in every class. My friend is very* ***bad*** *at drawing.* **2** naughty: *You are a* ***bad*** *boy for telling a lie to the teacher.* **3** not good to eat: *The bananas have gone* ***bad****.* **4** nasty; serious: *Paul has a* ***bad*** *cold and must stay in bed. You have made some* ***bad*** *mistakes in your sums.*

> - bad, worse, worst
> - Same as **evil** or **wicked**.
> - The opposite is **good**.

badge

a small piece of plastic, metal or cloth with a picture or words on it, which you wear on your jacket or jumper: *Tim is wearing a* ***badge*** *with his name on it.*

badminton
a game in which two or four players use rackets to hit a small, light object called a shuttlecock: *You play* ***badminton*** *on a* ***badminton court****.*

bag
an object made of paper, plastic, cloth or leather in which you carry things: *I need a big* ***bag*** *for my shopping. Would you like a* ***bag*** *of crisps?*

bait
a small piece of food that you put on a hook to make fish bite, or in a trap to attract animals: *John uses worms as a* ***bait*** *for catching fish.*

bake
to cook something in an oven: *My mother **baked** a cake for my birthday.*

baked, baking, has baked

baker
a person who makes bread and cakes: *A shop where you can buy bread and cakes is called a **baker's**.*

balance
the skill of keeping yourself from falling: *Mark was walking along the wall when he lost his **balance** and fell.*

balance
1 to keep something steady so that it doesn't fall: *Susan can **balance** a jug full of water on her head.* **2** to keep yourself from falling: *Mark was **balancing** on the wall.*

balanced, balancing, has balanced

bald
having very little hair or no hair at all on the top of the head: *Bill's grandfather has a **bald** head, his father is going **bald** and his uncle is **bald** already.*

ball
a round object which you use for playing games: *Roger kicked the **ball** into the goal.*
ball-point pen a pen with a very small ball at the end which brings the ink on to the paper: *Do you like writing with a **ball-point pen**?*

ballet
a kind of dancing that needs a lot of skill and good balance: *Lorna is taking lessons in **ballet**.*

Say **bal**-ay.

ballerina
a woman who does ballet: *Nicola is training to be a **ballerina**.*

balloon
a large round object like a very light ball which is filled with air or gas: *The children blew up red, blue and green **balloons**.*

bamboo
a tall plant with hollow stems which are hard and strong like wood: ***Bamboo** can be used for making furniture.*

banana
a long yellow fruit which grows in hot countries: ***Bananas** are easy to peel and they taste sweet. Buy me a bunch of **bananas** from the grocer's.*

band
1 a group of musicians: *Tracey plays the drums in the school **band**.* **2** a group of people: *A **band** of robbers stole a lot of money from the bank.* **3** a thin piece of material to put round something: *Kate put a rubber **band** round the box to keep it closed.*

bandage

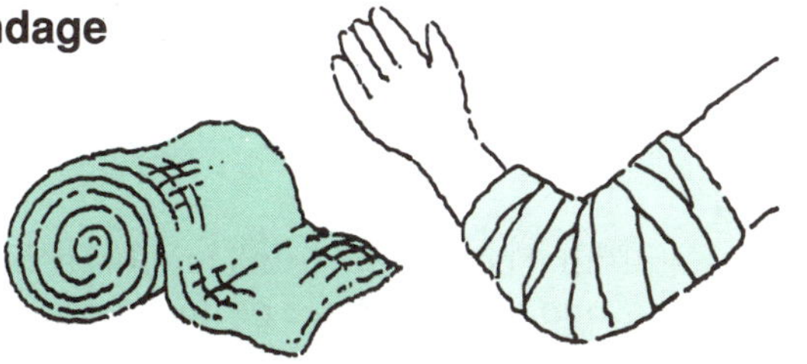

a long piece of cloth for tying round a part of your body which has been cut or hurt: *The doctor put a **bandage** round Mary's sore finger.*

bandage
to put a bandage round something: *Mum **bandaged** Pauline's cut knee.*

bandaged, bandaging, has bandaged

bang
1 a sudden loud noise: *The door shut with a **bang**.* **2** a blow; a knock: *David got a **bang** on the head when he fell off his bicycle.*

bang
1 to close with a loud noise: *Michael **banged** the door because he was very angry.* **2** to hit something, making a loud noise: *My little sister likes to **bang** her drum.*

bank
1 a place where money is lent or exchanged and where people can leave their money safely: *Mum puts all her money in the **bank**.* **2** the ground along the edge of a river or lake: *The river overflowed its **banks** after the heavy rain. We went for a walk along the river **bank**.*

bar
1 a long piece of metal or wood: *There are iron **bars** in front of the prison windows.* **2** a flat, oblong piece of something: *Mum gave each of the children a **bar** of chocolate. Jenny used a new **bar** of soap to wash her hands.*

barbecue
1 a special kind of cooker for cooking meat

and other food out of doors: *We grilled the steaks on the **barbecue** in the garden.* **2** a party at which you cook food on a barbecue: *Our neighbours invited us to a **barbecue** last night.*

barber
a person who cuts men's hair or shaves their beards: *My brother goes to the **barber's** once a month to get his hair cut.*

bare
1 not covered: *In hot weather we like to keep our arms and legs **bare**. When the teacher took down all the pictures, the walls looked very **bare**.* **2** with no leaves: *In winter many of the trees are **bare**.*

bark
the stuff that covers the trunk and branches of a tree: *Simon cut the **bark** off the branch with a small knife.*

bark
to make the noise of a dog: *Our dog always **barks** at the postman. The dog is **barking** at the cat.*

barrel
a round container for liquids or other goods, with curved sides and a flat top and bottom: *The fish were packed in **barrels** and loaded on to the lorry.*

baseball
an American game played by two teams of nine players using a hard ball: *In **baseball** you have to hit the ball with a bat and run round four sides of a big square.*

basement
the lowest level of a building, usually below the ground level: *The food department of this store is in the **basement**.*

basin
a large bowl: *You can wash your hands in the wash-**basin** in the bathroom.*

basket
an object for holding and carrying things, made of strips of wood or cane woven together: *Do you prefer a **basket** or a bag for carrying the shopping in?*

basketball
a game in which two teams of five players try to throw a large ball into a net on a high post: *In **basketball** the players are not allowed to carry the ball.*

bat

1 a piece of wood specially shaped for hitting the ball in certain games: *A baseball **bat** is long and narrow but a table-tennis **bat** is small, round and flat.* **2** a small animal with wings, that squeaks: ***Bats** fly about at night.*

bath
1 a long, deep container for water in which you can wash your whole body: *Mum filled the **bath** with warm water. We have a **bath** and a shower in our bathroom.* **2** the act of washing your body in a bath: *I had a **bath** this morning.*

bathe
1 to go swimming: *Do you like **bathing** in the sea?* **2** to clean with water: *The doctor **bathed** the cut on my finger.*

bathed, bathing, has bathed

bathroom
1 a room which contains a bath or a shower, a wash-basin, and sometimes a toilet: *We have a small **bathroom** with a shower.* **2** a toilet: *May I use your **bathroom**, please?*

bathtub
a bath: *Mike filled the **bathtub** with water and got in.*

baton
a light stick used by a conductor of an orchestra or a choir: *The music teacher uses a **baton** to help us sing in time to the music.*

battery
an object which stores electric power and is used to make something work: *I need new **batteries** for my radio.*

Two **batteries**

battle
a fight between armies: *Many soldiers were killed in the **battle**.*

battleship
a very large ship with big guns: ***Battleships*** *were used during the war.*

be
1 you use **be** to tell people how to behave: ***Be*** *brave — don't cry. The teacher told the children to* ***be*** *good while she went out of the classroom.* **2** you use **be** to say what job you want to do: *Emma wants to* ***be*** *a doctor when she grows up.* **3** you use **be** with **shall** and **will** to say what is going to happen: *I shall* ***be*** *angry if you behave badly. You will* ***be*** *late if you don't hurry. You will* ***be*** *taken to the zoo by bus.*

- was or were, being, has been
- These other words belong to the word **be**: **am**, **are**, **is**, **was**, **were**.

beach
a strip of land beside the sea, which is covered with sand or pebbles: *We like playing on the* ***beach.*** *I'm going down to the* ***beach*** *to have a swim.*

bead
a little ball of glass, wood or plastic with a hole through the middle: *You can make a necklace out of* ***beads***.

beak
the hard pointed part of a bird's mouth which it uses for picking up food: *The bird had a worm in its* ***beak***.

bean

a small round vegetable of many different kinds which grows in a pod: *Some* ***beans*** *have to be soaked in water and cooked for a long time before they can be eaten. We'll open a tin of baked* ***beans*** *for lunch.*

bear
a large wild animal with thick fur and sharp claws: *We watched the* ***bears*** *climbing rocks in the zoo. A polar* ***bear*** *is white. A baby* ***bear*** *is called a cub.*

bear
to have to suffer something or put up with something that you don't like: *Rosie* ***bore*** *the pain bravely when she hurt her leg. I can't* ***bear*** *that stupid television programme.*

bore, bearing, has borne

beard
the hair that grows on a man's chin and cheeks: *My father is growing a* ***beard.*** *My uncle has shaved off his* ***beard.***

beast
an animal, especially a large, dangerous wild animal: *Would you dare to live among the* ***beasts*** *of the jungle?*

beat
1 to hit: *My little brother likes* ***beating*** *his drum. Joe* ***beat*** *his dog because it stole some meat.* **2** to win against someone: *Sarah* ***beat*** *her brother in the competition. Our team was badly* ***beaten*** *in the football match.* **3** to make the noise that your heart makes: *Your heart* ***beats*** *fast when you run.*

beat, beating, has beaten

beautiful
1 very nice to look at; pretty: *Mary's mother is very* ***beautiful.*** *What a* ***beautiful*** *dress you are wearing!* **2** very nice; very pleasant: *We had* ***beautiful*** *weather for our holiday in New Zealand.*

Meaning 1: the opposite is **ugly**.

beauty
being beautiful: *The film-star was famous for her* ***beauty***.

because
for this reason: *Peter can't go to school today* ***because*** *he is ill.*

become
1 to grow or change; to turn into something: *Sally has* ***become*** *very tall, hasn't she? Robert wants to* ***become*** *a doctor. Sue and I* ***became*** *good friends.* **2** to happen to someone or something: *What* ***became*** *of your old teddy-bear?*

became, becoming, has become

bed
the piece of furniture on which you sleep: *It's*

*time to go to **bed.** Mother put the baby to **bed**. Do you make you own **bed** in the mornings?*

bedroom
a room for sleeping in: *Do you have your own **bedroom**? Angela shares a **bedroom** with her little sister.*

bee
an insect which makes honey: *Some **bees** live in hives. The **bees** were flying from flower to flower.*

beef
the meat of a bull or cow: *Mum has bought some **beef** to cook for dinner.*

beehive

a kind of small, wooden house in which bees are kept: *There were thousands of bees in the **beehive.***

been
see **be**: *Where have you **been**? The weather has **been** bad all week. Have you ever **been** to the zoo? We have **been** living in this house for five years. Have the books **been** handed in to the teacher? Sally was punished because she had **been** naughty.*

beetle

an insect with two hard covers over its wings: *A ladybird is a small, round, red **beetle** with black spots.*

before
1 earlier: *I have seen this film **before**. It's too late to take you to the doctor now — why didn't you ask me **before**?* **2** earlier than: *Tim guessed the answer **before** the other children. Please come **before** three o'clock. Wash your hands **before** you start eating.*

> The opposite is **after**.

beg
1 to ask someone for money or food: *The old man was so poor that he had to **beg** in the street.* **2** to ask someone very eagerly: *Sarah **begged** Lucy not to go.*

> begged, begging, has begged

beggar
a person who lives by begging: *The **beggar** asked for money to buy food.*

begin
to start: *The lesson **begins** at 9.30. It **began** to rain.*

> - began, beginning, has begun
> - Same as **start**.
> - The opposite is **end** or **finish**.

beginning
the start of something: *At the **beginning** of the music lesson we sang a few songs. I have read only the **beginning** of my new book.*

> - Same as **start**.
> - The opposite is **end**.

behave
to act in a good way or a bad way: *If you come shopping with me, you must **behave** yourself. The children **behaved** very well at the concert. The teacher was angry with John because he **behaved** badly during the lesson.*

> behaved, behaving, has behaved

behaviour
the way you behave: *The headmaster praised the pupils for their good **behaviour.***

> Same as **conduct**.

behind
1 at the back of something: *Jack is hiding **behind** the door. The playground is **behind** the school. A car has two wheels in front and two **behind.*** **2** left in a place; not taken with you: *Joanne left her purse **behind** in the classroom.*

> Meaning 1: the opposite is **in front of** or **in front**.

being
a person; something that is living: *We are all human **beings**. This story is about some strange **beings** from another world.*

being
see **be**: *You are all **being** far too noisy today.*

belief
a feeling that something is true; believing in

someone or something: *Many people have a strong **belief** in God.*

believe
1 to feel that something is true, although you don't really know it is: *Do you really **believe** this story? I **believe** what Peter told me. Mark said he didn't break the computer and I **believed** him.* 2 to feel certain that someone or something is real: *I **believe** in God. I don't **believe** in ghosts.* 3 to think: *I **believe** the train leaves at half past two.*

believed, believing, has believed

bell
1 a hollow metal object which has a bit of metal hanging inside it that hits the sides and makes a sound when it is swung backwards and forwards: *The church **bells** were rung for the wedding.* 2 any other object for making a ringing sound: *When the door **bell** rang Judy went and opened the door. The **bell** rang at the end of the lesson. Do you have a **bell** on your bicycle?*

bellow
to make the noise of a bull: *The bull was **bellowing** in the field.*

belly
the part of a person's or animal's body between the chest and the legs: *Dave put the saddle on the horse and fastened it under its **belly**.*

The **bellies** of animals

belong
1 to be owned by someone: *This book **belongs** to me. Whom does this bicycle **belong** to?* 2 to be a member of some group: *Which football club does Peter **belong** to?*

below
lower than something; in a lower place: *Your foot is **below** your knee. The plane flew **below** the clouds. We climbed up the tower and looked at the houses down **below**.*

The opposite is **above.**

belt
a long piece of leather or cloth that you wear round your waist: *You need a **belt** to keep your trousers up.*

bench
a long seat, usually made of wood: *My friend and I sat on a **bench** in the park and ate our sandwiches.*

bend
a curve: *There are a lot of **bends** in this road.*

bend

1 to curve; to make something curved: ***Bend** your arm. The road **bends** to the right. The strong man could **bend** an iron bar.* 2 to move the top part of your body downwards: *David **bent** down to pick up the coin.*

bent, bending, has bent

beneath
under: *The mouse was hiding **beneath** the sofa. Amy hid the key **beneath** the mat.*

The opposite is **above**, **over** or **on top of**.

bent
see **bend**: *I've **bent** the handle of the spoon.*

bent
with a bend in it: *A **bent** pin is useless.*

berry
any small round juicy fruit such as a strawberry or raspberry: *Are those green **berries** poisonous?*

A lot of **berries**

beside
at the side of someone or something; next to: *Kate sat **beside** her sister. The lamp is **beside** the bed.*

besides
1 as well as: *Is anyone coming **besides** Steve? **Besides** the dog, we have two cats and a canary.* 2 also: *I don't want to go for a walk — **besides**, it's raining.*

best
better than all the others: *Liz is my **best** friend. Which is the **best** football team? Jane did **best** in the English exam.*

The opposite is **worst.**

do your best to try as hard as you can: ***Do your best** to win the race.*

bet
1 to gamble money, for example on a horse in a race: *Bob* ***bet*** *$10 on the grey horse.* **2** to be very certain: *I* ***bet*** *I can run faster than you.*

bet, betting, has bet

bet
the thing you agree to with someone when you bet on something: *Nicola made a* ***bet*** *with her father that she would finish her sums in ten minutes.*

better
1 good or well compared with someone or something else: *Our new car is much* ***better*** *than our old one. Mike is* ***better*** *at running than I am. Helen can sing* ***better*** *than her mother.* **2** not as ill as before; not as bad as before: *I feel much* ***better*** *today. My mother had a headache but she is* ***better*** *now. Is your headache* ***better*** *now?*

The opposite is **worse**.

had better it would be a good thing if: *You* ***had better*** *do your homework now if you want to watch television tonight. I'****d better*** *go before it starts raining again.*

between
1 in the space dividing two things: *There is a fence* ***between*** *our garden and our neighbours' garden. Could you come* ***between*** *2 o'clock and 2.30?* **2** dividing two people or things from each other: *There was an argument* ***between*** *Anne and Mark. Do you know the difference* ***between*** *a butterfly and a moth?* **3** giving some to one person and some to the other: *The twins divided the chocolate* ***between*** *them.*

beware
a warning that means 'look out!', 'be careful!': *There was a notice on the gate saying '****Beware*** *of the dog!'*

bicycle

a vehicle with two wheels and a seat for one person who makes it go forward by pushing the pedals: *Can you ride a* ***bicycle****?*

Called a **bike** for short.

big
large in size: *The Lee family has a* ***big*** *house with ten rooms.*

- Same as **large**.
- The opposite is **small** or **little**.
- big, bigger, biggest

bike
short for **bicycle**: *Martin got a new* ***bike*** *for his birthday.*

bill

1 a piece of paper showing how much money you have to pay: *After we had finished our meal we asked the waiter for the* ***bill****. My father pays the telephone* ***bill*** *every three months.* **2** a note worth a certain amount of money: *Mike changed a ten-dollar* ***bill*** *at the bank.*

bind
1 to tie; to fasten: *Kathy* ***bound*** *up the parcel. The robbers* ***bound*** *the bank-manager to a chair with a rope.* **2** to bandage: *The nurse will* ***bind*** *up your cut finger.*

bound, binding, has bound

bird
an animal with wings and feathers: *Early in the morning the* ***birds*** *sing in the trees. A penguin is a large sea-****bird*** *that cannot fly.*

birth
being born: *Daddy and I went to see Mummy in hospital after the* ***birth*** *of my little brother.*

birthday
the day on which you were born: *When is your* ***birthday****? My* ***birthday*** *is on February 24th. What do you want for your* ***birthday****? Are you having a* ***birthday*** *party?*

biscuit
a kind of small flat cake which is usually sweet: *Do you like chocolate* ***biscuits****?*

Same as a **cookie**.

bit
1 a piece: *There is only one* ***bit*** *of cake left. Mike tore a* ***bit*** *of paper out of his notebook.*

2 a little: *Wait a* ***bit*** *longer. These shoes are a* ***bit*** *too small.*

bit

see **bite**: *The dog* ***bit*** *Ruth's leg.*

bite

to cut through something with your teeth; to injure someone with the teeth: *That dog tried to* ***bite*** *me. Peter* ***bit*** *off a piece of his chocolate.*

> bit, biting, has bitten

bite

the action of biting: *The dog gave me a* ***bite*** *on the leg. Some snakes have a poisonous* ***bite****.*

bitten

see **bite**: *I was* ***bitten*** *by a mosquito.*

bitter

having a sharp taste; not sweet: *This juice tastes* ***bitter****.*

> The opposite is **sweet**.

black

the darkest colour; the opposite of white: ***Black*** *is the colour of the night. The teacher is wearing* ***black*** *shoes today. We have a colour TV in our living-room but I have a* ***black****-and-white TV in my bedroom.*

blackberry

a small soft berry that looks like a raspberry, but is black: ***Blackberries*** *grow on thorny bushes at the sides of roads and fields.*

> Lots of **blackberries**

blackboard

a large, dark-coloured board in a classroom: *The teacher writes with a piece of white chalk on the* ***blackboard****.*

blade

the cutting part of a knife or other tool: *The* ***blade*** *of this knife is made of steel.*

blame

1 to say that someone is the cause of something bad: *The car-driver* ***blamed*** *the cyclist for the accident. I didn't break the window — you can't* ***blame*** *it on me!* **2** to think someone is wrong to do something: *I don't* ***blame*** *you for getting angry with Alan — he was very rude to you.*

> • blamed, blaming, has blamed
> • The opposite is **praise**.

to blame being the cause of something bad: *You are not* ***to blame*** *for the accident.*

blank

with nothing written on it: *The teacher gave us each a* ***blank*** *sheet of paper to draw a picture on.*

blanket

a warm cover made of wool, usually used on a bed; a rug: *Here is an extra* ***blanket*** *for your bed in case you are cold in the night.*

blaze

a large fire that destroys a building: *A neighbour rescued the little girl from the* ***blaze****.*

blaze

to burn with flames: *A nice warm fire was* ***blazing*** *in the fireplace. The roof of the building was* ***blazing*** *by the time the firemen arrived.*

> blazed, blazing, has blazed

bleat

to make the noise of a sheep or goat: *The lamb* ***bleated*** *for its mother.*

bled

see **bleed**: *Amy's finger* ***bled*** *a little when she pricked it with a needle.*

bleed

to have blood flowing out: *Richard's nose is* ***bleeding****.*

> bled, bleeding, has bled

blew

see **blow**: *The wind* ***blew*** *very strongly.*

blind

not able to see: *Anna helped the* ***blind*** *man to cross the street.*

blindfold
to tie a piece of cloth round someone's head so that it covers their eyes: *The prisoner couldn't see anything because he had been* ***blindfolded****.*

block
1 a large piece of wood or stone: *Dad chopped the* ***block*** *of wood into small pieces.* **2** a tall building containing a lot of flats or offices: *We live in a* ***block*** *of flats. My father works in an office* ***block*** *in the city.* **3** buildings arranged in a square with streets along each side: *The taxi-driver drove round the* ***block****.*

block
to close up; to stop something from getting through: *The crashed cars* ***blocked*** *the road. My nose gets* ***blocked*** *when I have a bad cold.*

blood
the red liquid in your body: ***Blood*** *flowed from the wound in the soldier's leg.*

blouse
a kind of shirt worn by a girl or a woman: *Jennifer is wearing a blue skirt and a white* ***blouse****.*

blow
a hard knock: *In the fight Roger got a nasty* ***blow*** *on the head. The man knocked Harry down with one* ***blow*** *of his fist.*

blow
1 to move along as the wind does: *The wind is* ***blowing*** *more strongly now.* **2** to make something move, as the wind does: *The wind* ***blew*** *Mrs Lang's hat off.* **3** to make a sound on a musical instrument or a whistle by breathing hard into it: *Mary tried to* ***blow*** *her father's trumpet. The teacher* ***blew*** *his whistle at the end of the football game.*

blew, blowing, has blown

blow out to stop something burning by breathing hard at it: *Annabel* ***blew out*** *the candles on her birthday cake.*
blow up **1** to destroy by explosion: *The soldiers* ***blew up*** *the bridge. The old factory was* ***blown up****.* **2** to fill something with air: *Ben has* ***blown up*** *ten balloons already.*

blown
see **blow**: *The wind has* ***blown*** *the tree down.*

blue
the colour of the sky when there are no clouds: *Jenny has* ***blue*** *eyes and fair hair. Jack is wearing dark* ***blue*** *trousers and a light* ***blue*** *shirt.*

bluff
to trick: *The thief* ***bluffed*** *his way into the palace by pretending to be a policeman.*

blunt
not sharp; having an edge that does not cut well; having the point worn down: *This knife has gone* ***blunt****. You can't write with a* ***blunt*** *pencil.*

The opposite is **sharp**.

blush
to become red in the face because you feel ashamed or shy: *The new girl* ***blushed*** *when the teacher spoke to her for the first time.*

boar
a male pig: *The farmer has one* ***boar*** *and three sows on his farm.*

board
a flat piece of wood: *The headmistress pinned the list on the notice-****board****. Emma made a beautiful cheese-****board*** *out of different kinds of wood.*

board

to get on a ship, train or aircraft: *Passengers for Bangkok may now* ***board*** *their plane.*

The opposite is **alight**.

on board on a ship, train or aircraft: *The ship left the harbour when all the passengers were* ***on board****.*

boast
to talk too proudly: *Garry was always* ***boasting*** *about how rich he was. Sandra* ***boasted*** *that she was the best pupil in her class.*

boat
a small vessel for travelling over water; a ship: *Chris rowed the* ***boat*** *towards the shore. We'll cross the river by* ***boat****. The party of tourists went round the lake in a motor-****boat****.*

body
the whole of a person; the whole of an animal: *Athletes have to look after their* ***bodies****. A cat's* ***body*** *is covered with fur.*

Several **bodies**

boil
a painful red swelling on the skin: *Dad had to go to the doctor because he had a* ***boil*** *on his neck.*

boil
1 to heat water until it bubbles and changes into steam; to bubble and change from water into steam: ***Boil*** *the water. The water is* ***boiling*** *now.* **2** to cook by boiling in water: *Have you* ***boiled*** *the potatoes? I like my egg* ***boiled*** *for five minutes.*

bold
not afraid to do things that are dangerous; daring: *No-one was* ***bold*** *enough to go into the empty house in the dark. Bill thought of a* ***bold*** *plan for catching the thief.*

- Same as **daring**.
- The opposite is **shy** or **timid**.

bolt

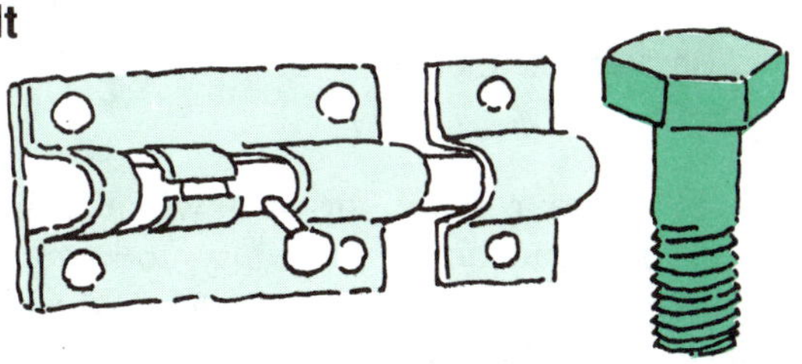

1 a small metal bar that slides across to fasten a door or window: *We have a* ***bolt*** *as well as a lock on the front door.* **2** a type of screw which is used to fasten things together: *The swing is held together by nuts and* ***bolts****.*

bomb
a weapon which explodes: *The pilot dropped a* ***bomb*** *on the factory and blew it up.*

bone
one of the hard pieces inside your body which form your skeleton: *Fish is difficult to eat when it has a lot of* ***bones*** *in it. Sally broke two* ***bones*** *in her foot when she fell off the wall.*

book
a number of printed or blank sheets of paper bound together; a story or whatever is printed in a book: *When I grow up I would like to write* ***books*** *for children. Write your homework in your exercise* ***book****.*

book
to reserve: *My mother* ***booked*** *four seats for the concert. Mr Smith has* ***booked*** *a table at the restaurant for this evening.*

boot
a shoe with a part that covers your ankle: *I have a pair of warm* ***boots*** *for wearing in the winter.*

border
a strip going round the edge of something: *This handkerchief has a red* ***border****.*

bore
see **bear**: *Susan* ***bore*** *the pain very bravely when she broke her leg.*

bore

to make a long or deep hole through something: *The engineers* ***bored*** *a long tunnel under the sea.*

bored, boring, has bored

bored

not interested; tired of something: *I get* ***bored*** *watching sport on television. You get* ***bored*** *when you have nothing to do. I'm* ***bored*** *of playing with my little sister.*

boring
not interesting: *Don't you think this film is* ***boring****?*

born
becoming a living person: *Michael was* ***born*** *on 1 April 1981. Most of the children in our class were* ***born*** *in Singapore.*

borrow
to take something away for a while, meaning to return it: *Ann* ***borrowed*** *a book from the*

*library. Could I **borrow** your bicycle, please?*

- I'm **borrowing** a book **from** Jane.
- Jane is **lending** a book **to** me.

boss
the person who is in charge: *Mr White is the **boss** of this firm. The **boss** will tell you what to do.*

both
the two; the one and the other: *Mary and I **both** like our new teacher. **Both** of us like her. **Both** girls are very nice. The girls are **both** very nice. **Both** are very nice. Nicola is **both** nice and intelligent.*

bottle
a container made of glass or plastic for holding liquids: *Lucy drank a whole **bottle** of lemonade. We had to buy drinking water in **bottles** when we were on holiday.*

bottom
1 the lowest part of anything: *Our house is at the **bottom** of the hill. John and Bob dived to the **bottom** of the lake. You'll find the answer at the **bottom** of the page.* **2** the part of your body that you sit on: *Peter slipped and fell on his **bottom**.*

Meaning 1: the opposite is **top**.

bought
see **buy**: *Sarah **bought** some flowers for her granny. Our parents have **bought** a new car.*

bounce
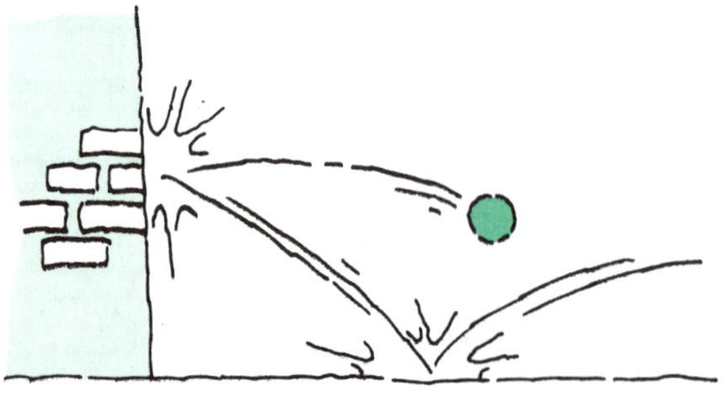

to spring back from the ground or something hard; to throw something against the ground so that it springs back again: *The ball **bounced** off the wall. Maggie is **bouncing** a red ball on the pavement.*

bounced, bouncing, has bounced

bound
see **bind**: *The prisoner's hands were **bound** together behind his back.*

bouquet

a nicely arranged bunch of flowers for carrying: *The bride carried a **bouquet** of red roses.*

Say boo-**kay**.

bow
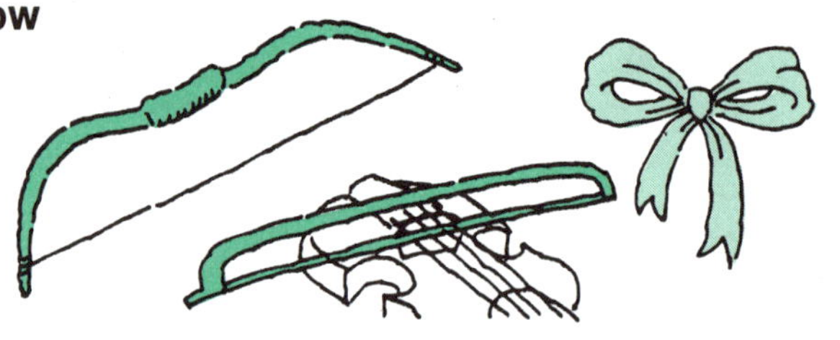

1 a curved rod bent by a string, with which arrows are shot: *The hunter went out to shoot animals with his **bow** and arrow.* **2** a knot with two loops and two loose ends: *Ann has a big **bow** in her hair. Have you learnt how to tie a **bow** yet?* **3** a special rod for playing a violin with: *I put my violin and **bow** back in the violin-case.*

Rhymes with **toe**.

bow
to bend your body forward when you are greeting someone very politely; to bend your head downwards: *The gentlemen **bowed** to the ladies. All the children **bowed** their heads in prayer.*

Rhymes with **now**.

bowl
a deep round dish: *Mum was making a salad in a big glass **bowl**. Lucy was so hungry that she ate three **bowls** of rice.*

box
a cardboard, plastic or wooden container: *Diana got a **box** of chocolates from her friend. My little brother keeps his toys in a large wooden **box**.*

box
to fight someone with your fists as a sport, wearing big leather gloves: *Peter goes to a club to learn how to **box**.*

boxer
a sportsman who boxes: *Both **boxers** were badly hurt in the fight.*

boy
1 a male child: *There are more* ***boys*** *than girls in our class.* **2** a son: *Mr and Mrs Black have two* ***boys*** *and a girl.*

bracelet
a chain or band that you wear around your wrist: *Helen got a gold* ***bracelet*** *for her birthday.*

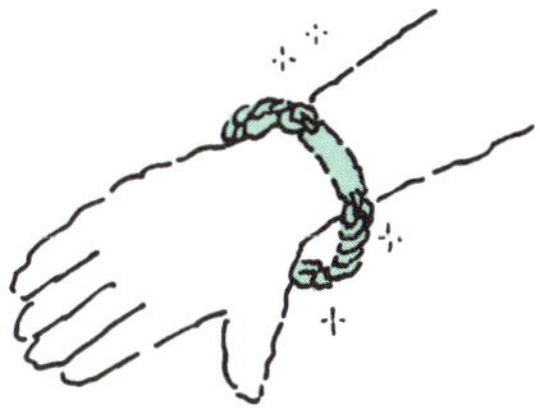

brain
the part of you inside your head, which you think with: *Dogs have smaller* ***brains*** *than human beings do.*

brake
the handle that is used to slow down or stop a car, train or bicycle: *Steve had to put on his* ***brakes*** *when a dog ran out on to the street in front of his bicycle.*

branch
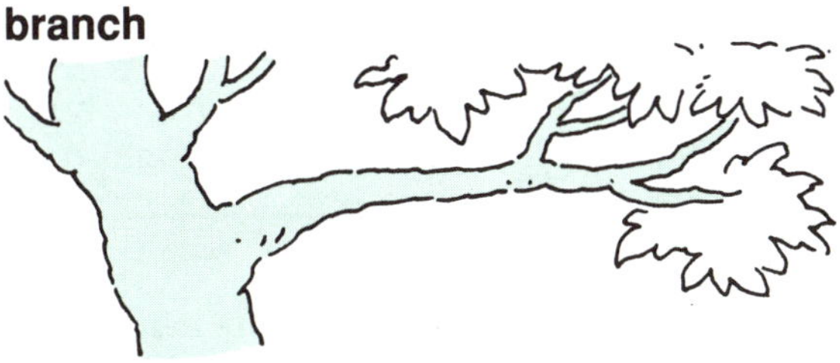

a part of a tree that grows out of the trunk: *My father cut some* ***branches*** *off the old apple tree.*

brave
not afraid of danger or pain; full of courage: *Mary is a very* ***brave*** *girl — when her little brother fell into the river she jumped in and saved him. It was* ***brave*** *of Robert not to cry when he burnt his hand.*

bravery
being brave: *The general praised the soldiers'* ***bravery****.*

Same as **courage**.

bread
a food made from flour and water, which is baked in an oven: *My mother asked me to go to the baker's and buy a loaf of* ***bread****. Bill cut a few slices of* ***bread*** *and spread them with butter.*

breadth
how wide something is; the distance from one side to the other side: *The swimming-pool is 20 metres in length and 7 metres in* ***breadth****.*

break
a short rest; a pause: *At school we have a 15-minute* ***break*** *at 10 o'clock. Let's stop work and have a* ***break*** *for tea.*

break
1 to divide into two or more pieces, especially with force: *Anne tried to* ***break*** *the stick in two. Tim* ***broke*** *off a piece of his chocolate bar and gave it to me. The cup fell on the floor and* ***broke****. Mike fell down the stairs and* ***broke*** *his arm.* **2** to damage something so that it does not work any more: *Bob* ***broke*** *his watch. The washing-machine is* ***broken****.* **3** to go against a law or a rule: *You mustn't* ***break*** *the school rules.*

broke, breaking, has broken

break away to go away suddenly; to escape: *My dog tried to* ***break away*** *from me when he saw the cat. The policemen caught the thief but he* ***broke away*** *from them.*

break down to stop going because something has gone wrong with the engine: *The bus* ***broke down*** *when it was taking us to school today, so we had to get out and walk.*

break in, break into to get into a house by force: *A thief* ***broke in*** *during the night and stole the video recorder. Our neighbours' house was* ***broken into*** *last night. The burglars were caught by the police while they were trying to* ***break into*** *the bank.*

break open to get something open by using force: *John had lost his key for the front door and tried to* ***break*** *it* ***open****.*

breakfast
the first meal of the day: *I had tea and toast for* ***breakfast****. When do you have* ***breakfast****?*

breath
the air that goes into and out of your body through your nose or mouth: *Your* ***breath***

*smells of oranges. Joe took a deep **breath** and dived into the water. Granny was out of **breath** after running up the stairs.*

Say **breth.**

breathe
to take air into your lungs and let it out: *Do you **breathe** through your nose or your mouth? I could hardly **breathe** because of the smoke all around me.*

- Say **breeth.**
- breathed, breathing, has breathed

breeze
a gentle wind: *I like it when there's a cool **breeze**. There is a **breeze** blowing from the sea.*

brick
a hard block made of clay that is used to build walls and houses: *Our house is made of **bricks**, not stone. There is a red **brick** wall round our school yard.*

bride
a woman who is getting married: *The **bride** wore a beautiful white dress and a long veil.*

bridegroom
a man who is getting married: *The **bridegroom** wore a grey suit for the wedding.*

bridesmaid
a girl who looks after the bride at a wedding: *The **bridesmaids** wore long pink dresses and had flowers in their hair.*

bridge
a part of a road or railway that is built over a river or road, so that people and vehicles can cross from one side to the other: *We had to take a ferry across the river because there was no **bridge**. The new railway **bridge** is built out of steel.*

brief
short: *The doctor only came for a **brief** visit. My aunt sent us a **brief** note telling us that she had moved house.*

briefcase
a flat case for carrying papers: *My father has a black leather **briefcase** which he takes to his office.*

bright
1 shining with a strong light: *The sun is very **bright** today because there are no clouds.* **2** having a very strong colour: *A tomato is **bright** red. Do you like **bright** colours?* **3** cheerful: *Our granny greeted us with a **bright** smile.* **4** clever: *The **brighter** children in the class will probably go to a university when they are older.*

Meanings 1 and 2: the opposite is **dull** or **dark.**

brim
1 the top edge of a cup, glass or bowl: *Don't fill the glass right up to the **brim** or you may spill it.* **2** a broad piece round the edge of a hat: *If the sun is too bright and hot for you, you can wear a hat with a wide **brim**.*

bring
to carry something with you; to make someone come with you: *Could you please **bring** a few of your records along? I have **brought** two friends home with me for lunch. **Bring** your exercise books to me. You may borrow my umbrella, but please **bring** it back tomorrow.*

brought, bringing, has brought

bring up to look after children while they are growing up: *My granny had ten children to **bring up**. Jenny has been **brought up** by her aunt because her parents live abroad.*

broad
wide: *The streets in the centre of the city are very **broad**, with big shops on each side. The river is almost a kilometre **broad** here.*

- Same as **wide.**
- The opposite is **narrow.**

broadcast
to send out a programme from a radio or television station: *The Prime Minister's speech was **broadcast** on television last night.*

broadcast, broadcasting, has broadcast

broke
see **break**: *The mirror dropped and **broke**. Kate **broke** a window today.*

broken
see **break**: *My watch is **broken**. Thomas has **broken** the window.*

brooch
a piece of jewellery that is fastened by a pin:

*Mum sometimes wears a gold **brooch** on her dress.*

Rhymes with **coach**.

broom
a brush with a long handle for sweeping the floor: *Could you please fetch the **broom** and sweep up all these little bits of paper?*

brother
a boy who has the same parents as you do: *I have two sisters and one **brother**. Tom has no **brothers** or sisters.*

brought
see **bring**: *Susan took three books back to the library and **brought** five home. I have **brought** you your tea.*

brown
a colour like the colour of earth: *Lisa's eyes are dark **brown**. This bear has **brown** fur. Some people like to lie in the sun and get **brown**.*

brush
an object with stiff hairs that you use for cleaning, scrubbing or painting: *You use a hair**brush** for tidying your hair and a tooth**brush** for cleaning your teeth. A painter uses a large **brush** to paint walls and ceilings.*

brush
to clean with a brush; to tidy with a brush: *Don't forget to **brush** your hair. Dad **brushed** the dust off his jacket with a clothes-**brush**. Your shoes need **brushing**.*

bubble

a little ball of air: *You get soap **bubbles** all over your hands when you wash them with soap. There are lots of tiny **bubbles** in lemonade that rise to the top of your glass.*

bubble
to be full of bubbles: *The water will begin to **bubble** as soon as it boils.*

bubbled, bubbling, has bubbled

bucket
a large container with a handle, for carrying water: *My mother filled a **bucket** with water and took it outside to wash the car.*

Same as a **pail**.

buckle
an object that fastens a belt or strap: *Jill is wearing a belt with a silver **buckle**.*

buckle
to fasten with a buckle: *Wait for me while I **buckle** my sandals.*

buckled, buckling, has buckled

bud
a little round shoot on a tree or plant, from which a leaf or flower will grow: *Are there any **buds** on these fruit-trees yet?*

budgerigar

a small bird that has brightly-coloured feathers and is kept as a pet: *My aunt has a green **budgerigar** that can say 'hello'.*

Called a **budgie** for short.

buffalo
a large kind of ox: *Wild **buffaloes** live in large herds in Africa.*

Many **buffaloes** or **buffalos**

bug
1 a small insect that lives in dirty houses and beds: *A **bug** can bite you and suck a little bit of blood.* **2** any small insect: *There's a **bug** crawling up your arm.*

build
to make something by putting pieces together: *Our neighbours want to **build** a new house in the country. My brother has **built** a little car for himself out of old pieces of metal. A new road has been **built** round the city.*

built, building, has built

building
something that has been built, such as a house, school or store: *I don't like the new high **buildings** in the city centre.*

built
see **build**: *My father **built** a wall round our garden last year. When was this house **built**?*

bulb
1 a glass object that is shaped like a pear and used in an electric lamp: *I need a new **bulb** for my desk lamp.* **2** a root shaped like a ball: *Some kinds of flowers are grown from **bulbs**.*

bull
the male of the animals that belong to the ox family; the male of the elephant: *The cows were kept in one field and the **bulls** in another. A **bull** can be dangerous because it can attack people with its horns.*

bulldog
a large dog with a short, thick neck and a broad flat face: ***Bulldogs** are fierce dogs, so some people keep them to protect their houses.*

bullet
a piece of metal that is fired from a gun: *The policeman was wounded in the arm by a **bullet**.*

bully
a person who hurts or frightens other weaker people: *The headmaster punished the **bullies** who had been frightening the new pupils.*

Two **bullies**

bully
to behave like a bully: *Some of the older boys **bullied** the two little girls as they were walking home. Stop **bullying** your little brother!*

bullies, bullied, bullying, has bullied

bump
1 a knock or the sound it makes: *The car hit the tree with a loud **bump**.* **2** a swelling or lump on your body: *Mike got a **bump** on his head when he hit it against the edge of the table.*

bump
to knock against something: *I didn't look where I was going and **bumped** into a lamp-post. The ceiling was so low that Dad **bumped** his head against it.*

bun
a kind of small round cake: *I bought some **buns** with raisins in them, and we ate them with butter and jam for tea.*

bunch
a group of things that are tied or joined together: *My father bought a **bunch** of flowers for my mother. I found a **bunch** of keys in the street. Bill ate a whole **bunch** of grapes at lunchtime.*

bundle
a group of things that are tied together: *The children collected some firewood and tied it in **bundles** to take home.*

bungalow
a low house that has only a ground floor: *You can't go upstairs in a **bungalow**, can you?*

burglar
a person who breaks into a building to steal things: *Last night a **burglar** broke into our school and stole a computer.*

Same as a **thief**.

burn
1 to destroy or damage by fire; to be destroyed or damaged by fire: *There was a fire in the factory and one of the buildings **burnt** down. My father **burnt** the toast this morning.* **2** to injure by fire: *Be careful not to **burn** your fingers on the hot iron.* **3** to catch fire: *Paper **burns** easily.*

burnt, burning, has burnt

burnt
see **burn**: *I don't like eating **burnt** toast. The match dropped on the tablecloth and **burnt** a hole in it.*

burrow
a hole made in the ground by an animal: *Rabbits dig **burrows** to live in.*

burst
1 to break suddenly, especially with a bang: *Peter **burst** the balloon with a pin. Bubbles **burst** after a short while.* **2** to come suddenly: *A boy **burst** into our classroom without knocking.*

burst, bursting, has burst

burst into tears to start crying: *Jenny **burst into tears** when she heard that her dog had been injured.*

bury
1 to put a dead body in a grave: *The children **buried** the dead bird in the garden.* **2** to hide something in the ground: *The thief **buried** the*

jewellery in a metal box under the big oak tree.

buries, buried, burying, has buried

bus

a large vehicle for carrying a lot of passengers by road: *I go to school by* ***bus****. Can you tell me which* ***bus*** *goes to the railway station?*

bus-stop

a place where buses stop to let you get on or off: *My mother sometimes walks with me to the* ***bus-stop****. There are always long queues at the* ***bus-stops*** *when the shops close in the evening.*

bush

a plant that looks like a small tree without a trunk: *We have rose* ***bushes*** *in our garden.*

business

1 buying and selling things: ***Business*** *was good at the shop today. This company does* ***business*** *with many foreign firms.* **2** a shop, a firm: *My uncle runs two hairdressing* ***businesses****.*

Say **biz**-nis.

businessman, businesswoman

a person who buys and sells things; a person who runs a business: *Some* ***businessmen*** *have to travel a lot. My aunt is a very good* ***business-woman*** *— she knows how to make a lot of money.*

- Say **biz**-nis-man, **biz**-nis-woo-man.
- Two **businessmen**, two **businesswomen**

busy

1 having a lot of work to do: *The headmaster is too* ***busy*** *to see you now. I am very* ***busy*** *today.* **2** full of traffic or people: *The roads are very* ***busy*** *in the mornings and also in the evenings.*

busy, busier, busiest

but

1 a word you use to show that there is a difference between two things you want to say: *Mr Li is rich* ***but*** *not happy. I invited Lisa and Amy to tea* ***but*** *Lisa couldn't come.* **2** except: *There was nobody in the house* ***but*** *me.*

butcher

a person who sells meat: *You can buy meat, pies and sausages at the* ***butcher's****.*

butter

a kind of fat that is made from cream: *Louise spread her toast with* ***butter*** *and marmalade. Would you like another slice of bread and* ***butter****?*

butterfly

an insect with large coloured wings: *We stood and watched the beautiful blue* ***butterfly*** *as it flew from flower to flower.*

Two **butterflies**

button

1 a small, round object for fastening clothing: *My blouse has seven* ***buttons*** *down the front. A* ***button*** *came off my coat and I asked my mother to sew it on again.* **2** a small object that you press to switch something on or to ring a bell: *Press this* ***button*** *to turn the television on.*

button

to fasten with buttons: ***Button*** *up your jacket — it's cold outside.*

buy

to get something by paying for it with money: *I should like to* ***buy*** *a new radio but I don't have enough money. My aunt* ***bought*** *me an interesting book for my birthday. Roger has* ***bought*** *himself a football.*

- The opposite is **sell**.
- bought, buying, has bought

by

1 next to someone or something; near: *Paul is sitting* ***by*** *his sister. My grandparents live* ***by*** *the sea.* **2** showing who or what does something or causes something: *Joe was hit on the head* ***by*** *a golfball. This model aeroplane was made* ***by*** *Jane and Peter. This is a good story — who is it* ***by****?* **3** using some kind of transport: *We travelled home* ***by*** *car, not* ***by*** *train. This letter came* ***by*** *hand, not* ***by*** *post. You'll have to send that letter* ***by*** *airmail if you want it to get to America in time for your aunt's birthday.* **4** not later than: *Be home* ***by*** *five o'clock.* **5** during: *I don't like travelling* ***by*** *night.* **6** you use **by** when you measure things: *If the table is 3 metres long and 2 metres wide, you can say it is 3 metres* ***by*** *2 metres.*

by yourself **1** alone: *I don't like being all* ***by myself*** *in the house.* **2** without help from anyone else: *Did you write this story* ***by yourself****?*

cab
a car that you can hire with a driver, for short journeys: *Dad called a **cab** to take us to the station.*

Same as a **taxi**.

cabbage
a vegetable that looks like a big ball of leaves: *You can either cook **cabbage** or chop it up and eat it raw.*

cable

a thick, strong rope made of wires: *The new bridge is held up by **cables**.*

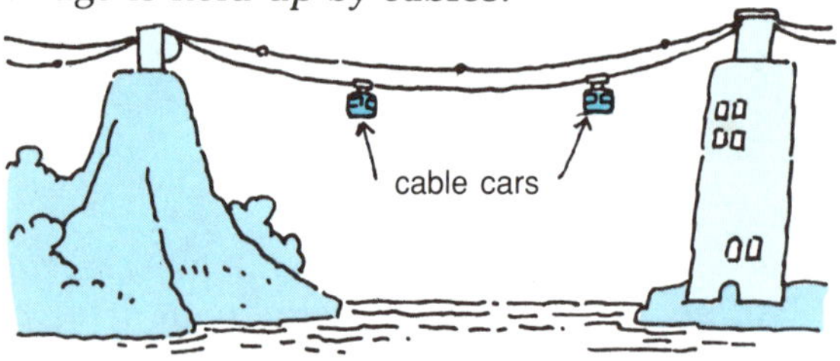

cable car a vehicle for passengers that is pulled by a moving cable: *The **cable car** took us all the way from the valley to the top of the mountain.*

café
a small restaurant where you can have a snack and a drink of tea or coffee: *After we had done our shopping we went to a **café** for tea.*

Say **kaf**-ay.

cage
a container made of wire, or a small area closed in by metal bars, in which birds or animals are kept: *The canary flew away when I opened its **cage**. The tiger was walking about its **cage** roaring.*

cake
a sweet food made by mixing and then baking flour, fat, eggs, sugar and other things: *Would you like a piece of chocolate **cake**? No, thank you, I prefer these cream **cakes**.*

calculate
to work out a sum: *Can you **calculate** the number of hours in a week?*

calculated, calculating, has calculated

calculator

a small machine for calculating, that you can carry in your pocket: *Andy used a **calculator** to add up all the numbers.*

calendar
a card, or a set of pages, printed with the months and days of the year: *Thomas has a **calendar** hanging in his room with photographs of animals in it — a new photograph for each month.*

calf
1 the baby of a cow, elephant, giraffe, whale or seal: *The **calf** followed the mother cow around the field.* **2** the back part of your leg, below your knee: *My **calves** are aching after all that running I did yesterday.*

Two **calves**

call
1 a telephone message; a talk with someone on the telephone: *There were two phone **calls** for you while you were out. I'll give you a **call** tomorrow.* **2** a shout: *We heard a **call** for help coming from the river.*

call
1 to give a name to someone or something: *What are you going to **call** the baby? I'm **called** Pauline. What are you **called**? My brother's name is Robert but his friends **call** him Bob. 'What do you **call** a baby cat?' 'A kitten.'* **2** to shout to someone to get them to come to you: *Mum says she will **call** us when it is time for dinner.* **3** to telephone someone: *I'll **call** you this evening. 'Hello, I'd like to speak to Helen, please.' 'Who is **calling**?' My mother **called** a doctor because my sister was very ill.* **4** to visit someone for a short time: *Richard **called** on us last night. I'll **call** at your house tomorrow morning with the book I promised you.*

call for to come and fetch someone: *Joe* ***calls for*** *me in the mornings and we walk to school together.*
call out to shout something: *Stand up as I* ***call out*** *your names.*

calm
1 not anxious; not excited: *Please keep* ***calm*** *— there is nothing to worry about. Our teacher is a very* ***calm*** *person — she never shouts at us.* 2 still; without any wind: *The sea was very* ***calm*** *— there were no waves. The weather has been* ***calm*** *today.*

Same as **quiet**.

came
see **come**: *David* ***came*** *home very late last night.*

camel

a desert animal with one or two large humps on its back, that carries goods and people: *A* ***camel*** *can walk for many days without eating or drinking anything.*

camera
the instrument that you take photographs or make films with: *Claire took lots of pictures with her new* ***camera****. I put a new film in my* ***camera****.*

camp
a group of tents or huts in which people live for a short time: *The children spent their holidays in a* ***camp*** *by the sea. Soldiers have to go to an army* ***camp*** *to train.*

camp
to live in a tent for a short time: *I would like to go* ***camping*** *with my friends during the summer holidays. We* ***camped*** *on the beach last year.*

can
1 to be able to do something: ***Can*** *you carry this big box or is it too heavy for you? I asked Peter if he* ***could*** *carry the big box.* 2 to know how to do something: *My little sister* ***can*** *already ride a bicycle. I* ***could*** *not do that when I was her age. Most children in my class* ***can*** *swim.* 3 to be allowed to do something: *Hello,* ***can*** *I speak to David, please? You* ***can*** *go to the cinema if you are good. Mum said we* ***could*** *go to the cinema.*

can, could

can
a metal container for food, drink, oil or paint: *We'll open a* ***can*** *of meat balls for supper. I took two* ***cans*** *of lemonade with me to drink during the journey.*

canal
a kind of river which has been made by men for boats to pass along: *The Panama* ***Canal*** *links the Pacific Ocean with the Atlantic Ocean.*

canary
a small yellow singing bird which people keep as a pet: *My friend has a* ***canary*** *which sings beautifully.*

Two **canaries**

candle
a stick of wax with a string through the middle, that you burn to give light: *We had to use* ***candles*** *when the electric lights went out. Rosie blew out all the* ***candles*** *on her birthday cake in one go.*

cane
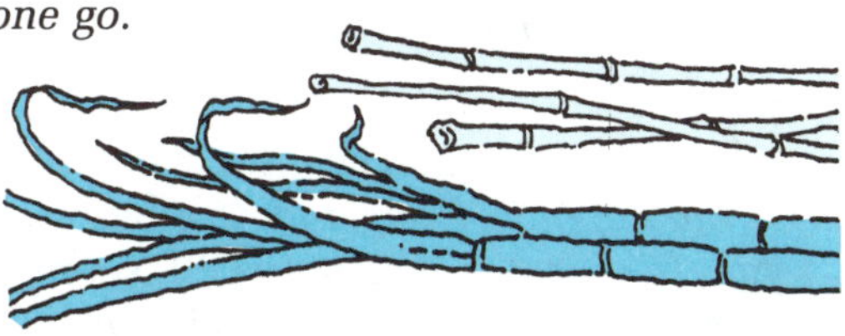

1 the long hollow stem of a plant such as bamboo: *Sugar is made from sugar* ***cane****. Baskets are made from* ***cane****.* 2 a long thin stick which teachers used to use for hitting schoolchildren when they were naughty: *The teacher kept a* ***cane*** *in his cupboard.*

cane
to hit with a cane: *The headmaster* ***caned*** *the boy who had been bullying the younger children.*

caned, caning, has caned

canned
stored in cans: *We took a lot of* ***canned*** *food with us when we went camping.*

cannot
can and **not**, written as one word: *Jane* ***cannot*** *walk to school because she has hurt her leg.*

cannot, could not

can't
short for **cannot**: *Sorry, I **can't** hear what you are saying. You can swim, **can't** you?*

> can't, couldn't

canteen

a place in a factory or office where people can buy and eat meals: *The workers eat their lunch in the **canteen**.*

cap
1 a hat with a peak at the front: *Policemen wear a **cap** with a special badge.* **2** a hat that fits closely round your head: *In some swimming-pools you have to wear a swimming **cap**.* **3** the cover or top of a bottle or pen: *Put the **cap** back on your pen when you have finished writing.*

capital
1 the most important city in a country: *London is the **capital** of England.* **2** a big letter that you find at the beginning of sentences or names: *THESE ARE **CAPITALS**.*

captain
1 the person who is in charge of a ship or an aeroplane: *The **captain** welcomed the passengers on board the ship.* **2** the leader of a team: *The school football team chose Peter as their **captain**.*

capture
1 to catch: *The leopard was **captured** and taken to the zoo. A prisoner escaped from prison but the police **captured** him again.* **2** to attack a place and get control of it: *The soldiers **captured** the fortress after a long battle.*

> - Meaning 1: same as **catch.**
> - captured, capturing, has captured

car
a motor vehicle with four wheels, for carrying people: *My big brother is learning how to drive a **car**. Mum takes us to school by **car**. Do you prefer to walk to school or go by **car**?*

card
1 a piece of stiff, folded paper with a picture and greetings on it: *Don't forget to send a birthday **card** to your grandmother.* **2** a small printed piece of cardboard or plastic: *All the new pupils were given **cards** with their names on.* **3** a small oblong piece of stiff paper with a number or picture on it, which you use for playing games: *There are 52 **cards** in a pack of **cards**. Would you like a game of **cards**?*

cardboard
a stiff, hard material that is made from paper, and is used especially for making boxes: *Our new television set arrived in a big **cardboard** box. At school today we cut animal-shapes out of **card-board** and put them up along the shelf.*

cardigan
a knitted jacket that is fastened at the front, usually with buttons: *Diana put her **cardigan** on because the room was very cold.*

care
1 attention: *Carry the cups with **care**.* **2** worry: *All headmasters and headmistresses have a lot of **cares**. My granny is always full of **care**.*
take care to be careful: ***Take care** when you cross the road. **Take care** or you will fall!*
take care of to look after someone or something: *Our aunt **took care of** us while our mother was in hospital.*

care
1 to worry about something: *Every mother **cares** a lot about her own children.* **2** to mind about something: *I don't **care** if I lose the game.*

> cared, caring, has cared

care for **1** to like: *Would you **care for** another cup of tea?* **2** to look after: *A nurse's job is to **care for** sick people.*

careful
making sure that you do not have an accident or make a mistake: *Please be **careful** when you're riding your bicycle. My mother is a very **careful** driver. You should be more **careful** with your toys. I've made a **careful** copy of the teacher's notes.*

> Same as **cautious.**

careless
not careful: *Peter did not listen to what the teacher said and made some **careless** mistakes.*

*This work is very **careless**, Jonathan! It was **careless** of you to drop the plate.*

cargo
the goods that are carried by a ship or plane: *The ship was carrying a **cargo** of sugar to New Zealand. A **cargo** plane does not carry passengers.*

Many different **cargoes**

carol
a song that people sing at Christmas: *We sang a lot of **carols** on Christmas Day.*

carpenter
a person whose job is making and repairing the wooden parts of buildings: *The **carpenter** is going to fit a new door in our kitchen.*

carpet
a thick piece of material for covering the floor: *My parents bought a large woollen **carpet** for our living-room.*

carrot
a long, thin, orange-coloured vegetable that grows under the ground: *Rabbits like to eat **carrots**.*

carry
to take something from one place to another: *I have to **carry** my books to school every day in my schoolbag. That box is too heavy for one person to **carry** alone.*

carries, carried, carrying, has carried

carry on to continue: ***Carry on** with your homework. John's mother told him to go to bed, but he **carried on** watching television.*
carry out to do or finish something: *Mark **carried out** his plan. The children **carried out** the teacher's orders.*

cart
a vehicle with two wheels, that is pulled by a horse: *Farmers sometimes use **carts** for carrying heavy loads.*

carve
1 to cut an object out of a piece of wood or stone: *The statue was **carved** out of wood.* **2** to slice a large piece of meat: *Dad **carved** the ham with a long, sharp knife.*

carved, carving, has carved

case
1 a container for holding your clothes when you are travelling: *We shall have to pack our **cases** the day before we go on holiday.* **2** a firm container for holding something: *Keep your glasses in their **case** when you're not wearing them.*
in case because something may happen: *Take an umbrella **in case** it rains.*

cash
paper money and coins, not cheques: *Do you wish to pay in **cash** or by cheque? I don't have any **cash** on me at the moment.*

cashier

a person who receives and pays out money, for example in a bank: *Lisa's mother works as a **cashier** in a supermarket.*

castle
a large building that has strong walls and towers to protect the people inside against attacks: *The **castle** stood on top of a high mountain.*

cat
an animal with soft fur and a long tail that people keep as a pet: *A **cat** likes to catch mice and birds. **Cats** can see in the dark. **Cats** love being stroked.*

catapult
a stick that looks like the letter Y, fitted with an elastic band for shooting little stones at things: *It can be very dangerous to play with a **catapult** because you might hurt someone.*

catch
1 to capture animals or fish: *The fishermen **caught** a lot of fish last night.* **2** to capture or get hold of a person: *Did the police **catch** the thief?* **3** to get hold of something that is falling or being thrown, and keep hold of it: *Philip could not **catch** the ball.* **4** to get on a bus or train before it leaves: *I have to **catch** the train at 10 o'clock. Julie had to run to **catch** the bus for school.* **5** to surprise someone while they are doing something wrong: *The policeman*

caught *the man stealing a bicycle.* **6** to get an illness: *Mark* ***caught*** *a cold because he stayed too long in the cold water.* **7** to be able to hear: *Sorry, I didn't* ***catch*** *what you said.* **8** to start burning: *The dry grass* ***caught*** *fire when Peter dropped the match on it.*

- Meanings 1 and 2: same as **capture.**
- caught, catching, has caught

caterpillar

a creature that looks like a worm, and turns into a butterfly or moth: *A* ***caterpillar*** *eats leaves. Some birds like to eat* ***caterpillars.***

cattle
cows and bulls: *The farmer on the hill owns a large herd of* ***cattle.*** *The* ***cattle*** *are kept in the field during the day but they go into the shed at night.*

caught
see **catch**: *Sarah* ***caught*** *the ball. Andrew has* ***caught*** *a bad cold, so he has to stay in bed.*

cauliflower
a vegetable which looks like a large white ball with green leaves around it: *Have you tried eating* ***cauliflower*** *with oyster sauce?*

cause
the reason why something happens: *Nobody knows what the* ***cause*** *of the accident was.*

cause
to make something happen: *What* ***caused*** *the explosion? Helen's illness* ***caused*** *her mother a lot of worry.*

caused, causing, has caused

cautious
taking care not to make mistakes or get into trouble: *My father is a* ***cautious*** *driver. You must be more* ***cautious*** *and not talk to strangers.*

Same as **careful.**

cave
a large hole in a rock or mountain, or under the ground: *Many thousands of years ago people lived in* ***caves.*** *The children were longing to explore the big dark* ***cave.***

ceiling
the roof inside a room: *The walls and* ***ceiling*** *of my room are white. My father fixed the lamp to the* ***ceiling.***

celebrate
to have a party because something special is happening: *Tracy is* ***celebrating*** *her birthday today.*

celebrated, celebrating, has celebrated

cement
1 a grey powder which is mixed with sand and water and used for sticking bricks together: *Dad needed ten sacks of* ***cement*** *to build the wall.* **2** a strong kind of glue for mending broken dishes and doing other jobs of that kind: *I tried to join the broken pieces of the vase with* ***cement.***

cement-mixer
a machine for making concrete: *A* ***cement-mixer*** *has a large container shaped like a barrel that turns round and round, in which sand, water, cement and little stones are mixed.*

cent
a coin that is worth one hundredth of a dollar: *This chewing-gum costs 20* ***cents*** *a packet.*

centimetre
one hundredth of a metre: *This piece of ribbon is seventy* ***centimetres*** *long and three* ***centimetres*** *wide.*

centipede

a tiny creature that is long and narrow in shape and looks like a worm with lots of short legs: *I've just seen a* ***centipede*** *crawling across the floor.*

centre
1 the middle of something: *We live near the* ***centre*** *of the city.* **2** a large building or a place that many people go to: *A shopping-****centre*** *is a place where a lot of shops have been built close together. A sports-****centre*** *is a place where you can practise lots of different sports.*

Meaning 1: same as **middle.**

century
one hundred years: *Many* ***centuries*** *ago, people lived in caves. Some trees live for several*

centuries. *We live in the 20th* ***century***.

Many **centuries**

cereal

1 a grain used as food: *Wheat, maize and rice are* ***cereals***. 2 a food that you eat for breakfast, made from a grain: *Many people eat their* ***cereal*** *with milk and sugar.*

ceremony

the actions and words that are used at a special event such as a wedding: *Exchanging rings is part of the marriage* ***ceremony***.

Some **ceremonies**

certain

1 knowing; not doubting; sure: *I'm* ***certain*** *Mike will come to the party. Joanne is* ***certain*** *to win the painting competition. Bill set the alarm clock for 7 o'clock to make* ***certain*** *that he would not be late for school.* 2 some: ***Certain*** *kinds of fruit, such as pineapples and bananas, only grow in hot countries. Always leave a* ***certain*** *amount of time for checking your homework when you have finished it.*

Meaning 1: same as **sure**.

certainly

1 without any doubt: *Sorry, I can't come today, but I'll* ***certainly*** *come tomorrow.* 2 of course: *You may* ***certainly*** *have a chocolate. 'May I come shopping with you?' '****Certainly****!'*

chain

a number of metal rings that are joined together in a line: *The dog was fastened to the railings by a long* ***chain***. *Audrey is wearing a silver* ***chain*** *round her neck.*

chain

to fasten with chains: *The prisoners were* ***chained*** *together in a long line. We had better* ***chain*** *the dog to the railings when we go into the shop.*

chair

a piece of furniture that you sit on, which has an upright part that supports your back: *There are four* ***chairs*** *around the table.*

chalk

a kind of crayon you use for writing on blackboards with: *The teacher picked up a piece of white* ***chalk*** *and wrote the word on the blackboard. She keeps a box of coloured* ***chalks*** *in her desk.*

challenge

to ask someone to take part in a contest, or do something difficult or dangerous: *Danny* ***challenged*** *his brother to a game of table-tennis. I* ***challenge*** *you to swim across the swimming-pool under water.*

challenged, challenging, has challenged

champion

a person who has beaten all the others in a contest or competition: *Lisa is the badminton* ***champion*** *of our school this year.*

chance

1 something that may happen: *Our football team has a good* ***chance*** *of winning the match. Is there any* ***chance*** *that you will be seeing Robert tomorrow?* 2 the time and ability to do something: *Vicky has never had a* ***chance*** *of going abroad. The bird flew away before I had a* ***chance*** *to take a picture of it.* 3 something you didn't plan: *I met Andrew by* ***chance*** *on my way to school.*

change

1 a difference; something new that happens to something: *There is no* ***change*** *in my plans — I still want to go to China. I usually have cereal for breakfast, but today I had a boiled egg and toast for a* ***change***. 2 coins, not paper money: *Do you have enough* ***change*** *for the telephone?* 3 money that you get back when you pay for something with more money than it costs: *Bob gave the taxi-driver three dollars and got ten cents* ***change***. *Always make sure you get the right* ***change*** *in a shop.*

change

1 to make different; to become different: *Catherine* ***changed*** *her name to Kate. Mark had* ***changed*** *so much that I didn't recognize him.* 2 to put on different clothes: *I always* ***change*** *into my jeans and sweater when I come home from school. Your shirt is dirty — you must* ***change*** *it straight away.* 3 to give one kind of money for another kind: *Could*

you please ***change*** *a dollar for two fifty-cent coins? My father* ***changed*** *$100 into Australian dollars at the bank.*

changed, changing, has changed

chapter
a part of a book: *This book is divided into 12* ***chapters****. Read* ***chapter*** *5 for homework.*

charge
1 a price: *What is the* ***charge*** *for a telephone call to Hong Kong?* **2** an attack: *The soldiers made a* ***charge****.*
in charge of looking after someone or something: *Mrs King will be* ***in charge of*** *this class while your teacher is away. The teacher put me* ***in charge of*** *collecting the books from the desks.*

charge
1 to ask for a certain amount of money for something: *They are* ***charging*** *$3.50 for a ticket to the football match.* **2** to rush forward and attack: *The lion* ***charged*** *at the zebra.*

charged, charging, has charged

chart
a drawing, map or diagram that gives you information about something: *This weather* ***chart*** *shows you how the weather is going to change during the next few days.*

chase
1 to run after someone or something: *Andrew* ***chased*** *after Paul but did not catch him. The police* ***chased*** *the robbers by car.* **2** to make a person or an animal run away: *Mr Black is always* ***chasing*** *cats out of his garden.*

chased, chasing, has chased

chat
a talk with someone: *Mrs Green walked home with me and stayed for a* ***chat*** *with my mother.*

Same as **conversation.**

chat
to talk with someone in an easy, friendly way: *My mother and the lady next door like* ***chatting*** *about their families. In Britain, people* ***chat*** *about the weather a lot.*

chatted, chatting, has chatted

chauffeur
a person whose job is to drive a car for someone else: *The Prime Minister has a* ***chauffeur*** *to drive him to meetings. Many* ***chauffeurs*** *wear uniforms.*

Say **show**-fer.

cheap
costing very little money; not expensive: *Buy a* ***cheap*** *pair of shorts for your camping trip. My old bicycle was much* ***cheaper*** *than my new one. Mike bought the* ***cheapest*** *ticket to New York.*

The opposite is **expensive** or **dear.**

cheat
to be dishonest or unfair; to break the rules: *Copying someone else's work in an exam is* ***cheating****. The ice-cream man tried to* ***cheat*** *me out of 20 cents. I never* ***cheat*** *at games.*

check
to make sure that something is correct: *Will you please* ***check*** *my sums? Before my mum left the house she* ***checked*** *that she had switched off the cooker.*
check in to arrive at a hotel and sign the guests' book: *We* ***checked in*** *last night.*
check out to leave a hotel: *My father gave back the key and paid the bill when he* ***checked out****.*
check up to make sure of something: *Please* ***check up*** *on the time that the train arrives.*

check
1 the checking of something: *Give these sums a quick* ***check****.* **2** another way of spelling **cheque:** *May I pay by* ***check****?*

checked
with a pattern of squares: *Susie is wearing a blue-and-white* ***checked*** *dress.*

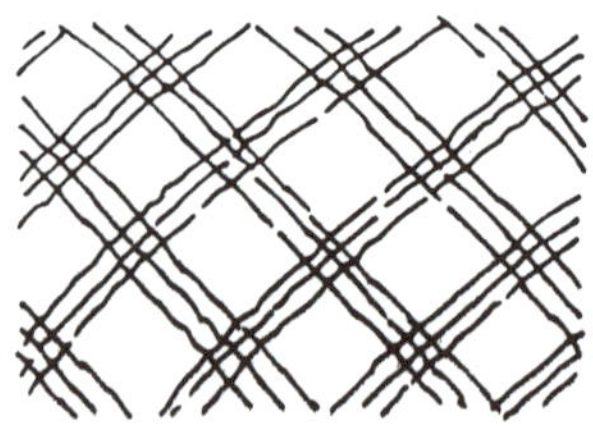

cheek
the side of your face: *Anna kissed her mother on both* ***cheeks*** *before she went to bed.*

cheer
a shout of joy, especially the shout 'Hooray!': *Three* ***cheers*** *for the winner!*

cheer
to shout loudly and joyfully; to shout 'Hooray!': *We all* ***cheered*** *to encourage our school team. The children* ***cheered*** *when George received the prize.*

cheerful
happy; joyful: *Emma is always **cheerful** and smiling. The children sang a **cheerful** song on their way home.*

cheese
a solid food made from milk: *There are many different kinds of **cheese**. Would you like some bread and **cheese** for lunch?*

cheetah
a large wild animal with black spots, that can run very fast: *A **cheetah** is a member of the cat family and lives in Africa.*

cheque
a special written form that people can use instead of money to pay for things: *My mother paid for my new shoes by **cheque**. You have forgotten to sign this **cheque**.*

Rhymes with **neck**.

cherry
a small, round, red fruit with a stone inside: ***Cherries** grow in bunches on a cherry-tree.*

A bunch of **cherries**

chest
1 the front part of your body between your neck and waist: *Your **chest** contains your heart and lungs.* 2 a large, strong wooden box: *My mother stores some of her old clothes in a large **chest** in the spare room.*

chew
to soften and break up food with your teeth so that it is easier to swallow: *You have to **chew** meat well before swallowing it.*

chewing-gum
sweet sticky stuff that you can chew for a long time but do not swallow: *We arc not allowed to chew **chewing-gum** during lessons.*

chick
a baby hen or cock: *Four little **chicks** have hatched out.*

chicken
1 a bird that is kept on a farm for its eggs and meat; a young hen or cock: *The **chickens** are fed on grain.* 2 the meat from a chicken: *I like fried **chicken**.*

chief
the leader of a group of people: *When there are problems, the people of the village go to their **chief** and ask him for help.*

chief
most important: *The **chief** reason for eating food is to stay alive. Name the **chief** cities of New Zealand.*

child
1 a baby or a young person, not an adult: *When my mother was a **child** she lived on a farm. Every **child** has to go to school.* 2 a son or daughter: *My aunt's youngest **child** is two years old.*

- Two **children**
- The opposite is an **adult**.

children
see **child**: *The **children** are playing in the garden. My aunt has six **children**.*

chimney
a tall tube of brick or stone through which the smoke from a fire goes up to the sky: *Smoke was pouring out of the factory **chimney**. In colder countries, every house used to have fireplaces and **chimneys**.*

chimpanzee
a small ape that has brown or black fur: *The **chimpanzees** at the zoo were so like people that they made us laugh. **Chimpanzees** are very intelligent animals.*

chin
the part of your face below your mouth: *Sarah rested her **chin** on her hands while she looked out of the window.*

chocolate
1 a sweet, solid, brown food that is eaten as a sweet or used in ice-cream or cakes: *A bar of **chocolate** is divided up into pieces or squares of **chocolate**. You'll get fat if you eat so many **chocolate** biscuits.* 2 a small hollow piece of chocolate that contains cream or toffee or a nut or something else: *I gave my mum a big box of **chocolates** for her birthday.*

choice
1 a number of things for you to choose from; a

variety: *I know an ice-cream shop where you can get a* ***choice*** *of 20 different flavours of ice-cream.* **2** choosing; being able to choose: *Here is some money to buy a book of your own* ***choice****. You must tell your mother the truth — you have no* ***choice****.*

choir

a group of singers: *Any pupil who enjoys singing may join the school* ***choir****. The* ***choir*** *is giving a concert at the end of term.*

Say **kwire.**

choke

1 to stop breathing, or stop someone breathing: *The thick smoke nearly* ***choked*** *the firemen. The firemen nearly* ***choked*** *in the thick smoke.* **2** to block: *This pipe is* ***choked*** *with dirt.*

choked, choking, has choked

choose

1 to take one thing rather than another from a number of things: *You can* ***choose*** *between lemonade and orange juice. James* ***chose*** *lemonade. Have you* ***chosen*** *what you want to drink yet?* **2** to decide: *If John* ***chooses*** *to stay at home today, he may do so.*

- Meaning 1: same as **select.**
- chose, choosing, has chosen

chop

to cut something into small pieces: *Could you please* ***chop*** *the carrots? George* ***chopped*** *the wood up into logs.*

chopped, chopping, has chopped

chose or **chosen**

see **choose**: *Mary* ***chose*** *a pink dress. Which record have you* ***chosen****?*

Christmas

a festival on 25 December (called Christmas Day) when the birthday of Jesus Christ is celebrated: *At* ***Christmas*** *people give each other presents and wish each other 'merry* ***Christmas****'. We all helped to decorate the* ***Christmas*** *tree and Mum prepared a special* ***Christmas*** *dinner. Mum sends a lot of* ***Christmas*** *cards to friends and relatives every year.*

church

a building where people meet to pray to God: *We go to* ***church*** *every Sunday morning. The largest* ***church*** *in town is St John's* ***Church****.*

cigar

a thick brown roll of dried tobacco leaves that people smoke: *My grandad sometimes smokes a* ***cigar****.*

cigarette

a tube of paper filled with tobacco for smoking: *Mr Jones could not smoke because he had no matches to light his* ***cigarette****.*

cinema

a building in which films are shown: *Would you like to go the* ***cinema*** *tonight? What's on at the* ***cinema****?*

circle

a round shape; a ring: *In this game we have to stand in a* ***circle*** *and hold hands. Can you draw a* ***circle****?*

circular

having the shape of a circle: *Plates are usually* ***circular****.*

Same as **round.**

circus

a travelling show with acrobats, clowns and animals: *A* ***circus*** *is held in a large, round tent. On my birthday my parents took me to the* ***circus****.*

city

a very large town: *Tokyo and Kuala Lumpur are capital* ***cities****.*

Two **cities**

clap

to strike your hands together several times: *When the singer appeared the audience* ***clapped*** *and cheered.* ***Clap*** *your hands in time to the music.*

clapped, clapping, has clapped

class

a group of pupils or students who are taught together: *Amy and I are in the same* ***class****. How many children are there in your* ***class****?*

classmate

a pupil in the same class as you: *Peter invited some of his* ***classmates*** *to his birthday party.*

classroom
a room in a school where a class is taught: *The pupils assemble in the* ***classroom*** *before the teacher comes in.*

claw
one of the sharp nails growing from an animal's foot: *The kitten scratched my hand with its* ***claws****.*

clay

a soft, sticky kind of earth that becomes hard when it is baked: *Bricks are made of* ***clay****, and so are some mugs and bowls and other dishes.*

clean
without any dirt; not dirty: *Are your hands* ***clean****? I always put on* ***clean*** *clothes after I have had a bath.*

> The opposite is **dirty.**

clean
to make something clean: *I* ***clean*** *my teeth after every meal. Mum is* ***cleaning*** *the kitchen.*

clear
1 easy to see, hear or understand: *That photo is a bit faint but this one is nice and* ***clear****. Our teacher has a* ***clear*** *voice. Dad made it* ***clear*** *to us that we have to do what he says.* **2** easy to see through; clean: *The water in this river is so* ***clear*** *that you can see the fish.* **3** with nothing in the way: *Dad likes to drive fast when the roads are* ***clear****.* **4** without clouds or rain: *We had* ***clear*** *weather most of the time during our sailing trip.*
clear up **1** to tidy: *Before I go to bed, I have to* ***clear up*** *my bedroom. Could you please* ***clear up*** *this mess?* **2** to get better: *If the weather* ***clears up****, we'll go for a picnic. My headache has* ***cleared up****.*

clerk
a person who works in an office or bank: *Susan's father is a* ***clerk*** *in a large bank.*

> Rhymes with **dark.**

clever
able to learn or understand quickly: *Helen is a* ***clever*** *girl and always does very well in her exams. Our dog must be very* ***clever*** *— he understands all our commands. Jean made a* ***clever*** *joke and we all laughed.*

climb
to go up a mountain, wall, tree, ladder or stairs: *The two children* ***climbed*** *up the tree and picked some cherries. This wall is too high to* ***climb****. Have you ever* ***climbed*** *that hill over there?*

clinic
a hospital where people go for advice or treatment: *My dad had a boil on his neck and had to go to the skin* ***clinic****.*

clock
an instrument for measuring time, that hangs on the wall, or sits on a table or shelf: *There is a large* ***clock*** *over the entrance to the railway station.*
o'clock the word you use after saying the time when it is exactly at the hour: *This morning I got up at eight* ***o'clock****. Mr Brown arrived at seven* ***o'clock*** *in the evening. It is exactly 12* ***o'clock****.*

close
to shut: *Please* ***close*** *the door. I always* ***close*** *my eyes when I wash my hair. This shop* ***closes*** *at seven o'clock.*

> - Same as **shut.**
> - closed, closing, has closed

close
1 near: *My new school is very* ***close*** *to my house. Emma stood* ***close*** *to her mother.* **2** very dear: *Andrew is a* ***close*** *friend of mine.*

closed
shut; not open: *Most shops are* ***closed*** *on Sundays. Make sure that all the windows are* ***closed*** *before you go out.*

> Same as **shut.**

close-up
a photograph of someone or something that is taken with the camera very close to them: *I tried to take a* ***close-up*** *of my cat sitting on the wall.*

cloth
1 material from which clothes and many other things are made: *My mother bought three metres of* ***cloth*** *to make a new dress.* **2** a piece of cloth that you use for cleaning: *I need a* ***cloth*** *to wipe the table with.*

clothes
things that you wear, such as a shirt, trousers or a dress: *Lucy always wears smart **clothes**, doesn't she? What a huge pile of dirty **clothes**! Where are my clean **clothes** for tomorrow? Sheets and blankets are called bed**clothes**.*

clothing
clothes: *In winter you need warm **clothing**. In the suitcase were a shirt, shorts, socks and other pieces of **clothing**.*

cloud
a patch of white or grey that floats in the sky, made of tiny little drops of water: *There are a lot of dark **clouds** in the sky — it looks as if it might rain.*

clown
a person who does funny things to make people laugh: *The **clown** in the circus was dressed in a funny costume and his face was painted white.*

club
1 a group of people who have the same interest and meet regularly to enjoy it together: *My sister and I have joined the tennis **club**. Are you a member of the gym **club**?* **2** the place where the members of a club meet: *I'll see you at the **club** at 6 o'clock.* **3** a thick, heavy stick that can be used as a weapon: *The robbers attacked the policemen with **clubs**.*

clue
something that helps to solve a problem or mystery: *After Clare had given me a **clue**, I knew the answer to the riddle at once.*

clumsy
careless in the way you move and use your hands: *Philip is very **clumsy** — he is always dropping things. It was **clumsy** of me to knock the vase over.*

coach

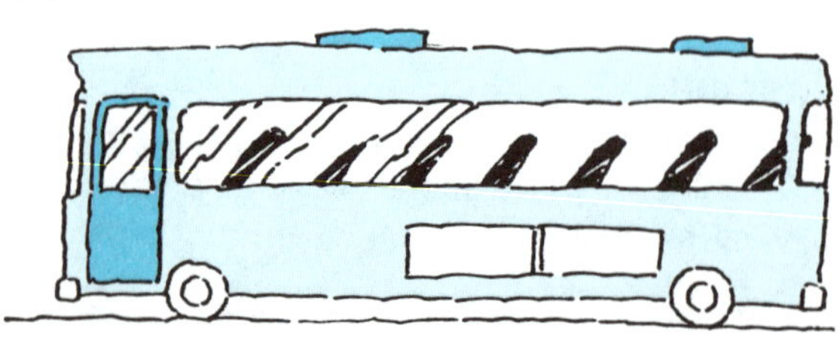

a large, comfortable bus for long journeys: *Do you prefer travelling by **coach** or by train? We took the **coach** to George Town.*

coast
the part of the land next to the sea: *The ship sailed along the **coast** of Sumatra.*

coat
1 a piece of clothing with long sleeves that you wear over other clothes: *It's cold outside — put on your **coat** before you leave.* **2** an animal's fur: *A bear has a very thick **coat**.*

cobbler
a person whose job is to mend shoes and other leather things: *My shoes need new heels — I'll have to take them to the **cobbler**'s.*

cobra
a long, poisonous snake which lives in India and Africa: *When it is frightened, a **cobra** spreads out the skin of its neck to look more dangerous.*

cock
a grown-up male chicken: *There were seven hens and one **cock** on the farm. A **cock** crows early in the morning.*

cockroach

a large brown insect like a beetle that lives in dirty kitchens: ***Cockroaches** come out at night and eat bits of food that are lying around.*

cocoa
1 a brown powder which is used for making chocolate: ***Cocoa** is made from the seeds of a tree that grows in hot countries.* **2** a drink made from this powder, mixed with milk or water: *Would you like a cup of hot **cocoa**?*

coconut
a very large nut that contains white solid flesh and clear juice that you can drink: ***Coconuts** grow on palm trees and have a hard shell. You can eat the white flesh of the **coconut**.*

coffee
a hot drink, dark brown in colour, made from the beans of a plant that grows in South America and Africa: *I like milk with my **coffee**. Would you like another cup of **coffee**?*

coin
a small round piece of metal that is used as money: *I need a few 50-cent **coins** for the telephone.*

cold
low in temperature; not hot or warm: *In winter it is very **cold** outside. My tea has gone **cold**. I*

feel ***cold****. We had* ***cold*** *meat for lunch today.*

The opposite is **hot** or **warm.**

cold
an illness which makes you sneeze and cough: *Jenny has caught a bad* ***cold*** *and has to stay in bed. A* ***cold*** *usually lasts only a few days.*

collar
1 the part of a shirt, jacket or coat which goes round your neck: *The* ***collar*** *of this shirt is too tight.* **2** a leather band or a chain which is put round the neck of a dog or cat: *Our dog has a* ***collar*** *with its name on it.*

collect
1 to bring together: *The boys are* ***collecting*** *wood for the camp-fire.* **2** to save up a lot of things of the same sort because you are interested in them: *Ann* ***collects*** *foreign stamps.* **3** to fetch someone or something: *My mum* ***collects*** *us from school every day by car. Please would you* ***collect*** *the fish from the shop on your way home?*

Meaning 1: same as **gather.**

collide

to come together with great force; to crash: *The two ships* ***collided*** *in the fog. The bus* ***collided*** *with a lorry.*

collided, colliding, has collided

colour
the quality that everything has, but which you can't see in the dark; any of the many shades that objects have: *Yellow, red, blue and green are* ***colours****. What* ***colour*** *is your new dress? Which is your favourite* ***colour****? Is the movie in* ***colour*** *or in black and white?*

colour
to put colour on a picture: *You can use crayons to* ***colour*** *your drawing.*

comb
a flat piece of plastic or metal divided into lots of teeth, which you use to tidy your hair: *Mike always carries a* ***comb*** *in his pocket.*

comb
to tidy your hair with a comb: *Joan* ***combed*** *her hair in front of the mirror.*

come
to move towards a place or person: *I'm* ***coming*** *to your house tomorrow.* ***Come*** *here at once! My friend* ***came*** *to see me. Have any letters* ***come*** *for me today?*

- The opposite is **go.**
- came, coming, has come

comfort
a pleasant state when you feel relaxed, and not too hot or too cold; something that makes life easy and relaxed: *Would you rather stay in the* ***comfort*** *of a hotel than sleep in a tent? We all enjoy the* ***comforts*** *of home, such as a shower, hot water and good food.*

comfort
to make someone who is unhappy feel better: *My mother* ***comforted*** *me when I failed my music exam. Jill was crying and Cathy tried to* ***comfort*** *her.*

comfortable
1 making you feel relaxed: *This big armchair is very* ***comfortable****. My new shoes don't feel* ***comfortable*** *— I think they're a bit too small.* **2** feeling relaxed: *When you are ill, you usually feel more* ***comfortable*** *in bed.*

comic
a children's magazine with stories, especially funny ones, told in rows of small pictures: *The adventures of Korky the Cat are on the front page of the* ***comic****.*

command
something you are told to do: *Soldiers have to obey* ***commands****.*

Same as **order.**

command
to tell someone to do something: *'Leave the room immediately!'* ***commanded*** *the teacher. The general* ***commanded*** *his soldiers to march to the next village.*

Same as **order.**

common
1 happening often; seen often; usual: *Seagulls are* ***common*** *here. It is quite* ***common*** *here to wear short trousers in summer.* **2** used by

everyone: *English is our **common** language.*

Meaning 1: the opposite is **rare.**

community
all the people who live in a town or village: *We must help to look after the old people in our **community**.*

Several **communities**

companion
a friend; a person who is with you for a while, or goes with you somewhere: *Mr and Mrs Lee are taking my sister with them on their trip as a **companion** for their own daughter.*

company
1 a business: *Bill's father works for a big oil **company**.* **2** being with someone: *I was glad that my mother kept me **company** when I had to go to the dentist. 'May I come with you?' 'Yes, of course, I'll be glad to have your **company**.'*

Meaning 1: two **companies**

compare
to look at two or more things to find out how much they are alike, or which is better: *Mike **compared** his bicycle with mine and decided his was better. You can't **compare** the taste of a lemon with the taste of a banana — they are completely different. People often **compare** diamonds to stars.*

compared, comparing, has compared

compass
an instrument which you use to find directions: *A **compass** has a needle which always points to the north.*

compete
to try to beat others in a contest or a game: *Our team is **competing** against the Hong Kong team in the tennis contest. Paul and Mark **competed** with each other for first prize in the quiz.*

competed, competing, has competed

competition
a test that many people take part in to find out which of them is the best: *The winner of a **competition** usually gets a prize. How many children took part in the painting **competition**?*

Same as a **contest**.

complain
1 to tell someone that you think something is bad, or unfair: *Kenneth is always **complaining** about the weather. Our neighbour **complained** to my mother about the noise we were making.* **2** to say that you have a pain or feel ill: *My grandfather has been **complaining** of a pain in his chest.*

complete
to finish: *Have you **completed** Exercise 3?*

completed, completing, has completed

complete
1 whole; with nothing missing: *I've got a **complete** set of the new stamps.* **2** total: *My parents didn't tell me anything about my new bicycle till my birthday — it was a **complete** surprise.* **3** finished: *My model aeroplane will soon be **complete**.*

completely
in every way: *Let's do something **completely** different today. My drawing is **completely** finished.*

composition
a piece of written work that you do as an exercise at school: *The teacher asked us to write a **composition** about our visit to the zoo.*

computer

a machine that can calculate numbers and sort out a lot of information in a very short time: *A lot of work can be done by **computer**. Do you know how to operate this **computer**?*

concert
a performance of music or singing: *The school orchestra and choir are giving a **concert** next week in the school hall.*

concrete
very hard stuff for building, made of cement, sand, small stones and water, all mixed together: *A lot of modern buildings are made of **concrete** and steel.*

conduct
the way someone behaves: *Simon's teacher told his parents that his* ***conduct*** *in school was not very good.*

> Same as **behaviour.**

conduct
to keep time for an orchestra while it is playing, or for a choir while it is singing: *The music teacher uses a baton to* ***conduct*** *the choir.*

conductor
1 a person who sells tickets on a bus: *I paid the fare to the bus* ***conductor***. **2** a person who keeps time for an orchestra or a choir: *A* ***conductor*** *stands facing the musicians.*

cone

1 the hard, brown, pointed fruit of a pine-tree or a fir-tree: *You can find* ***cones*** *on the floor of a forest.* **2** a solid shape that is round at one end and pointed at the other; something of this shape: *The police put traffic-****cones*** *round the hole in the road.* **3** a thin hollow kind of biscuit in the shape of a cone, filled with ice-cream: *Mark bought an ice-cream* ***cone*** *on his way home.*

connect
to join together; to link: *This road* ***connects*** *the two farms. Please show me how to* ***connect*** *the printer to the computer. Health is* ***connected*** *with good food and exercise.*

consider
to think about something: *My parents are* ***considering*** *moving to another part of the city. I shall* ***consider*** *your advice carefully.*

considerate
thinking of the feelings and wishes of other people: *It was very* ***considerate*** *of you to bring flowers for your granny.*

contain
to have something inside: *This box* ***contains*** *some old letters.*

container
1 something made to contain things: *My mother put our sandwiches in a plastic* ***container***. **2** a very large metal box for carrying goods on lorries, trains or ships: *A* ***container*** *lorry is used for transporting goods in* ***containers***.

contest
an event that lots of people take part in, to see which of them is the best: *The winner of the swimming* ***contest*** *received a gold medal.*

> Same as a **competition**.

continent
one of the great areas of land on the earth: *There are five* ***continents*** *— Asia, Africa, America, Australia and Europe.*

continue
1 to keep on doing something, without stopping: *If this rain* ***continues****, we shan't be able to have our picnic. Angela* ***continued*** *talking after the lesson had begun.* **2** to go on with something after stopping: *Jane* ***continued*** *with her homework after dinner. The story* ***continues*** *on page 24.*

> continued, continuing, has continued

continuous
going on without stopping: *We've had* ***continuous*** *rain for two whole days.*

control
power over someone or something; being completely in charge: *Linda has no* ***control*** *over her dog — it does just what it likes. She should keep her dog under* ***control****. The teacher should always be in* ***control*** *of the class. The car went out of* ***control*** *on the slippery road.*

control
1 to be in charge of someone or something: *The captain* ***controls*** *the whole ship.* **2** to make someone behave well: ***Control*** *yourselves, children — there's too much noise!* ***Control*** *your dog, please!* **3** to guide; to direct: *Yesterday a policeman had to* ***control*** *the traffic at the corner because the traffic lights weren't working.*

> controlled, controlling, has controlled

conversation
a talk between people: *Pat and I had a long* ***conversation*** *about our plans for the holiday.*

> Same as a **chat.**

cook
a person whose job is cooking: *There is a very good* ***cook*** *at the new restaurant.*

cook
1 to prepare and heat food: *My mother **cooks** three meals every day. My granny **cooked** a chicken for dinner. Do you know how to **cook** these fish?* **2** to become ready to eat by heating: *The chicken is **cooking** in the oven. How long does rice take to **cook**?*

cooked
prepared for eating by being heated, baked, fried or boiled: *Do you like carrots **cooked** or raw?*

The opposite is **raw.**

cooker
a kitchen stove with an oven and heated metal surfaces on top for cooking food: *My mother has an electric **cooker**. I put the frying-pan on the **cooker**.*

cookery book a book that tells you how to cook different kinds of food: *Elizabeth looked at the **cookery book** to find out how to make a chocolate cake.*

cookie
a kind of hard, flat cake: *Mrs Liu gave us tea and **cookies** when we went to see her.*

Same as a **biscuit.**

cool
1 not too hot; cold; fresh: *Although the sun is hot, there's a **cool** breeze today. It's always **cooler** in the shade than in the sun. How do you keep **cool** in hot weather?* **2** calm: *If a wasp starts flying round you, just stand still and keep **cool**.*

Meaning 1: the opposite is **warm** or **hot.**

copy
to make something like something else; to do something like someone else: ***Copy** these words into your exercise books. The teacher told the children not to **copy** one another's work. Liz did a somersault and her little brother tried to **copy** her. There is a machine in Dad's office for **copying** letters.*

copies, copied, copying, has copied

copy
1 something that is made exactly the same as something else: *This picture is a **copy** of a famous painting. Bill made five **copies** of the list on the copying machine.* **2** one of a large number of books or magazines that are all the same: *There are two **copies** of the dictionary in the school library.*

Several **copies**

coral

hard white, pink or red stuff that forms at the bottom of the sea: ***Coral** is used for making jewellery. My granny has a **coral** necklace.*

cork
1 very light, brown-coloured stuff that forms the bark of a certain kind of oak-tree: ***Cork** is used for making mats.* **2** a piece of cork that is put into the top of a bottle: *Put the **cork** back in the bottle.*

corn
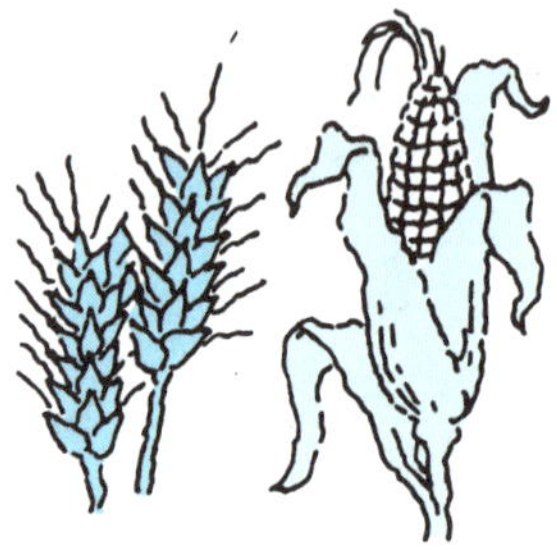

plants such as wheat, oats or maize, especially maize; grain from these plants: ***Corn** is made into flour in a mill.*

corner
the place where two walls or streets meet: *Our television stands in a **corner** of the kitchen. A **corner** shop is a small shop on the **corner** of a street.*

correct
1 to put the mistakes right in something: *You've spelt this word wrong — **correct** it, please. You must **correct** this sentence.* **2** to mark the mistakes in something: *The teacher **corrected** our exercises.*

correct
without a mistake; not wrong: *Jenny's answer was **correct**. You were quite **correct**, Jenny! There are no mistakes in Mike's sums — they are all **correct**.*

- Same as **right.**
- The opposite is **wrong.**

corridor
a long, narrow passage in a building: *There are lots of doors on each side of the **corridor**. Don't run along the **corridor**.*

cost
the amount of money that you have to pay for something: *What was the **cost** of the meal?*

cost
to have a price: *This bicycle **costs** $160. Our new car **cost** a lot of money.*

cost, costing, has cost

costume
1 the clothes which an actor or actress wears: *All the children in the play wore **costumes** — some were dressed as animals and some as fairies.* **2** clothing for a special purpose: *Remember to bring your swimming **costumes**.*

cot
a small bed for a baby: *A **cot** has high sides so that the baby cannot fall out.*

cottage
a small house, especially in the country: *Joe's grandparents live in a **cottage** near the sea.*

cotton
a soft material that comes from a plant and is used for making cloth or thread: *This shirt is made of **cotton**. You need a lot of **cotton** clothes if you live in a hot country.*
cotton wool soft, white, fluffy cotton: *The doctor wiped the wound with some liquid on a piece of **cotton wool**.*

cough
to make a sudden loud, rough noise in your throat: *Tom is **coughing** a lot because he has a bad cold. The smoke made me **cough**.*

cough
an illness which makes you cough often: *Kim has a bad **cough** and cannot go to school today.*

could
1 see **can**: *Helen asked me if I **could** swim.* **2** you use **could** to say that something is possible: *We **could** have a picnic this afternoon, if you like. I **could** do it if I had more time.* **3** you use **could** to ask someone politely about something: ***Could** you please open the window? Hello, **could** I speak to Andrew, please?*

couldn't
short for **could not**: *I **couldn't** come yesterday because I was very busy. You could help me do the dishes, **couldn't** you?*

count
to say the numbers one by one; to find out the total by doing this: ***Count** up to ten. I **counted** the number of children in the room.*

counter
a long narrow table in a shop where you are shown the things that you buy: *The shop assistant put the watches on the **counter** so that my mother could try them on.*

country
1 any land in the world: *Great Britain is a **country** in Europe. Canada is a larger **country** than the United States of America.* **2** the part of the land that is away from the town, where you find fields, hills, woods and wild animals: *My grandparents like to spend their holidays quietly in the **country**.*

Meaning 1: two **countries**

couple
1 a man and a woman; a boyfriend and a girlfriend: *The young **couple** next door have a baby.* **2** two; a few: *Could you please lend me a **couple** of eggs? I had to wait a **couple** of minutes while Sarah got ready to go.*

courage
the ability to do something dangerous even if you are afraid: *The fireman was praised for his **courage** in saving the children from the fire.*

Same as **bravery**.

course
1 a number of lessons: *Ann is doing a **course** in Chinese. Do you like the other people on your computer **course**?* **2** a part of a meal: *The first **course** of our meal was tomato soup.*
of course yes; certainly: *'Can you swim?' '**Of course** I can.' 'Could you please hold the baby for a few minutes?' '**Of course**!'*

court
an area marked with white lines, where you play a game such as badminton, tennis or squash: *Our club has five tennis **courts**.*

courteous
having good manners: *Michael is a **courteous** boy — he always says 'please' and 'thank you'. Always be **courteous** to older people.*

Same as **polite**.

courtesy
good manners: *You must show **courtesy** by thanking somebody who helps you.*

cousin
the child of your aunt and uncle: *How many **cousins** do you have?*

cover

1 a thing that you put over something: *My mother put a **cover** over the fruitbowl to keep the flies away. 'Have you seen my book? It has a red **cover**.' Take off the bed**cover** before you get into bed.* **2** the top of something: *We've lost the **cover** of the dustbin.*

Meaning 2: same as **lid**.

cover

to put something over something: *Jenny didn't want to see the cruel part of the film, so she **covered** her eyes with her hands. In the evenings I **cover** my canary's cage with a dark cloth. My shoes were **covered** in mud after our walk through the fields. The furniture is **covered** with dust.*

cow

a large animal that produces milk and is kept on a farm: *The **cows** are eating grass in the field.*

coward

a person who is easily frightened: *The children called Joe a **coward** because he didn't dare jump over the ditch.*

The opposite is a **hero**.

cowboy

a man who looks after cattle, especially in America: *The **cowboys** that we see on television are all very good at riding horses and very quick at firing their guns.*

crab

a sea animal with a hard shell and five pairs of legs, the first pair with large claws: ***Crabs** usually walk sideways.*

crack

a split; a narrow gap: *There is a **crack** in this cup. You can look through this **crack** in the wall.*

crack

to break, but not into pieces: *The stone hit the window and **cracked** it. One of the eggs in the box was **cracked**.*

cradle

a baby's bed which can be rocked gently from side to side: *The baby is asleep in her **cradle**.*

crane

1 a machine with a long arm and a chain, that moves heavy things by lifting them in the air: *A **crane** is used by workmen.* **2** a large bird with a long neck and long legs: *A **crane** eats mainly fish.*

crash

1 an accident in which a vehicle gets damaged: *Nobody was injured in the car **crash**.* **2** a sudden loud noise: *There was an awful **crash** when the waiter dropped all the plates.*

crash

1 to go against something with great force: *The two cars **crashed** into each other at the corner. Mr Smith **crashed** his car into a wall. The aeroplane **crashed** in the mountains.* **2** to fall down, making a loud noise: *The plate **crashed** to the floor.*

crawl

1 to move on your hands and knees: *My little sister can't walk yet, but she **crawls** everywhere.* **2** to move slowly: *The beetle **crawled** up the wall.*

crazy

1 mad: *It's sometimes nice to do something **crazy**. Everyone thought Mr Green had gone **crazy** when he started dancing in the street.* **2** liking something or someone very much: *Peter is **crazy** about football.*

crayon

a coloured pencil that is used for drawing: *Take out your **crayons** and draw me a picture of the person sitting next to you.*

cream

1 the thick white liquid that forms on top of milk, from which butter and cheese are made: *When you whip **cream** it becomes solid. I like strawberries and **cream**.* **2** soft stuff that you rub into your skin: *Mother put some **cream** on her face after she had washed it.*

creature

any thing that lives and can move about, such as an animal, a bird, a fish or an insect: *A wolf is a wild **creature** that looks like a dog.*

creep

1 to move slowly, quietly or secretly: *Bill was late, so he tried to **creep** quietly into the classroom without the teacher noticing. I **crept** towards the bush because I didn't want the birds to fly away.* **2** to move with your body close to the ground; to crawl: *Martin **crept** under the sofa to hide. The cat was **creeping** towards the bird.*

crept, creeping, has crept

crept
see **creep**: *Kate* ***crept*** *up the stairs.*

crew
the people who work on a ship, aeroplane or spaceship: *There were 350 passengers and a* ***crew*** *of 40 on board the ship.*

croak
to make the sound of a frog: *In the evenings you can hear frogs* ***croaking*** *by the lake.*

crocodile
a large reptile with a long tail and long pointed jaws with sharp teeth: ***Crocodiles*** *live in lakes and rivers.*

crooked
1 bent: *The old man's back was so* ***crooked*** *that he had to walk with a stick.* **2** not straight: *That picture on the wall is* ***crooked*** *— could you please put it straight?*

> The opposite is **straight**.

cross
1 a shape formed by two lines that go across each other like this, + : *Mary is wearing a little gold* ***cross*** *on a chain round her neck.* **2** a written mark like this, × : *The teacher put a* ***cross*** *beside the sums that were wrong, and a tick beside the ones that were right.*

cross
1 to go from one side to the other: *Let's* ***cross*** *the street now — there are no cars coming. We* ***crossed*** *the river in a boat. This bridge* ***crosses*** *the river.* **2** to put one leg or arm over the other: *Mike sat down and* ***crossed*** *his legs.*
cross out to draw a line through something written: *The teacher* ***crossed out*** *the words that were wrongly spelt and wrote the correct words on top.*

cross
angry: *Helen was* ***cross*** *with me because I wouldn't let her ride my bicycle. Don't be* ***cross*** *— I didn't mean to hurt you.*

crossroads
a place where two roads meet and cross each other: *Many* ***crossroads*** *have traffic lights for controlling the traffic.*

crossword
a puzzle in which small squares have to be filled with letters to make words: *The clues help you to work out the answers to the* ***crossword****.*

crow
a large black bird: *A* ***crow*** *has a loud cry.*

crow
to make the noise of a cock: *A cock* ***crows*** *early in the morning.*

crowd
a large number of people who have come together in one place: *There was a big* ***crowd*** *waiting in front of the palace gates to see the Queen.*

crown
the precious, circular object that kings and queens wear on their heads at special ceremonies: *The Queen was wearing a golden* ***crown*** *covered with diamonds.*

cruel
wanting to cause pain: *The man was very* ***cruel*** *to his dog — he often kicked it, and he didn't give it enough to eat.*

> - Same as **wicked**.
> - The opposite is **kind**.

crunchy
hard and firm, so that you make a lot of noise when you bite it: ***Crunchy*** *apples are nicer to eat than soft ones.*

crush
1 to squeeze; to spoil by untidy folding: *Cotton clothes get* ***crushed*** *easily.* **2** to pound into small pieces: *You make peanut butter by* ***crushing*** *peanuts.*

cry
1 a shout: *A man heard Jenny's* ***cries*** *for help and pulled her out of the water.* **2** the sound that some birds and animals make: *Have you ever heard the* ***cry*** *of a wolf?*

> Frequent **cries**

cry
1 to let tears come from your eyes when you are sad; to weep: *David* ***cried*** *when he broke his watch.* **2** to shout: *Jenny* ***cried*** *out when she fell into the river.*

> - Meaning 1: the opposite is **laugh**.
> - cries, cried, crying, has cried

cub
the baby of certain animals such as bears, foxes

or lions: *The lion **cubs** were playing with their mother.*

cube

a shape like a square box, with six equal sides: *My little sister has some **cube**-shaped toy bricks.*

cucumber

a long narrow green vegetable: *My mother sliced a **cucumber** to put into the salad.*

cunning

clever in a bad, sly way: *The **cunning** wolf pretended to be Red Riding Hood's granny. I've thought of a **cunning** plan for finding out the answer to the test.*

cup

1 a small bowl-shaped object with a handle, from which you drink tea or coffee: *I put four **cups** and saucers on the table.* **2** the drink inside a cup: *Would you like a **cup** of tea?* **3** a gold or silver bowl that is given as a prize for winning a sports competition: *Our football team won the **cup** this year.*

cupboard

a piece of furniture with shelves and doors, in which things can be kept: *My mother keeps the cakes and biscuits in a **cupboard** in the kitchen. We have a shoe **cupboard** in the hall.*

cure

to make better; to heal: *A good sleep will **cure** your headache. The doctor **cured** my little sister when she was ill.*

cured, curing, has cured

curious

1 always wanting to know things about other people: *Our new neighbours are very **curious** — they keep watching us out of their windows. I'm **curious** to find out whether Mike has passed his exams.* **2** unusual; odd: *Robert has a **curious** habit of staring at people.*

curl

a twisting bit of hair; a wave: *The baby's hair is full of **curls**.*

curly

full of curls: *Tim has fair **curly** hair.*

curtain

a long piece of material that hangs from the top of a window: *At night my mother draws my bedroom **curtains**.*

curve

a bend, like part of a circle: *An S has two **curves** in it.*

curved

bending round; like part of a circle: *The letter D is **curved** on one side and straight on the other.*

cushion

an object like a square bag stuffed with feathers or some other soft material, for putting on a seat to make it more comfortable: *We have a green sofa with four white **cushions**.*

custom

something that people do regularly: *It is a common **custom** to have a cake with candles on for your birthday.*

customer

a person who buys things from a shop: *The shopkeeper asked the assistant to serve the **customers**.*

cut

the result of cutting something: *You ought to put a bandage over that **cut** on your finger. Elizabeth went to the hairdresser's for a hair**cut**.*

cut

1 to divide something, or make an opening in something, with a knife or a pair of scissors: ***Cut** the paper in half. **Cut** a hole in the middle of the paper. Jenny **cut** a few slices of bread for her sandwiches. My little brother likes to **cut** out pictures from magazines.* **2** to make something shorter by cutting it: *The hairdresser **cut** Elizabeth's hair. I **cut** my fingernails after my shower this evening.* **3** to wound with something sharp: *I **cut** my finger on a piece of broken glass, and it wouldn't stop bleeding.*

cut, cutting, has cut

cycle

to ride a bicycle: *I **cycle** to school when the weather is fine.*

cycled, cycling, has cycled

cyclist

a person who rides a bicycle: ***Cyclists** have to ride very carefully when there is a lot of traffic.*

cymbal

a musical instrument that looks like a metal plate: *Joe plays the **cymbals** in the school orchestra.*

Say **sim**-bal.

Dd

dad or **daddy**
children's words for father: *I went shopping with my mum and* ***dad****. May I stay up late tonight,* ***Daddy****?*

daily
1 every day: *Bob and I see each other* ***daily****. My grandfather takes his dog for a* ***daily*** *walk in the park.* **2** produced every day: *We get a* ***daily*** *newspaper.*

daisy
a small flower with a yellow centre and white petals: *I picked a bunch of* ***daisies*** *in the meadow.*

Lots of **daisies**

damage
to cause harm to something: *The storm has* ***damaged*** *a lot of trees. The picture got* ***damaged*** *when it fell off the wall.*

damaged, damaging, has damaged

dance
to move with special steps in time to music: *The teacher played some music on the tape-recorder for us to* ***dance*** *to. I like watching ballet-****dancing*** *on television.*

danced, dancing, has danced

dance
1 a special set of steps and movements that you learn and remember: *We have been learning some Thai* ***dances*** *at school. Have you done this* ***dance*** *before?* **2** a party at which people dance: *My parents are going to a* ***dance*** *tonight.*

danger
1 harm or trouble that might be coming: *If a lion escaped from the zoo, the people of this town would be in great* ***danger****, wouldn't they? There was a big notice on the electric fence, saying* ***DANGER****! You're always in* ***danger*** *of losing your way if you go too far from home. Children soon learn about the* ***dangers*** *of busy streets.* **2** something that may cause harm or injury: *Don't leave knives and scissors lying about — they can be a* ***danger*** *to small children.*

The opposite is **safety**.

dangerous
able to cause harm or injury: *That dog is* ***dangerous*** *— it might bite you. There have been a lot of accidents on that* ***dangerous*** *road.*

The opposite is **safe**.

dare
1 to be brave enough to do something: *Granny wouldn't* ***dare*** *touch a snake. The last time someone* ***dared*** *to tell the teacher she was wrong, she got very angry. How* ***dare*** *you tell me I'm wrong! Don't you* ***dare*** *say such a thing again!* **2** to ask someone if they are brave enough to do something: *I* ***dare*** *you to jump off that wall.*

dared, daring, has dared

daring
eager to do dangerous things: *It was very* ***daring*** *of you to climb up that rock.*

Same as **bold** and **brave**.

dark
1 without light: *I couldn't see anything in the* ***dark*** *room. It's getting* ***dark*** *— we should be going home now.* **2** not pale in colour; nearer to black than to white: *Pine needles are* ***dark*** *green. My brother has fair hair and my sister has* ***dark*** *hair. Some people have* ***dark*** *skins and some have pale skins.*

- Meaning 1: the opposite is **bright**.
- Meaning 2: the opposite is **light**, **fair** or **pale**.

dark
the time between sunset and sunrise, when there is no light: *We must get home before* ***dark****. Are you afraid of the* ***dark****? Cats can see in the* ***dark****.*

darling
a word that you use for a person whom you love very much: *Mum calls Dad '****darling****'.*

dart
an object like a very short arrow that you throw at a round target called a **dartboard**, marked with numbers: *In the game of **darts**, you aim your **darts** at the parts of the dartboard that give you the highest score.*

dash
to go very quickly; to rush: *I have to **dash** off now and catch the bus. Mike **dashed** into the room and told us that a helicopter had landed outside.*

Same as **rush**.

date
what day it is, in what month and in what year: *I can't read the **date** on this letter. What is your **date** of birth? What's the **date** today? The **date** is the 17th of January, 1990.*

daughter
a female child: *My teacher has two **daughters** and one son.*

Rhymes with **water**.

dawn
the beginning of the day, when the sun begins to rise; daybreak: *Some birds start singing at **dawn**.*

day
1 the 24 hours from one midnight to the next midnight: *What **day** is it today — is it Friday? I met Susan the **day** before yesterday. Our next exam is in three **days'** time.* **2** the time between sunrise and sunset: *Dad works all **day**. The nurses looked after the patient **day** and night.*

The opposite is **night**.

daybreak
the beginning of the day; the dawn: *The soldiers left the camp at **daybreak**.*

daylight
the light that you get during the day, when the sun is up: *I hope we'll get home in **daylight** — we might lose our way in the dark.*

dead
no longer living; having died: *The children found a **dead** bird and buried it in the garden.*

The opposite is **alive**.

deaf
not able to hear: *My grandfather is getting **deaf** — you have to shout so that he can hear you.*

dear
1 loved or liked by someone: *Linda is my **dearest** friend.* **2** nice; attractive: *What a **dear** little puppy!* **3** very expensive; costing a lot of money: *Schoolbooks are getting very **dear**.*

- Meaning 3: same as **expensive**.
- Meaning 3: the opposite is **cheap**.

December
the twelfth month of the year.

decide
to make up your mind to do something: *I have **decided** to learn to play the guitar. I could not **decide** what to do next. 'Have you **decided** what you'd like for your birthday?' 'Yes, I've **decided** on a bike.'*

decided, deciding, has decided

decision
something you decide: *It was difficult to choose between the two colours, but I think I made the right **decision** in choosing the red dress.*

deck
a floor on a ship or bus: *The cars are on the lower **deck** of the ship. Let's sit on the top **deck** of the bus.*

decorate

1 to make something more beautiful by adding something to it: *We **decorated** the Christmas tree with glass balls and golden stars. Mum **decorated** the cake with pink icing.* **2** to put paint or wallpaper on the walls of a room: *All the rooms had to be **decorated** before we moved into the new flat.*

decorated, decorating, has decorated

deep
1 going down a long way: *This lake is very **deep**.* **2** measuring a certain amount down-

wards: *The swimming-pool is 3 metres **deep** at the **deep** end.* **3** dark: *The sea is a **deep** blue colour.* **4** low: *My uncle has a **deep** voice.*

Meaning 1: the opposite is **shallow**.

deer

a large grass-eating animal that can run fast: *A stag is a male **deer** and it has horns, called antlers, on its head.*

Two **deer**

defend

to protect someone or something against attack: *In the story, the prince **defended** the girl against the wicked dragon. The soldiers **defended** the castle.*

The opposite is **attack**.

degree

a unit of temperature: *The temperature today is 32 **degrees** (32°).*

delay

1 to put off something till a later time: *We had to **delay** our holiday for a week because my brother was ill.* **2** to make someone or something late: *We were **delayed** by the traffic, so we arrived late at the theatre. The bus was **delayed** for ten minutes because of the accident.*

delay

the amount of time by which something is delayed; the amount of time you have to wait for something: *The train arrived after a **delay** of half an hour. The doctor came without **delay** when my mother rang him.*

delicious

tasting very nice: *Please may I have some more chocolate cake? It's **delicious**.*

Say di-**lish**-us.

delight

joy; happiness: *The baby laughed with **delight** when we gave him the balloon to play with.*

delight

to please someone very much: *The teacher was **delighted** with the beautiful gift from her pupils. My parents were **delighted** that I had won first prize in the reading competition.*

deliver

to bring something to the person who has asked for it, or whom it is being sent to: *A postman **delivers** letters and parcels. Dad bought a new washing-machine on Monday and the shop **delivered** it to our house on Tuesday.*

demand

to ask very firmly: *The teacher **demanded** to know why John was an hour late for school. My mother **demanded** her money back from the butcher because the meat was bad.*

dentist

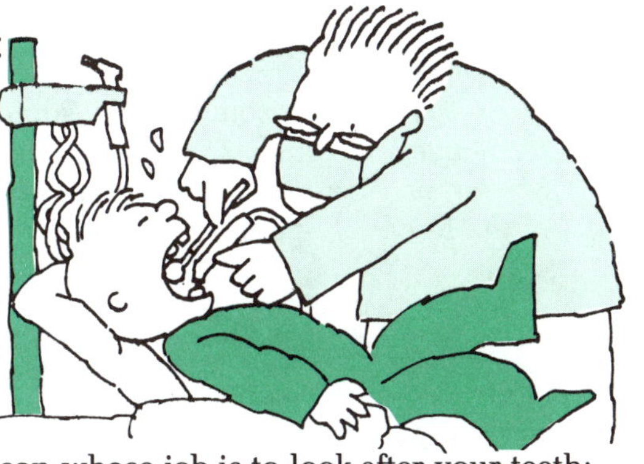

a person whose job is to look after your teeth: *Some people go to the **dentist** only when they have toothache. The **dentist** filled a hole in one of my teeth.*

depart

to go away; to leave: *The plane to Kuala Lumpur **departs** from Singapore at 7.50 p.m. and arrives at 8.35 p.m.*

- Same as **leave**.
- The opposite is **arrive**.

department

a part of a business, shop, office or university: *My uncle works in the export **department** of a large firm. Where is the shoe **department** in this store?*

department store a large shop with different departments where lots of different kinds of goods are sold: ***Department stores** have escalators and lifts to take you to all the different floors.*

depend

1 to be decided by something: *I don't know whether we'll have a picnic tomorrow — it **depends** on the weather. Success **depends** on hard work.* **2** to need the help of someone: *Babies and little children **depend** on their parents to feed them and dress them.* **3** to know that someone will do what you want them to: *Jane will remember to bring your umbrella back — you can **depend** on her.*

depth
the distance from the top downwards: *The submarine was travelling at a **depth** of 200 metres below the surface of the water.*

describe
to say what someone or something is like: *Is your sister tall or short — can you **describe** her to me? Billy **described** his father as a strict but friendly man. The teacher asked the children to **describe** their own bedrooms.*

described, describing, has described

description
the describing of someone or something: *I recognized the man from your **description**. My father gave the policeman a **description** of the thief.*

desert

a large area that is very dry and covered with sand: *The Sahara **Desert** in Northern Africa is the largest **desert** in the world. Hardly any plants grow in a **desert** because there is very little rain.*

deserve
to be good enough to get something nice; to do something bad enough to get punished: *Amy has worked very hard and **deserves** a good mark. Pauline **deserves** to be punished for stealing Maureen's money.*

deserved, deserving, has deserved

design
1 a plan prepared for something before it is made: *In a clothes factory, hundreds of dresses are made from the same **design**.* **2** a pattern; a picture: *I like the **design** on the front of your sweater.*

design
to prepare a plan of something before it is made: *Joe's father is **designing** a new kind of computer. The teacher asked us to **design** a poster to advertise the school play.*

desk
a table for writing: *The headmaster likes to see pupils sitting quietly at their **desks** in their classrooms. My father has a large **desk** with lots of drawers in his office.*

destroy
to smash something to pieces; to spoil something completely: *The house was **destroyed** by a bomb during the war.*

detective
a police officer who investigates robberies and murders: *After the bank robbery, two **detectives** went to the bank to look for clues.*

dew
tiny drops of water that cover the ground on a cool morning: *On some mornings the grass is wet with **dew**.*

diagram
a drawing that explains something that is difficult to understand: *This book has **diagrams** showing the parts of a car.*

dial
to get a number on the telephone by touching the right numbers with your finger: *I'm so sorry — I must have **dialled** the wrong number.*

dialled, dialling, has dialled

diamond
a very hard, precious stone that sparkles: *My father gave my mother a beautiful ring with five small **diamonds** in it. **Diamonds** are used not only as jewellery but also to cut glass.*

diary
a small book in which you write what has happened each day or what you have planned: *Jane keeps a **diary** that nobody is allowed to read. I make notes about important things in my **diary** so that I don't forget them.*

Two **diaries**

dictionary
a book that has words of a language in the order of the alphabet and gives their meanings or translates them into another language: *If you don't understand a word, look it up in a **dictionary**. I have an English **dictionary**.*

Lots of **dictionaries**

did
see **do**: *I **did** what you told me. **Did** you see Steven yesterday?*

didn't
short for **did not**: *Ann **didn't** come to school yesterday because she was ill. You liked that movie, **didn't** you?*

die
to stop living; to become dead: *Those flowers are **dying**. Our cat was very old when she **died**.*

- The opposite is **live**.
- died, dying, has died

die away to become more difficult to hear: *The noise of the aeroplane soon **died away**.*
die down to become less strong: *I think the wind has **died down** a bit.*
die out to disappear from the world: *The panda is in danger of **dying out**.*

difference
the way in which two things are different: *Can you see any **difference** between these two pictures? What is the **difference** between a monkey and an ape?*

different
not the same: *When I am twelve, I shall go to a **different** school. You can choose between thirty **different** flavours of ice-cream at this shop. Indoor games are quite **different** from outdoor games.*

The opposite is **same**.

difficult
hard to do; hard to understand; not easy: *These sums are very **difficult**. The teacher asked me a **difficult** question. That high wall would be very **difficult** to climb over.*

- Same as **hard**.
- The opposite is **easy** or **simple**.

difficulty
anything that is difficult for you: *My brother has **difficulty** getting up in time for school.*

A lot of **difficulties**

dig
to turn over earth or sand with a spade; to make a hole in the ground: *Our dog has **dug** a lot of holes in our garden. I'm going to **dig** the garden this afternoon. We had to **dig** the car out of the mud. Some men are **digging** up the road outside our house.*

dug, digging, has dug

dim
not bright; not clear: *We saw a **dim** light in the distance. I couldn't see who it was — I only saw a **dim** shape in the fog.*

dine
to have dinner: *We usually **dine** at 7 o'clock.*

dined, dining, has dined

dining-room
a room that is used for eating in: *In our **dining-room** there is a round dining-table and six chairs.*

dinner
the main meal of the day, usually eaten in the evening: *Is it time for **dinner** yet? We always have **dinner** at seven o'clock.*

direct
straight: *Is this the most **direct** way to the airport? The bus goes **direct** from the airport to the city centre.*

direct
1 to tell someone where to go; to guide someone: *Could you please **direct** me to the railway station?* **2** to be in charge of something that is being done; to control; to organize: *Mr Gold is **directing** our school play.*

direction
the way you go to get somewhere: *'Am I going in the right **direction** for the city centre?' 'No, it is in the opposite **direction**.' What **direction** did Mike go in?*

dirt
stuff that is not clean, such as mud or dust: *The children's clothes were covered with **dirt** after they had been playing on the muddy river-bank.*

dirty
not clean: *Your hands are very **dirty** — please go and wash them. My white trousers got **dirty** when I sat on the ground.*

- dirty, dirtier, dirtiest
- The opposite is **clean**.

disagree
not to agree: *I thought the film was good, but John and Paul **disagreed** with me about it. My sister and I often **disagree** with each other.*

The opposite is **agree**.

disappear
1 to go out of sight; not to be able to be seen any more: *The rabbit **disappeared** into a hole. The sun **disappeared** behind the clouds.* **2** to go away so that people do not know where

you are: *A little boy **disappeared** from his home two days ago.*

The opposite is **appear**.

disobey
not to obey: *If pupils **disobey** their teacher, they must be sent to the headmaster straight away.*

discover
1 to be the first person who finds something: *Christopher Columbus **discovered** America.* **2** to find out: *In the story the children tried to **discover** where the treasure was hidden.*

discuss
to talk about something: *Yesterday my friends and I **discussed** our plans for the holiday. We were **discussing** where we should go.*

disease
an illness: *Measles is a nasty **disease**, so you have to have an injection to stop you catching it. Grandad has heart **disease**, so he can't walk very far.*

disguise
to change the way you look so that people will think you are someone else: *The thief **disguised** himself as a workman by putting on a workman's clothes and helmet.*

- Say dis-**gize**.
- disguised, disguising, has disguised

dish
1 a plate or a bowl in which food is brought to the table: *Mum put the soup in a large **dish**.* **2** food prepared for eating: *At the restaurant we had a very nice **dish** made of chicken and ginger.*

dish rack a place for wet dishes: *I washed the dishes and left them on the **dish rack** to dry.*

dishes
all the plates, cups, knives and other things that you use during a meal: *It's your turn to wash the **dishes** — I did the **dishes** yesterday.*

dishonest
not honest: *You can't trust a **dishonest** person. A person who cheats or tells lies is **dishonest**.*

dislike
not to like: *Most people **dislike** having to get up early. Dishonest people deserve to be **disliked**.*

disliked, disliking, has disliked

dismiss
to send away: *The pupils will be **dismissed** at 12.30 p.m.*

distance
the space between things or places: *Some of the pupils have to walk a long **distance** to school. What is the **distance** between Singapore and Kuala Lumpur?*

disturb
to interrupt someone when they are busy or asleep: *I'm sorry to **disturb** you when you're working, but could I borrow two chairs? The baby's asleep — please don't **disturb** her.*

ditch
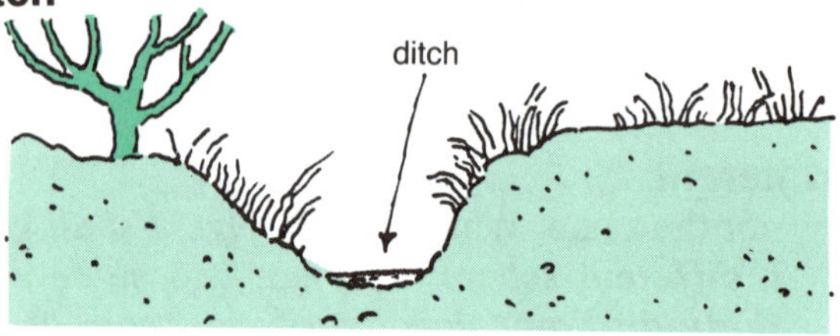

a hollow that is dug in the ground along the side of a road or field, to drain water away: ***Ditches** are often full of water.*

dive
1 to go into the water with your head first: *Have you ever **dived** off the highest **diving-board** at the swimming-pool?* **2** to go swimming under water wearing a special container with oxygen, so that you can breathe: *My father goes **diving** so that he can study different kinds of fish.* **3** to go under water: *We watched the submarine **dive**.*

dived, diving, has dived

diver
a person who dives, especially someone who works under water: *A group of **divers** have been down to the bottom of the harbour today to look for a ship that sank there many years ago.*

divide
1 to separate into parts or groups: *The teacher **divided** the children into two teams for a game of football. Draw a square and then **divide** it in half. There's a little wall **dividing** our garden from our neighbours' garden.* **2** to share: *We **divided** the sweets between us.* **3** to find out how many times one number contains another: *If you **divide** 6 by 3, you get 2.*

divided, dividing, has divided

division
one of the parts you get if you divide something up: *A school is divided up into several **divisions** called classes.*

do
1 used in sentences with **not**: *I **do** not want to go. We **don't** have a dog, but the people next door **do**.* **2** used in questions and in some answers: *'**Do** you know where Marie lives?' 'Yes, I **do**.' **Do** you have the time, please? You don't speak Chinese, **do** you?* **3** to carry out some action: *What shall I **do**? Sarah is **doing** her homework. Mum **does** the cooking and I **do** the washing-up. Never run across the road — that's a dangerous thing to **do**! Jill is **doing** her hair in front of the mirror.* **4** to get on well or badly: *'How are you **doing**?' 'I'm **doing** well, thank you.'*

does, did, doing, has done

doctor
a person who is trained to treat ill people: *Mum called the **doctor** when I was ill in bed. My dad went to see **Dr** Brown because he didn't feel well.*

doctor is written **Dr** before a name.

dodge

to avoid something by a sudden clever movement: *The ball nearly hit Tim but he **dodged** just in time. He managed to **dodge** the ball.*

dodged, dodging, has dodged

doe
the female of the **deer**: *A **doe** has no horns, but a male deer does.*

does
see **do**: ***Does** Helen live near you? What **does** this word mean? Martin **does** not want to come, **does** he?*

doesn't
short for **does not**: *Lily **doesn't** like potatoes. Robert collects stamps, **doesn't** he?*

dog
an animal that is kept as a pet or used to guard something: *Our **dog** barks whenever someone comes to our front door. I have to take the **dog** for a walk twice a day. In the street **dogs** must always be kept on a lead.*

doll
a toy in the shape of a small person: *Sue has a **doll** that can cry and talk.*

dollar
the main unit of money in America, Canada, Australia, Singapore and other countries, often written $: *This book costs ten **dollars** ($10).*

done
see **do**: *Have you **done** your homework yet? 'What have you **done** with my shoes? I can't find them anywhere.'*

donkey
a grey animal with long ears, that is like a small horse: *Have you ever ridden a **donkey**? **Donkeys** are good at carrying heavy loads.*

don't
short for **do not**: *I **don't** want to do my homework.*

door
a large, flat piece of wood for closing the entrance to a house, room or cupboard: *Could you please open the **door** for me? Please close the cupboard **doors**. The front **door** is the main entrance to a house.*

next door in the next house: *A neighbour is someone who lives **next door** to you. Sometimes we can hear the dog barking **next door**.*

doorstep
a step just outside the door of a house: *There is a doormat on the **doorstep** for people to wipe their shoes on.*

doorway
the opening in the wall where the door is: *Don't stand in the **doorway** — please come in!*

dot
a small round mark: *Anne is wearing a white blouse with pink **dots**.*

double
1 twice: *My room is **double** the size of your room. If Jane is four years old and James is **double** her age, how old is James?* **2** into two halves: *The blanket has been folded **double**. The old, old man was bent nearly **double**.*

3 for two people: *My parents have a* ***double*** *bed in their bedroom.*

double-decker or double-decker bus

a bus with two floors: *You get a good view of the city from the top of a* ***double-decker****. There are a lot of red* ***double-decker buses*** *in London.*

doubt

the feeling of not being sure: *Sometimes you know what to do, and sometimes you are full of* ***doubt****. I've no* ***doubt*** *that Peter will win the drawing prize.*

doubt

to think that something is not probable: *It's very late — I* ***doubt*** *whether Mark will come now. I* ***doubt*** *if he'll come. He might come later, but I* ***doubt*** *it.*

doughnut

a cake that is cooked by frying and then covered with sugar: *When you eat a* ***doughnut*** *you get sticky fingers.*

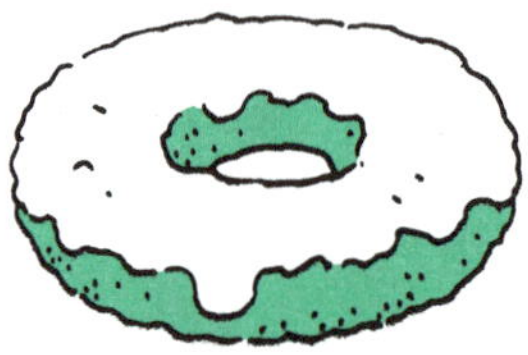

Say **doe**-nut.

dove

a large bird, usually grey in colour.

Same as a **pigeon**.

down

1 towards a lower place; to the ground: *David climbed* ***down*** *the ladder. I sat* ***down*** *on the chair. Julie fell* ***down*** *and cut her knee.* **2** in a lower place: *My bicycle is* ***down*** *in the basement. We climbed the tower and looked at the houses* ***down*** *below.* **3** along: *We walked* ***down*** *the street to the bus-stop.*

The opposite is **up**.

downstairs

1 to a lower floor: *I went* ***downstairs*** *to get some water from the kitchen.* **2** on a lower floor: *I've left my book* ***downstairs****. The sitting-room is* ***downstairs*** *and the bedrooms are upstairs.*

The opposite is **upstairs**.

downwards or downward

towards a lower place; to a lower position: *When you nod, you move your head upwards and* ***downwards****. The path led* ***downward*** *to the sea.*

dozen

twelve: *There are two* ***dozen*** *children in the class. Half-a-****dozen*** *of them speak Chinese.*

Two **dozen**

drag

to pull something that is heavy or difficult to move: *Paul* ***dragged*** *the heavy box across the floor. Mum sometimes has to* ***drag*** *Peter away from the television and make him do his homework.*

dragged, dragging, has dragged

dragon

a creature that you find in stories and pictures; it usually breathes fire, its body is covered with scales and it has wings and a long tail: *In this fairy tale the treasure is guarded by a fierce* ***dragon****.*

dragonfly

an insect with a long thin body and two pairs of wings: *There are many brightly coloured* ***dragonflies*** *by the pond.*

Two **dragonflies**

drain

a pipe that carries away water: *The* ***drain*** *under the kitchen sink is blocked.*

drain

1 to remove liquid from something: *The noodles have to be* ***drained*** *after they have been boiled.* **2** to flow away: *The rain* ***drains*** *off the road into the ditch.*

drank

see **drink**: *I was very thirsty and* ***drank*** *a whole bottle of lemonade.*

draw

1 to make a picture with a pencil or crayons: *Emma is* ***drawing*** *a dog. Can you* ***draw*** *a straight line?* **2** to pull something: *The cart was being* ***drawn*** *by a donkey.* **3** to close or open curtains: *Please* ***draw*** *the curtains — it's getting dark. In the morning I jump out of bed and* ***draw*** *the curtains.*

drew, drawing, has drawn

drawer

part of a desk or chest that can slide out and in, which you keep things in: *The letter is in the bottom* ***drawer*** *of my desk. Mum keeps her jewellery in the top* ***drawer*** *of her chest of* ***drawers****.*

drawing
a picture drawn by someone: *The teacher liked my **drawing** so much that she pinned it on the wall for everyone to see.*

drawn
see **draw**: *I have **drawn** a picture of my dad. Every night the curtains are **drawn** and the door is locked.*

dream
1 events that you see while you are asleep: *Joe had a horrible **dream** last night. When I go to bed Mum says to me: 'Good night, sweet **dreams**.'* **2** something that you wish will come true: *It's Lisa's **dream** to become a famous actress.*

dream
to see events while you are asleep: *I often **dream** about my dog. I was just **dreaming** that I had won a lot of money when my mum woke me up.*

dreamt, dreaming, has dreamt

dreamt
see **dream**: *I can't remember what I **dreamt** about last night. Have you ever **dreamt** about school?*

Say **dremt.**

dress
a piece of clothing worn by a girl or woman that has a top and skirt in one piece: *Jenny is wearing a pink **dress**. Shall I wear a blouse and skirt or a **dress**?*

dress
1 to put clothes on: *Get up and get **dressed**! In the morning my mum **dresses** my little sister, but I can **dress** myself. Mrs Jones is **dressed** all in black today.* **2** to clean a wound and cover it with a bandage: *Peter burnt his hand and had to go to hospital to get it **dressed**.*
dress up to put on special clothes, especially when you want to pretend to be someone else: *Timothy **dressed up** as a policeman. Susan likes **dressing up** in her mother's clothes.*

dressing
1 a bandage for a wound: *The doctor changed the patient's **dressing**.* **2** a sauce that is poured over a salad to make it taste nicer: *Mum made a **dressing** out of oil, vinegar, salt and pepper.*

dressing-table
a table in a bedroom with a mirror and drawers: *Mum is sitting at her **dressing-table** combing her hair.*

drew
see **draw**: *Who **drew** this beautiful picture?*

drink
a liquid that you swallow: *Are you thirsty — would you like a **drink**? No, thank you, I've just had a **drink** of tea. Lemonade is a nice cool **drink**.*

drink
to swallow a liquid: ***Drink** plenty of water. The cat is **drinking** some milk.*

drank, drinking, has drunk

drip
to fall in drops: *Rain **dripped** off the roof.*

dripped, dripping, has dripped

drive
1 to be in control of a car, bus or lorry: *My sister is learning how to **drive**. Can you **drive** a car?* **2** to take someone in a car: *My mother **drives** me to school in the morning.*

drove, driving, has driven

driven
see **drive**: *I have never **driven** a car.*

driver
a person who drives a car, bus, lorry or train: *Mum told the taxi-**driver** where we wanted to go. Richard's father is a bus-**driver**.*

drop
1 to let something fall, usually by accident: *Nicola **dropped** a box of pins all over the floor.* **2** to go down; to fall: *The coins must have **dropped** through the hole in my pocket. The cat **dropped** on to its paws.*

- Meaning 2: same as **fall**.
- dropped, dropping, has dropped

drop
a small amount of liquid that is dropping or spilling: *I didn't get wet — there were only a few **drops** of rain. A **drop** of wine has been spilt on the tablecloth.*

drove
see **drive**: *Mum **drove** the car into the garage.*

drown
to sink in water and die: *A man fell off the ship and **drowned** because he couldn't swim.*

drug
1 a medicine: *The doctor gave the patient a new* ***drug*** *to cure her pain.* **2** a dangerous kind of liquid or powder that some people take to feel happy and excited: *It is very dangerous to take* ***drugs****.*
drug store a shop where medicines and many other things are sold and where you can also buy snacks: *Do you know where the nearest* ***drug store*** *is?*

drum
a round musical instrument covered with a tight skin, which you beat with sticks or with your hands: *Jim plays the* ***drums*** *in the school band.*

drunk
see **drink**: *I have* ***drunk*** *a lot of tea today.*

dry
not **wet**: *The ground is very* ***dry*** *— it hasn't rained for several weeks. Rub yourself* ***dry*** *with a towel.*

The opposite is **wet.**

dry
to make something dry; to become dry: *You use a towel to* ***dry*** *yourself. I prefer* ***drying*** *the dishes to washing them. Has the paint* ***dried*** *yet?*

dries, dried, drying, has dried

duck
1 a water-bird with short legs, a short neck and a broad flat beak: *We took some stale bread with us to feed the* ***ducks*** *in the pond.* **2** the meat of a duck: *We are having roast* ***duck*** *with rice for dinner.*

dug
see **dig**: *The gardener* ***dug*** *a hole so that he could plant the apple tree. The men have* ***dug*** *up the road to lay new drains.*

dull
1 not interesting; boring: *This is a* ***dull*** *film — I don't want to watch it any more.* **2** not bright; not clear: *The weather is very* ***dull*** *today. Yesterday was a* ***dull*** *day, but today is sunny.*

Meaning 2: the opposite is **bright.**

dumb
not able to speak: *The little girl was born deaf and* ***dumb****. Mike was* ***dumb*** *with fright when he saw Joe dressed up as a ghost.*

dump
a place where rubbish is taken: *Take all this junk to the rubbish* ***dump****.*

dump
1 to put something down heavily: *Mum* ***dumped*** *the heavy shopping bags on the table.* **2** to get rid of something: *You are not allowed to* ***dump*** *your rubbish wherever you like.*

during
1 for the time that something lasts: *I stayed with my granny* ***during*** *the holidays.* **2** in the middle of something: *I met Joe twice* ***during*** *the holidays.*

dusk
the time of evening when the light is disappearing, after the sun sets: *The park closes at* ***dusk****.*

dust
dirt that is like powder: *The furniture was covered with* ***dust****. Dad brushed the* ***dust*** *off his black suit.*

dust
to wipe dust off furniture: *Could you give me a cloth to* ***dust*** *these shelves?*

dustbin
a large round container for rubbish: *The* ***dustbin*** *is kept outside the house.*

duster
a cloth for dusting: *Get a* ***duster*** *out of the cupboard and dust the furniture.*

dusty
covered with dust: *When we came back from our holiday the furniture looked very* ***dusty****.*

duty
1 something that you ought to do: *It is your* ***duty*** *to work hard at school. Are you really doing your* ***duty****?* **2** a job that you have been given: *It is my* ***duty*** *to take the dog for a walk every evening.*

Too many **duties**

dwarf
a creature like a tiny man that you find in stories or fairy tales: *Snow White lived with the seven* ***dwarfs*** *in the forest.*

The opposite is a **giant.**

dying
see **die**: *This plant looks as if it's* ***dying****.*

each
every thing; every person: *Dry **each** dish carefully after you have washed it. We **each** have a dictionary. The teacher gave us **each** a sheet of paper for writing our answers on. The doctor will examine **each** of you in turn. **Each** of the pupils has been given a letter to take home.*

each other doing the same to someone as they do to you: *Daniel and Paul looked at **each other**. The twins always try to help **each other**. Sarah and I have known **each other** for two years.*

eager
wanting something very much: *Robert was **eager** to win first prize in the drawing competition.*

eagle

a large bird that attacks and eats small wild animals: *An **eagle** has very good eyesight.*

ear
the part of you that you hear with: *Does your hair cover your **ears**? An elephant has large **ears** that it can move backwards and forwards. If you can hear very well, people say you have 'sharp **ears**'.*

early
1 not late; sooner than usual; sooner than expected: *We shall have to get up very **early** tomorrow morning to catch the plane. David arrived ten minutes **early** because his watch was fast.* **2** near the beginning of a period: *My father comes home from work in the **early** evening. The birds wake us in the **early** morning.*

- The opposite is **late**.
- early, earlier, earliest

earn
to get money for work: *My elder sister **earns** some money by baby-sitting.*

earring
a piece of jewellery that you attach to your ears: *Lucy got a pair of gold **earrings** for her birthday.*

earth
1 the planet on which we live: *The **earth** goes round the sun. The blue whale is the largest animal on **earth**.* **2** soil: *Fill the plant-pot with **earth**.*

easel

a wooden support for a blackboard or an artist's picture: *The artist set up his **easel** on the beach and started to paint a picture of the sea.*

east
the direction from which the sun rises: *The wind is blowing from the **east**. There is a strong **east** wind. Taiwan lies to the **east** of China. New York is on the **east** coast of America.*

easy
not difficult: *These sums are **easy**. You will know the answer to this **easy** question. It is **easier** to climb a tree than a wall. The **easiest** way to get to the top floor is to take the lift.*

- easy, easier, easiest
- Same as **simple**.
- The opposite is **difficult** or **hard**.

eat
to chew and swallow; to take food: *What would you like to **eat**? I **ate** too much ice-cream at the party.*

ate, eating, has eaten

eat in to have a meal at home, not at a restaurant: *I would prefer to **eat in** today.*

eat out to have a meal at a restaurant: *Shall we we **eat out** tonight? We **eat out** a lot.*

eat up to eat everything that you are given to eat; to finish your food: ***Eat up** your rice! 'I'm going to **eat** you **up**,' said the tiger to the monkey.*

eaten
see **eat**: *We haven't **eaten** our dinner yet.*

echo
the repeating of a sound: *The children shouted into the cave and listened to the* ***echoes****.*

- Say **eck**-oe.
- A lot of **echoes**

edge
1 the side of something: *Don't put that glass so near the* ***edge*** *of the table — it will fall off. The children played at the* ***edge*** *of the river.* **2** the cutting side of something sharp, such as a knife or sword: *The* ***edge*** *of a razor blade is very sharp.*

eel

a long, thin fish that looks like a snake: *Some kinds of* ***eel*** *can be eaten.*

egg
1 an object with a hard shell that is laid by a female bird, from which a baby bird is hatched: *The bird is sitting on the* ***eggs*** *in the nest.* **2** one of these laid by a hen and used as food: *Would you like a boiled* ***egg****?*

eight
1 the number 8: *Four and four are* ***eight****.* **2** 8 in number: *Bill is* ***eight*** *years old.*

eighteen
1 the number 18: *Nine and nine are* ***eighteen****.* **2** 18 in number: *My sister is* ***eighteen*** *years old.*

eighty
1 the number 80: *Forty and forty are* ***eighty****.* **2** 80 in number: *David's granny is* ***eighty*** *years old.*

either
1 the one or the other: *You may borrow* ***either*** *of these books. Mum offered John tea or coffee but he didn't want* ***either****. I can write with* ***either*** *hand, but I write better with my right.* ***Either*** *Pat or Joe is coming with me.* ***Either*** *you apologize to Dad right now, or you get no ice-cream.* **2** used with **not** to mean 'as well': *If you don't go, I won't* ***either****. 'Have you been to New Zealand?' 'No.' 'I haven't,* ***either****.'*

elastic
a kind of tape that contains rubber and stretches easily: *Karen put a piece of* ***elastic*** *through the top of her skirt to hold it up.*

elbow
the place where your arm bends in the middle: *Steven leant on his* ***elbows*** *and looked out of the window.*

elder
older: *Mark has two* ***elder*** *sisters. Joanne is the* ***elder*** *of the two.*

eldest
oldest: *Susan is the* ***eldest*** *of the four children.*

electric
worked by electricity: *Is this cooker* ***electric****? We have an* ***electric*** *fan in our kitchen.*

electricity
a form of energy from which we get light, heat and power: *This machine is worked by* ***electricity****. Don't leave all the lights on — you are wasting* ***electricity****.*

elephant
a very large, grey animal with a long trunk, large ears and two tusks: ***Elephants*** *are found in Africa and India.* ***Elephants*** *live in herds. An* ***elephant*** *uses its trunk to bring food and water up to its mouth.*

eleven
1 the number 11: *Five and six are* ***eleven****.* **2** 11 in number: *There are* ***eleven*** *players in a football team. Peter is* ***eleven*** *years old.*

else
other than the person or thing that has already been named: *'I've invited Bob and Paul to my party.' 'Oh good — who* ***else*** *is coming?' I don't like this film — let's watch something* ***else*** *instead.*
or else because if not: *Go to bed now,* ***or else*** *you'll be too tired to get up in the morning.*

employ
to pay someone to do some work: *I'd prefer to* ***employ*** *a gardener to work in my garden than do all the gardening myself. Mrs Jones is* ***employed*** *as a cashier at the supermarket.*

employee
a person who is paid to work for a firm or for another person: *This firm has fifty* ***employees****.*

employer
a person who gives work to people and pays them for it: *Some* ***employers*** *don't pay their employees enough money.*

empty
having nothing or no one inside: *This bottle is*

empty — who drank all the lemonade? Please throw the ***empty*** *boxes away. The bus was nearly* ***empty*** *this morning.*

The opposite is **full**.

empty

to make empty; to become empty: *Mum couldn't find the car keys in her bag, so she* ***emptied*** *it on to the table. The classroom* ***empties*** *quickly at lunch-time. I opened my purse and* ***emptied*** *the coins out on to the table.*

empties, emptied, emptying, has emptied

encourage

1 to make someone feel good and full of hope: *Teachers should* ***encourage*** *their pupils by praising them whenever they can.* **2** to give someone courage to do something; to persuade: *Nicola's parents* ***encouraged*** *her to take part in the reading competition.*

encouraged, encouraging, has encouraged

end

the last part of something: *We are on holiday until the* ***end*** *of the month. Go to the* ***end*** *of this street and then turn right. At the* ***end*** *of the story the prince marries the princess.*

The opposite is **beginning** or **start**.

end

to finish; to come to an end: *How does the film* ***end****? We* ***ended*** *our sports lesson with a run round the field.*

- Same as **finish**.
- The opposite is **begin** or **start**.

enemy

1 a person who hates you and wants to harm you: *Everybody likes Kate — she has no* ***enemies***. **2** an army that is fighting against the army of your country in a war: *The soldiers waited for the* ***enemy*** *to attack. The* ***enemy*** *aircraft dropped a bomb on the factory.*

- A lot of **enemies**
- The opposite is a **friend**.

energy

1 strength: *The old man next door has a lot of* ***energy*** *— he goes jogging in the morning and digs his garden in the afternoon. Athletes must eat a lot so that they keep up their* ***energy***. **2** power that makes machines work: *Electricity is a form of* ***energy***. *It's a waste of* ***energy*** *to wash such a small pile of clothes in the washing-machine.*

engine

1 a machine that makes a vehicle move: *The* ***engines*** *of most cars run on petrol.* **2** a large vehicle that pulls a train: *Michael wants to become an* ***engine****-driver when he grows up.*

engineer

1 a person who designs and makes machines; a person who designs roads, railways and bridges: *Christina's father works as an* ***engineer*** *with a building firm.* **2** a person who repairs machines: *A telephone* ***engineer*** *had to come when our telephone was not working.*

enjoy

to get pleasure from something: *Dad and I* ***enjoy*** *swimming in the sea. Did you* ***enjoy*** *your meal? Peter said he* ***enjoyed*** *the film very much.*

enjoy yourself to have a good time; to feel happy: *Did you* ***enjoy yourself*** *at the party? We were all* ***enjoying ourselves*** *at the picnic when it began to rain.*

enlarge

to make something larger: *Our neighbours* ***enlarged*** *their house by building two extra bedrooms on to it. We looked at the holiday photographs and decided which ones we would like to have* ***enlarged***.

enlarged, enlarging, has enlarged

enormous

very large: *The new buildings in the city centre are* ***enormous***. *I am not hungry yet because I had an* ***enormous*** *lunch.*

Same as **huge**.

enough
1 as much as you need: *Do you have **enough** money to go to the cinema? There is **enough** food for everyone. Have you had **enough** to drink? Is the tea hot **enough** for you? This car isn't big **enough** for six people. If you don't practise, you'll never swim well **enough** to be chosen for the team.* **2** as much as you can bear: *Mum said she had had **enough** of the loud music and turned off the radio. You've been watching television quite long **enough** — go to bed now.*

enter
1 to go or come into a place: *There was a notice on the door saying: 'Private — do not **enter**'. The children stopped talking when the teacher **entered** the classroom.* **2** to join something; to become a member of something: *Angela **entered** the school last term.*

The opposite is **leave**.

entertain
to do things or say things that are interesting for people to watch or listen to; to amuse people: *The clowns **entertained** the audience while the acrobats were changing their costumes. Joe **entertained** us with a funny story while we waited for the bus.*

entrance
the way into a place; an opening; a door or gate: *The **entrance** to the tunnel was blocked by a large rock. We arranged to meet at the main **entrance** to the school.*

The opposite is **exit**.

entry
permission to enter: *We can't go in — the sign says: 'No **entry**'.*

envelope

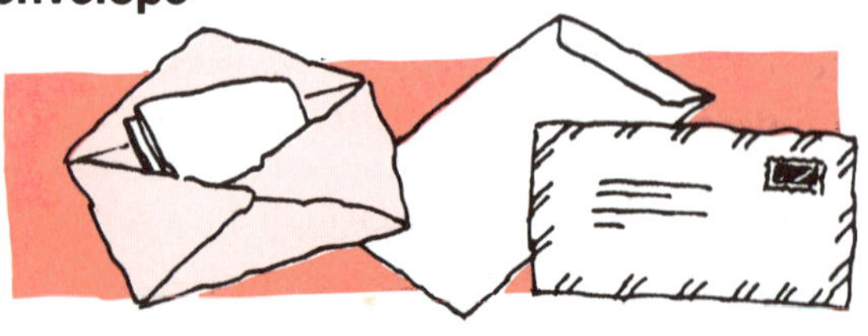

the paper cover that you put a letter into: *Don't forget to put a stamp on the **envelope**.*

equal
the same in size, amount or number: *Mum cut the cake into eight **equal** pieces. Mum gave us each an **equal** amount of ice-cream. Jerry's and Janet's marks came out **equal**. Janet's marks were **equal** to Jerry's. They scored **equal** marks.*

erase
to rub out pencil marks: *Jenny, please **erase** that silly drawing from your exercise book.*

erased, erasing, has erased

eraser
a piece of rubber that you use for rubbing out pencil marks: *I have a pencil, a ruler and an **eraser** in my pencil-case.*

escalator

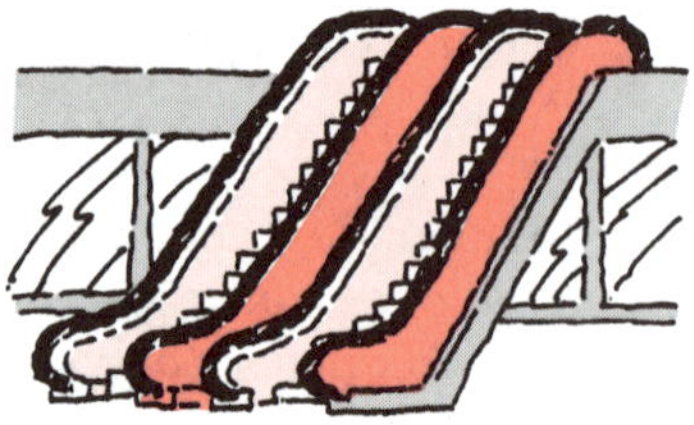

a moving staircase: *There are **escalators** and lifts in department stores so that you don't have to walk up and down the stairs.*

escape
getting away: *The prisoner made his **escape** through a window. There have been far too many **escapes** from the jail.*

escape
to get away: *A prisoner has **escaped** from the jail. The bank robbers **escaped** before the police arrived.*

escaped, escaping, has escaped

especially
most of all: *I like sweet things, **especially** ice-cream. My parents and I often go swimming, **especially** when it is very hot.*

estate
a person's land: *Mr Robinson employs 150 workers on his **estate**.*

eve
the day before a festival: *Christmas **Eve** is on December 24.*

even
1 you use **even** to point out something surprising in what you are saying: *'Have you finished your homework yet?' 'No, I haven't **even** started.' **Even** the best pupil in the class didn't pass the exam.* **2** still: *David is very strong, but his brother is **even** stronger. Today the weather was **even** better than it was yesterday.*

even

1 smooth; flat: *The surface of a road should be smooth and* ***even****.* **2** all the same length or amount: *When you walk, you usually take* ***even*** *steps.*

even number a number that can be divided by two: *2, 4, 6, 8 and 10 are* ***even numbers****.*

The opposite is an **odd number**.

evening

the part of the day between the afternoon and the night: *We have our dinner in the* ***evening****. There is a good film on TV tomorrow* ***evening****. On Saturday* ***evenings*** *I'm allowed to stay up late.*

event

1 something that happens, especially something unusual or important: *The first day at school is a big* ***event*** *for every child.* **2** a happening that is planned: *At the school sports there will be races, competitions and several other* ***events****.*

ever

1 at any time: *Have you* ***ever*** *been abroad? It hardly* ***ever*** *rains here in summer. Susan has done better than* ***ever*** *in her exams. That was the best film I have* ***ever*** *seen.* **2** always: *I'll love you for* ***ever****.*

ever after for the rest of your life: *Then the prince and princess got married and they lived happily* ***ever after****.*

ever since all the time since: *Mr and Mrs Lee have known me* ***ever since*** *I was a baby.*

every

1 each; all: ***Every*** *house should have a fire-extinguisher. We go on holiday* ***every*** *summer. I clean my teeth after* ***every*** *meal. The dog barks* ***every*** *time someone comes to our front door. Not* ***every*** *family has a car.* **2** after a regular amount of time: *I get my hair cut* ***every*** *six weeks.*

every other day on one day, not on the next, but on the day after that: *My granny comes to see us* ***every other day****.*

everybody

all the people: ***Everybody*** *on the bus has to buy a ticket. I can't invite* ***everybody*** *to my party.*

The opposite is **nobody**.

everyone

all people; each person: ***Everyone*** *knows that it is wrong to tell lies. The teacher handed* ***everyone*** *a sheet of paper.*

The opposite is **no-one**.

everything

all the things: *Do you have* ***everything*** *you need?* ***Everything*** *in the old house was covered in dust. Be patient — I can't do* ***everything*** *at once.*

The opposite is **nothing**.

everywhere

in every place; to every place: *The flies are* ***everywhere****.* ***Everywhere*** *I go, the puppy follows me.*

The opposite is **nowhere**.

evil

very bad; wicked: *In the story, the country was ruled by an* ***evil*** *king who treated the people very badly.*

Same as **bad** or **wicked**.

exact

correct: *What is the* ***exact*** *time, please? Dad is about 1.70 metres tall, but I don't know his* ***exact*** *height.*

exactly

1 in every way; quite: *This tool is* ***exactly*** *what I need for mending my bike. This dress is nice, but it's not* ***exactly*** *what I wanted.* **2** on the point of: *It's* ***exactly*** *ten o'clock.* **3** in a completely correct way: *Tell me* ***exactly*** *what all the shopping cost.*

exam

short for **examination**: *I passed the English* ***exam****.*

examination

a test you are given to see what you have learnt: *The pupils have to take* ***examinations*** *in most subjects every term.*

examine

1 to look at something carefully: *I* ***examined*** *the strange stone and wondered where it had come from.* **2** to look at someone carefully to find out whether they are healthy: *A doctor comes to the school once a year to* ***examine*** *all the children. The doctor* ***examined*** *my throat. The dentist* ***examined*** *my teeth and discovered a small hole in one of them.*

examined, examining, has examined

example
something that shows you what other things of the same kind are like: *Ants and bees are good* ***examples*** *of insects that live in large groups. The teacher laid out some* ***examples*** *of the children's work for the parents to see. Can you give me an* ***example*** *of how this word is used?*

for example such as: *Some animals,* ***for example*** *dogs, are kept as pets.*

excellent
very good: *Maria is an* ***excellent*** *pupil. We had* ***excellent*** *weather when we were on holiday. The meal was* ***excellent****.*

except
leaving out; apart from: *All my friends came to my birthday party* ***except*** *Paul.*

exchange
to give something and get something else in return: *At the end of the holiday we* ***exchanged*** *addresses with our new friends. Mum went back to the department store to* ***exchange*** *the shirt she bought me for a larger one.*

exchanged, exchanging, has exchanged

excited
very lively and happy, usually because you are looking forward to something: *The children were* ***excited*** *about going to the circus. I was too* ***excited*** *to sleep.*

exciting
very interesting: *I am reading an* ***exciting*** *book about the adventures of three children. This film is very* ***exciting****.*

excursion
a trip; an outing: *Today our class had an* ***excursion*** *to the museum. The party of tourists went on an* ***excursion*** *to the little island.*

excuse
a good reason or explanation for something wrong you have done: *What is your* ***excuse*** *for being late this time?*

excuse
to forgive: *I'll* ***excuse*** *you for being late this time, but don't be late again.*

excused, excusing, has excused

excuse me I beg your pardon: ***Excuse me*** *— do you have the time?*

exercise
1 a piece of written work that you do as practice: *Finish* ***Exercise*** *7 for homework. We write our homework in our* ***exercise*** *books.* **2** things you do that keep you fit, such as gym, games, walking, jogging, swimming and cycling: *People who sit at a desk all day don't get enough* ***exercise****. Swimming is a healthy form of* ***exercise****.* **3** one of a number of movements that you do to strengthen your body: *Dad does* ***exercises*** *every morning when he gets up.*

exercise

to do exercises or go jogging to keep fit: *My dad* ***exercises*** *every morning before he goes to his office.*

exercised, exercising, has exercised

exhibition
things collected together and put out in a public place for people to come and look at: *The teacher took us to an* ***exhibition*** *of model ships at the museum.*

exit
a way out of a building: *In large buildings there are signs saying 'fire* ***exit****', that show you the way to go out if there is a fire.*

The opposite is **entrance**.

expect
1 to know that something is going to happen, or someone is going to come: *Dad is* ***expecting*** *an important telephone call tonight. We* ***expect*** *my aunt tomorrow afternoon.* **2** to suppose: *I* ***expect*** *you are tired after the long journey.*

expensive
costing a lot of money: *My new bicycle was very* ***expensive****. I can't afford* ***expensive*** *toys.*

- Same as **dear**.
- The opposite is **cheap**.

experience
1 something important that happens to you: *The fire was a terrible* ***experience*** *for the children. My grandfather told us about his* ***experiences*** *during the war.* **2** practice at doing something: *How much* ***experience*** *have you had at looking after children?*

explain
1 to make something easy to understand: *Can you* ***explain*** *to me how this machine works? The teacher* ***explained*** *the meanings of the difficult words.* **2** to give a reason for something: *Steve* ***explained*** *why he was late.*

explanation
a reason for something: *The teacher asked Paul for an* ***explanation*** *of his bad behaviour. There is no* ***explanation*** *for the strange objects that appeared in the sky yesterday.*

explode
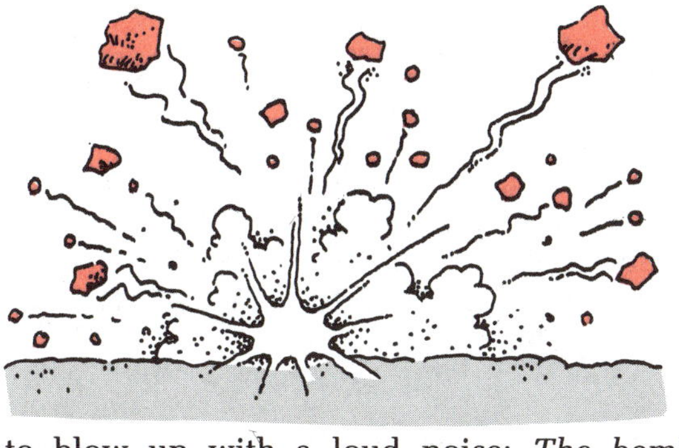

to blow up with a loud noise: *The bomb* ***exploded*** *and destroyed a lot of buildings.*

exploded, exploding, has exploded

explore
1 to look all round a place that you haven't been to before: *The children* ***explored*** *the cave.* **2** to visit and look at a place that no-one has been to before: *The oceans have not been completely* ***explored*** *yet.*

explored, exploring, has explored

explosion
the exploding of something; the noise made by something exploding: *The* ***explosion*** *of the bomb could be heard many miles away.*

export
to send goods to another country for sale: *Japan* ***exports*** *cars to many countries.*

The opposite is **import**.

export
1 the exporting of goods: *In the Philippines sugar is grown for* ***export***. **2** something that is exported: *Rubber is one of Malaysia's most important* ***exports***.

The opposite is **import**.

extra
1 more than usual; more than you need or is necessary: *This week I got an* ***extra*** *$2 pocket money so that I could go to the zoo. I'll give you an* ***extra*** *blanket in case you feel cold in the night.* **2** very; especially: *My dad takes an* ***extra****-large size of jumper. We had an* ***extra****-special meal for my birthday.*

extract
to pull out: *The dentist had to* ***extract*** *one of my teeth.*

eye
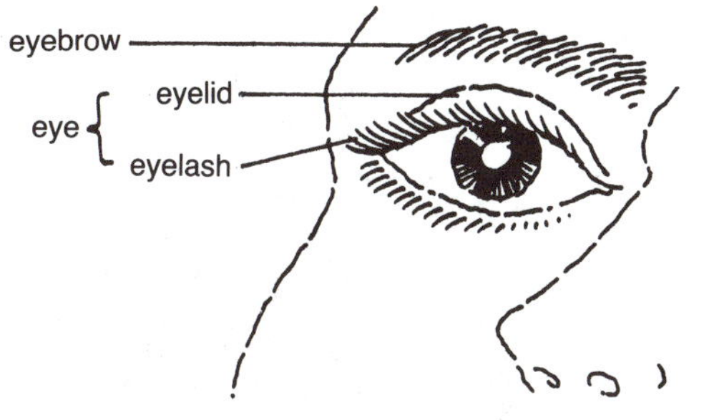

that part of you that you see with: *Peter has brown* ***eyes***. *You close your* ***eyes*** *when you go to sleep. If you are good at noticing things, people say you have 'sharp* ***eyes***'.

eyebrow
the curved line of hair above your eye: *My grandad's* ***eyebrows*** *have turned grey.*

eyelash
one of the hairs that grow along the edge of your eyelid: *My little sister has beautiful long* ***eyelashes***.

eyelid
the piece of skin that covers your eye when you shut it: *Some women put coloured stuff on their* ***eyelids*** *to make their eyes look prettier.*

eyesight
the ability to see: *You don't need glasses if you have good* ***eyesight***.

Ff

face
1 the front of your head where your eyes, nose and mouth are: *Peter and Jane were both red in the* ***face*** *after running down the hill. Why have you all got such sad* ***faces*** *today?* **2** the front of something: *On a clock-****face*** *the hands are in the middle and the numbers 1 to 12 round the edge. I put the piece of paper* ***face*** *down on the table so that nobody could read it.*

face to face close enough to speak to each other: *I'd like to meet a famous actor* ***face to face*** *some day.*

face
to be opposite to something; to look towards something: *The kitchen window* ***faces*** *the street. The teacher told the naughty boy to* ***face*** *the wall.*

faced, facing, has faced

fact
something that is true and can be proved: *It is a* ***fact*** *that daily exercise is good for your health.*
in fact really: *I expected to enjoy the film but* ***in fact*** *I hated it.*

factory
a building where goods are made in large numbers: *There are 250 people working in the clothes* ***factory****. Ten thousand cars a year are produced by this* ***factory****.*

Two **factories**

fade
1 to become less bright: *The colours of the curtains have* ***faded*** *in the sun.* **2** to become less loud: *The noise* ***faded*** *away after a while.*

faded, fading, has faded

fail
1 not to be successful in an exam or test: *Five of my classmates* ***failed*** *their English exam.* **2** not to manage to do something: *The horse* ***failed*** *to jump the second fence.*

- Meaning 1: the opposite is **pass**.
- Meaning 2: the opposite is **succeed**.

failure
failing to do something; not a success: *My big sister was upset by her* ***failure*** *to pass her driving test. My cake is a* ***failure*** *— it tastes horrible!*

The opposite is **success**.

faint
1 not strong; difficult to notice: *I could hear a* ***faint*** *sound coming from behind the cupboard and wondered what it was. There was a* ***faint*** *smell of garlic in the kitchen.* **2** not clear; difficult to see properly: *This photograph is very* ***faint****.*

faint
to lose your senses for a moment, and fall down, usually because of a pain or a shock: *Liz* ***fainted*** *when she saw blood coming from the cut in her finger. The woman* ***fainted*** *on hearing the bad news.*

fair
a kind of large market with stalls where you can buy or win things, and big machines with seats that you can have exciting rides on: *The* ***fair*** *was held in a big field. I won this doll at the* ***fair****.*

fair
1 treating everyone the same: *It was a* ***fair*** *test — everybody was treated alike. 'Why have you eaten all the chocolates and left none for me? It's not* ***fair****!' It's not* ***fair*** *that I have to go to bed when Amy is allowed to stay up.* **2** light-coloured: *Andrew has* ***fair*** *hair and blue eyes.* **3** fine, without rain: *We had* ***fair*** *weather most of the time during our sailing trip.*

Meaning 2: the opposite is **dark**.

fairy

a creature in a story that looks like a tiny girl with wings: *In this story a **fairy** helps a boy to escape from a wicked giant. My little brother believes in **fairies**.*

Two **fairies**

fairy tale a story for children with fairies, dwarfs, magicians or other creatures: *My mum sometimes reads me a **fairy tale** before I go to bed.*

fall

1 tumbling by accident: *Mr Brown had a **fall** on the slippery path and hurt his leg.* **2** dropping through the air: *When you are using a parachute, you don't open it until you are in the middle of your **fall**.* **3** autumn: *Leaves change colour in the **fall**.*

fall

1 to lose your balance and tumble over: *Don't **fall** into the water! Michael slipped and **fell** on the pavement. Mary laughed so much that she **fell** off her chair.* **2** to drop down: *The cup **fell** off the table and broke. The patient's temperature has **fallen**.*

- Meaning 1: same as **tumble**.
- Meaning 2: same as **drop**.
- Meaning 2: the opposite is **rise**.
- fell, falling, has fallen

fall asleep to begin to sleep: *My granny often **falls asleep** while she is watching television.*

fallen

see **fall**: *A lot of apples have **fallen** from the tree.*

false

1 not true; wrong: *The man gave a **false** name to the police instead of his real name. Is this story true or **false**?* **2** not natural: *Both my grandparents have **false** teeth.*

Meaning 1: the opposite is **true**.

familiar

well-known; not strange: *Your face looks **familiar** to me — we must have met before. This song is **familiar** to most children.*

The opposite is **strange**.

familiar with knowing something well: *Mr Green is **familiar with** this city — he has lived here for six years.*

family

1 parents and their children: *The Grey **family** live next door to us. There are many **families** with small children in this street.* **2** a group of people related to each other; your cousins, aunts, uncles and grandparents: *All the **family** came to my granny's birthday party.* **3** a group of animals or plants that are like each other in certain ways: *The tiger is a member of the cat **family**.*

Two **families**

famous

known to many people: *Lewis Carroll was a **famous** writer. He wrote a **famous** book called 'Alice in Wonderland'. Robert Louis Stevenson is also **famous** for his books.*

fan

1 a person who admires someone famous, such as a singer or an actress; a person who likes a certain sport very much: *Some pop stars have thousands of **fans** all over the world. The football **fans** were very noisy after the match.* **2** a thin, flat object that you wave in front of your face to keep you cool in hot weather: *Sometimes I use my exercise book as a **fan**.* **3** a machine that has several blades which turn round fast and make the room cooler: *Switch on the electric **fan** — it's far too hot in here!*

fan

to cool yourself with a fan: *I **fanned** myself with my exercise book.*

fanned, fanning, has fanned

far

1 a long way away: *I don't live **far** from school. The prince and princess sailed away to a **far** country.* **2** a certain length or distance: *How **far** can you throw the ball? How **far** is it to* *school from your house?* **3** very much: *My sister can sing **far** better than my dad.*

- Meanings 1 and 2: far, further, furthest
- Meanings 1 and 2: the opposite is **near**.

far away, far off a long way away: *Don't go **far away**. My grandmother lives **far away**, in America. The school is not **far off**.*

so far up to now: *Have you enjoyed this film **so far**? **So far**, I haven't found the answer to the question you asked me.*

fare
the price of a journey in a bus, train or taxi; the money that you have to pay for a journey: *What is the **fare** to the station? My father spends a lot of money on **fares** to and from work.*

farewell
an old word that means goodbye: *In the story the prince said, '**Farewell**, dear father, I shall return in a year and a day.'*

farm
a piece of land, together with the buildings on it, that is used for growing food and keeping animals such as cows, pigs and hens: *In the country there are lots of small **farms**. Mark would like to work on a **farm** when he grows up.*

farmer
a person who has a farm: *My uncle is a **farmer** — he has a large farm with a lot of cattle.*

farming
the business of growing food or keeping animals on a farm: *Matthew is interested in **farming**. My uncle uses all the modern **farming** methods.*

fashion
the way of dressing or doing your hair that is liked by a lot of people at a certain time: *The **fashions** in clothes and shoes are always changing. For boys, short hair is in **fashion** and long hair is out of **fashion** at the moment.*

fast
1 quick; quickly: *My uncle has a **fast** car. My dad drives very **fast** on the motorway. Angela speaks so **fast** that I can't understand her.* **2** showing a time that is later than the correct time: *My watch is three minutes **fast**.*

The opposite is **slow**.

fast food food that can be quickly prepared, such as hamburgers: ***Fast food** is useful when you're in a hurry, but you shouldn't have it at every meal.*

fasten
1 to close: *This dress **fastens** up the back with a zipper. Look out — your safety belt isn't **fastened** properly.* **2** to fix; to attach: *Susan **fastened** a red flower to her dress.*

fat
white grease that you have under your skin; the white stuff that you see attached to meat; other kinds of grease such as oil and butter: ***Fat** is used in cooking and baking. Bacon contains a lot of **fat**.*

fat
large, heavy and round in shape; not slim: *You will get **fat** if you go on eating too much. Mrs Green has the **fattest** cat I've ever seen.*

- The opposite is **thin**.
- fat, fatter, fattest

father
a man who has children: *I call my **father** Daddy. I think my **father** and mother are very good parents.*

fault
1 a mistake; something for which you are to blame: *It's your **fault** we missed the bus because you didn't hurry.* **2** something wrong: *An engineer is trying to mend the **fault** in our telephone.*

favour
a kind action: *Will you do me a **favour** and fetch me my glasses?*

favourite
liked best of all; preferred: *Strawberries are my **favourite** fruit. Which is your **favourite** television programme? My **favourite** colour is pink. I like most colours, but pink is my **favourite**.*

fawn

a baby deer: *A **fawn** is light brown and has very thin legs.*

fear
a strong, unhappy feeling that you have when you think you are in danger: *The boy tried not*

to show his ***fear*** *of the big dog. The people lived in* ***fear*** *of another flood.*

fear
to be afraid of something: *There is no need to* ***fear*** *the exam if you have been working hard and learnt everything.*

feast
a large, special meal: *The king invited a lot of people to a* ***feast*** *in the palace to celebrate his daughter's birthday.*

feather
one of the long light objects that grow from a bird's skin and cover its body: *I found a white seagull's* ***feather*** *on the shore. My pillow is filled with soft goose* ***feathers.***

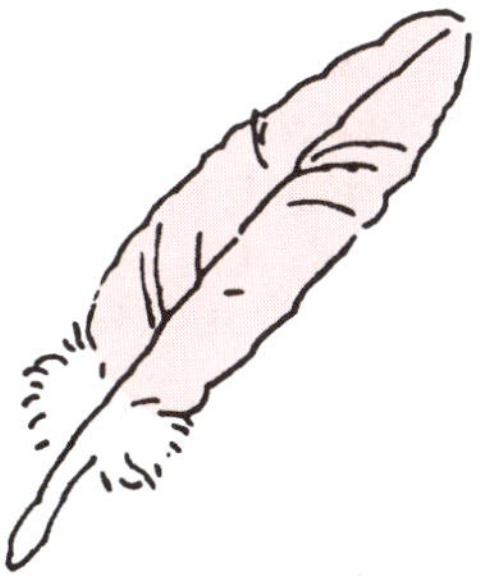

February
the second month of the year.

fed
see **feed**: *Mum* ***fed*** *the baby and then put her to bed. Have you* ***fed*** *the dog yet?*
fed up bored or unhappy because you have had too much of something: *I am* ***fed up*** *with doing my homework.*

feeble
weak: *The old lady is getting very* ***feeble*** *and has to stay in bed all day.*

feed
1 to give food to a baby, a weak person or an animal: *Mum is* ***feeding*** *the baby. The baby is still too small and weak to* ***feed*** *himself.* **2** to eat: *Horses, cows and sheep* ***feed*** *on grass.*

fed, feeding, has fed

feel
1 to have some kind of feeling: *I* ***feel*** *hungry. 'How do you* ***feel****?' 'I* ***feel*** *better now.' 'Do you* ***feel*** *cold?' 'No, I* ***feel*** *quite warm.' Jenny* ***felt*** *very unhappy. I've eaten too much and now I* ***feel*** *sick. Mark was* ***feeling*** *lonely so he went to call on Robert.* **2** to find out what something is like by touching it with your hands: *The blind man* ***felt*** *the object carefully.* ***Feel*** *how soft the cat's fur is.* **3** to notice something on your skin: *I* ***felt*** *a drop of rain on my leg. We could* ***feel*** *the cold wind through our clothes.*

felt, feeling, has felt

feelers

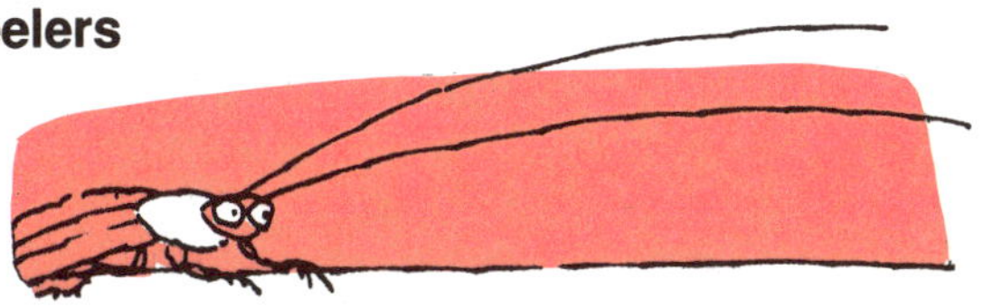

the two long, thin parts on the head of an insect, with which it can feel things around it: *An insect can move its* ***feelers*** *in all directions.*

feeling
something that you feel, such as happiness, unhappiness, fear, anger, pain or hunger: *Do you get a* ***feeling*** *of being lonely when you're on your own in the house? Some people like to hide their real* ***feelings****.*

feet
see **foot**: *It's nice to run on the sand with bare* ***feet****.*

fell
see **fall**: *Michael* ***fell*** *down and hurt his knee.*

felt
see **feel**: *I* ***felt*** *so happy when my parents told me they were going to buy a puppy. Have you ever* ***felt*** *lonely?*

female
an animal or bird that can have babies or lay eggs: *The* ***female*** *is usually smaller than the male. A* ***female*** *bird lays the eggs.*

The opposite is **male**.

fence
a line of wooden or metal posts round a piece of land, joined together with wire or pieces of wood, to stop people or animals getting in or out: *The garden was surrounded by a wooden* ***fence****. There was a* ***fence*** *round the field where the cows were kept.*

fern
a plant with soft curly leaves like feathers: *We are growing different kinds of* ***fern*** *in our classroom.* ***Ferns*** *do not have flowers.*

ferry
a boat that takes people and also cars, coaches and lorries across a river or a narrow bit of sea: *We went by* ***ferry*** *from Singapore to Sentosa.*

Two **ferries**

fertile
producing a lot of crops: *The land is so **fertile** here that we have three harvests every year.*

festival
a time of the year when people have a holiday and celebrate a special event: *Christmas is an important **festival** that takes place in December.*

fetch
to go and bring something or someone: *Could you please **fetch** me my briefcase from the hall? I must hurry — it's time to **fetch** the children from school.*

fever
an illness that causes the temperature of your body to be higher than usual and makes your heart beat faster: *Matthew has a **fever** today so he must stay in bed.*

few
not many: ***Few** people would be willing to eat worms. There are **few** trees in a desert.*

The opposite is **many** or **a lot.**

a few some: *I have borrowed **a few** books about animals from the library. There are only **a few** sweets left in the jar! I'll be back in **a few** minutes.*

fewer
not as many: *There are **fewer** girls in my class than in my brother's class. There are **fewer** boys than girls in the choir.*

The opposite is **more.**

field
1 a piece of land that is used for growing food or keeping animals: *The sheep are kept in this **field**. The farmer is out working in the **fields**.* **2** a piece of land covered with grass that is used for playing games such as football or hockey: *The players assembled on the **field** ready for the match.*

fierce
very angry; always wanting to attack: *Our neighbour has a **fierce** dog that everybody is afraid of.*

fifteen
1 the number 15: *Three times five is **fifteen**.* **2** 15 in number: *Ian is **fifteen** years old.*

fifty
1 the number 50: *Five times ten is **fifty**.* **2** 50 in number: *The fare is **fifty** cents.*

fig

a soft, sweet fruit that has a lot of tiny seeds inside: ***Figs** can be eaten fresh or dried in the sun and stored.*

fight
a struggle; a battle: *There was a **fight** going on in the street between two gangs.*

fight
to attack each other with hands or with weapons: *The two boys were **fighting** each other when the teacher came into the classroom. Stop **fighting** with your little brother! The two armies **fought** a fierce battle.*

fought, fighting, has fought

figure
1 the numbers 0 to 9: *'275' has three **figures**. Write today's date in **figures**.* **2** the shape of a person: *It was very dark and all I could see was the **figure** of a man running across the street.*

file

1 a line of people walking one behind the other: *The children walked in single **file** into the school hall.* **2** a container for keeping papers together and in order: *My dad keeps all his business letters in a large **file**.*

fill
to make something full; to become full: *Ann **filled** the bottle with water. The playground began to **fill** up with children as soon as the bell rang.*

film
1 moving pictures that are shown on television or at a cinema: *Did you watch the **film** about elephants yesterday? Shall we go and see a **film**?* **2** a thin strip of material on which photographs are taken: *I need a new **film** for my camera.*

filthy
very dirty: *The children's clothes were **filthy** after they had been playing in the mud.*

fin

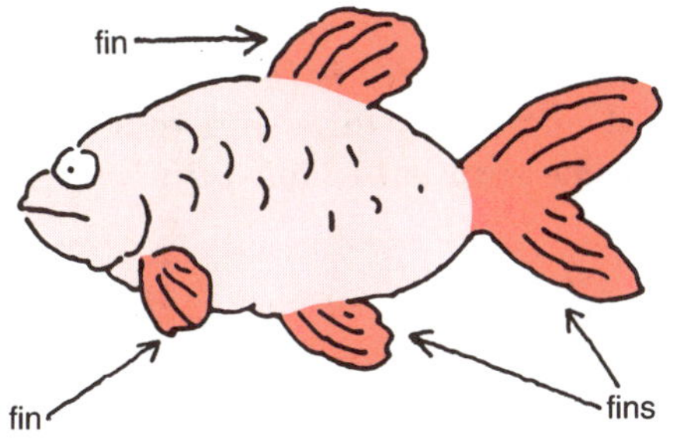

one of the thin parts on a fish's body, that are used for balancing and swimming: *The sailors saw a shark's **fin** above the water.*

find
1 to get what you have been looking for; to get something by accident: *I **found** the missing shoe under my bed. Sue **found** some beautiful shells on the beach. Mike **found** a $5 note in the street. I couldn't **find** my sister because she was hiding behind the curtain.* **2** to feel a certain way about something: *I **find** this book very exciting. Robert **finds** his homework too difficult.*

- Meaning 1: the opposite is **lose**.
- found, finding, has found

find out to get the answer to something you wanted to know: *Paul is trying to **find out** the result of the football match. I've **found out** who stole my bicycle.*

fine
1 well; healthy: *I had a cold yesterday but I am feeling **fine** today. 'How are you?' 'I'm **fine**, thank you.'* **2** good; all right: *There's nothing wrong with your work — it's **fine**. 'I'll come and see you at four o'clock.' '**Fine**.'* **3** very thin: *My sister has **fine** hair. You need a sharp pencil to draw a **fine** line.* **4** bright; not raining: *We'll go to the beach if it's **fine** tomorrow. It was a **fine** day yesterday.*

fine
money that must be paid as a punishment: *Dad had to pay a **fine** for driving too fast.*

finger
one of the five parts that the end of your hand is divided into; not counting your thumb, one of the other four of these: *You can say that you have five **fingers**, or four **fingers** and a thumb, on each hand. Your first **finger**, next to your thumb, is your 'index **finger**', your second **finger** is your 'middle **finger**', your third finger is your 'ring **finger**', and your fourth finger is your 'little **finger**'.*

fingerprint
the mark made by the tip of a finger, showing the lines on the skin: *The police could find no **fingerprints** because the burglar had worn gloves.*

finish
the end of a race: *The two runners were almost together at the **finish**. It was a close **finish**.*

The opposite is **start**.

finish
1 to bring to an end; to complete; to come to an end: *I've **finished** my homework. The music **finished** suddenly.* **2** to eat or drink the last of something: *We went for a walk after we had **finished** our meal.* **3** to stop using something: *Have you **finished** with my pencil yet?*

Meanings 1 and 2: the opposite is **start** or **begin**.

finish up **1** to eat, drink or use the last of something so that there is nothing left: ***Finish up** your dinner.* **2** to come at last: *We went on a trip through Malaysia and **finished up** in Penang.*

finishing-line
the line that marks the end of a race: *Which horse was the first to cross the **finishing-line**?*

fir
a tall, pointed tree with thin, sharp leaves called 'needles' that don't fall off in winter: *A **fir** has cones in which the seeds are stored.*

fire
1 something that is burning by accident: *Several houses were destroyed in the **fire**.* **2** a pile of wood that is burning to give heat: *The scouts collected some dry wood and lit a **fire** to cook a meal.* **3** a gas or electric heater: *Switch on the **fire** if you feel cold.*
fire alarm a bell that makes a loud noise to warn people when there is a fire: *Everybody*

*has to leave the building when the **fire alarm** rings.*
fire brigade a group of firemen: *The house is on fire! Call the **fire brigade**!*

fire engine a large vehicle that carries firemen and all the things that are needed for putting out fires: *Six **fire engines** were driving as fast as possible to the burning building.*
fire station a building for firemen and fire engines: *The firemen wait in the **fire station** until they are called to put out a fire.*
on fire burning: *The building is **on fire**!*

fire
to use a gun; to shoot: *The soldier **fired** his gun three times. The men each **fired** three bullets at the target. The thief **fired** at the policeman.*

fired, firing, has fired

fire-extinguisher
a metal container that is filled with water or foam for putting out fires: *There are red **fire-extinguishers** on every floor of this office.*

fireman
a man whose job is to put out fires: *A **fireman** wears a helmet and special clothes to protect himself from fire.*

Two **firemen**

fireplace
a space in the wall of a room where a fire is burnt for heating: *The smoke from the **fireplace** goes up the chimney.*

firework

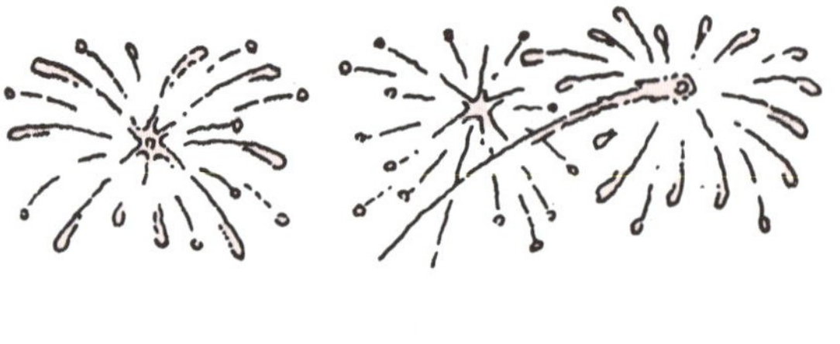

an object that explodes with a loud noise and a lot of flashes that make brightly coloured patterns: *There will be a show of **fireworks** to celebrate the Queen's visit.*

firm
a business; a company: *My father works for a large **firm**. His **firm** employs over 200 people.*

firm
1 hard; difficult to bend: *I prefer a **firm** mattress to a soft one.* **2** strong and not shaking: *Make sure that the ladder is **firm** before you climb it.* **3** strong, not gentle and quiet: *Teachers have to be **firm** with their pupils.*

first
1 before all others: *January is the **first** month of the year. Peter was the **first** child to arrive at the party. Who came **first** in the race?* **2** before doing anything else: *I'll help you with the cooking but I have to wash my hands **first**.* **3** for the first time: *I didn't like badminton when I **first** played it, but now I like it very much.*

The opposite is **last**.

at first at the beginning: ***At first** John was afraid to go into the dark cave, but soon he felt braver and went in.*
first aid treatment of a wounded or sick person before a doctor arrives: *All car-drivers ought to know how to give **first aid**.*

fish
1 a creature that lives in the water and breathes through gills: *There are plenty of **fish** around the coast. How many **fish** did you catch?* **2** the flesh of a fish, which is eaten as food: *Do you prefer meat or **fish**? There are a lot of bones in this **fish**.*

Two **fish**

fish
to catch fish: *My uncle showed me how to **fish** with a fishing-rod.*

fisherman
a man who fishes as a job or as a hobby: *The **fishermen** returned to the harbour with a big load of fish.*

Two **fishermen**

fishing
the catching of fish, as a job or as a hobby: *We're going **fishing** this afternoon. A lot of people in this village earn their living from **fishing**.*

fishmonger
a person who sells fish: *Please would you call*

*at the **fishmonger's** and collect the fish I ordered for dinner?*

fist
a tightly closed hand: *The two boys were punching each other with their **fists**.*

fit
1 to be the right size or shape: *This coat **fits** very well. These shoes don't **fit** me — they are too small. This lid won't **fit** on that jar.* **2** to fix something: *The man **fitted** a new lock to our front door.*

fitted, fitting, has fitted

fit
healthy and able to do exercises without getting tired: *I feel very **fit**. My dad does exercises to keep himself **fit**.*

- Same as **healthy**.
- fit, fitter, fittest

five
1 the number 5: *Two and three are **five**.* **2** 5 in number: *I'll be back in **five** minutes. Sam is **five** years old today.*

fix
1 to fasten something: *Dad **fixed** the shelf to the wall. How can I **fix** the cover back on this book?* **2** to mend; to repair: *My father knows how to **fix** the car.*

flag
a piece of cloth with a design on it that can be attached to a pole: *Every country has its own **flag**.*

flame
the bright light that leaps up from something that is burning: *The **flames** and smoke from the burning factory could be seen a mile away.*

flamingo

a large bird with pink feathers, long legs, a long neck and a curved beak: ***Flamingos** live in large groups near water.*

flash
a sudden bright light: *The **flash** of lightning was followed by loud thunder.*

flash
to shine for a short time: *The blue light on the police car was **flashing**. Peter **flashed** his torch three times as a signal.*

flask
a special container for keeping hot drinks hot or cold drinks cold: *We took a **flask** of hot tea with us for our picnic.*

flat
an apartment for living in, on one floor of a building: *We live in a **flat** on the third floor.*

Same as an **apartment**.

flat
1 level; even: *A table-top is **flat**. You need a **flat** surface for skating. Shoes without high heels are called **flat** shoes.* **2** having lost all its air: *My bicycle has a **flat** tyre.* **3** used up, having no power left: *The batteries in my radio have gone **flat**.*

flat, flatter, flattest

flavour
taste: *Do you like the **flavour** of this drink? There are many different **flavours** of ice-cream.*

flesh
1 the muscles and fat that cover the bones of human beings, animals, birds and fish: *The **flesh** of animals and birds is called meat.* **2** the soft part of fruit: *The **flesh** of a peach is sweet and juicy.*

flew
see **fly**: *The **bird** flew back to its nest. The plane **flew** above the clouds. The pilot **flew** over the sea.*

flight
1 a journey in a plane: *How long is the **flight** from Singapore to London?* **2** a plane that is taking passengers on a certain journey: *The **flight** to Frankfurt leaves in 20 minutes. We had to wait for an hour for our **flight** to Hong Kong. There are two **flights** a day to Tokyo.* **3** the action of flying: *Have you ever seen swans in **flight**?* **4** a set of stairs: *We have to go up six **flights** of stairs to get to our flat on the third floor.*

flippers

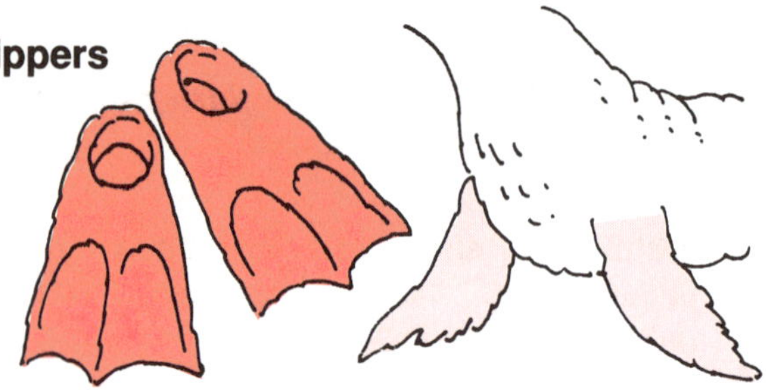

1 rubber shoes with wide flat pieces at the end, for helping you to swim under water: *I can swim much faster with my **flippers** on.* 2 the short, flat limbs of a seal, sea-lion or walrus, that are used for swimming: *In the circus we saw a sea-lion that could slap its **flippers** together as if it was clapping its hands.*

float

to stay on the surface of a liquid; not to sink: *A piece of wood was **floating** in the river. Tim made some little boats out of cork to **float** on the water.*

The opposite is **sink**.

flock

a group of animals or birds: *A shepherd looks after a **flock** of sheep.*

flood

a large amount of water lying on land that is usually dry: *If it goes on raining like this we shall have **floods**.*

flood

to cover a place with a large amount of water: *The fields were **flooded** after the heavy rain. A pipe burst and **flooded** the bathroom.*

floor

1 the surface in a room on which you stand or walk: *Some children had to sit on the **floor** because there were not enough chairs. The pencil fell on the **floor**.* 2 all the rooms on one level in a building: *We live on the third **floor**. The **floor** that is level with the street is called the ground **floor**.*

florist

a person who sells flowers and plants: *A shop where you can buy flowers is called a **florist's**.*

flour

a white powder that is made by crushing grains of wheat, and is used for making bread, rolls, cakes and other food: *The baker makes bread out of **flour**, water and salt.*

flow

to move along in the way that water does: *This river **flows** into the sea. The water **flowed** down the drain.*

flower

a plant that has a coloured part formed of petals, which attracts bees; the coloured part of a plant: *A raspberry plant has small white **flowers**. Sue went into the garden and picked a bunch of **flowers**. The gardener has planted a lot of **flowers**.*

flown

see **fly**: *The canary has **flown** away.*

flu

short for **influenza**: *I don't feel very well — I think I must be getting **flu**.*

fluffy

soft like fur: *Cotton wool is a **fluffy** material. Baby chickens are yellow and **fluffy**.*

flute

one of the instruments of the orchestra, a long metal pipe with holes: *My sister is learning to play the **flute**.*

fly

a small insect with two wings: *A **fly** is crawling up the window. In warm weather there are **flies** everywhere and they annoy people.*

Lots of **flies**

fly

to move through the air on wings; to travel in an aircraft: *A penguin is a bird but it cannot **fly**. The birds will **fly** away if you go too close to them. Joe is **flying** to New York in the summer. A pilot knows how to **fly** a plane.*

flies, flew, flying, flown

flyover

a bridge that carries a road over another road: *There is a new **flyover** in the city centre.*

foal
a baby horse: *A **foal** likes to stay near its mother.*

foam

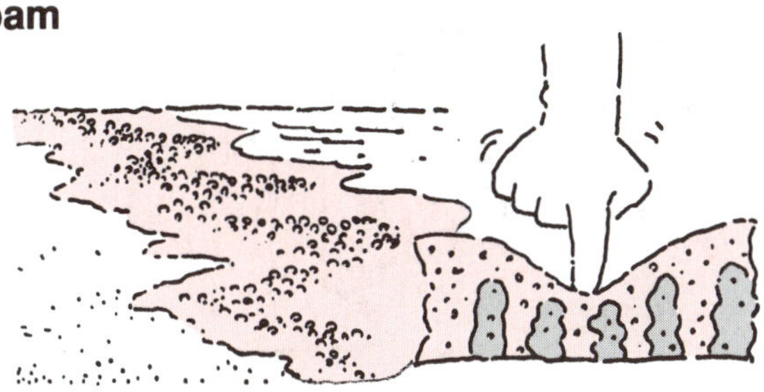

1 lots and lots of tiny little bubbles all joined together, like the kind that soap sometimes makes in the bath: *There was a lot of **foam** at the edge of the sea.* **2** a soft rubber or plastic material that looks like a sponge and it is used for making seats, mattresses and cushions: *My bed has a thick **foam** mattress on it.*

fog
thick cloud near the ground that makes it difficult to see anything: *We had to wait for five hours at the airport because the aeroplane could not take off in the **fog**.*

fold
1 to bend one part of a piece of paper or cloth so that it covers another part: *I carefully **folded** the letter and put it in an envelope. Mum ironed the shirts, **folded** them up and put them away in the drawer.* **2** to put your arms across your chest so that one arm goes over and under the other one: *Kate leant back in her chair and **folded** her arms.*

follow
1 to go behind someone or something: *The puppy **followed** its mother into the garden.* **2** to chase: *The police **followed** the burglars down the motorway.* **3** to come after something: *The rain was **followed** by sunshine.* **4** to go along a road: *If you **follow** this road you will come to the city centre.* **5** to carry out something: *Michael **followed** the teacher's advice and learnt five new words every day.*

Meaning 1: the opposite is **lead**.

fond
liking someone or something very much: *Even though they are **fond** of you, your parents sometimes get angry with you. I am very **fond** of swimming.*

food
things that people and animals eat: *Mum buys most of our **food** in the supermarket. My little sister eats baby **food**. Grass is the only **food** that sheep and cows need.*

fool
a stupid, silly person: *You can't get toothpaste back into the tube, you silly **fool**! Don't be such a **fool**!*

foolish
silly; not wise: *It is **foolish** to cross the road without first making sure there is no traffic coming.*

The opposite is **wise** or **smart**.

foot
1 the part of your leg on which you stand or walk: *I've hurt the big toe on my left **foot**. You keep needing new shoes as your **feet** grow bigger.* **2** the lowest part; the bottom of something: *There was a small house at the **foot** of the hill. Tom left his shoes at the **foot** of the stairs.* **3** a unit of length that is equal to 30 centimetres: *Sue is five **feet** tall. The bed is six **feet** long. This hill is about 900 **feet** high.*

Two **feet**

on foot walking: *I had to come home **on foot** because I missed the last bus.*

football
1 a game between two teams of eleven players who try to kick a ball into a goal: ***Football** is played on a large field.* **2** the ball that is used in this game: *A **football** is a large leather ball that is filled with air.*

footpath
a path for walking, not for bicycles or cars: *We walked along a **footpath** by the river.*

footstep
the sound that is made by someone walking: *I heard **footsteps** outside the door and looked out to see who it was.*

for
1 to be given to someone: *This present is **for** you. There are two letters **for** Mum and one **for** you.* **2** during a certain time; over a certain distance: *I worked **for** two hours and then went outside to play with my friends. After we had driven past the village we saw no houses **for** seven kilometres.* **3** as payment: *I paid $1 **for** my ticket. You can get a piece of chewing-gum **for** 10 cents.* **4** with a certain purpose: *Mum gave me money **for** my bus fare. Amy is saving up her money **for** a bicycle.* **5** in order

to help someone: *What can I do **for** you?* **6** as the employee of someone: *Steven's father works **for** a large clothing firm.*

for example as an example; such as: *Some flowers, **for example** roses, have a lovely scent.*

forbade
see **forbid**: *My father **forbade** me to play football in the street.*

forbid
to tell someone not to do something: *There is a law that **forbids** people to drop litter.*

- The opposite is **permit**.
- forbade, forbidding, has forbidden

forbidden
see **forbid**: *My mother has **forbidden** me to watch television before I've finished my homework. It is **forbidden** to smoke in the theatre.*

force
1 to make someone do something that they do not want to do: *A big boy **forced** Jean to give him all her money. The heavy rain **forced** us to give up our walk and go home.* **2** to use your strength to break something: *The burglars **forced** the door open.*

forced, forcing, has forced

force

1 strength: *A lot of trees were blown over by the **force** of the wind.* **2** strong and violent action: *The burglars used **force** to make the bank manager give them all the money.*

forehead
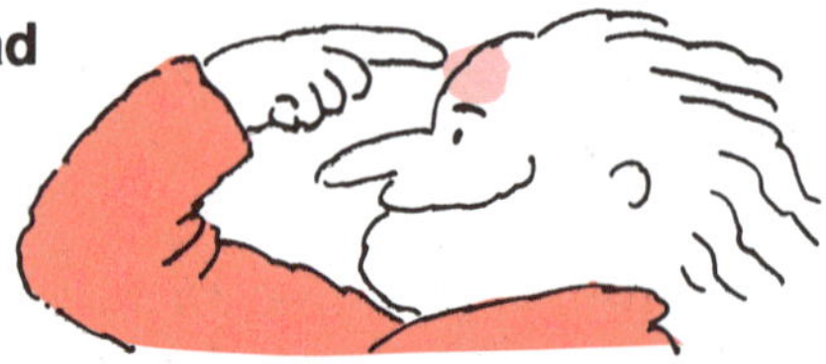

the part of your face above your eyebrows: *Susan's hair covers her **forehead**.*

foreign
belonging to a country that is not your own: *My parents have a lot of **foreign** friends. A person who belongs to a **foreign** country is called a **foreigner**.*

Say **for**-en.

forest

a large piece of land where trees grow close together: *A lot of birds and small animals, such as mice and squirrels, live in the **forest**.*

forever or for ever
always: *I wish we could be on holiday **forever**. I like this town very much and I would like to stay here **for ever**.*

forgave
see **forgive**: *I **forgave** Jack for taking my bike without asking. My mum **forgave** me when I said I was sorry that I had been rude to her.*

forget
not to remember: *Don't **forget** to lock the door when you go out. Peter keeps **forgetting** to return my pen to me. Don't **forget** your coat when you're leaving.*

- The opposite is **remember**.
- forget, forgetting, has forgotten

forgive
to stop being angry with someone who has done something wrong: *I'll **forgive** you if you are really sorry for being naughty. My mother would never **forgive** me if I told her lies.*

forgave, forgiving, has forgiven

forgiven
see **forgive**: *The teacher has **forgiven** my bad behaviour.*

forgot
see **forget**: *I **forgot** my towel when I went swimming.*

forgotten
see **forget**: *I am sorry, I have **forgotten** your name. Mum has **forgotten** her umbrella. I've **forgotten** how to do these sums.*

fork
an eating tool with three or four points that you use for lifting food to your mouth: *You*

*hold your knife in your right hand and your **fork** in your left.*

form

1 a school class: *I am in the third **form**. Which **form** are you in?* 2 a shape: *Paul thought he saw the **form** of a tall man in the fog. Jenny has an alarm clock in the **form** of a mouse.* 3 a kind: *Gym is a healthy **form** of exercise.*

form

to make a shape: *The children **formed** a circle and held hands. The people **formed** a queue at the bus-stop.*

fortnight

two weeks: *I haven't seen Peter for a **fortnight**. We are going on holiday for a **fortnight**.*

fortress

a great, strong building such as a castle, which can be defended against enemies: *The people built a large **fortress** on a mountain to protect themselves against attack.*

fortunate

lucky: *It was very **fortunate** that nobody was injured in the accident.*

fortune

1 a lot of money: *Lorna hopes to become a pop star and make her **fortune**.* 2 good or bad luck: *I made a mistake in my homework, but by good **fortune** the teacher didn't notice it.*

forty

1 the number 40: *Four times ten is **forty**.* 2 40 in number: *Mark's father is **forty** years old.*

forwards or **forward**

in a direction that is in front of you; not backwards: *The teacher asked Mary and Kate to come **forward** to the blackboard and write their answers on it. When I'm in a train I like sitting in a seat that faces **forwards**.*

fought

see **fight**: *When I was younger, I often **fought** with my brother. The warriors **fought** a fierce battle.*

found

see **find**: *Have you **found** your missing glove? Steven **found** a foreign coin in the street.*

fountain

a statue or some other shape made of metal or stone, from which water shoots out: *In the garden there was a pool with a **fountain** in the middle of it.*

fountain pen a pen with a nib and a small container of ink inside: *Do you prefer to write with a **fountain pen** or a ball-point pen?*

four

1 the number 4: *Two and two are **four**.* 2 4 in number: *My little sister is **four** years old.*

fourteen

1 the number 14: *Seven times two is **fourteen**.* 2 14 in number: *A fortnight is the same as **fourteen** days.*

fowl

a bird, especially a chicken, duck or goose: *My uncle keeps **fowls** and a few pigs on his farm.*

fox

a wild animal that looks like a dog, with a pointed face and ears and a long, thick tail: *A **fox** lives in a hole in the ground called an 'earth'.*

fraction

an amount that is not a whole number: $\frac{1}{2}$ *and* $\frac{3}{4}$ *are **fractions**.*

fracture

to break a bone in part of your body, especially an arm or a leg: *Jenny fell down the stairs and **fractured** her arm.*

fractured, fracturing, has fractured

frame

1 an edge around something: *Granny has a photograph of me in a silver **frame** in her sitting-room. Dad sat on his glasses and broke the **frames**.* 2 the shape of a building or a vehicle, which is built first out of metal or wood, so that the rest can be built over it: *An aeroplane has a strong steel **frame**.*

free

1 allowed to do what you want; not controlled;

not kept prisoner: *You are **free** to go where you like. We live in a **free** country. The prisoner was set **free** because he was innocent.* **2** not working; not busy: *My mum doesn't have much **free** time. Are you **free** this afternoon?* **3** not being used; not occupied: *Is that seat **free**?* **4** costing nothing: *My parents got two **free** tickets for a concert.*

freeze
1 to become ice: *When the weather is very cold, the river **freezes** and we can skate on it.* **2** to make food very cold so that it will keep fresh for a long time: *I've made two pies, so that we can eat one today and **freeze** the other one for later.*

froze, freezing, has frozen

frequent
happening often: *Mr Smith makes **frequent** journeys to France. There are **frequent** buses to the city centre.*

frequently
lots of times: *Jennifer is **frequently** late for school.*

Same as **often**.

fresh
1 just made: ***Fresh** bread has a lovely smell.* **2** just gathered: *We buy **fresh** fruit and vegetables every day at the market.* **3** still good to eat; not stale: *Meat will keep **fresh** for a few days if it is stored in a refrigerator.* **4** not used; clean: *Here is a **fresh** towel for you. I need a **fresh** piece of paper.* **5** cool; refreshing: *I went outside to get some **fresh** air. I like the **fresh** breeze by the sea.* **6** not salty: *Sea-water is salty, but the water in rivers is **fresh**.*

Meaning 3: the opposite is **stale**.

Friday
the sixth day in the week, the day after Thursday: *My parents often go to the cinema on **Friday** evenings.*

fridge
short for **refrigerator**: *We keep most of our food in the **fridge**.*

friend
someone whom you know well and like: *Carol is my best **friend**. We soon made **friends** with the new children next door.*

The opposite is **enemy**.

friendly
kind: *Amy is very **friendly** to everybody. I like going to the library because the librarian has such a **friendly** smile.*

friendly, friendlier, friendliest

fright
a sudden feeling of fear: *Bill gave me a **fright** by suddenly jumping out from behind the door.*

frighten
to make someone afraid: *The children were **frightened** by the thunder. The large dog **frightened** Martin when it barked at him. I'm not **frightened** of snakes.*

frog
a small animal with smooth, slippery skin and long back legs that it uses for jumping: *A lot of **frogs** live near this pond and you can hear them croaking in the evenings.*

from
1 leaving a place: *I caught the 11 o'clock plane **from** Singapore to Hong Kong.* **2** starting at a time: *The shop is open **from** 8 o'clock in the morning till 7 o'clock in the evening.* **3** sent by someone; given by someone: *This doll was **from** my granny. I got a letter **from** my aunt today.* **4** belonging to a place: *I come **from** Malaysia.* **5** out of someone's hands: *Mum took the scissors **from** my little sister.* **6** out of a place: *The teacher took a book **from** the shelf and showed it to the children. Did you collect the newspaper **from** the shop?* **7** because of: *My dad got ill **from** working too hard.* **8** you use **from** with **different**: *Our house is different **from** yours.*

from time to time sometimes: ***From time to time** the teacher takes us to the museum.*

front
the part of anything that faces forwards: *The **front** of a house is the part that faces the street. Remember to lock the **front** door. The **front** of a car is the part where the driver sits. The **front** page of a newspaper is the first page. You've spilt ice-cream down the **front** of your dress.*

The opposite is **back**.

in front of in a position just ahead of someone

or something; not behind: *Susan sits **in front of** me in the classroom. There is a small garden **in front of** the house. Never run **in front of** a car.*

The opposite is **behind**.

frown

to make your eyebrows come together when you are annoyed: *The teacher **frowned** at Tim when he wouldn't stop talking in the classroom.*

froze

see **freeze**: *The water in the pond **froze** during the night.*

frozen

see **freeze**: *Get me a packet of **frozen** spinach at the supermarket.*

fruit

the part of a plant that contains seeds or a stone and has flesh that you can eat: *We often have fresh **fruit** at the end of a meal. Bananas, mangoes and oranges are my favourite **fruits**.*

fry

to cook food in hot fat: *Mum is **frying** some onions.*

fries, fried, frying, has fried

frying-pan

a shallow pan with a long handle that is used for frying: *The cook used a heavy **frying-pan** for roasting the spices.*

fuel

something such as petrol, oil or wood that is burned to get power or heat: *Motor vehicles cannot run without **fuel**.*

full

1 containing as much as possible: *Is your cup **full** or empty? The bus was **full** of people. 'Could you please open the door for me? My hands are **full**.'* **2** having had enough to eat or drink: *I'm **full** — I can't eat any more.* **3** complete: *A child pays half fare and an adult pays **full** fare on a bus. Please tell me the **full** story.*

Meaning 1: the opposite is **empty**.

full stop a point (.) that marks the end of a sentence: *A **full stop** is always followed by a capital letter.*

full up having no space left for any more people or things: *The bus is **full up**.*

fun

the feeling that you are enjoying yourself: *We had a lot of **fun** at the party. It's great **fun** playing in the sea.*

funeral

the ceremony of burying a dead person: *A large number of people attended Mr Jones's **funeral**.*

funny

1 amusing; making you laugh: *Peter told us a **funny** story about his puppy. The clown in the circus did a lot of **funny** tricks.* **2** strange: *I heard a **funny** noise coming from the flat above. There is a **funny** smell in the kitchen.*

funny, funnier, funniest

fur

the thick hair on an animal: *Mary's cat has soft black **fur**.*

furious

very angry: *Mum was **furious** with me because I went out without telling her.*

furnish

to put furniture into a room or house: *My parents allowed me to **furnish** my own bedroom when we moved to a new flat.*

furniture

things in a house such as tables, chairs and beds: *We bought a new sofa and some other pieces of **furniture** for our sitting-room.*

further

1 a greater distance: *Andrew lives **further** away from school than I do. I cannot walk any **further** — I am too tired.* **2** more: *The police are trying to get **further** information about the robbery.*

furthest

the greatest distance: *Who lives **furthest** away from school?*

future

the time that will come after now: *Nobody knows what will happen in the **future**.*

The opposite is the **past**.

in future from now on: *Don't be late **in future**.*

gaiety
a feeling of being happy and cheerful: *New Year is a time of **gaiety**.*

gain
1 to get something good from something: *You won't **gain** much from school if you never listen to the teacher.* **2** to get more of something; to increase in something: *The old man slowly **gained** strength after his illness. The bicycle **gained** speed as it went down the hill.*

gallop

to run very fast: *The horse was **galloping** round the field.*

gamble
to bet money on things like card games and horse races: *Some people waste a lot of their money on **gambling**.*

gambled, gambling, has gambled

game
1 something that children do together for fun: *The children are playing a **game** in which each child has to pretend to be an animal.* **2** a sport or a pastime with rules, in which you try to win: *My dad usually wins at card **games**. Football, baseball, basketball, hockey and tennis are **games** that need a lot of energy.* **3** a match: *Would you like a **game** of badminton?*

gang
1 a group of young people who are friends with each other: *There are about ten of us in our **gang**.* **2** a number of people who join together to do something bad: *A **gang** of robbers planned to attack the van that was carrying the money to the bank.*

gap
an empty space: *My father has a **gap** between his two front teeth. David got into the garden through a **gap** in the fence.*

garage
1 a building in which a car is kept: *We have a **garage** next to our house.* **2** a building where cars are repaired and petrol is sold: *Mum has taken our car to the **garage** to be repaired.*

garden
a piece of land beside a house, where flowers, vegetables and other plants are grown: *The children are playing in the **garden**. There is a wall round the **garden**.*

gardener
a person whose job is to work in someone else's garden: *Some people who have a large garden employ a **gardener**. A **gardener** is planting some flowers in the park.*

garlic
a plant that has a small white bulb that you can use in cooking; it has a strong taste and smell: ***Garlic** is added to food to give it a strong flavour.*

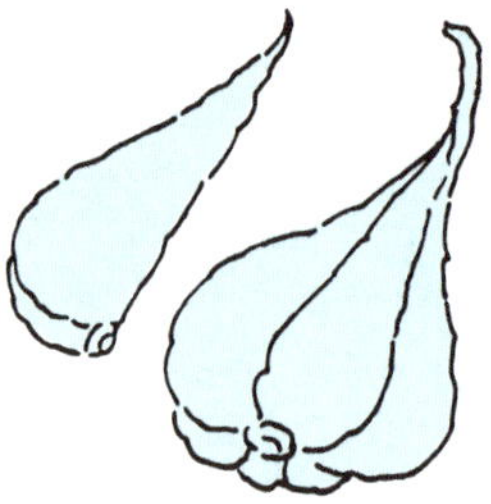

gas
1 stuff like air that is used as a fuel for cooking and heating: *Does your mum cook with **gas** or electricity? We have a **gas** cooker in our kitchen. My granny has a **gas** fire in her sitting-room.* **2** an American word for petrol: *A **gas** station is a place where people can buy **gas** for their cars.*

gate
an outside door in a wall or fence: *The park **gates** are locked in the evening. Please close the **gate** after you so that the dog does not escape on to the road.*

gather
1 to come together in a group: *A lot of children **gathered** around the cage where the monkeys were playing.* **2** to bring things together; to collect: *Please **gather** your books together now. We **gathered** blackberries from the bushes along the road.*

- Meaning 1: same as **assemble**.
- Meaning 2: same as **collect**.

gave

see **give**: *Mum **gave** me money for the bus fare. I **gave** my mum a bunch of flowers for her birthday.*

gay

1 happy: *The children were **gay** and cheerful.* **2** brightly coloured: *Marie is wearing a very **gay** dress.*

gaze

to look at something for a long time: *The children **gazed** at the strange animal in the cage. The teacher told Robert to listen to her instead of **gazing** out of the window.*

- Same as **stare**.
- gazed, gazing, has gazed

geese

see **goose**: *Today we had to stop our car and wait for a flock of **geese** to cross the road.*

general

an officer who is very important in the army: *The **general** commanded his troops to attack.*

generous

kind and helpful to people; giving people more than they expect: *It was very **generous** of you to pay for my ticket to the cinema. Linda was given a bicycle by a **generous** uncle.*

The opposite is **selfish**.

gentle

1 behaving and talking in a kind, quiet way; touching things softly and carefully: *The doctor was very **gentle** with the patient. Everybody likes Mrs Johnson because she is such a **gentle** old lady.* **2** quiet; not loud or strong: *Anne has a **gentle** voice. There was a **gentle** breeze.*

gentleman

1 a man who speaks and behaves politely and kindly: *A **gentleman** usually opens the door for a lady.* **2** a polite word for a man whose name you don't know: *There is a **gentleman** waiting to see you.*

Two **gentlemen**

germ

a very tiny living thing that causes diseases: *You should stay at home when you have a bad cold so that you don't pass your **germs** on to other people.*

get

1 to become: *Please don't **get** angry. It is **getting** warm in here. You'll have to wait until it has stopped raining if you don't want to **get** wet.* **2** to receive: *What did you **get** for your birthday? Did you **get** my message?* **3** to bring; to buy: *Please **get** me a bottle of lemonade from the fridge. Could you please **get** me a loaf of bread from the baker's?* **4** to go; to take: *There was no bridge so we couldn't **get** across the river. I tried to **get** the book down from the top shelf.* **5** to persuade someone; to ask someone to do something: *I'll try and **get** my aunt to lend us the money. My dad **got** a gardener to plant the bushes.* **6** to arrive: *When did you **get** home?* **7** to catch a disease: *I hope I don't **get** measles.* **8** to hear; to understand: *I didn't quite **get** what you said. Peter didn't **get** the joke.*

got, getting, has got

get about to be able to move about; to travel about: *The old lady doesn't **get about** much nowadays.*

get along with to be friendly with someone: *We **get along** very well **with** our neighbours.*

get away to leave without getting caught; to escape: *The thieves stole thousands of dollars from the bank and **got away** in a van.*

get away with to escape the punishment you should have for doing something wrong: *I won't punish you this time for telling a lie, but you won't **get away with** it next time!*

get hold of **1** to grab: *Tom **got hold of** his sister's arm and pulled her back on to the pavement.* **2** to find; to borrow: *Can you **get hold of** the magazine for me? I'll try to **get hold of** my brother's bike.* **3** to manage to speak to someone: *It is very difficult to **get hold of** the headmaster because he is often at meetings.*

get in **1** to go inside: *The car's waiting — hurry up and **get in**! How did you **get in** without a key?* **2** to arrive: *When does the train **get in**?*

get into **1** to begin having: *You'll **get into** trouble if you don't tell your parents the truth. Tom **got into** a fight with a bigger boy.* **2** to climb inside: *I **got into** the bath. **Get into** the car!*

get off to leave a train or bus: *We **got off** the train as soon as it stopped. I have to **get off** at the next stop.*

get on **1** to work or live with someone in a friendly way: *We **get on** very well together. I*

***get on** well with Joe.* **2** to enjoy what you are doing: *How are you **getting on** with your English lessons?* **3** to continue doing something: *I must **get on** with my homework.* **4** to board; to get into: *Where did you **get on** the bus?*

get out of **1** to leave a place; to climb out of something: *I'd like to **get out of** the house and go for a walk. I don't like **getting out of** bed in the morning.* **2** to avoid doing something: *You can't always **get out of** washing the dishes.* **3** to take off clothes: *Tim **got out of** his school uniform and into his jeans.*

get through **1** to pass an exam or test: *Paul **got through** his exam easily.* **2** to finish work: *We **got through** a lot of work today.*

get together to meet: *Our club **gets together** once a week.*

get up **1** to get out of bed: *I **got up** at seven o'clock.* **2** to stand up: *Please don't **get up**. Bob **got up** off the floor.*

ghost
the figure of someone who is dead, which seems to appear in front of you: *I am not afraid of **ghosts** because there aren't any **ghosts**. Do you believe in **ghosts**? Lesley thought she saw a **ghost** last night.*

giant
an imaginary person who is huge and strong: *The **giant** in the fairy tale was so tall that he could step over a river.*

The opposite is a **dwarf**.

gift
something given; a present: *I bought some flowers as a **gift** for my mother.*

gigantic
huge; very large: *There are some **gigantic** buildings in the city centre.*

giggle
to laugh in a silly way: *The children couldn't stop **giggling** at the joke. The funny song made us all **giggle**.*

giggled, giggling, has giggled

gill
one of the openings on the side of a fish's head: *A fish breathes by taking in water through its **gills**.*

ginger
a kind of root that is used to give a strong flavour to food: *Mum chopped some **ginger** and added it to the food in the pan.*

giraffe
a tall animal with a very long neck, long legs and dark patches on its skin: ***Giraffes** live in Africa and feed on leaves from trees.*

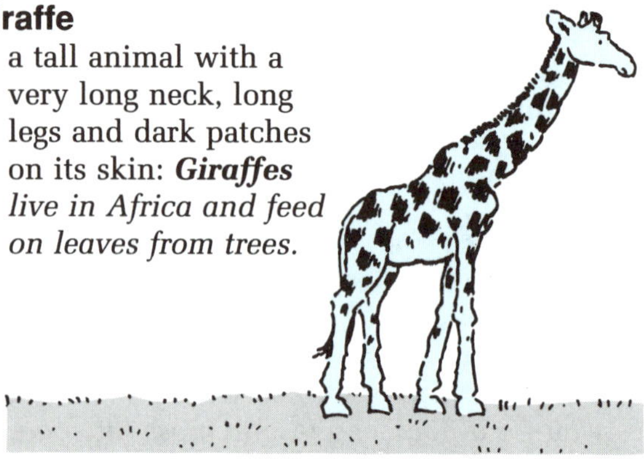

girl
1 a female child: *Most of the **girls** like playing football with the boys.* **2** a daughter: *My aunt has five children — three **girls** and two boys.*

give
1 to hand something to someone: *Please **give** me your pencil. Did you **give** Amy the key to the front door?* **2** to hand something to someone as a gift: *My parents **gave** me a toy train for my birthday.* **3** to offer: *Can you **give** me an example of how this word is used? Let me **give** you a piece of advice. I don't know the answer — **give** me a clue.* **4** to organize some event: *We are **giving** a party tomorrow.* **5** to make a noise or movement: *She **gave** a sudden cry.*

- Meaning 1: the opposite is **take**.
- gave, giving, has given

give away **1** to give something to others without wanting money for it: *The new shop is **giving away** balloons to all the children who come in.* **2** to tell a secret: *One of the robbers **gave away** the place where the money was hidden.*

give back to return something: *Helen **gave** me **back** the book that she borrowed last month.*

give in **1** to surrender: *The soldiers **gave in** to the enemy after a long fight.* **2** to stop trying to do something: *'Have you guessed the answer to the riddle?' 'No, I **give in**.'*

give off to produce something such as a smell

or smoke: *The bad eggs **gave off** a terrible smell.*

give up 1 to stop: *My dad wants to **give up** smoking. Suzanne never **gave up** hope of finding her missing cat.* 2 to surrender: *The robber **gave** himself **up** to the police.*

give way 1 to break: *The old bridge might **give way** soon.* 2 to agree against your will: *Should children always **give way** to their parents' wishes?*

glad

pleased; happy: *I'm so **glad** that you have come. I'm **glad** you like the gift. I shall be **glad** to help you.*

glance

to look quickly at someone or something: *Mr Black kept **glancing** at the clock. I **glanced** at my sister to see if she was smiling.*

glanced, glancing, has glanced

glass

1 a hard transparent material that breaks easily: *This bottle is made of **glass**.* 2 a container made of glass, from which you can drink: *A **glass** fell off the table and broke.* 3 the drink inside a glass: *I drank three **glasses** of lemonade.* 4 a mirror: *A **glass** or a looking-**glass** are old words for a mirror.*

glasses

metal or plastic frames with special lenses that you wear over your eyes to help you to see better; spectacles: *My grandad has two pairs of **glasses** — one for reading and one for looking at things that are further away. Where are my sun**glasses**?*

glide

1 to move smoothly and easily: *A long snake **glided** across the path.* 2 to float in the air: *An eagle was **gliding** above us.*

glided, gliding, has glided

glove

a piece of clothing that you wear on your hand: *I have got a new pair of **gloves**. Mum wears rubber **gloves** when she washes the dishes.*

glow

to give out a red light: *I can see a cigarette **glowing** in the dark.*

glue

sticky stuff that you use for sticking things together: *You can mend the broken handle of the cup with **glue**.*

glue

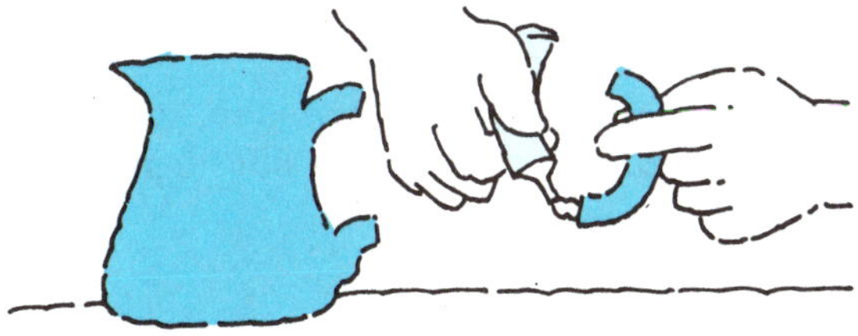

to stick things together with glue: *My mum **glued** the pieces of the broken vase together.*

glued, gluing, has glued

go

1 to move from one place to another: *Peter is **going** across the street. **Go** straight ahead. Shall we **go** by car or by bus?* 2 to attend; to visit: *My little sister doesn't **go** to school yet. Let's **go** to the movie.* 3 to lead somewhere: *Where does this road **go**?* 4 to leave: *I think it's time we were **going**. Please **go** now.* 5 to disappear: *My purse has **gone**!* 6 to do some action: *I am **going** for a walk with my dog. Would you like to **go** swimming?* 7 to be put; to fit: *The spoons **go** in the top drawer. That big box won't **go** into the cupboard.* 8 to become: *These apples have **gone** bad. My dad's hair is **going** grey.*

- Meaning 4: the opposite is **come**.
- went, going, has gone

go against to do something different from what you have been told to do: *I don't want to **go against** my parents' wishes.*

go ahead 1 to go in front of someone: *Please **go ahead** and I'll follow you.* 2 to begin to do something: *'Shall I tell you a funny story?' 'Yes, **go ahead**.' We **went ahead** with our plan.*

go off 1 to explode: *The bomb **went off**.* 2 to ring: *When the alarm **went off** the thieves ran away.* 3 to become rotten or sour: *That meat has **gone off**. Put the milk in the fridge so that it won't **go off**.*

go on 1 to continue: *Don't **go on** reading when I'm talking to you! We'll **go on** with our game after dinner.* 2 to happen: *What's **going on** here?*

go out 1 to stop burning; to stop shining: *Our camp-fire kept **going out** because of the rain. The lights suddenly **went out**.* 2 to go somewhere, such as a party, in the evening: *My parents don't **go out** a lot.*
go over to read carefully; to examine: *My dad sometimes **goes over** my homework.*
go with to look right with something; to taste right with something: *Your tie **goes** nicely **with** your shirt. I don't think chocolate **goes** well **with** chips.*
going to doing something soon; wanting to do something: *I am **going to** have a shower. It is **going to** rain soon.*

go
a turn at something; an attempt: *Would you like a **go** at this computer game? I've had my **go**. Jill blew out ten candles in one **go**.*

goal
1 in football, the two posts that you have to kick the ball between: *The man who guards the **goal** is called a **goal**-keeper.* 2 the point you score if you manage to kick the ball between the posts: *Phil has scored another **goal**! Our team won by three **goals** to two.*

goat
an animal of the sheep family, with horns and a hairy coat: *A baby **goat** is called a kid. The mother **goat** was bleating for her kid.*

God
the highest being of all, who made everything on earth and in heaven: *I believe in **God**. Pray to **God** for help.*

god
one of several beings that are believed to have power over nature: *Some people pray to many different **gods**. Brahma, Vishnu and Shiva are the three chief Hindu **gods**.*

goddess
a female god: *Kali is a Hindu **goddess**.*

goggles

special tightly-fitting glasses that you use to protect your eyes from water or dust: *Many people wear **goggles** when they go swimming. Where are my **goggles**? There is a pair of **goggles** beside the swimming-pool.*

gold
a precious, shiny yellow metal that is used for making jewellery and money: *This ring is made of **gold**. A **gold** coin is worth a lot of money.*
gold medal the medal that is given as first prize in a sports contest: *The winner receives a **gold medal**.*

golden
1 like gold; having the colour of gold: *The princess had **golden** hair.* 2 made of gold: *The princess was wearing a **golden** crown.*

gone
see **go**: *My friends have just **gone**. This banana has **gone** bad.*

good
1 behaving well; not naughty: *Be **good**! Sarah is a **good** girl.* 2 kind: *You've been very **good** to me. Mr Johnson is a **good** neighbour.* 3 able to do something well: *Jill is **good** at tennis. David is very **good** at English. Dr Kelly is a **good** doctor. Mum is a **good** cook.* 4 of high quality: *This is a **good** bicycle. Mum always buys **good** food. Is that book **good**?* 5 correct: *We're learning to speak **good** English. Bill has **good** manners.* 6 cheerful; happy: *I am in a **good** mood today.* 7 pleasant: *Ice-cream is **good** to eat. It is **good** to see you.* 8 fit; healthy; strong: *My grandparents are in **good** health. You don't need glasses if you have **good** eyesight.* 9 helpful; giving health: *Vegetables are **good** for you. Swimming is **good** for your health.*

- The opposite is **bad**.
- good, better, best

no good no use: *A broken watch is **no good** to anyone. It's **no good** shouting for help when there's no-one to hear you.*

good-looking
pretty; handsome: *Sue is a **good-looking** girl. Do you think Bob is **good-looking**?*

goodbye
a word that you use when you are leaving someone: *I have to go now — **goodbye**!*

goods
things that are sold; products: *This shop sells leather **goods**. A train that transports **goods**, not people, is called a **goods** train.*

goose
a large bird with a long neck that makes a loud noise: *A* ***goose*** *is similar to a duck. Some* ***geese*** *are wild, but others are kept on farms. This pillow is filled with soft* ***goose*** *feathers.*

Two **geese**

gorilla
the largest kind of ape; it has black fur and lives in the forests of Africa: *A* ***gorilla*** *is very big and strong.*

got
see **get**: *Jenny* ***got*** *a letter from America this morning. Steve* ***got*** *a football from his parents for his birthday.*
have got means the same as **have**: ***Has*** *Jane* ***got*** *blue eyes or brown eyes? We* ***have*** *only* ***got*** *two days to finish the work.* ***Have*** *you* ***got*** *everything you need? Goodbye —* ***I've got*** *to go now.*

gown
a woman's dress for dances and parties: *My mum has a beautiful* ***gown*** *made of blue silk.*

grab
to seize something suddenly: *My little sister* ***grabbed*** *a biscuit from the plate. Peter was going to run across the busy road but his mother* ***grabbed*** *his arm.*

grabbed, grabbing, has grabbed

grade
1 a mark for an examination: *My brother always gets good* ***grades*** *at school.* **2** an American word for a school class: *We are in the third* ***grade*** *now.*

grain
1 the seeds of rice, wheat, oats or maize: *The sacks of* ***grain*** *were stored in a shed.* **2** one of these seeds: *There are only a few* ***grains*** *of rice left in the jar.*

gramme, gram
a unit of weight: *One thousand* ***grammes*** *are equal to one kilogramme (1000 g = 1 kg). This packet contains 100* ***grams*** *of peanuts.*

grand
1 splendid; large and beautiful: *It would be nice to live in a* ***grand*** *house.* **2** very pleasant; great: *We had a* ***grand*** *day by the sea.*

grandad
a grandfather: *My* ***grandad*** *used to be a policeman.*

grandchild
the child of a person's son or daughter: *I am my grandparents' oldest* ***grandchild****.*

Lots of **grandchildren**

granddaughter
the daughter of a person's son or daughter: *My grandparents have three* ***granddaughters*** *— my sister Sue, my cousin Nancy, and me.*

grandfather
the father of your father or mother: *I have two* ***grandfathers*** *— one is a businessman, and the other is retired.*

grandmother
the mother of your father or mother: *I got some money from both my* ***grandmothers*** *for my birthday.*

grandparents
the parents of your father or mother: *I have four* ***grandparents*** *— my mother's parents and my father's parents.*

grandson
the son of a person's son or daughter: *My grandparents have five* ***grandsons*** *— my cousins John and Adrian, and my three brothers.*

granny
a name for a grandmother: *I am drawing a picture for* ***Granny****.*

Two **grannies**

grape
a small, sweet, juicy fruit that grows in bunches: *Jenny likes green* ***grapes*** *but I like purple* ***grapes*** *.* ***Grapes*** *are also dried to make raisins.*

grapefruit
a large, round, yellow fruit that is similar to an orange but not so sweet: *This **grapefruit** is very sour. Would you like a glass of **grapefruit** juice?*

grass
a green plant with very thin leaves, that covers meadows, parks and gardens: *Sheep, goats and cows eat **grass**. We sat on the **grass** and ate our picnic.*

grasshopper

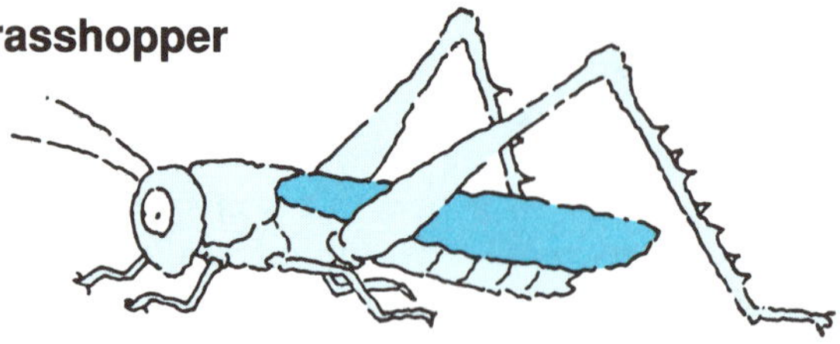

an insect with long back legs that can jump very high: ***Grasshoppers** make a noise by rubbing their legs against their wings.*

grateful
wanting to thank someone for something: *I am very **grateful** for your help. I would be **grateful** if you could take the dog for a walk.*

grave
a place where a dead person is buried: *There were a lot of flowers on the **grave**.*

gravy
a sauce made from the liquid that comes out of meat when it is being cooked: *Would you like more **gravy** with your rice?*

grease
thick oil or soft fat: *I've put some **grease** on my bicycle chain to stop it getting rusty.*

great
1 very large: *There was a **great** crowd of people outside the palace waiting for the Queen.* **2** a lot of something: *Please take **great** care of the baby.* **3** very important; famous: *Shakespeare was a **great** writer. Charlie Chaplin was one of the **greatest** actors of all time.* **4** very good; very pleasant: *We had a **great** time at the zoo. Swimming in the sea is **great** fun. I've got a **great** idea.*

greedy
wanting a lot of food; wanting more than you need: *Don't be **greedy** — leave some of the ice-cream for your sister.*

green
the colour of fresh grass: *The new leaves of most plants are bright **green**.*

greengrocer
a person who sells fruit and vegetables: *Please could you get me a kilo of apples at the **greengrocer's**?*

greet
to say or do something friendly when you meet someone; to show that you are pleased to see them, such as saying 'hello', or 'good morning', or shaking hands, or kissing them: *James **greeted** Mrs Smith politely when he met her on his way to school. My dog **greeted** me by jumping up on me and licking my face. My aunt came out of the house to **greet** us when we arrived.*

greetings
a kind message; kind wishes: *My dad received a lot of **greetings** on his birthday.*
greetings card a folded card with a picture on the front and greetings inside: *This shop sells birthday cards, Christmas cards, Good Luck cards and many other kinds of **greetings cards**.*

grew
see **grow**: *The puppy **grew** very fast in its first three months.*

grey
the colour of the street; the colour of dark clouds: *A donkey is **grey**. My dad is wearing a dark **grey** suit. Granny's hair is going **grey**.*

grief
a feeling of being very sad; great sorrow, like the kind you feel when a friend or relation dies: *The whole family was filled with **grief** at the sad news.*

The opposite is **joy**.

grieve
to be very sad: *Mrs Barker **grieved** for her dead husband.*

- The opposite is **rejoice**.
- grieved, grieving, has grieved

grill
to cook food directly over or under very strong heat: *We **grilled** steaks and sausages on the barbecue.*

grind
to crush something into tiny pieces: *You have*

*to **grind** these spices before you use them. This machine is for **grinding** coffee.*

ground, grinding, has ground

grip

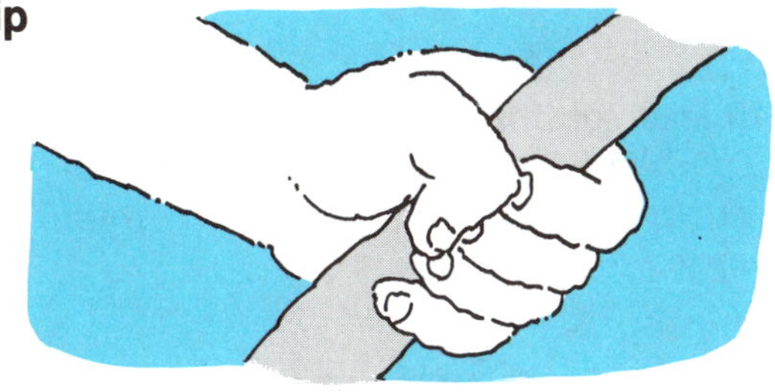

to take hold of something firmly with your hand: *The old man **gripped** his walking-stick. The policeman **gripped** the thief's arm.*

gripped, gripping, has gripped

groan

to make a deep sound in your throat because you are in pain or unhappy: *The patient **groaned** when the doctor touched her injured leg.*

grocer

a person who sells food and other things that you use in your home: *Goods that you buy at the **grocer's** are called groceries.*

ground

1 the solid surface of the earth; the soil: *A bird landed on the **ground** near my feet. The **ground** is very dry because it hasn't rained for many days.* **2** a piece of land for a special purpose: *Most schools have a play**ground**. Football matches are played on a football **ground**.*

ground

see **grind**: *These spices are freshly **ground**.*

groundnut

a peanut: ***Groundnut** oil is made by crushing **groundnuts**.*

group

1 a number of people or things that are together in one place: *A **group** of children stood by the pond and fed the ducks. The children are playing in small **groups** in the school playground. The Philippines are a **group** of islands.* **2** a group of musicians who play pop music together: *Which is your favourite pop-**group**?*

group

to form into a group: *The children **grouped** round the teacher.*

grow

1 to become bigger: *Whenever I meet my aunt, she tells me I've **grown** a lot since she last saw me. The small puppy soon **grew** into a big dog.* **2** to let your hair get longer; to get longer: *Your hair has **grown** a lot. My dad is **growing** a beard.* **3** to get bigger, and produce leaves, flowers and seeds, as a plant does: *There are a lot of fir-trees **growing** in this forest. Firs **grow** very tall. Carrots **grow** well in this soil.* **4** to put seeds or young plants in the ground: *My mother **grows** lots of different kinds of roses in our garden. The farmer **grows** rice in his fields.* **5** to become: *It's **growing** dark — we had better get home.*

grew, growing, has grown

grow up to become an adult: *I want to be a doctor when I **grow up**.*

growl

to make a deep, angry sound in the throat: *The dog **growled** at the little girl when she pulled its tail.*

growl

a deep angry noise like the kind that a bear or dog makes when it is angry: *The dog gave a **growl** when it saw the strangers.*

grown

see **grow**: *I've **grown** five centimetres in one year. The tree in our garden has **grown** very tall.*

grown-up

an adult: *The **grown-ups** stay up late but I have to go to bed early.*

growth

becoming bigger: *The gardener has been measuring the **growth** of this tree in the last year.*

grub

the worm-like form of an insect after it hatches from its egg: *A caterpillar is the **grub** of a butterfly or moth.*

grunt

to make the noise of a pig: *The pigs **grunted** when the farmer brought their food.*

guard
1 someone whose job is to protect a person or a place from attack: *The King always has a body**guard** with him.* 2 a person whose job is to stop prisoners from escaping: *The prisoners escaped when their **guards** fell asleep.* 3 a person who is in charge of a train: *The **guard** blew his whistle and the train started to move.*

guard
1 to protect a place or a person from danger: *The soldiers were **guarding** the palace. Our neighbours have a big dog to **guard** their house.* 2 to stop someone from escaping by watching them all the time: *The soldiers **guarded** their prisoners night and day.*

Meaning 1: same as **protect**.

guardian
a person who takes care of someone or something: *The young orphan's uncle became his **guardian**. The **guardian** of the castle was the only person who knew where the treasure was hidden.*

guess
an answer you make when you don't know the right answer: *Have a **guess** at the number of people who live in this city. Your **guess** was nearly right. That's a good **guess**.*

guess
1 to say what you think might be nearly the right answer: *If you don't know the answer, just **guess**. **Guess** who is coming to see us? I **guessed** that the number of children in the school was 850. How did you **guess** the right answer?* 2 to suppose; to think: *I **guess** you're right. I **guess** I'll have to go now.*

guest
a person who comes to see you and has a meal with you, or stays in your home: *We are having three **guests** to stay with us at the weekend. My parents invited twenty **guests** to their New Year's party.*

guidance
help and advice: *The children made a model of the school under the **guidance** of their teacher. The teacher gave the children **guidance** on how to use a dictionary.*

guide
1 a person who shows tourists the way to go, and points out interesting things: *A **guide** will show you round the castle. You will need a **guide** in the mountains because it is dangerous if you lose your way.* 2 a book that contains information for tourists: *My dad bought a **guide** to London before he went there.*

guided, guiding, has guided

guide
to lead someone; to show someone the way: *The blind man was **guided** by his dog. The teacher **guided** the children round the museum.*

guilty
having done something wrong: *The judge said the man was **guilty** of murdering the old lady.*

The opposite is **innocent**.

guinea-pig
a small animal like a rabbit but with short ears and no tail: ***Guinea-pigs** are often kept as pets in cages.*

guitar

a musical instrument with six strings that you play with your fingers: *My sister is learning to play the **guitar**.*

gum
1 a sweet that you chew; chewing-gum: *Do you like fruit **gums**? You are not allowed to chew **gum** in the classroom.* 2 a type of glue: *You use **gum** for sticking pieces of paper together.* 3 the firm pink flesh round your teeth: *My **gums** sometimes bleed if I brush my teeth too hard.*

gun
a weapon that fires bullets: *The robber fired his **gun** at the bank manager. Do policemen carry **guns** in your country?*

gymnastics
exercises and movements that you are taught for making you strong, healthy and good at moving your body like an acrobat: *Our **gymnastics** teacher is teaching us how to climb a rope.*

Called **gym** for short.

habit
something that you do usually: *My dad has the **habit** of doing exercises before breakfast. Mr Jones is trying to get out of the **habit** of smoking. I got up at seven o'clock out of **habit**, forgetting I was on holiday.*

had
see **have**: *We **had** a good time at the zoo. Have you **had** lunch yet? I **had** just come back from school when Peter rang. You'**d** better finish your homework.*

> You can shorten:
> - **I had** to **I'd**
> - **you had** to **you'd**
> - **he had** to **he'd**
> - **she had** to **she'd**
> - **we had** to **we'd**
> - **they had** to **they'd**

had better it would be a good thing if: *We **had better** wash the dishes.*

hadn't
short for **had not**: *My parents wouldn't allow me to watch television because I **hadn't** finished my homework.*

hair
1 one of the very fine, thin objects that grow from your skin, especially on your head: *My dad is beginning to get some grey **hairs**.* **2** all the hairs on your head: *Paul has very short **hair**. I am going to have my **hair** cut.*

hairbrush

a brush for tidying your hair: *I keep a comb and a **hairbrush** on my dressing-table.*

haircut
1 the cutting of your hair: *Your hair is too long — you need a **haircut**.* **2** the way your hair is cut: *I like your new **haircut**.*

hairdresser

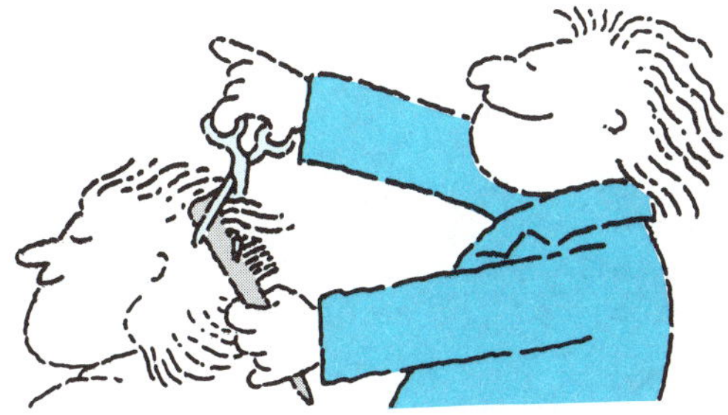

a person whose job is to wash and cut people's hair: *A shop in which **hairdressers** work is called a **hairdresser's**. My mum goes to the **hairdresser's** every week.*

hairdryer
an electric machine that blows out hot air for drying your hair: *At the hairdresser's there are big **hairdryers** that fit over your head, but at home we have a little **hairdryer** that you hold in your hand.*

hairy
covered with hair: *Some caterpillars are very **hairy**.*

half
one of the two equal parts of anything: *Mum cut the mango into two **halves** and gave one **half** to me. I've only read the first **half** of this book.*

> Two **halves**

half past thirty minutes past the hour: *I got home at **half past** three. My aunt came to see us at **half past** nine in the morning.*
in half in two equal parts: *Mum cut the mango **in half**. The pencil broke **in half**.*

half
partly: *This cup is only **half** full. The lemonade bottle is **half** empty.*

hall
1 a room at the entrance to a house: *There are a lot of doors leading from the **hall** to other rooms in the house. We left our coats in the **hall**.* **2** a large room for meetings or concerts: *The children assembled in the school **hall**.*

halve
to divide something into two equal parts: *I **halved** the apple and gave one half to my sister.*

> halved, halving, has halved

ham
salty meat from the back leg of a pig: *I had three slices of **ham** with my salad. Would you like a **ham** sandwich?*

hamburger
a round flat piece of beef that is fried and then put into a bread roll with slices of onion: *I sometimes buy a **hamburger** for lunch.*

hammer
a tool with a heavy metal head that you use for hitting things such as nails, to make them go into wood: *Mum used a **hammer** to break open the coconut.*

hammer
to hit with a hammer: *Dad **hammered** a nail into the door of the shed.*

hamster

a small animal with pale brown fur that is similar to a mouse but has a tiny tail: *A **hamster** is often kept as a pet in a cage. **Hamsters** sleep during the day.*

hand
1 the part of your body at the end of your arm: *Guess what I'm holding in my left **hand**. Jenny carried the heavy bag with both **hands**.* **2** one of the two fingers on a clock or watch that point to the numbers: *The short **hand** of a clock is called the 'hour **hand**' and the long one the 'minute **hand**'.* **3** help: *Please give me a **hand** with this heavy box. Do you need a **hand** with your work?*

hands up! raise your hands above your head: *The bank robber had a gun and shouted, "**Hands up!**"*

shake hands to shake someone's right hand when you greet them or when you say goodbye to them: *Do you always **shake hands** when you meet someone for the first time? The Queen **shook hands** with each of her 200 guests.*

hand
to pass something; to give: *Mike **handed** the book to Paul. The teacher **handed** out an exercise book to each child.*

handkerchief
a small square piece of cloth or soft paper that you use for wiping your nose: *You use a lot of paper **handkerchiefs** when you have a bad cold.*

handle
the part of an object that you hold in your hand to pick it up or to open it: *The tea is very hot, so hold the cup by its **handle** and you won't burn your fingers. A broom has a very long **handle**. You have to press down the door-**handle** to open the door.*

handsome
good-looking; attractive to look at: *The prince in the story was young, tall and very **handsome**.*

handwriting
the way you write: *My father's **handwriting** is very difficult to read. Karen has beautiful **handwriting**.*

hang
1 to fix something above the ground on a hook, string or chain; to be fixed above the ground: *I'll **hang** the picture on that wall. **Hang** your coat on the hook. A light was **hanging** from the ceiling. My new calendar is **hanging** over my desk.* **2** to be loose; to swing about: *The dog's tongue was **hanging** out. Julie's long hair **hung** down over her shoulders.*

hung, hanging, has hung

hangar

a large building in which aeroplanes are kept: *The plane was taken into the **hangar** for repairs.*

happen
to take place: *The accident **happened** on the motorway late at night. How did the accident **happen**? What **happened** next?*

happiness
being happy: *The message in the greetings card said, 'I wish you all the **happiness** in the world'.*

happy
1 very pleased: *I'm so **happy** that Granny is coming to stay with us. Your parents will be **happy** to hear that you got such a good mark in your exam. I feel **happy** today. The day my*

*parents bought me a puppy was the **happiest** day of my life.* **2** willing to do something: *I'll be **happy** to help you if you need me.*

- happy, happier, happiest
- Meaning 1: the opposite is **sad**.

harbour

a port for ships; a place where ships can shelter from the wind, and where people can land and where cargoes can be loaded and unloaded: *All the ships stayed in the **harbour** during the storm. When does this ferry reach Singapore **harbour**?*

Same as a **port**.

hard

1 very firm; not soft: *The pears are still too **hard** to eat. The ground was very **hard** and dry because it hadn't rained for three weeks.* **2** not easy; difficult: *Is English a **hard** language to learn?* **3** doing something a lot; doing something with speed and energy: *Dad has been working **hard** in the garden all day. If you study **hard**, you will pass your exams. It is still raining **hard**. You have to pull **hard** to open the garage door.*

- Meaning 1: the opposite is **soft**.
- Meaning 2: same as **difficult**.

hardly

almost not; almost none; almost never; almost nobody: *I was so tired, I could **hardly** keep my eyes open. I can **hardly** walk because my feet are so sore. There is **hardly** any rice left. My mum **hardly** ever gets angry. There was **hardly** anybody on the beach early in the morning.*

hardworking

working eagerly and well: *It's nice to be clever, but you have to be **hardworking** too, if you want to pass your exams.*

hare

an animal with long ears, that looks like a large rabbit: ***Hares** can run very fast.*

harm

to hurt someone; to damage something: *Don't be frightened — the dog won't **harm** you. The dry weather is **harming** the young plants.*

harm

injury: *Be careful with that knife — you might do yourself a lot of **harm** with it. The ball hit David's head, but it didn't do him any **harm**. A bit of hard work will do you no **harm**. The burglar told the woman that she would come to no **harm** if she kept quiet.*

harmful

bad for your health: *A medicine can be **harmful** if you take too much of it. Looking directly at the sun may be **harmful** to your eyes.*

harmless

not dangerous: *Our dog is quite **harmless** — he wouldn't bite anybody. A cold is usually a **harmless** illness.*

harvest

1 the gathering in of ripe cereals, vegetables or fruit: *When is the rice **harvest**? A lot of people were working in the fields at **harvest**-time.* **2** the cereals, vegetables and fruit that have become ripe and are ready to gather: *Everybody at the farm had to help bring in the **harvest**.*

harvest

to gather in the ripe cereals, vegetables or fruit: *We **harvested** all the mangoes before the storms began.*

has

see **have**: *Anne **has** a lot of toys. **Has** Pat got a bike? Joe'**s** got blue eyes and brown hair. It **has** stopped raining now. What'**s** happened? That'**s** been done.*

You can shorten:

- **he has** to **he's**
- **she has** to **she's**
- **it has** to **it's**
- **what has** to **what's**
- **that has** to **that's**
- **Joe has** to **Joe's**

hasn't

short for **has not**: *Rachel **hasn't** seen this film yet. Bill has a new bicycle, **hasn't** he? Linda **hasn't** got a cat, has she?*

haste
the doing of something very quickly; a rush: *Joe did his homework in too much* ***haste*** *because he wanted to play football afterwards.*

hat
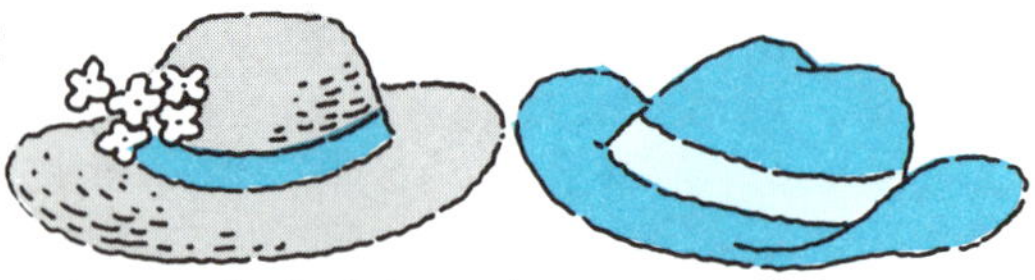

a piece of clothing that you wear on your head: *My* ***hat*** *has a wide brim to keep the sun out of my eyes. In winter I wear a woollen* ***hat*** *to keep my head and ears warm.*

hatch
to produce baby birds from eggs; to break out of an egg: *The hen has* ***hatched*** *three chicks. These chickens* ***hatched*** *this morning. All the eggs have* ***hatched****.*

hate
to dislike very much: *In the fairy tale, the evil queen* ***hated*** *Snow White because of her beauty, and wanted to kill her. I* ***hate*** *getting up early in the morning. I* ***hate*** *drinking cold tea.*

- The opposite is **love**.
- hated, hating, has hated

have
1 you use **have** when you are talking about actions that are in the past, or began in the past: *I* ***have*** *just heard the news.* ***Have*** *you read that book yet? I* ***have*** *never flown in an aeroplane before.* ***Have*** *you ever been abroad? Kate and Anna* ***have*** *taken the dog for a walk — they'll be back soon. We'****ve*** *been learning English for two years.* **2** to possess: *I* ***have*** *a bicycle. We* ***have*** *a dog. Do you still* ***have*** *my pencil? Joe* ***has*** *brown eyes. I* ***have*** *two sisters and one brother. Do you* ***have*** *a lot of friends?* **3** to be suffering from something: *I* ***have*** *a headache. Mark* ***has*** *a cold.* **4** to eat or drink something; to do something: *Dad is* ***having*** *his breakfast. I've just* ***had*** *a cup of tea. I am going to* ***have*** *a bath.* ***Have*** *a rest.* ***Have*** *a try. Mrs Phillips is* ***having*** *another baby in June.* **5** to get something done: *I am* ***having*** *my hair cut. Dad* ***had*** *the car washed.* **6** to get something: *Have you* ***had*** *any news from your aunt in Paris?* **7** you often use **have** with **got** in meanings 2 and 3: ***Have*** *you* ***got*** *a bicycle? Jenny* ***has got*** *brown eyes, hasn't she?*

You can shorten:
- **I have** to **I've**
- **you have** to **you've**
- **we have** to **we've**
- **they have** to **they've**

- has, had, having, has had

have to or **have got to** must: *It's late — I* ***have to*** *go now. I'****ve*** *still* ***got to*** *do my homework. We* ***had to*** *run to catch the bus.*

haven't
short for **have not**: ***Haven't*** *you finished your sums yet?*

hawk

a large bird with a short curved beak, that hunts small birds and other animals: *A* ***hawk*** *has very good eyesight.*

hawker
a person who sells goods in the street, or goes from house to house selling goods: *My mum never buys anything from* ***hawkers****.*

hay
grass that has been cut and dried and is used as food for cattle: *In winter the farmer feeds the cows with* ***hay****.*

he
you use **he** when you are talking about a boy or man: *When I met Paul yesterday,* ***he*** *told me* ***he*** *was feeling ill. Our neighbour is a friendly man —* ***he*** *always tries to help other people.*

head
1 the top part of your body, where your face and hair are; the same part of an animal's body: *Can you stand on your* ***head****? Why do people scratch their* ***heads*** *when they feel puzzled? Carol patted the dog's* ***head****.* **2** the first place; the top part of something: *At last I reached the* ***head*** *of the queue.*

headache
a pain in your head: *I went to bed early because I had a* ***headache****.*

headmaster
a man who is in charge of a school: *A girl in*

*my class was sent to the **headmaster** today because she shouted at the teacher.*

headmistress
a woman who is in charge of a school: *Our **headmistress** is very friendly, so we are not afraid of her.*

headquarters
the place where the leaders of a group of people, such as the police, work: *The man was taken to police **headquarters** to tell his story to the police. The company's **headquarters** are in Paris.*

heal
to make healthy; to become healthy: *This scratch on your leg will **heal** in a few days. Doctors are trained to **heal** sick people.*

health
being well; not being ill: *The doctor examined me and told me that I was in good **health**.*

healthy
1 having good health: *I am feeling fit and **healthy**. My granny is hardly ever ill — she is very **healthy**.* **2** helping to keep you healthy: *Fresh vegetables and fruit are **healthy**. Swimming is one of the **healthiest** forms of exercise.*

healthy, healthier, healthiest

heap

a large pile: *There were **heaps** of stones and soil on the pavement after the street had been dug up. Please tidy that **heap** of papers on your desk.*

heap
to put things into a heap: *Some old newspapers were **heaped** up in a corner of the room. Tom **heaped** rice on to his plate.*

hear
1 to receive sound with your ears: *Speak louder — I can't **hear** you! I didn't **hear** you come in. Dogs can **hear** very well.* **2** to get information or news: *I **hear** that you are moving house. I haven't **heard** anything from my friend in America. I've never **heard** of Mr Green — who is he?*

heard, hearing, has heard

heard
see **hear**: *Emma **heard** a strange noise. Have you **heard** the news?*

heart
1 the part in your chest that pumps blood through your body: *Your **heart** beats faster when you run.* **2** the centre: *We live in the **heart** of the city.* **3** your feelings: *If someone is very kind, you say they have a kind **heart**. If someone is very sad about something, you say their **heart** is broken.*
by heart from memory: *The teacher told us to learn the words **by heart**. You have to know the poem **by heart** if you are going to recite it.*

heat
1 warmth; being hot: *The **heat** from the electric heater will soon dry our wet clothes. I can feel the **heat** of the sun on my skin.* **2** very hot weather: *I could hardly sleep last night because of the **heat**.*

heat
to make something hot: *The water will have to be **heated** before you can take a shower. **Heat** the pie for twenty minutes in the oven.*
heat up **1** to become hot: *The air **heats up** quickly once the sun has risen.* **2** to make something hot again: *Mum **heated up** the soup for me when I came home late for dinner.*

heater
an instrument for heating a room, or for heating water: *It's cold in here — could you switch on the electric **heater**? Please remember to switch off the water **heater**.*

heating
all the heaters that heat a building: *In a house with central **heating** all the rooms are heated by hot water from one big tank.*

heaven
the place where God lives and where good people are believed to go when they die: *Do you believe that animals go to **heaven** as well as people?*

The opposite is **hell**.

heavy
1 having a lot of weight: *This bag is too **heavy** for me to carry. Dad carried the **heaviest** suitcase.* **2** having a certain weight: *How **heavy** are you?* **3** falling in great quantity: *There was a **heavy** shower of rain as we were walking home from school.* **4** falling with a lot of weight:

*The falling brick gave the workman a **heavy** blow on the shoulder.*

- The opposite is **light**.
- heavy, heavier, heaviest

he'd
short for **he had** or **he would**: *John said **he'd** already been to the circus, but **he'd** like to go again.*

heel

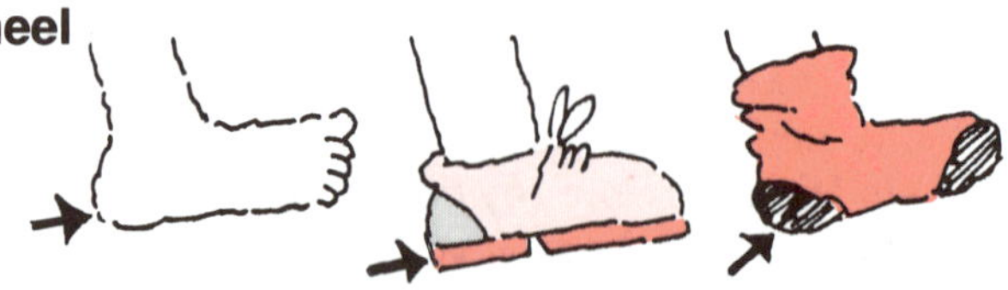

1 the back part of your foot: *My **heels** hurt because my new shoes are rubbing against them.* **2** the part of a shoe or boot that is under your heel: *Mrs Jones is wearing black shoes with very high **heels**. The **heel** has come off this shoe.* **3** the part of a sock that covers your heel: *I have a big hole in the **heel** of my sock.*

height
the distance from the bottom to the top of something: *What **height** are you? This wall is three metres in **height**. Some trees grow to a **height** of 100 metres.*

held
see **hold**: *Amy **held** her little sister by the hand. Have you ever **held** a mouse in your hand?*

helicopter

an aircraft without wings that is kept in the air by long blades fixed to its roof, that go round very fast: *A **helicopter** can rise straight up from the ground, it can stay in the same position in the air for a time, or move through the air.*

hell
the place where evil people are believed to go when they die, to be punished for ever and ever: *Nobody wants to go to **hell**.*

The opposite is **heaven**.

he'll
short for **he will**: *Ask John — **he'll** know what to do.*

hello
a word you say when you greet someone: *'**Hello**, Kelly! How are you?' '**Hello**. This is Mike. Could I speak to David, please?'*

helmet

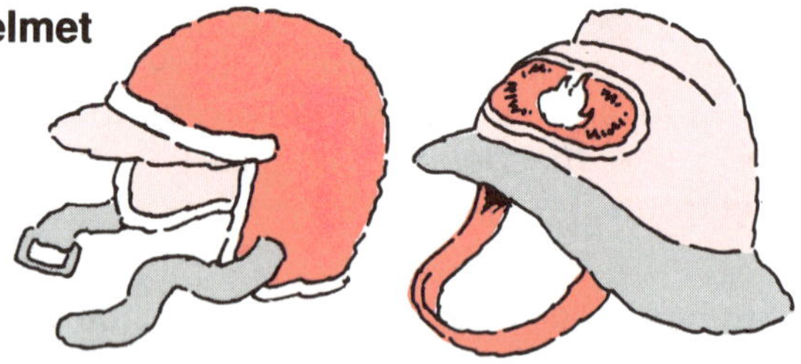

a metal or plastic hat that you wear to protect your head: *You have to wear a **helmet** when you're riding a motorbike. Firemen wear large **helmets**.*

help
to make it easier for someone to do something: *My elder sister **helped** me to write the letter. Could you please **help** me with my work? Can I **help** you? An old man fell down in the street and I **helped** him up.*
help yourself to serve yourself some food or drink: ***Help yourself** to another piece of cake. Peter **helped himself** to more lemonade.*
can't help not to be able to prevent something: *Mark looked so funny with the paint on his nose that I **couldn't help** laughing. I **can't help** it if the bus is late. 'We're going to be very late for school.' 'Oh well, it **can't be helped**.'*

help
1 the action of helping someone; something that helps you: *Do you need any **help** with the housework? Thank you for washing the floor — that was a big **help**. You are a great **help** to me.* **2** a word you shout when you are in danger, to make someone come and rescue you: ***Help! Help!** I'm locked in the cupboard!*

helpful
useful; giving help: *The teacher gave us some **helpful** advice on how to avoid making mistakes. The people here are very friendly and **helpful**. Thank you very much for the information, you have been most **helpful**.*

helpless
unable to do anything for yourself: *A baby is completely **helpless** when it is born.*

hem
the edge of a piece of clothing that is folded

over and sewn: *The **hem** of your dress has come undone.*

hen
a female chicken that lays eggs: *There are twenty **hens** and one cock on this farm.*

her
1 you use **her** when you are talking about a girl or woman: *'Have you seen Jenny?' 'No, I haven't seen **her**.' Could you please tell Mrs Smith that there was a phone call for **her**?* **2** belonging to a girl or woman: *My mother has **her** own car. Susan invited all **her** friends to **her** birthday party.*

herd

a group of animals of one kind that stay together: *Elephants live in **herds**. There is a large **herd** of cattle in the field.*

here
at this place; to this place: *Paul is **here** with us. The sea is not far from **here**. 'Did you find the missing shoe?' 'Yes, **here** it is.' Please come **here**.*

The opposite is **there**.

here and there all around: *My little sister's toys were scattered **here and there**.*

hero
1 a person who has done something brave and is therefore admired by a lot of people: *Jeff's a **hero** — did you hear that he saved Paul from drowning yesterday?* **2** the most important person in a book, play or film: *The **hero** of this book is a boy called Peter Pan.*

- Two **heroes**
- Meaning 1: the opposite is **coward**.

heroine
a female hero: *The **heroine** of this story is a beautiful girl called Snow White.*

heron

a large grey bird with long legs and a long neck: ***Herons** live near water and eat fish.*

hers
you use **hers** for something that belongs to a girl or woman: *'Is this Lisa's book?' 'No, that one isn't **hers** — **hers** is on her desk.' 'I've come to see Helen — I'm a friend of **hers**.'*

herself
1 you use **herself** in sentences where girls or women do something to or for themselves: *Michelle looked at **herself** in the mirror. Sally fell down and hurt **herself**. Mrs Lee bought **herself** a new dress. My little sister can already dress **herself**.* **2** without help: *Did Sarah really draw that picture **herself**?* **3** sometimes used to show who you mean more clearly: *Teresa couldn't go to the concert **herself**, so she gave me her ticket.*

he's
short for **he is** or **he has**: *Richard says **he's** coming to see me when **he's** finished his homework.*

hid
see **hide**: *Jenny **hid** behind the door.*

hidden
see **hide**: *Where have you **hidden** my jacket? The house was **hidden** behind a high wall.*

hide
1 to put something in a place where it cannot be seen, or is difficult to find: *Andy **hid** my book behind his back. My dog **hid** a bone in the garden.* **2** to go somewhere where you cannot be seen, or are difficult to be found: *You **hide**, and I'll come and look for you. Paul was **hiding** in the cupboard.*

hid, hiding, has hidden

high
1 rising a long way above the ground: *Have you ever dived off the **high** diving-board? Mount Everest is the **highest** mountain in the world.* **2** having a certain height: *This building*

is about 100 metres ***high****.* **3** much more than usual: *The patient has a* ***high*** *temperature. The ambulance drove to the hospital at* ***high*** *speed.* **4** not deep in sound: *Children have* ***high*** *voices.*

- The opposite is **low**.
- Meanings 1 and 2: same as **tall**.

highway
a main road: *We drove at a speed of 100 kilometres an hour along the* ***highway****.*

hill
1 a piece of land that rises up above the land all round it: *We climbed up the* ***hill*** *and looked down at the fields below.* **2** an upward slope: *Do you get off your bicycle when you come to a* ***hill****?*

Meaning 1: the opposite is a **valley**.

him
you use **him** when talking about a boy or man: *When you see Daniel, please ask* ***him*** *to ring me.*

himself
1 you use **himself** in sentences where men or boys do something to or for themselves: *Michael looked at* ***himself*** *in the mirror. My dad cut* ***himself*** *with his razor.* **2** without help: *Did Sam write that story* ***himself****?* **3** sometimes used to show who you mean more clearly: *Mr Philips gave me a message to take to the headmistress because he couldn't leave the classroom* ***himself****.*

hip
the part of you between your waist and the top of your legs; the left or right side of this part of you: *Women have wider* ***hips*** *than men do. Granny broke her left* ***hip*** *and had to go to hospital.*

hippo
short for **hippopotamus**: ***Hippos*** *like standing in the water.*

hippopotamus
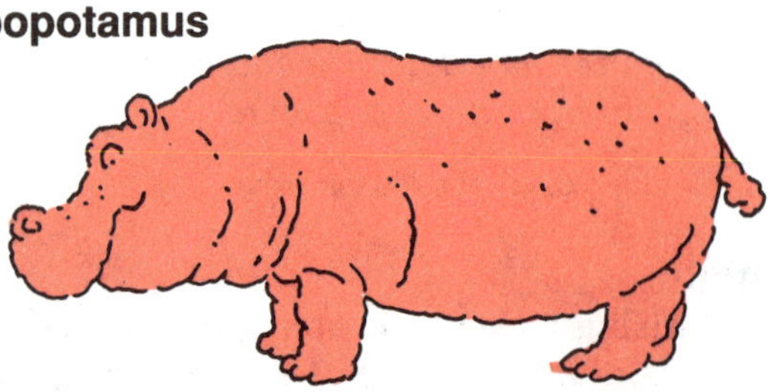

a large, dark grey animal with short legs, a big mouth, small ears and thick skin, that lives near rivers in Africa: ***Hippopotamuses*** *eat grass and water-plants.*

- Two **hippopotamuses**
- Called a **hippo** for short.

hire
to pay money to borrow something for a certain time: *My parents* ***hired*** *a car for a week when they were on holiday in Java.*

hired, hiring, has hired

his
belonging to a boy or man: *David has* ***his*** *own bedroom. Peter is inviting all* ***his*** *friends to* ***his*** *party. 'Is this Paul's pen?' 'No, that one isn't* ***his*** *—* ***his*** *is on the desk.' 'Could I talk to Mark, please — I'm a friend of* ***his****.'*

hit
1 to give someone or something a blow; to knock: *The ball* ***hit*** *Joe on the head. Susan* ***hit*** *her foot against a big stone. The car* ***hit*** *a lamp-post. Stop* ***hitting*** *the dog! The soldier was* ***hit*** *by a bullet. In table-tennis, you have to* ***hit*** *the ball over the net with your bat.* **2** to reach: *The second arrow* ***hit*** *the target.*

- The opposite is **miss**.
- hit, hitting, has hit

hive
a wooden container like a small hut, in which bees live and store up honey: *There are thousands of bees in a* ***hive****.*

hobby
something that you enjoy doing when you are not working: *My dad's* ***hobby*** *is fishing. Do you have any* ***hobbies****? My* ***hobbies*** *are swimming, reading and collecting stamps.*

A lot of **hobbies**

hockey

a game for two teams of eleven players, who use long, curved sticks to hit a hard white ball into a goal: ***Hockey** is played on a large field like a football field.*

hoe

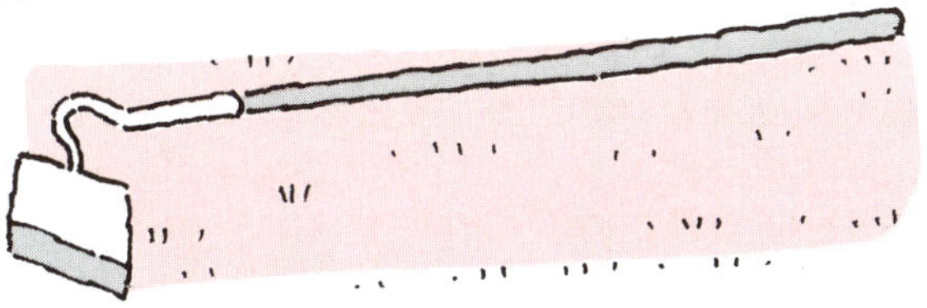

a tool with a long handle and a sharp blade, that you use for getting weeds out and breaking up hard ground: *My grandad has a **hoe**, a rake and other tools in his garden shed.*

hold

1 to have something in your hand: *Sarah is **holding** a pencil in her right hand. Could you **hold** my bag while I put on my jacket? **Hold** that dish with both hands. Catherine is **holding** her little brother by the hand. The children stood in a circle and **held** hands.* **2** to keep something in one position: ***Hold** out your hand and I'll give you some sweets. **Hold** your hands above your head.* **3** to contain: *This bottle **holds** one litre of lemonade. This bag isn't big enough to **hold** all our shopping.*

held, holding, has held

hold on **1** to keep holding: ***Hold on** to the railings so that you don't slip.* **2** to wait for a short time, especially on the telephone: ***Hold on** a moment, please — I'll get Mr Johnson to speak to you.*

hold up **1** to make someone late: *I'm sorry I'm late — I got **held up** in the traffic.* **2** to support something: *The shelf was **held up** by a pile of bricks.* **3** to rob someone by saying you will hurt or kill them if they don't give you money: *A gang of robbers **held up** the staff at the bank.*

hold

the gripping of something with your hands: *Take **hold** of this rope. I tried to run away but my mum got **hold** of my arm. Keep **hold** of your little brother's hand while you cross the road.*

hole

an opening in something; a gap or tear: *The cat went through a **hole** in the fence. There are big **holes** in these old socks. The dentist found a small **hole** in my tooth. Many animals live in **holes** in the ground.*

holiday

a time when you do not have to work or go to school: *We are going to Penang for our **holidays**. How long are your summer **holidays**? My dad is taking two weeks' **holiday** in June. Our neighbours have gone on **holiday**. My aunt is on **holiday** in Japan.*

hollow

having an empty space inside: *Bottles, pipes and tubes are **hollow**.*

home

1 the place where you live with your family: *Emma invited me to her **home**. She has a lovely **home** with a big garden. Mr Jones works in the city, but his **home** is in the country. Singapore is my **home**.* **2** to or at the place where you live: *I'm going **home** now. May I bring some friends **home** for tea? 'Is your dad at **home**?' 'No, he's still at work.' 'What time will he be **home**?' 'About 6 o'clock.' When does Paul come **home** from school?*

homeless

without a place to live in; having no home: *There are a lot of **homeless** people in this city.*

homework

work that teachers give to their pupils to do at home: *Have you done your English **homework**? I haven't got any **homework** today.*

honest

always telling the truth; not cheating: *Andrew is an **honest** boy — you can trust him completely. Be **honest** and tell me what you really think.*

honesty

being honest: ***Honesty** is the most important quality that human beings should have.*

honey

a sweet, sticky, golden food that is made by bees: *I took some **honey** out of the jar and spread it on my toast.*

hoof

the hard part of the foot of an animal such as a horse, cow or sheep: *An animal's **hooves** are made of the same stuff as fingernails and toenails are.*

Four **hooves** or **hoofs**

hook

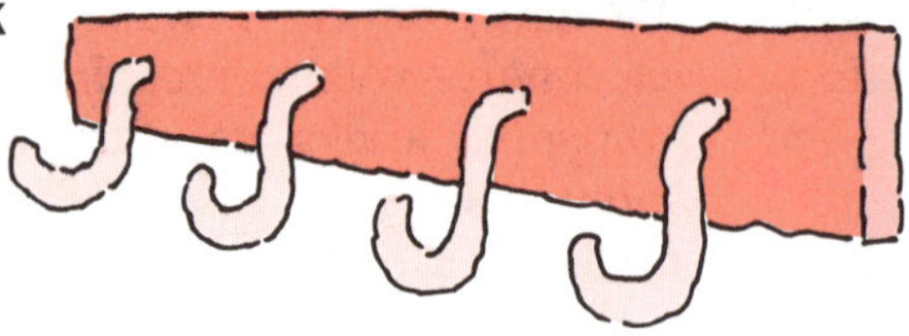

a curved piece of metal or plastic that is used for hanging things on, or for holding or fastening things: *Hang your jacket on that **hook**. Please could you fasten this **hook** at the back of my dress? A fish-**hook** is tied to the end of a fishing-line to catch fish.*

hoop
a large ring made of wood, metal or plastic: *At the circus we saw a lion jumping through a **hoop**.*

hop
1 to jump on one foot: *John dropped a hammer on his left foot, so he had to **hop** about on his right foot.* 2 to jump: *A bird was **hopping** across the grass.*

hopped, hopping, has hopped

hope
to want something to happen and believe that it may happen: *It's late but I am still **hoping** Bob will come. I **hope** you will come and see me soon. We **hope** to be back home by five o'clock. 'Do you think it will be fine today?' 'I **hope** so.' 'Is it going to rain today?' 'I **hope** not.'*

hoped, hoping, has hoped

hope
something that you hope: *After failing two exams Peter lost all **hope** of getting a good grade. The teacher told Peter not to give up **hope**.*

hopeful
believing that something that you want to happen will happen: *The police are **hopeful** that they will soon find the bank robbers.*

hopeless
without hope; impossible: *It's **hopeless** to try and repair this old bicycle.*

horizon
the line at which the earth and sky seem to meet: *The sun went down below the **horizon**. The sailors saw another ship on the **horizon**.*

horn
1 one of the two hard, pointed things that grow on the heads of cows, goats, deer and other animals: *A bull uses its **horns** to attack other bulls.* 2 the instrument in a car, bus or train that a driver uses to make a loud noise as a warning or signal: *The taxi-driver sounded his **horn** because the car in front of him stopped suddenly.* 3 an instrument that is made out of metal and played by blowing into it: *There are three **horns** in this orchestra.*

hornet
a kind of large wasp: *A **hornet**'s sting is very painful.*

horrible
1 terrible; very unpleasant: *What a **horrible** smell! The weather was **horrible** in England — it was cold and wet all the time.* 2 causing horror: *The ghost gave a **horrible** cry and disappeared.*

horror
1 great fear: *My sister has a **horror** of spiders. A **horror** story tries to frighten you.* 2 a nasty feeling of shock: *I was filled with **horror** when I heard the bad news.*

horse
a large animal that people ride on, which is also used for pulling carts and other vehicles: *A baby **horse** is called a foal, a female **horse** is a mare and a male **horse** a stallion. **Horses** are kept in stables. The **horse** neighed because it was frightened. A pony is a small **horse**.*
on horseback riding on a horse: *Ten policemen **on horseback** accompanied the president's car.*

hose

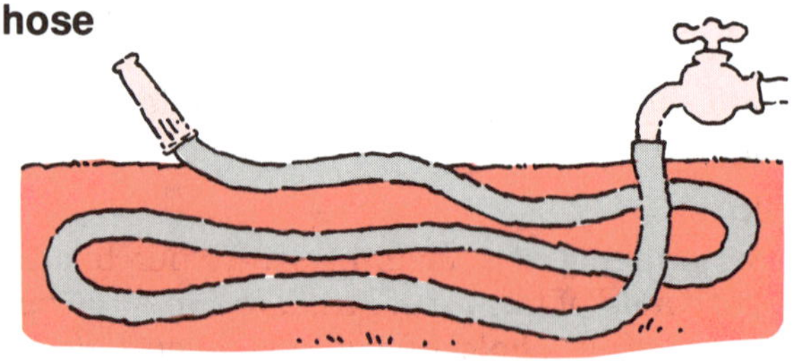

a long rubber tube that is used for spraying water: *The gardener fixed the **hose** to the tap, turned on the water and watered the plants in the garden.*

hospital
a building where people who are ill or injured are looked after by doctors and nurses: *Nurses and doctors look after the patients in a **hospital**. We visited my little sister every day when she was in the children's **hospital**.*

host
a person who invites guests and looks after them when they come: *The **host** welcomed the guests and offered them something to drink.*

hostess
a female host: *The **hostess** greeted the guests and introduced them to each other.*

hot
1 very warm; full of heat: *Be careful, the tea is still very **hot**. In our house there is always plenty of **hot** water for a shower. We have **hot** weather in summer and cold weather in winter. Running makes me feel **hot**.* **2** having a very strong taste that makes your mouth feel hot: *Pepper is **hot**.*

- Meaning 1: the opposite is **cold**.
- hot, hotter, hottest

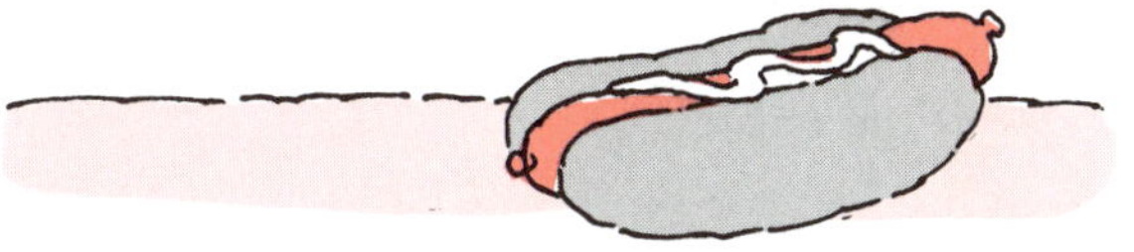

hot dog a long bread roll with a hot sausage inside: *A **hot dog** is one kind of fast food. My mum bought me a **hot dog** from a stall in the park.*

hotel
a building where people rent rooms for a few nights, and buy meals: *We stayed in a **hotel** while we were on holiday. My parents booked a double room and a single room in a big **hotel**.*

hour
a period of sixty minutes: *There are 24 **hours** in a day. I spent over an **hour** drawing this picture. We'll have dinner in half an **hour**. We walked for two **hours**.*

house
a building in which people live: *This **house** has five bedrooms, a sitting-room, a kitchen, two bathrooms and a garage. There is a garden at the back of the **house**.*

housewife
a woman who spends most of her time looking after her family and her home: *My mum is a **housewife** now, but she used to work in an office.*

Two **housewives**

housework
work that you need to do to keep the house clean and tidy: *This morning we've got to wash the breakfast dishes, dust the furniture, sweep the floors, and do lots of other **housework**.*

hovercraft

a vehicle that can move over land and water: *A **hovercraft** floats above the land or water on a layer of air. A **hovercraft** can move much faster than a ferry.*

how
1 you use **how** in questions about size, distance, time and quantity: ***How** big is your bedroom? **How** long does it take you to walk to school? **How** far is the city centre from your house? **How** often do you go to the hairdresser's? **How** old are you?* **2** in what way: ***How** do you make bread? Tell me **how** you did it. I know **how** to do this sum. I know **how** the burglar got into our neighbours' house.* **3** you use **how** to show surprise: ***How** silly of me to forget to bring my exercise book! **How** hot it is today! **How** nice of you to give me your last chocolate! **How** pretty you look today!*

how about words you use when you suggest something or ask what someone else thinks: *'What shall we do this afternoon?' '**How about** going swimming?' I think I'll go to the cinema — **how about** you?*

how are you? words you use when you greet someone you know: *Hello, Sarah! **How are you?***

how do you do? a polite way of greeting someone when you meet them for the first time: *'I am Mary.' '**How do you do?** I am Jane Brown.'*

howl
to make the long, crying sound of a wolf or dog: *The dog **howled** because he didn't like the loud music.*

hug

to put your arms round someone and hold

them tight: *My dad **hugged** and kissed us when he returned from his trip abroad.*

hugged, hugging, has hugged

huge
very large: *Our neighbour has a **huge** dog that is almost as big as a pony. The new supermarket is **huge**.*

- Same as **enormous**.
- The opposite is **tiny**.

hum
to make a singing sound with your mouth closed: *Mary was **humming** a tune to herself.*

hummed, humming, has hummed

human or human being
a person: *A lot of animals are afraid of **humans**. A chimpanzee and a **human being** are similar to each other in many ways.*

hump
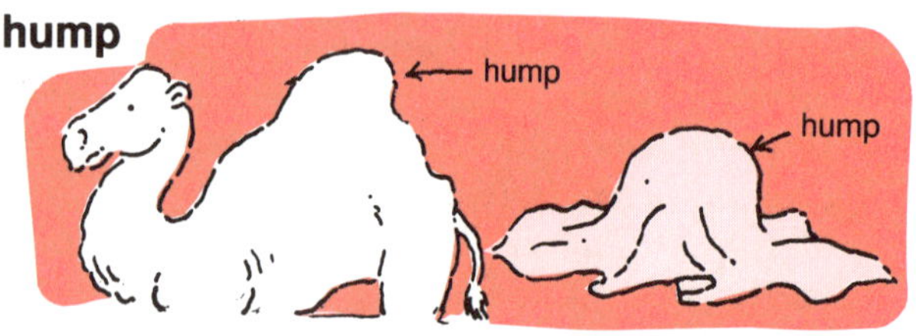

a large lump: *Camels store fat in their **humps**. Sally thought we wouldn't be able to see her in the bed, but we noticed the **hump** under the blanket.*

hundred
1 the number 100: *Ten times ten is one **hundred**. Fifty and fifty is a **hundred**.* **2** 100 in number: *There are about a **hundred** children in the choir. There are five **hundred** children in this school.*

Two **hundred**

hung
see **hang**: *Katie **hung** her coat on a hook. I have **hung** the picture over my bed.*

hunger
not having enough to eat: *Poor people in many parts of the world are dying of **hunger**.*

hungry
wanting something to eat: *Are you **hungry**? I'm very **hungry** — I haven't eaten anything since breakfast.*

hunt
to chase and catch wild animals: *A group of lionesses were **hunting** a zebra. In the past, people spent a lot of time **hunting** deer and other animals.*

hunter
a person who hunts animals: *The **hunter** shot a deer and two hares.*

hurry
1 to be quick; to go quickly: *You'd better **hurry** if you want to catch the bus. I **hurried** home.* **2** to make someone be quick: *If you **hurry** me, I'll make mistakes.*

hurries, hurried, hurrying, has hurried

hurry up to be quick: *Please **hurry up** or we'll be late.*
in a hurry **1** quickly: *Steve did his homework **in a hurry** because he wanted to play outside.* **2** wanting to be quick: *I can't wait — I'm **in a hurry**. Mum was **in a hurry** to get home and feed the baby.*

hurt
1 to harm; to injure: *Nobody was **hurt** in the accident. I **hurt** myself on that nail. Bob **hurt** his knees when he fell down.* **2** to be painful: *My finger **hurts**.* **3** to upset: *Sarah was **hurt** by her friend's cruel words. I'm sorry, I didn't mean to **hurt** you.*

- Meaning 1: same as **injure**.
- hurt, hurting, has hurt

husband
the man that a woman is married to: *A **husband** and wife are a married couple. Mrs Black usually drives her **husband** to his office in the mornings.*

hut
a small house, usually made of wood: *In the story, the children built themselves a **hut** out of some old pieces of wood.*

hutch
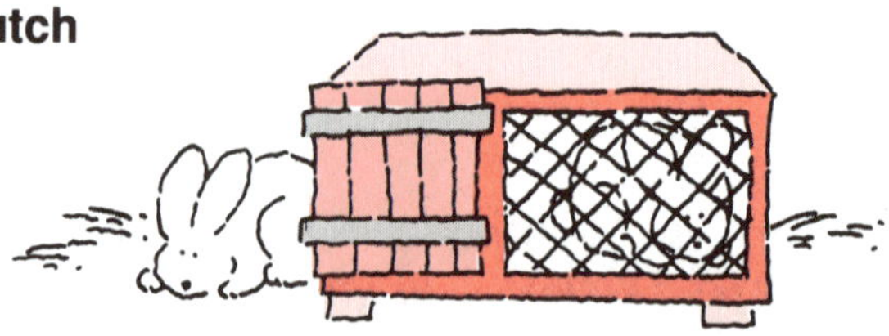

a wooden box with a wire front for keeping rabbits in: *If you buy a rabbit, you will have to build a rabbit **hutch** for it.*

hymn
a song that people sing to praise God: *I liked the **hymns** that we sang in church today.*

I
the word used for talking about myself: ***I*** *am eight years old. My sister and* ***I*** *go to the same school.*

ice
frozen water: *The pond was covered with* ***ice****.*

ice
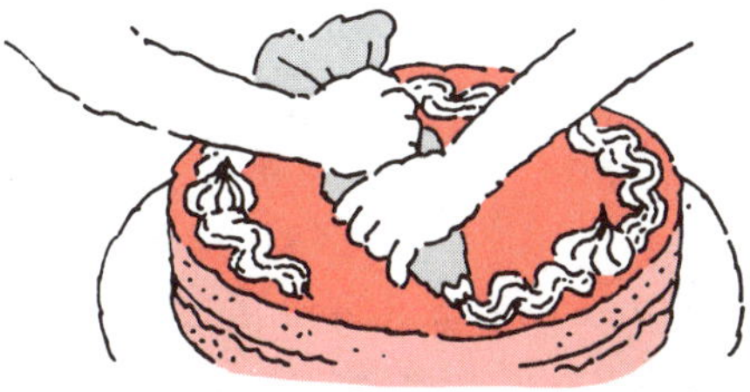
to cover a cake with icing: *Mum* ***iced*** *the birthday cake.*

iced, icing, has iced

ice-cream
a sweet, soft, frozen food that is made from cream or milk with some flavour: *May I have a chocolate* ***ice-cream****, please?*

ice-cube
a small, square piece of ice that you put into a drink to cool it: *Would you like a few* ***ice-cubes*** *in your lemonade?*

icing
a kind of liquid sugar that is used to cover and decorate cakes: *The birthday cake had pink* ***icing*** *and eight candles on top.*

I'd
short for **I should**, **I would** or **I had**: ***I'd*** *like to help you.* ***I'd*** *come to the party if I could. I went home when* ***I'd*** *finished my work.*

idea
something that you think of; a plan: *'I've had an* ***idea*** *— let's all go to the beach instead of to the park.' 'What a good* ***idea****!'*

if
1 you use **if** when you are talking about what may happen: ***If*** *you don't hurry up, we shall miss the train. We shan't be able to have a picnic* ***if*** *it rains. I'll go to the playground only* ***if*** *you come with me.* **2** whether: *I wonder* ***if*** *I could borrow your pen? Do you know* ***if*** *John is coming or not? Ask Peter* ***if*** *he is ready.*

ill
not well; having a disease: *Paul has to stay in bed because he is* ***ill****. I feel* ***ill*** *— I think I've caught a cold. Julie is very* ***ill*** *with a fever.*
fall ill or **be taken ill** to become ill suddenly: *My dad* ***fell ill*** *at his office and had to see a doctor immediately. Mrs Smith* ***was taken ill*** *in a shop and was rushed to hospital in an ambulance.*

I'll
short for **I shall** or **I will**: *Goodbye —* ***I'll*** *see you tomorrow.* ***I'll*** *make the tea today.*

illness
bad health; a disease: *Many pupils are absent because of* ***illness****. Mumps is one of the* ***illnesses*** *that you usually get when you're young.*

I'm
short for **I am**: ***I'm*** *glad that I don't have to go to school today.* ***I'm*** *very hungry.*

imaginary
not real; living only in stories: *Fairies, dwarfs, giants and dragons are* ***imaginary*** *creatures.*

The opposite is **real**.

imagine
to see or hear something in your mind: ***Imagine*** *you have won lots of money — what would you buy first? Can you* ***imagine*** *what the teacher would say if we all refused to do our homework? 'Mum, there's a tiger under my bed.' 'Nonsense, you're* ***imagining*** *things!'*

imagined, imagining, has imagined

imitate
to do the same as someone or something else; to copy: *Michael was trying to* ***imitate*** *his father's voice. Can you* ***imitate*** *the way a monkey walks? My brother often tries to* ***imitate*** *me.*

imitated, imitating, has imitated

immediately
at once; without delay: *If the fire alarm rings, you must leave the building* ***immediately****. The fire brigade came* ***immediately*** *after they had received the telephone call.*

impolite
not polite; rude: *You must not be* ***impolite*** *to the teacher. It is* ***impolite*** *to leave without saying goodbye.*

- Same as **rude**.
- The opposite is **polite** or **courteous**.

import
to bring in goods from other countries for sale: *Britain* ***imports*** *radios from Japan.*

The opposite is **export**.

import
1 the importing of goods: *The country had terrible floods recently, so it had to increase its* ***import*** *of rice.* **2** something that is imported: *Steel and other* ***imports*** *are brought to our country by sea.*

The opposite is **export**.

important
1 mattering a lot: *It is* ***important*** *that you should understand the exam questions before you answer them. Good teaching is very* ***important*** *for a child. The headmaster has some* ***important*** *news to announce.* **2** having a lot of power: *The Prime Minister is a very* ***important*** *man.*

impossible
not able to be done; too difficult: *It is* ***impossible*** *to watch television and read a book at the same time.*

imprison
to put someone in prison: *The burglar was* ***imprisoned*** *for two years for breaking into a house and stealing some jewellery.*

improve
to get better; to make something better: *I hope the weather will* ***improve*** *soon. Robert has* ***improved*** *a lot in English. Mr Thomas was very ill but he is* ***improving*** *now. Do you think that sugar* ***improves*** *the taste of coffee?*

improved, improving, has improved

in
1 inside; within: *Dad is* ***in*** *the living-room. My brother is still* ***in*** *bed. We live* ***in*** *Singapore. Mrs Clark came to the meeting* ***in*** *her car.* **2** into something: *Peter put his hands* ***in*** *his pockets. The taxi stopped and we got* ***in****. May I come* ***in****?* **3** during a certain time: *I'll come and see you* ***in*** *the afternoon. We went on holiday* ***in*** *July. I was born* ***in*** *1980.* **4** at the end of a certain time: *I'll be back* ***in*** *ten minutes.* **5** at home, or at the place where you work: *Is your mother* ***in****? Is the manager* ***in*** *today?* **6** here are some other ways of using **in**: *We were walking* ***in*** *the rain. Lucy is dressed* ***in*** *a blue coat. I'm* ***in*** *a hurry. This letter is written* ***in*** *English. The little boy was* ***in*** *tears because he had lost his toy car. This room is* ***in*** *a terrible mess.*

Meaning 2: the opposite is **out of** or **out**.

inch
a unit of length that is equal to 2.5 centimetres: *Helen is four feet three* ***inches*** *tall. This box is ten* ***inches*** *long, five* ***inches*** *wide and two* ***inches*** *high.*

including
adding someone or something to a group; with: *The whole family went on holiday,* ***including*** *the dog.*

increase
to become more, or bigger; to make something bigger: *The number of children in this school has* ***increased*** *a lot in the last two years. My parents have just* ***increased*** *my pocket money by $2.*

increased, increasing, has increased

indoor
suitable for inside a building: *Do you know any good* ***indoor*** *games for a wet day?*

The opposite is **outdoor**.

indoors
inside a building: *We rushed* ***indoors*** *when it began to rain. I must stay* ***indoors*** *until I've finished my homework.*

The opposite is **outdoors**.

infant
a very young child: *At Christmas people celebrate the birth of the* ***infant*** *Jesus.*

influenza
an illness that gives you a headache and a fever, and usually a cough and a cold as well:

*Mrs Wood had to stay in bed for two weeks when she had **influenza**.*

Called **flu** for short.

inform

to tell someone: *You must **inform** the police that your bicycle has been stolen.*

information

facts that you want to know, or facts that you are able to give: *Could you please give me some **information** about trains to Kuala Lumpur? I'm sorry, I have no further **information** about the accident.*

injection

the putting of some special liquid into your blood through a hollow needle which makes a tiny hole in your skin: *You get **injections** to stop you getting certain illnesses, and to make you better when you are ill. The doctor gave my granny an **injection** against influenza.*

injure

to damage some part of your body: *George **injured** his arm when he fell down. Three people were **injured** in the accident.*

- Same as **hurt**.
- injured, injuring, has injured

injury

a wound; a cut: *After the accident, the car-driver was taken to hospital with a broken leg and head **injuries**.*

A lot of **injuries**

ink

a coloured liquid that is used for writing or printing: *Please write in blue or black **ink**. I need some **ink** for my pen.*

innocent

having done nothing wrong; not being to blame for something: *This man is **innocent** — he didn't steal the money.*

The opposite is **guilty**.

insect

any small creature with six legs and a body that is divided into sections: *Beetles, flies, butterflies, bees, wasps and ants are **insects**. Frogs, lizards and some birds feed on **insects**.*

inside

1 in something: *What is **inside** this cupboard? There is nothing **inside** this box. Mike closed the front door and left his key **inside** by mistake. We stayed **inside** because it was raining.* **2** into something: *I know where that shop is but I haven't been **inside** it yet. We found a cave and crawled **inside**.*

The opposite is **outside**.

inside

the part that is in something: *The **inside** of this apple is rotten.*

The opposite is the **outside**.

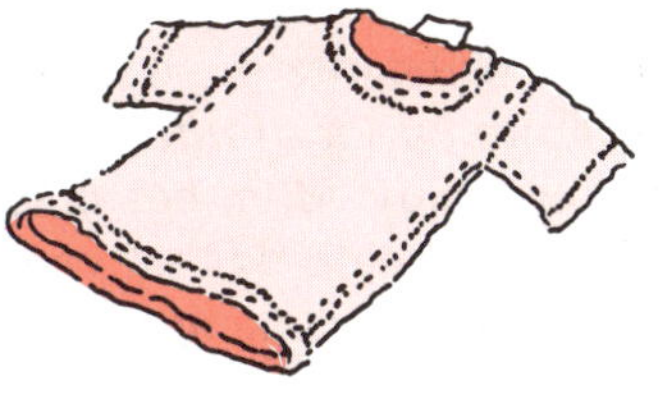

inside out with the inside part of a piece of clothing turned outside: *I think you are wearing your jumper **inside out**.*

inspect

to examine something carefully: *The detective **inspected** the fingerprints on the door-handle.*

instant

a moment; a certain moment: *The fire spread in an **instant**. I got into the bath and at that **instant** the telephone rang.*

instant

able to be prepared in a very short time: *You just have to add boiling water to **instant** coffee. **Instant** noodles need to be boiled only for a few minutes.*

instead

in place of something or someone else: *I don't like coffee — please could I have tea **instead**?*

*I want to go swimming today **instead** of playing football. My sister didn't want to go shopping, so I went **instead**.*

instruct
1 to teach someone a subject or a skill: *The teacher **instructed** us in the use of a calculator.* 2 to order someone to do something: *The headmaster **instructed** the pupils to assemble in the school hall at ten o'clock.*

instrument
1 a tool, especially one that is used by a doctor or a scientist: *A stethoscope is an **instrument** that a doctor listens to your heart with.* 2 an object such as a guitar, piano, or flute, that you make music with: *Our music teacher can play the piano, the violin and several other **instruments**. Do you play an **instrument**?*

intelligent
clever; able to learn and understand quickly: *Emma is an **intelligent** pupil. My dog is quite **intelligent**.*

intend
to plan to do something: *Do you still **intend** to go to Hong Kong? David is **intending** to train as a doctor.*

interest
1 attention; being interested in something: *The pupils showed a lot of **interest** in the idea of performing a play. Mum has no **interest** at all in football.* 2 something that you enjoy doing; a hobby: *Reading is one of my main **interests**.*

interest
to attract someone: *Football doesn't **interest** me at all.*

interested
1 wanting to know more about something: *My elder brother is very **interested** in computers.* 2 wanting to do something: *Michael is **interested** in becoming an actor.*

interesting
attracting your attention: *This film about chimpanzees is very **interesting**. I am reading an **interesting** book about China.*

interfere
to play with something that has nothing to do with you: *Please stop **interfering** with my computer — you'll break it.*

interfered, interfering, has interfered

interrupt
1 to stop someone while they are saying or doing something: *Please don't **interrupt** me while I'm talking on the telephone. I'm sorry to **interrupt** you but I need your help urgently.* 2 to disturb something; to make a break: *The lesson was **interrupted** by a loud noise in the passage.*

interval
1 a passing of time: *The storks returned in the spring after an **interval** of six months.* 2 a short break during a play or concert: *We had an ice-cream in the **interval**.*

into
1 to the inside of something: *We went **into** the house. Mum put the dish **into** the oven.* 2 against: *The car crashed **into** the wall.* 3 to something different: *A tadpole turns **into** a frog. A caterpillar changes **into** a butterfly. Lucy translated the story **into** Chinese.*

introduce
to announce the name of one person to the other person when they meet each other for the first time: *The hostess **introduced** the guests to each other.*

introduced, introducing, has introduced

invent
1 to make something that has never been made before: *Alexander Graham Bell **invented** the telephone. Fireworks were **invented** in China many hundreds of years ago.* 2 to think up something that is not true: *Richard **invented** a story to explain why he was late for school.*

invention
something invented: *The world has changed a lot since the **invention** of the computer.*

inventor
a person who invents something: *James Watt was the **inventor** of the steam engine.*

investigate
to examine an event carefully: *The police are **investigating** the robbery.*

investigated, investigating, has investigated

invitation
a request to come to a party or a meal: *Thank you for the **invitation** to dinner. I don't know whether to accept or refuse the **invitation**.*

invite
to ask someone politely to come to your house,

to a party or meal: *I **invited** all my friends to my birthday party.*

> invited, inviting, has invited

iron

1 a very hard metal that is used for making tools, gates and other things: *Steel is made from **iron**. A prison has **iron** bars over its windows.* **2** an electric instrument that is heated up and used for making clothes smooth: *Don't touch the **iron** — it's very hot.*

iron

to make clothes smooth with an iron: *I asked my mum to **iron** my shirt. My jeans don't need to be **ironed**.*

is

you use **is** with **he**, **she** and **it**: *Alice **is** my best friend. She'**s** ten. Peter'**s** a nice boy. He'**s** very tall. John **is** practising football. What **is** the date today? **Is** it the tenth of June? 'What'**s** the time?' 'It'**s** two o'clock.' Where'**s** the soap? When **is** your birthday? There'**s** Mummy! That'**s** good!*

> You can shorten:
> - **he is** to **he's**
> - **she is** to **she's**
> - **it is** to **it's**
> - **that is** to **that's**
> - **there is** to **there's**
> - **what is** to **what's**
> - **where is** to **where's**

island

a piece of land that is surrounded by water: *Sumatra is a large **island**. We went across to the **island** on a ferry.*

> Say **eye**-land.

isn't

short for **is not**: *That **isn't** a true story. John **isn't** coming with us to the zoo. Jean is very nice, **isn't** she?*

it

1 a thing; an animal; a baby: *You must read this book — **it**'s very interesting. I shouted at the dog and **it** ran away. The baby is crying because **it**'s hungry.* **2** a fact that you are talking about: *'I forgot to bring back your umbrella.' '**It** doesn't matter.' Peter says he can swim a mile but I don't believe **it**.* **3** you use **it** when you talk about the weather, distance, time or temperature: *Is **it** raining very hard? **It**'s cold in here. **It**'s two miles to the city centre. **It** is six o'clock.* **4** you use **it** to say what you think of something: ***It** was very nice of you to come. **It**'s easy to jump over this ditch.*

itch

to have an unpleasant feeling on your skin that makes you want to scratch: *My back is **itching**. Wool can make your skin **itch**.*

itchy

itching: *My skin feels **itchy**.*

it'll

short for **it will**: ***It'll** be difficult to find the ring again.*

its

belonging to it: *The puppy is running along beside **its** mother.*

it's

short for **it is** or **it has**: ***It's** half past two. **It's** been very hot all day.*

itself

1 you use **itself** in sentences where animals or machines do something to themselves: *A cat licks **itself** to keep **itself** clean. The washing-machine will turn **itself** off when it's finished.* **2** without help: *'How did the dog get in?' 'It can open the gate **itself**.'* **3** sometimes used to show the thing you mean more clearly: *I haven't been to the school **itself**, but I've met the headmaster.*

I've

short for **I have**: ***I've** seen this film before. **I've** got a good idea! **I've** no time to listen to nonsense.*

ivory

the hard white stuff that elephants' tusks are made of: ***Ivory** is very valuable and is used for making jewellery.*

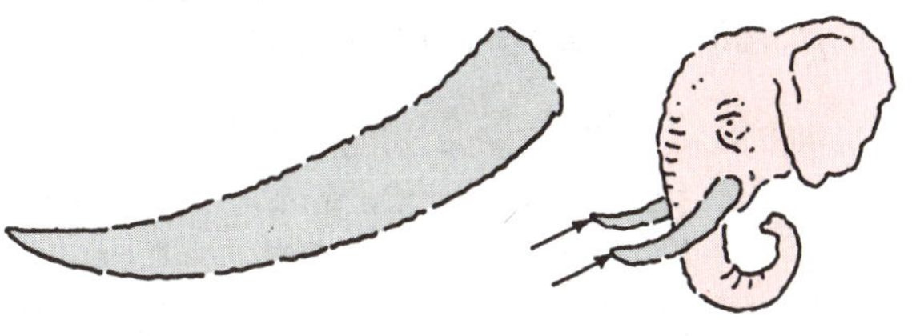

jack
a tool that is used to lift part of a motor car off the ground: *Dad had to use a **jack** when he changed the front wheel of the car.*

jacket

a short coat: *Michael is wearing jeans and a blue **jacket**. A suit is a **jacket** and trousers made of the same material.*

jail
a prison: *The man was sent to **jail** for stealing cheques and money.*

jail
to put someone in jail: *The thief was **jailed** for two years.*

jam
a sweet, sticky food that is made by cooking fruit with a lot of sugar: *Would you like some **jam** on your toast? There is a jar of raspberry **jam** on the table.*

jam
1 to get stuck; to make something get stuck: *This drawer has **jammed** — I can't pull it out. If you get too fat, you may get **jammed** in the doorway.* **2** to fill completely; to block: *The road to the city centre was completely **jammed** with traffic. The passage was **jammed** with people so that we couldn't get through.*

jammed, jamming, has jammed

traffic jam a large number of vehicles all trying to go in different directions, but not able to move because there are so many of them: *Dad came home very late because he had been held up in a **traffic jam**.*

January
the first month of the year.

jar
a glass container that has a wide top: *Please put the lid back on the jam-**jar**.*

jaw
one of the two bones in your mouth that hold your teeth: *The two **jaws** are called the 'upper **jaw**' and the 'lower **jaw**'. One of the boxers got his **jaw** broken in the fight.*

jealous
feeling annoyed because someone has something that you would like to have: *Peter is **jealous** of his little sister because she always gets what she wants. I'm not **jealous** of Ann's good marks.*

jeans
trousers that are made of strong, blue, cotton cloth: *I always change into **jeans** and a shirt when I come back from school.*

jeep

a small motor vehicle that can travel over rough ground: ***Jeeps** are used a lot by the army.*

jelly

1 a sweet, transparent food with a fruit flavour: *My mum made a raspberry **jelly** for my birthday party.* **2** a kind of jam that is made by boiling fruit juice and a lot of sugar: *I like apple **jelly** on toast.*

Lots of **jellies**

jet
1 an aeroplane that is driven by engines which work by sucking in air and forcing it out behind: *Most modern aeroplanes are **jets**. We flew by **jet** to America.* **2** a strong stream of

liquid or gas that is forced through a narrow opening: *The firemen directed **jets** of water at the burning house.*

jewel

a precious stone, such as a diamond or pearl; a brooch, ring or necklace with precious stones in it: *My mum gave her **jewels** to the bank to look after when we went on holiday.*

jewellery

objects such as bracelets, necklaces, brooches or rings that are made of gold or silver and decorated with jewels: *We are not allowed to wear any **jewellery** at school. A burglar broke into the house next door and stole all Mrs Scott's **jewellery**.*

jigsaw

a puzzle that is made up of lots of small pieces that you have to fit together correctly to make a picture: *This is a difficult **jigsaw**, with 500 pieces. Shall we do this **jigsaw** together?*

job

1 the regular work that a person gets paid for: *Mr Smith has got a **job** in a bank. Mrs Lee is looking for a new **job** as a shop assistant.* **2** a piece of work; a task: *Mum has several **jobs** to do before she can take us to the beach. I have a little **job** for you in the garden.*

jog

1 to run at an easy speed: *Mr Stevens goes **jogging** round the park every morning to keep fit.* **2** to push something so that it moves a bit: *Paul **jogged** my arm and I spilt some of my lemonade.*

jogged, jogging, has jogged

join

1 to put two things together; to connect: *You must **join** this piece to that piece. I **joined** the two pieces together. The children **joined** hands in a circle.* **2** to meet someone: *I have to finish my homework first, but I'll **join** you in the park in half an hour.* **3** to meet something else: *This road **joins** the motorway.* **4** to become a member of a group: *Mark **joined** a swimming club. Mr Hart **joined** the fire brigade.*

Meaning 1: the opposite is **separate**.

joke

something that is said or done to make people laugh: *John dressed up as a ghost for a **joke**. 'Do you know the **joke** about the elephant in the refrigerator?' 'Yes, it's an old **joke**.' The children thought it was a great **joke** when the cat stole the fish.*

joke

to make a joke; to say something as a joke: *I was only **joking** when I said it was snowing.*

joked, joking, has joked

journey

travelling from one place to another; a trip: *You must be very tired after your **journey** on the train. It's a two-hour **journey** by train from here to the coast.*

joy

great happiness: *Jim jumped for **joy** when he saw his birthday presents. A new baby brings a family a lot of **joy**.*

The opposite is **sorrow** or **grief**.

joyful

very happy: *I could tell from the children's **joyful** faces that they were very excited about going abroad.*

judge

1 a person whose job is to decide whether someone is guilty or not: *The **judge** said that the man was guilty of murdering the old lady and must go to jail for the rest of his life. The man was ordered by the **judge** to pay $200 for driving too fast.* **2** a person who decides who is the winner of a competition: *Our teacher is going to be one of the **judges** in the reading competition.*

judge

to decide who is the winner of a competition: *The music competition was **judged** by our music teacher.*

judged, judging, has judged

jug

a container with a handle, for holding and pouring liquids: *I poured some milk from the **jug** into a glass.*

juice

1 the liquid from fruit or vegetables; a drink made from this: *Add some lemon **juice** to your tea. Fresh orange **juice** is made by squeezing oranges. Do you like tomato **juice**?* **2** the liquid that comes out of meat when you cook it: *Gravy is made from the **juices** of meat.*

Rhymes with **goose**.

juicy

having a lot of juice in it: *This peach is very **juicy**.*

July

the seventh month of the year.

jump

1 to spring off the ground; to leap: *Grass-hoppers and frogs can **jump** a long way. Peter **jumped** off the wall. Sarah **jumped** into the swimming-pool. Can you **jump** across this ditch?* **2** to move quickly; to rise: *The bank robbers **jumped** into a car and drove off very fast. When the bell rang, Andrew **jumped** to his feet and opened the door.*

jumper

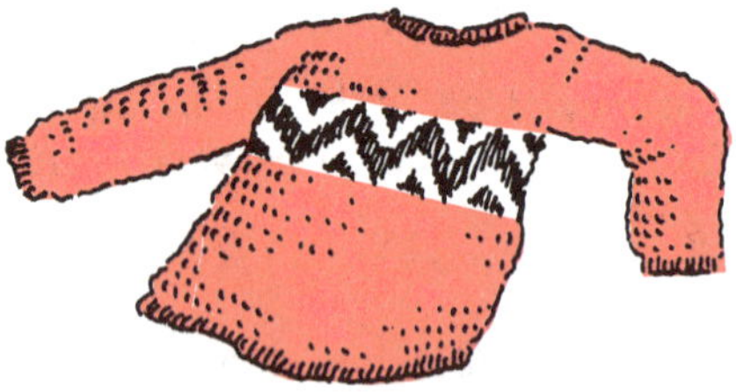

a knitted piece of clothing that covers the top part of your body; a sweater: *My granny has knitted me a warm **jumper**.*

junction

a place at which roads or railway lines meet: *There was an accident at the new road **junction**.*

June

the sixth month of the year.

jungle

a large piece of land in a hot country where tall trees and other plants grow very close together: *There are still tigers in the **jungles** of India.*

junk

old things that are useless; rubbish: *I threw away a lot of **junk** when I tidied my bedroom.*

just

1 a very short time ago; very recently: *Robert has **just** left. I've **just** seen Joe going into a shop.* **2** at this moment: *Mike is **just** coming upstairs.* **3** at a certain moment: *The telephone rang **just** as we were leaving the house. **Just** then, the door opened and in walked Jack.* **4** only: *Could you wait **just** a moment?* **5** exactly: *This knife is **just** what I needed. Your drawing is **just** as good as Peter's.*

Kk

kangaroo

a large Australian animal with a long, very strong tail and large, strong back legs that help it to jump: *A female **kangaroo** carries her baby in a pocket of skin called a 'pouch' on the front of her body.*

keen

1 wanting to do something very much; eager: *The children are **keen** to go to the zoo. Mandy is **keen** to do well at school.* **2** liking something very much: *Becky is **keen** on swimming. Tim is a **keen** footballer.*

keep

1 to make someone or something stay a certain way: *Please **keep** the window open. This coat will **keep** you warm. Last night I was **kept** awake by the thunder. Joe **kept** us waiting for half an hour.* **2** to have something for ever or for a very long time: *I don't need that book any more — you can **keep** it. Julie gave me the picture to **keep**.* **3** not to give away or throw away: *I gave some of my toy cars to my brother but I **kept** my toy train. Do you want to **keep** these old jeans or shall I throw them away?* **4** to continue to do something: *I **keep** thinking about the film I saw yesterday.* **5** to store; to have in a certain place: ***Keep** your money in a safe place. You can **keep** your books on this shelf.* **6** to have animals: *This farmer **keeps** cows, pigs and sheep. Our neighbour **keeps** rabbits.* **7** to stay fresh: *That meat won't **keep** for long in this heat.* **8** to stay a certain way: *Good morning, Mrs Roberts — I hope you're **keeping** well? I've got something to tell you, but you must **keep** quiet about it and not tell anyone else.*

kept, keeping, has kept

keep in to make someone stay indoors; to make someone stay late at school: *My mum **kept** me **in** and made me tidy up my bedroom. The teacher told Garry he would be **kept in** if he went on being naughty.*
keep off to stay away from something: *There is a notice in the park saying '**Keep off** the grass.'*
keep on to continue: ***Keep on** trying — never give up! We **kept on** playing football although it was raining.*
keep out not to enter: *The notice on the gate said 'Private Land. **Keep out**'.*
keep up **1** to move at the same speed as someone else: *Don't run — I can't **keep up** with you.* **2** to continue to do something: *I hope you're **keeping up** your piano practice. You're doing well — **keep** it **up**!* **3** to continue to look after something: *You must eat to **keep up** your strength.*

kennel

1 a small hut for a dog to sleep in: *Jack has built a **kennel** for his dog in his back garden.* **2** a place where dogs can be looked after: *We left our dog in **kennels** when we went on holiday.*

kept

see **keep**: *We **kept** all the windows open to get fresh air. Jenny has **kept** the book that I lent her.*

kerb

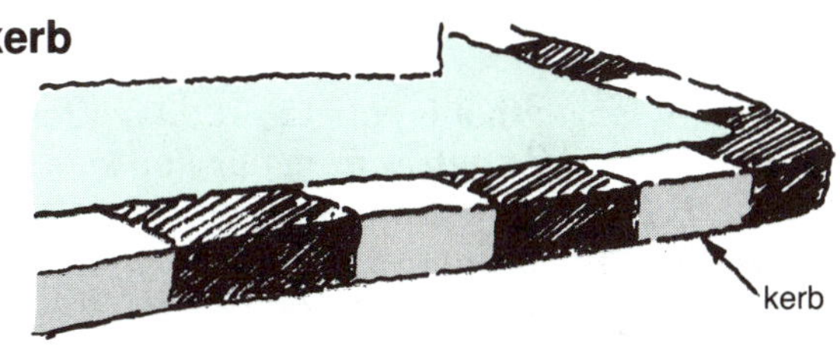

the row of stones that form the edge of a pavement: *Dad always tries to park the car as close to the **kerb** as possible.*

kettle

a metal pot for boiling water in: *A **kettle** has a lid and a handle on the top. We have a new electric **kettle**. I've just put the **kettle** on to make some tea.*

key

1 a small metal object that you use to open or close a lock: *Where is the front-door **key**?*

Dad has lost his car ***keys***. **2** one of the small parts of a typewriter, calculator or piano that you press with your fingers: *You don't have to press the* ***keys*** *hard — just touch them.*

kick
to hit something with your foot: *Tom* ***kicked*** *the ball into the goal. The dog will bite you if you* ***kick*** *it.*

kick
a blow with the foot: *The pony gave Sharon a* ***kick*** *on the leg.*

kid
1 a word for a child: *We often go and play football with the* ***kids*** *next door. My* ***kid*** *sister is four years younger than I am.* **2** a baby goat: *The* ***kid*** *is bleating for its mother.*

kill
to make a person, animal or plant die: *Two people were* ***killed*** *in the car crash. My mother saw a rat in the garden, and a man with some poison came round to* ***kill*** *it. The gardener tried to* ***kill*** *the weeds with a special spray.*

killer
a person who has killed someone: *The police are looking for the* ***killer*** *of the old man who was found murdered yesterday.*

kilo or **kilogramme**
a unit of weight that is equal to 1000 grammes: *Half a* ***kilogramme*** *is 500 grammes. Mum bought one and a half* ***kilos*** *of apples. I weigh 27* ***kilos***.

Written **kg** for short

kilometre
a unit of length that is equal to 1000 metres: *It is about two* ***kilometres*** *from our house to the school. Dad drove along the motorway at a speed of 110* ***kilometres*** *an hour.*

Written **km** for short

kind
a sort; a type: What kind of *dog do you have? There are thousands of different* ***kinds*** *of insects.*

kind
gentle and good to other people; friendly and helpful; generous: *My granny is very* ***kind*** *to me. It's very* ***kind*** *of you to help me with the shopping. Thank you for your* ***kind*** *invitation.*

The opposite is **cruel, unkind** or **wicked**.

kindly
1 in a gentle manner: *The doctor talked* ***kindly*** *to the frightened little boy. The teacher* ***kindly*** *lent me her pencil.* **2** please!: *Would you* ***kindly*** *stop talking.*

kindness
being kind: *Thank you very much for all your* ***kindness***. *The headmistress treats all the pupils with great* ***kindness***.

king
a man who rules a country: ***King*** *George VI was the father of Queen Elizabeth II. Prince Charles will be the next* ***king***.

kingdom
a country that is ruled by a king or queen: *King Charlemagne ruled over a large* ***kingdom***.

kingfisher

a bird with bright blue feathers that feeds on fish: *A* ***kingfisher*** *lives near rivers and lakes and catches fish.*

kiss
to touch someone's face or lips with your lips to show that you love them: *The girl* ***kissed*** *her parents good-night before she went to bed. My aunt likes us to* ***kiss*** *her on the cheek.*

kiss
a touch with your lips on someone's face or lips: *Dad gave me a* ***kiss*** *on the forehead. He always gives Mum a* ***kiss*** *when he goes off to work.*

kitchen
a room where food is cooked: *There's a cooker, a sink, a fridge and lots of cupboards in our* ***kitchen***.

kite
a light frame that is covered with paper or plastic and is attached to a long string: *The children were flying their* ***kites*** *in the park.*

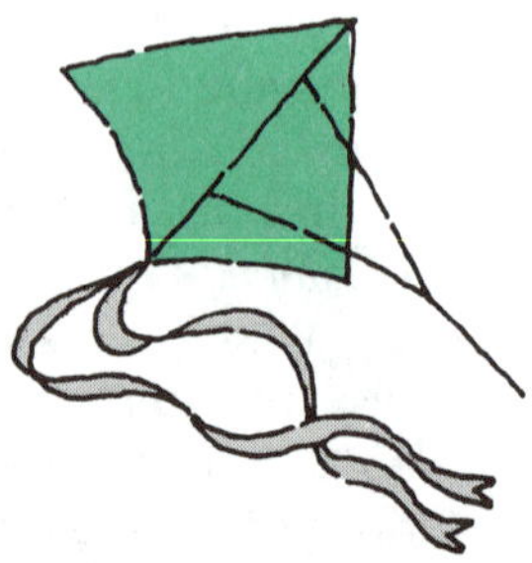

kitten
a baby cat: *Our cat had five* ***kittens***. *A* ***kitten*** *is blind for a few days after it is born.*

kiwi

a bird that lives in New Zealand and cannot fly: ***Kiwis*** *have very short wings, brown feathers, long beaks, and they lay very large eggs.*

Say **kee**-wee.

kiwi-fruit

an oval fruit with thin brown skin and juicy green flesh: *The easiest way to eat a* ***kiwi-fruit*** *is to cut it in half and eat the flesh with a spoon.*

knee

the part of your leg where it bends: *Mike fell down and cut both his* ***knees****. The little boy sat on his father's* ***knee****.*

kneel

to go down on your knees; to be on your knees: *In church people* ***kneel*** *down to pray. Mary was* ***kneeling*** *on the floor picking up pins.*

knelt, kneeling, has knelt

knelt

see **kneel**: *Laura* ***knelt*** *down to look for her hamster under the bed.*

knew

see **know**: *Nobody* ***knew*** *where Paul was. I* ***knew*** *all the children at the party.*

knife

a tool with a sharp blade that you use to cut things: *The waiter in the restaurant gave each person a* ***knife****, fork and spoon.*

Two **knives**

knit

to make something out of wool, using two thin sticks called 'knitting needles': *My mother* ***knitted*** *me this sweater.*

knitted, knitting, has knitted

knob

a round handle on a door or a drawer; a button on a radio or television that you turn to change the programme: *You must turn the* ***knob*** *to open the door. Stop playing with the* ***knobs*** *on the radio.*

knock

1 to make a noise by tapping on a door: *Someone has just* ***knocked*** *at the door — shall I go and see who it is? Please go and answer the door — someone's* ***knocking****.* **2** to hit something or someone so that they fall: *Sue* ***knocked*** *over the vase when she was dusting. One of the boxers* ***knocked*** *the other one down with a single blow. A car almost* ***knocked*** *me down when I tried to cross the road.*

knock out to hit someone so that they lose their senses and can't feel anything for a while: *In boxing, you try to* ***knock*** *the other person* ***out****.*

knock

the sound of knocking; a blow: *We heard a loud* ***knock*** *at the door. Philip got a nasty* ***knock*** *on the head when he fell downstairs.*

knot

a place where two pieces of thread, string or cloth are tied together; a place where one piece is tied round itself: *Make a* ***knot*** *in the thread before you start sewing. You should tie your shoelaces in a bow, not a* ***knot****! I can't undo this* ***knot*** *— I'll have to cut the string instead.*

know

1 to have information about something: *Do you* ***know*** *Nick's telephone number? Tracy* ***knows*** *all about our secret. I don't* ***know*** *where David is. We* ***know*** *that the earth is round, not flat.* **2** to have learnt something: *Ann* ***knows*** *a few words of Chinese. My dad* ***knows*** *a lot about computers. Do you* ***know*** *how to knit?* **3** to be certain: *I* ***know*** *I can win if I try.* **4** to be familiar with someone or something: *I* ***know*** *Liz very well — she lives near me. Do you* ***know*** *this story already?*

knew, knowing, has known

knowledge

information; understanding: *Teachers are full of* ***knowledge****. We still have very little* ***knowledge*** *about the universe. Paul has a good* ***knowledge*** *of computers.*

known

see **know**: *How long have you* ***known*** *Mike?*

koala

an Australian animal with grey fur that looks like a small bear: *A female* ***koala*** *carries her baby in a pocket of skin called a 'pouch', on the front of her body.*

Ll

label
a small written note that is fixed on something to say what it is, or whose it is: *The **label** on this jar says 'Strawberry Jam'. Dad tied a **label** to his suitcase with his name and address on.*

labourer
a man who does hard work such as digging up a street or helping on a farm: *A **labourer** doesn't need any training for his job.*

lace

1 a string for fastening shoes: *I need a new pair of **laces** for my running shoes.* **2** a net-like material with patterns, that is made with fine thread: *The table had a white tablecloth with **lace** round the edge.*

ladder
a set of steps fitted between two long pieces of wood or metal that you use for climbing up to a high place: *The firemen climbed up their long **ladders** to put out the fire at the hotel.*

ladle
a large round spoon with a long handle: *You use a **ladle** for serving soup.*

lady
1 a polite word for a woman: *Please stand up and let that **lady** sit down. Mrs Hart is a kind old **lady**. This shoe-shop sells **ladies'** shoes only. The first words of a speech are often '**Ladies** and gentlemen'.* **2** a woman who has good manners: ***Ladies** do not shout in public.*

Two **ladies**

ladybird
a small round red beetle with black spots: ***Ladybirds** are very useful because they eat tiny insects that damage plants.*

lagoon
a place of calm water that is cut off from the ocean: *We went swimming in the **lagoon**.*

laid
see **lay**: *Helen **laid** down her pencil. Have you **laid** the table?*

lain
see **lie**: *This big stone has **lain** in our garden for as long as we can remember.*

lake
a large area of water that is surrounded by land: *The water in a **lake** isn't salty. A lot of people go sailing on this **lake**.*

lamb
1 a baby sheep: *The **lamb** is bleating for its mother.* **2** the meat from a lamb: *We had roast **lamb** for dinner.*
lamb chop a slice of lamb that contains a bone: *Mum grilled **lamb chops** on the barbecue.*

lame
not able to walk properly: *The old man was **lame** in one leg after his accident.*

lamp
an object for giving you light, in a building or a street: *Mum has a reading-**lamp** on her desk. We had to use a gas-**lamp** in our tent at night.*

lamp-post
a tall metal pole beside a street, that has a light at the top: *A car hit the **lamp-post** at the corner of our street.*

land
1 the dry, solid part of the world: *The sailors were glad to be on **land** again after they had spent three months at sea.* **2** an area of ground: *This **land** is good for farming. All the **land** round here belongs to a rich farmer.* **3** a country: *The traveller told the children about the foreign **lands** he had visited.*

land
to come down to the ground: *The plane from Hong Kong is just **landing**. The pilot **landed** the helicopter in a field.*

lane
1 a narrow road: *We walked along the* ***lane*** *to the village. There is a* ***lane*** *joining Black Street to Green Street, but it's too narrow to drive along.* **2** you sometimes find **lane** in the name of a road: *We stayed in a hotel in Park* ***Lane***. **3** a part of a road for one line of traffic: *The new motorway has three* ***lanes*** *in each direction.*

language
the words that people of a certain country speak or write: *English is the first foreign* ***language*** *that we learn at school. How many* ***languages*** *do you speak?*

lantern
a container for carrying a light to help you see your way: *A long time ago, people carried* ***lanterns*** *at night with candles inside them.*

lap
the top part of your thighs when you are sitting: *Mum is holding the baby on her* ***lap***. *The little girl fell asleep on her father's* ***lap***.

lap

to drink like a cat: *The cat* ***lapped*** *up the milk from a saucer.*

> lapped, lapping, has lapped

large
big in size or amount: *We live in a* ***large*** *flat. An elephant is a very* ***large*** *animal. A* ***large*** *number of people go to work by car. This flat is too small for a* ***large*** *family.*

> - Same as **big**.
> - The opposite is **small**.

lark
a small brown bird that usually sings while it is flying high in the air: *Have you ever heard a* ***lark*** *singing?*

last
1 the one before this one; the one or ones before the present: *Our* ***last*** *flat was much smaller than this one. I went to bed very late* ***last*** *night. It has been raining for the* ***last*** *three hours. We went to Greece* ***last*** *summer. When was the* ***last*** *time you had your hair cut?* **2** the one or ones at the end; after all the others: *Mark lives in the* ***last*** *house on this street. I only saw the* ***last*** *ten minutes of the film. The grey horse came* ***last*** *in the race.* **3** the only one left: *Amy gave her friend her* ***last*** *piece of chocolate.*

> Meaning 2: the opposite is **first**.

at last after a long delay: *There you are* ***at last***! *— I've been waiting for you for more than an hour.*

last
to continue: *I hope this fine weather* ***lasts***. *The film* ***lasted*** *three hours.*

late
1 after the expected or usual time: *The bus is* ***late*** *today. I was* ***late*** *for school this morning. Hurry or you'll be too* ***late***. *Neil arrived* ***late*** *at the party.* **2** far on in a part of the day or night: *It was very* ***late*** *when Tim got to bed. The accident happened in the* ***late*** *morning, at about 11.30. The roads get full of traffic in the* ***late*** *afternoon. It's dangerous to walk about in the streets* ***late*** *at night.*

> The opposite is **early**.

lately
in the time just before the present; recently: *Have you seen Keith* ***lately***? *I used to be the smallest in the class, but I've grown a lot* ***lately***.

later
afterwards; some time after the present: *Mum went shopping and came back half an hour* ***later***. *See you* ***later***!

laugh
to make a sound that shows you are amused: *We all* ***laughed*** *loudly at Jack's joke. John kept making us* ***laugh*** *by making funny noises. You shouldn't* ***laugh*** *at people when they make mistakes.*

> The opposite is **cry**.

laughter
the sound of laughing: *We could hear* ***laughter*** *in the classroom next door.*

laundry
the clothes, sheets and towels that need to be washed; the clean clothes, sheets or towels that have been washed: *Do you have any* ***laundry*** *to be washed? Mum is hanging out the* ***laundry*** *in the garden.*

law
1 a set of rules by which people live: *Stealing is against the **law**. You must not break the law. The police have to keep **law** and order.* **2** a rule that you must obey: *There is a **law** that tells you not to drop litter.*

lawyer
a person whose job is to know about the law and advise people about it: *When Mr Jones was arrested by the police he sent for his **lawyer** immediately.*

lay
see **lie**: *We **lay** on the beach for a while and then went swimming.*

lay
1 to put carefully: *Please could you fold these towels and **lay** them on the cupboard shelf? Mother **laid** her baby gently in its cot.* **2** tc arrange the plates, knives, forks, spoons and glasses on a table before a meal: *Could you please **lay** the table?* **3** to produce eggs: *My hen **lays** an egg every day.*

> laid, laying, has laid

layer
a flat section of something; a covering on top of something: *The cake was made in two **layers**, with a **layer** of cream in the middle.*

lazy
not wanting to work; not wanting to take exercise: *My sister is very **lazy** and watches television all the time. Vicky takes the bus to school because she is too **lazy** to walk.*

> lazy, lazier, laziest

lead
1 to go in front of someone or something: *Follow my car and I'll **lead** you to my house. A police car **led** the procession.* **2** to take a person or animal somewhere; to guide: *Katie took her little brother by the hand and **led** him across the street. Joe was **leading** the pony into the stable. A waiter **led** us to an empty table in the restaurant.* **3** to go to a certain place: *This road **leads** to the city centre.* **4** to be ahead of the others: *Which horse is **leading**?* **5** to be the leader of a group: *The troops were **led** by General Brown.* **6** to cause: *Disobeying the teacher usually **leads** to trouble.*

> - Rhymes with **need**.
> - Meaning 1: the opposite is **follow**.
> - led, leading, has led

lead
1 the front position: *David has taken the **lead** in the race.* **2** a long leather strap for leading a dog: *You must keep your dog on a **lead** in the town.*

> Rhymes with **need**.

lead
1 a heavy grey metal: ***Lead** is used to make batteries.* **2** the black centre of a pencil: *Pencil-**leads** are always breaking or getting blunt.*

> Rhymes with **head**.

leader
a person who is in charge of a group: *Mr Brown is the **leader** of a group of scouts.*

leaf
one of the flat, thin, green parts of a plant: *Giraffes feed on **leaves** from the tops of trees. You can eat lettuce **leaves**.*

> Lots of **leaves**

leak
a hole through which liquid or gas gets out; water or gas that gets out through a hole: *Water was dripping on to the floor from a **leak** in the pipe. There's a smell of gas — is there a gas-**leak**?*

leak
1 to have a leak: *This bucket is **leaking** — we need a new one.* **2** to pass through a leak: *Gas was **leaking** from the cracked pipe.*

lean
1 to bend yourself in a certain direction: *Don't **lean** out of the train window when the train is moving. Nicola **leant** across the table to talk to me.* **2** to rest the weight of something on something else: *Dad **leant** the ladder against the wall. Don't **lean** your elbows on the table.*

> leant, leaning, has leant

lean
1 thin; not fat: *Most athletes need to be **lean**.* **2** not having much fat: *Chicken-meat is very **lean**.*

leant
see **lean**: *Dad **leant** on the gate and broke it.*

> Rhymes with **sent**.

leap
to jump: *Have you ever watched a kangaroo*

***leaping**? The dog **leapt** over the fence.*

leapt, leaping, has leapt

leap

the action of leaping: *The dog got over the stream in one big **leap**.*

leapt

see **leap**: *The cat **leapt** off the chair when Richard pretended to sit on her.*

Rhymes with **kept**.

learn

to gain knowledge about something; to gain skill to do something: *We **learn** English at school. My little brother is **learning** to swim. Sarah is **learning** to play the guitar.*

- The opposite is **teach**.
- learnt, learning, has learnt

learnt

see **learn**: *Mum **learnt** Chinese at school. Granny has never **learnt** to drive a car.*

least

the smallest amount: *Philip has the most food on his plate, then Mary, and Paul has the **least**. Of all the subjects I learn at school, I like arithmetic the **least**.*

The opposite is **most**.

at least 1 not less than; perhaps more than: *There are **at least** 60 people on this bus. This box is very heavy — it weighs **at least** ten kilos.* 2 you use **at least** when you mention one thing that is good: *It's cold, but **at least** it isn't raining.*

leather

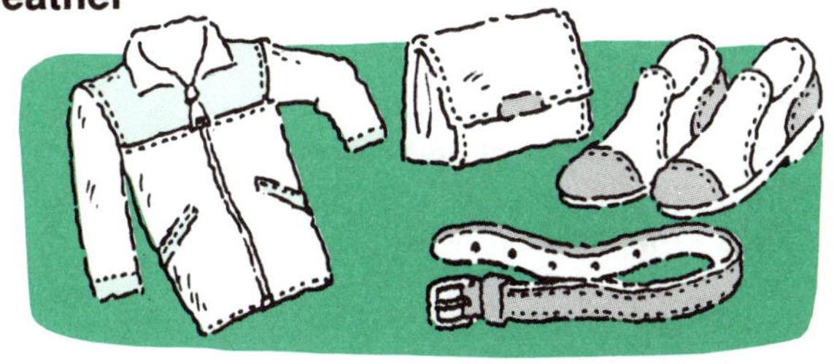

the skin of an animal that has had the hair removed and has been made smooth: ***Leather** is used to make shoes, bags, purses, clothes and lots of other things. Are these gloves made of **leather**?*

Rhymes with **weather**.

leave

1 to go away; to depart: *You must **leave** the house at seven o'clock to get to the airport in time. When does your train **leave**?* 2 to go away for ever: *Linda wants to go to university when she **leaves** school.* 3 to go without taking something: *Mum **left** the dog in the car when she went shopping. I **left** my umbrella on the bus.* 4 to let something stay a certain way: *Mike **left** his toys lying on the floor. Don't **leave** the lights on when you go out.* 5 to let something remain: *Please **leave** some ice-cream for me. Three from eight **leaves** five.*

left, leaving, has left

leave out not to put in; to forget to put in: *You've **left out** the 'a' in 'weather'.*

led

see **lead**: *I **led** my little brother across the road.*

left

1 see **leave**: *Neil **left** the room for a moment. Claire has already **left**.* 2 remaining: *I've only got ten cents **left**. You have five minutes **left** to finish the exam. How many balloons were **left** over from the party?*

left

the same side as the hand that you use less: *In Britain, people still drive on the **left**. Most people wear their watch on the **left** wrist. Turn **left** at the next corner and you'll see the museum on your **left**.*

The opposite is **right**.

leg

1 one of the limbs that a person or animal uses to walk: *How long can you stand on one **leg**? This poodle can stand on its back **legs**.* 2 one of the parts of a table or chair that stand on the floor: *Most tables have four **legs**.*

legend

a very old story: *Nobody knows whether the **legend** of King Arthur is true or not. Do you know the **legend** of the Monkey God?*

leisure

time that you can spend as you like, when you

have no work to do: *At weekends we have plenty of* ***leisure*** *for doing what we want.*

Say **lezh**-er.

lemon
a sour, juicy fruit with a thick yellow skin: ***Lemon*** *juice is sour to drink, but you can use it in cooking.*

lemonade
a sweet drink that has a lemon flavour: *Lots of bubbles rise to the surface of* ***lemonade*** *when you open the bottle.*

lend
to give something to someone for a certain time: *Could you please* ***lend*** *me a dollar until tomorrow? Rachel had no umbrella so I* ***lent*** *her mine to go home with.*

- I have **lent** my umbrella to Rachel.
- Rachel has **borrowed** my umbrella.
- lent, lending, has lent

length
the distance from one end to the other of an object along the longest side: *This table is two metres in* ***length*** *and one metre in breadth.*

lens
a special piece of glass or transparent plastic that helps you to see better: *If you have bad eyesight you can either wear glasses, or you can wear tiny* ***lenses*** *on the surface of your eye.*

lent
see **lend**: *Emma* ***lent*** *me her book about dogs. I have* ***lent*** *Peter my pen.*

leopard

a large animal of the cat family that is similar to a tiger but has black spots on its coat, not stripes: *There are* ***leopards*** *in Africa and Asia.*

Say **lep**-ard.

less
not as much: *I got* ***less*** *ice-cream than the others — please could I have some more? We have* ***less*** *than a quarter of an hour to catch the bus, so we must hurry. Dad is trying to eat* ***less****, so that he will get slimmer.*

The opposite is **more**.

lesson
a period of time when you are taught something by a teacher: *Mathematics is our first* ***lesson*** *on Monday mornings. How many English* ***lessons*** *do you have each week?*

let
to allow; to permit: *My mum wouldn't* ***let*** *me go outside because I had a cold.* ***Let*** *me see your drawing.*

let, letting, has let

let's you use **let's** to suggest something: *'What shall we do?'* ***'Let's*** *go to the beach.' 'Yes,* ***let's****!'*
let go to stop holding someone or something: ***Let go*** *of me! Will you* ***let go*** *of my coat! The dog wouldn't* ***let go*** *of the bone.*
let in to allow someone to come in: ***'Let*** *me* ***in****!' shouted Mike, banging at the door.*

letter
1 a written message that you send to someone by post: *I am writing a* ***letter*** *to my friend in America. Did you post my* ***letter****?* **2** a sign used in writing: *'A' is the first* ***letter*** *of the alphabet.*

letter-box
1 a metal container in the street, with a hole that you post letters through: *Where is the nearest* ***letter-box****?* **2** a hole in a door or a box at the entrance to a building, which a postman puts letters into: *Have a look in the* ***letter-box*** *— perhaps there is a letter for you.*

lettuce
a plant with large green leaves that you put in a salad: *Please would you wash the* ***lettuce*** *leaves?*

Say **let**-is.

level
flat; not sloping: *The table keeps shaking because the floor isn't* ***level****. You ride your bike slowly up a hill, faster on* ***level*** *ground and fastest down a hill.*

The opposite is **uneven** or **sloping**.

lever
a handle that you pull or push to work a

machine: *A railway engine is operated by lots of **levers** and buttons.*

liar
a person who tells lies: *If Bob told you I lent him my bike, he's a **liar**, because he took it without asking.*

librarian
a person who is in charge of a library: *Ask the **librarian** to help you if you can't find the book you want.*

library
a building where a lot of books are kept, especially for people to borrow: *You can borrow four books for three weeks from this public **library**. I must go to the **library** to return these books.*

Two **libraries**

lick

to move your tongue over something: *You eat an ice-cream by **licking** it. The dog **licked** my hand.*

lid
a cover for a pot, jar, tin or box: *Nick lifted the **lid** of the box and looked inside. Please put the **lid** back on the jar. Where is the dustbin **lid**?*

Same as **cover**.

lie
something that someone says that is not true: *One of my classmates said he had been absent from school because he was ill, but he was telling a **lie** — he had really been down at the beach.*

lie
to tell a lie: *I know you've been **lying** — please tell me the truth now. The man **lied** to the police about the robbery.*

lied, lying, has lied

lie
to be in a flat position; to get into a flat position: *You'll get dirty if you **lie** on the floor. The cat is **lying** on a cushion. The book is **lying** on your desk. Peter went to his bedroom and **lay** on his bed.*

lay, lying, has lain

lie down to get into a flat position: *I told my dog to **lie down**. Tracy was very tired and **lay down** on the sofa.*

life
the time when you are alive; being alive: *The old man has had a long and happy **life**. Angela saved her brother's **life** by pulling him out of the river. We shall remember the adventure for the rest of our **lives**.*

Many **lives**

lift
to raise up: *I can't **lift** this box — it's too heavy for me. The mother **lifted** the child on to her back.*

lift
1 a kind of cage like a little room that moves up and down between the floors of a tall building, carrying people or goods: *We took the **lift** to the third floor. You have to press this button to call the **lift**.* **2** a ride in someone's car: *Our neighbour gave me a **lift** to the city centre.*

light
1 the bright rays that come from the sun or the moon or a lamp, and help you to see things: *Have you enough **light** to read by? When dawn comes, the **light** gets stronger. The moon**light** shone on the sea.* **2** an electric lamp: *Please could you switch on the **light**? It's getting dark in here. Please turn off the **lights** before you go to bed. Suddenly all the **lights** went out.*

light
1 to make something start burning: *Could you please **light** the candles? Mum **lit** the gas on the cooker.* **2** to give light to a place: *The room was **lit** only by candles.*

lit, lighting, has lit

light
1 having plenty of light; not dark: *My bedroom is very **light** because it has two large windows.* **2** pale in colour: *The new leaves of this plant are **light** green. Mark is wearing a **light** blue*

shirt and dark blue trousers. **3** easy to lift or carry; not heavy; weighing little: *My schoolbag feels as* ***light*** *as a feather today. Cork floats easily because it is very* ***light****. Dad wears a* ***light*** *jacket in summer.* **4** gentle; not much: *There was a* ***light*** *wind by the sea. The rain was only* ***light****. I had a* ***light*** *lunch because I wasn't very hungry.*

- Meanings 1 and 2: the opposite is **dark**.
- Meaning 3: the opposite is **heavy**.

light sleep sleep that is easily disturbed: *Dogs and cats can fall into a* ***light sleep****, and a very small sound wakes them up again.*

lighthouse

a tower with a strong light that is built on the coast, or on a small island, to guide or warn ships: *We could see the flashing light of a* ***lighthouse*** *in the distance.*

lightning

the very bright flashes of light in the sky during a storm: *The flash of* ***lightning*** *was followed by loud thunder. A tall tree was struck by* ***lightning****.*

like

1 similar to; almost the same as: *Sarah looks* ***like*** *her mother. Tom can climb trees* ***like*** *a cat.* **2** you use **like** when you ask someone to describe a person or thing: *What is your new teacher* ***like****? What was the film* ***like****?*

like

1 to enjoy something; to find someone or something pleasant: *I* ***like*** *swimming. Which fruit do you* ***like*** *best? Do you* ***like*** *being at school? I* ***like*** *Helen very much.* **2** to want: *I would* ***like*** *to go to the zoo today. Would you* ***like*** *a cup of tea?*

liked, liking, has liked

lily

a tall plant that has large, usually white, flowers: *A* ***lily*** *is grown from a bulb. Dad bought Mum a bunch of white* ***lilies****.*

A bunch of **lilies**

limb

an arm or leg: *You have four* ***limbs****. A monkey has long* ***limbs****.*

lime

a sour, juicy fruit that is similar to a lemon: *Mum put a slice of* ***lime*** *in each glass of water.*

limp

to walk with difficulty, usually because you have hurt your foot or your leg: *Paul is* ***limping*** *because he has twisted his ankle.*

line

1 a long, thin mark: *Linda drew straight* ***lines*** *across the piece of paper. There are* ***lines*** *on a tennis court to mark the area where the ball must hit the ground. When you frown you get* ***lines*** *across your forehead.* **2** a row of people or things that are next to each other: *The children stood in a* ***line****.* **3** a row of written or printed words: *This poem has twelve* ***lines****. Please read the next three* ***lines****.* **4** the words that an actor has to learn: *I hope I don't forget my* ***lines****.* **5** a long piece of string, rope or wire: *Mum is hanging the laundry on the* ***line*** *in the garden. You catch fish with a fishing-rod and* ***line****.*

link

to join up: *Jan and Lucy were walking along with their arms* ***linked****.*

lion

a large animal of the cat family that has light brown fur and lives in Africa: *A male* ***lion*** *has a thick mane.* ***Lions*** *sleep most of the time. Have you ever heard a* ***lion*** *roar? A baby* ***lion*** *is called a cub.*

lioness

a female lion: *A group of* ***lionesses*** *were hunting a zebra.* ***Lionesses*** *look after one another's cubs.*

lip

one of the two parts round the edge of your mouth: *Your two* ***lips*** *are called your upper* ***lip*** *and your lower* ***lip****.*

lipstick

a red or pink colouring stick material for making your lips brighter: *Mrs Jones was* *wearing bright red **lipstick**.*

liquid

1 something that flows, such as water: *Bottles are containers for **liquids**.* 2 able to flow; not solid: *The ice-cream quickly became **liquid** when it was left in the sun.*

> The opposite is **solid**.

list

a number of things that are written down one below the other: *Mum is making a **list** of the things she wants to buy. The headmaster has a **list** of all the pupils' names.*

list

to put something in a list: *Peter **listed** the things he still had to do. The names of the winners are **listed** in the newspaper.*

listen

to pay attention to what you hear: *Please **listen** carefully to what I'm saying. **Listen** to this music — isn't it great? I enjoy **listening** to the radio.*

> Say **lis**-en.

lit

see **light**: *Mr Lee **lit** his pipe while he waited for the bus. Have you **lit** the candles?*

litre

a measure of liquid: *This bottle contains one **litre** of lemonade.*

> Say **lee**-ter.

litter

1 rubbish: *Don't drop **litter** in the streets. Put your **litter** in a rubbish bin.* 2 a number of animals that are born to the same mother at the same time: *There were six kittens in the **litter**.*

little

1 small; not big: *I live in a **little** village with only twenty houses. The last toe on your foot is called your **little** toe.* 2 very young: *When I was **little** I was afraid of dogs. My **little** sister is three years younger than me.* 3 not much: *The storm did very **little** harm. I have very **little** money left.*

> Meaning 3: little, less, least

a little a small amount; not much: *'Is there any soup left?' 'Yes, **a little**.' My granny only speaks **a little** English.*

live

1 to have your home in a certain place: *Where do you **live**? I **live** in Main Street. Keith went to **live** in London. Lions **live** in Africa.* 2 to be alive; to stay alive: *Nobody can **live** without water.*

> - Say **liv**.
> - Meaning 2: the opposite is **die**.
> - lived, living, has lived

live

broadcast while the event is taking place: *I watched the football match **live** on television. The concert will be broadcast **live** on the radio.*

> Rhymes with **five**.

lively

cheerful; full of energy: *Granny is still very **lively** although she's nearly 80.*

living

the money that people need to earn, to be able to live: *Mr Davis earns his **living** as a gardener. Mr Miller makes a **living** by selling old cars. What do you do for a **living**?*

living-room

the room in a house or flat where people sit and relax: *The whole family was sitting in the **living-room** watching television.*

lizard

a small reptile with four short legs and a long tail: ***Lizards** live in hot countries.*

load

something that is being carried: *The lorry was carrying a **load** of wood. Mum was walking up the street with a heavy **load** of shopping.*

load

1 to put a load into a vehicle: *Two men **loaded** the furniture into a lorry.* 2 to put bullets into a gun: *The soldier **loaded** his gun and fired at the target.*

loaf

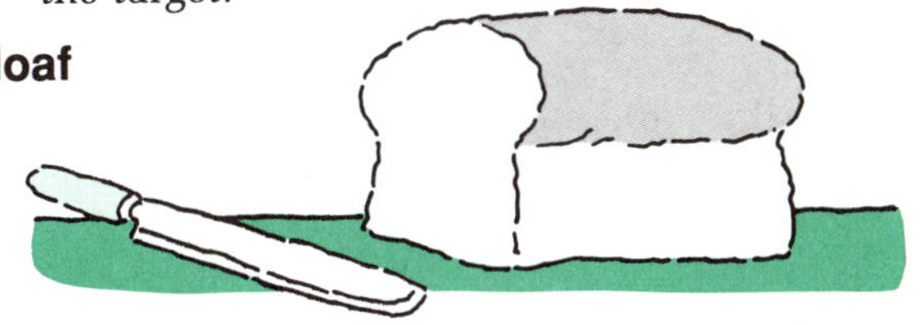

bread formed into a regular shape by being baked in a tin: *Could you buy me a **loaf** of* *brown bread at the baker's? Do you want a sliced **loaf**?*

Two **loaves**

lobster

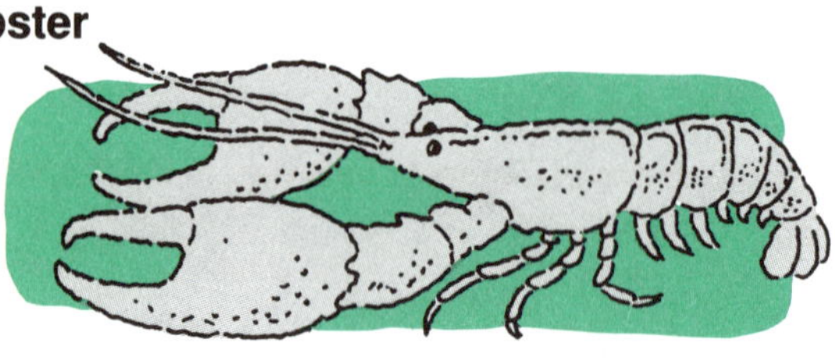

a sea creature that has a hard red shell and two large front limbs that are similar to scissors: *The flesh inside a **lobster**'s shell can be eaten after it has been cooked.*

local

belonging to the area in which you live: *My mum buys most of our food in the **local** shops. You can read about **local** events and news in a **local** newspaper.*

lock

1 an object for fastening doors, drawers and cases safely, so that they can't be opened without a key: *Tom closed the front door and turned the key in the **lock**.* **2** a piece of hair: *Mum has kept a **lock** of my hair that she cut off when I was a baby.*

lock

1 to fasten something with a key; to fasten the lock on something: *Don't forget to **lock** the front door. I always **lock** my bicycle when I leave it standing outside, so that nobody can steal it.* **2** to stop someone getting through a door by locking it: *Prisoners are **locked** in so that they cannot escape. I lost my key today, so I was **locked** out of the house till Mum came home.*

log

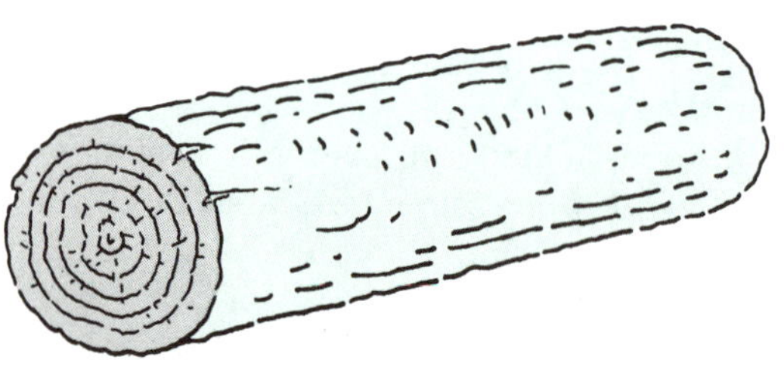

1 a thick piece of wood: *The tree was sawn into **logs**.* **2** a fallen tree-trunk: *We sat on a **log** to have a rest.*

loiter

to stand somewhere doing nothing: *A group of boys were **loitering** outside the shop.*

lollipop

a sweet on a stick: *Julie is sucking a **lollipop**.*

lonely

1 sad because you are alone, or because you have no friends: *Peter felt **lonely** in his new school because he didn't know anybody.* **2** far away from busy places: *We spent our holiday on a **lonely** island where there were no other tourists.*

long

1 a lot of time: *Have you been waiting **long**? It won't take me **long** to get ready.* **2** taking a lot of time: *Mum and Mrs Peters had a **long** chat in the supermarket. I took a **long** time to do my homework tonight.* **3** measuring a lot from one end to the other: *A giraffe has **long** legs and a very **long** neck. It's a very **long** journey to Australia.* **4** measuring a certain length; lasting a certain time: *The bed is two metres **long** and one metre wide. How **long** was the film?*

Meanings 2 and 3: the opposite is **short**.

all day long for the whole day: *It has been raining **all day long**.*

all night long for the whole night: *Have you ever stayed awake **all night long**?*

no longer not now; not any more: *This cinema is **no longer** being used.*

long

to want something very much: *In winter people **long** for the summer. I am **longing** to go on holiday.*

longing

a great wish for something: *My dog looked at my hamburger with **longing**.*

look

1 to turn your eyes to see something: *Bob **looked** at his watch. Stop **looking** out of the window, Jenny! Mary and Susan **looked** at each other. **Look** what the baby is doing!* **2** to seem; to appear: *It **looks** as if it's going to rain soon. It **looks** like rain. You **look** tired — you must go to bed early. Hello! You're **looking** well! That cloud **looks** like a fish. 'What does Mrs Smith **look** like?' 'She is tall, has black hair and wears glasses.'* **3** to search: *I've **looked** everywhere, but I still haven't found my purse.*

look after to take care of someone or something: *Our aunt **looked after** us while our mum was in hospital. Could you **look after** my things while I go swimming? You must*

look after *your plants and water them regularly.*

look for to search for someone or something: *I've been **looking for** you everywhere. Sue is **looking for** her glasses.*

look forward to to wait happily for something that is going to happen: *We are **looking forward to** the holidays. I am **looking forward to** seeing my friend again.*

look out! be careful!: ***Look out*** *— there's a car coming!*

look round to walk about looking at things: *I **looked round** the shop but didn't buy anything. We **looked round** the museum.*

look through to look at books, magazines or newspapers without reading them carefully: *Please **look through** this pile of comics and decide which ones you want to keep.*

look up to search for some information in a book: *If you don't know what this word means, you can **look it up** in your dictionary. Paul **looked up** Joseph's telephone number in the telephone book.*

look

1 the action of looking: *Take a **look** at this picture. Let me have a **look** at the baby. Mr Johnson had a quick **look** at his watch.* **2** appearance: *The garden had an untidy **look**. I don't like the **look** of those black clouds.*

loose

1 not firmly fastened: *This button is **loose**. Sometimes Julie ties her hair back, and sometimes she wears it **loose**.* **2** not fitting tightly: *This skirt is too **loose** round the waist.* **3** free; not tied: *I let my dog run **loose** in the park.*

> Meaning 2: the opposite is **tight**.

loosen

to make loose; to become loose: *The screw had **loosened** and fallen out. Jim **loosened** the knot in the string.*

lord

a man or animal that has powers over others: *The tiger is the **lord** of the jungle.*

lorry

a large vehicle that is used for carrying heavy loads by road; a truck: *Goods are transported to the supermarket by **lorry**. Dad overtook lots of **lorries** on the motorway.*

> Lots of **lorries**

lose

1 not to be able to find something; to have something no longer: *Don't **lose** that key. I've **lost** my purse. Mr Brown **lost** his job.* **2** to get rid of: *My dad doesn't eat sweets because he's trying to **lose** weight.* **3** not to win: *Our team **lost** the match. I always **lose** at card games.*

> - Meaning 1: the opposite is **find**.
> - Meaning 3: the opposite is **win**.
> - lost, losing, has lost

loss

1 losing something: *Mum is worried over the **loss** of her purse, because it had a lot of money in it.* **2** the money that you lose when you sell something for less money than you paid for it: *Mr Jones made a **loss** of $5000 when he sold his car.*

> Meaning 2: the opposite is **profit**.

lost

see **lose**: *Mary **lost** her ring. I've **lost** my ticket.*

lost

1 no longer knowing where you are; unable to find your way: *I'm **lost** — could you please tell me the way to the railway station? You can easily get **lost** in a big city.* **2** missing: *The **lost** dog has been found again.*

lot

the whole of something; everything: *I asked Paul for one of his chocolates, but he had already eaten the **lot**.*

a lot of a large amount of something; a large number: *The children ate **a lot of** ice-cream. Amy has **a lot of** friends.*

lots of a large amount of something; a large number: *My uncle has got **lots of** money. There are **lots and lots of** restaurants in Singapore.*

lotus

a plant with large flat leaves and white flowers, which float on lakes or rivers in hot countries; the flowers of this plant: *The leaves of **lotuses** grow very quickly.*

loud
making a large amount of sound; not quiet: *The guide spoke in a* ***loud*** *voice so that all the tourists could hear what she was saying. My parents don't like* ***loud*** *music.*

> The opposite is **soft**.

loudspeaker
an instrument for making a sound louder: *When a singer sings into a microphone, the audience can hear his voice through* ***loud-speakers****.*

love
1 a feeling of being very fond of someone: *Parents and children need one another's* ***love****.* **2** a feeling of liking something very much: *Jenny has had a* ***love*** *of music since she was a small child.*

love
1 to be very fond of someone: *Parents* ***love*** *their children.* **2** to like something very much: *I* ***love*** *these flowers. We all* ***love*** *ice-cream. Margaret* ***loves*** *dancing. I would* ***love*** *to come with you but I must go home now.*

> - The opposite is **hate**.
> - loved, loving, has loved

lovely
beautiful; pleasant: *Katie is a* ***lovely*** *girl. You look* ***lovely*** *in your new dress. What a* ***lovely*** *day! Thank you very much for your* ***lovely*** *present.*

> lovely, lovelier, loveliest

loving
feeling and showing your love for someone: *Mum is a* ***loving*** *mother to me and a* ***loving*** *wife to Dad.*

low
1 not high: *This chair is too* ***low*** *for me — I can't reach the table. Play a* ***low*** *note on the piano. Mr Miller was so tall that he hit his head on the* ***low*** *ceiling. In Britain, temperatures are very* ***low*** *in winter.* **2** not loud: *Sally was talking to me in a* ***low*** *voice so that nobody else would hear. Dad turned the music down* ***low****.*

> Meanings 1 and 2: the opposite is **high**.

lower
1 not as high: *The bus fares are* ***lower*** *here than in Hong Kong.* **2** bottom: *Your* ***lower*** *lip is thicker than your upper lip.*

> - Meaning 1: the opposite is **higher**.
> - Meaning 2: the opposite is **upper**.

luck
1 chance: *In this card-game you win by* ***luck****, not by skill.* **2** good fortune: *I shall need lots of* ***luck*** *for my exam. Wish me good* ***luck****! What a bit of* ***luck*** *it was finding that money!*

lucky
1 having good luck: *Mrs Davies was the* ***lucky*** *winner of the crossword competition. The people in the two cars were* ***lucky*** *not to be injured in the accident.* **2** bringing good luck: *Seven is my* ***lucky*** *number.*

luggage

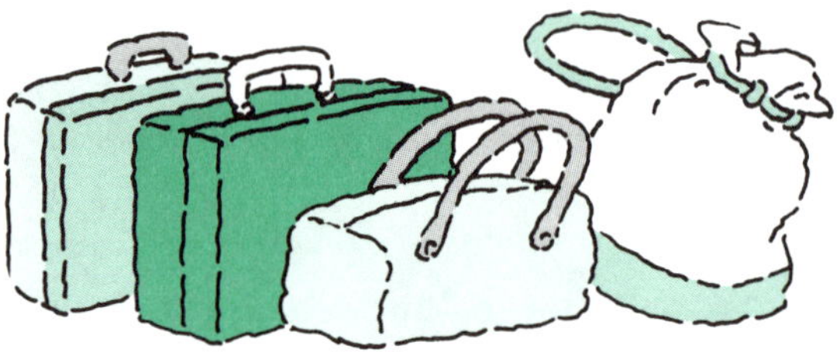

the suitcases and bags that you have with you when you are travelling: *We didn't take much* ***luggage*** *when we went on a short trip. Dad carries most of our* ***luggage****.*

lump
1 a big or small piece of solid stuff: *When Dad was working in the garden, he dug up a big* ***lump*** *of rock. Rachel put four* ***lumps*** *of sugar in her tea.* **2** a swelling: *I've got a* ***lump*** *on my head where the stone hit me.*

lunch
a meal that you eat in the middle of the day: *I had salad and a bread roll for* ***lunch****. We had* ***lunch*** *at half past twelve.*

lung
one of the two parts of your body inside your chest, that fill with air when you breathe in, and empty again when you breathe out: *When I had a bad cold the doctor listened to my* ***lungs*** *with her stethoscope.*

lychee
a small sweet fruit that has a hard red skin and soft white flesh, with a large stone in the centre: *I opened a can of* ***lychees****.*

lying
see **lie**: *I'm not* ***lying*** *— I'm telling the truth! The cat is* ***lying*** *in the shade.*

macaroni
a dried food in the shape of tubes that is cooked in boiling water and eaten with a sauce: *We had **macaroni** with tomato sauce for lunch.*

machine
an object that is designed to do a certain kind of work, so that people don't have to do it themselves: *A **machine** usually needs electricity to work. My mum has a washing-**machine** and a sewing-**machine**. A dish-washer is a **machine** that washes and dries the dishes.*

mad
1 crazy: *What a **mad** idea! The dog went **mad** when it was stung by a wasp. You must be **mad** to cross the road without looking. That noise is driving me **mad**!* **2** very angry: *My mum was **mad** at me for coming home late.* **3** liking something very much: *Mark is **mad** about pop music.*

mad, madder, maddest

Madam
a polite word to call a woman whose name you don't know: *Thank you, **Madam**! Waiters and shop assistants call female customers '**Madam**'.*

made
see **make**: *This camera was **made** in Japan. Have you **made** the tea yet?*

magazine
a paper that is published every week or every month, usually with a lot of photographs in it: *My mum sometimes buys a fashion **magazine**.*

magic
1 a power that makes things happen that cannot be explained: *In the fairy-tale, the dwarf spun the straw into gold by **magic**. The door suddenly opened, as if by **magic**.* **2** the skill of performing tricks, such as making things disappear: *Robert has promised to perform some **magic** for us, with a pack of cards.*

magician
a person who can perform magic: *In the story, the **magician** Merlin turned little Arthur into a fish. There was a **magician** on television who could produce rabbits and doves from his big black hat.*

magnet
a piece of iron that makes other pieces of iron move towards it: *You can find out whether a metal object is made of iron by holding a **magnet** close to it.*

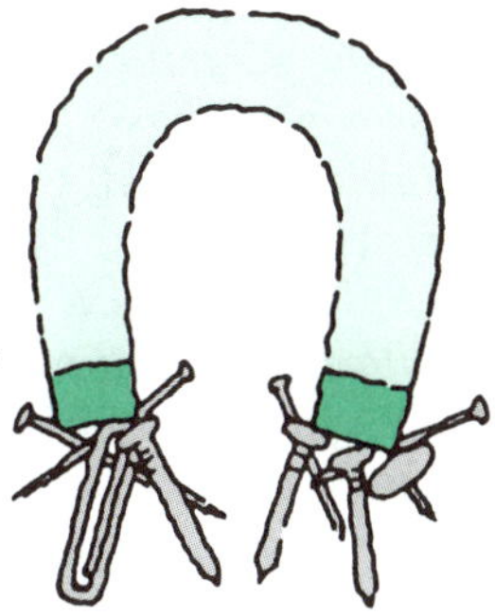

maid
a woman who works as a servant in a house or hotel: *Long ago, lots of people used to employ **maids** in their houses.*

mail
1 letters and parcels that are sent to you: *Is there any **mail** for me? The **mail** hasn't come yet.* **2** the collecting and delivering of letters and parcels: *I sent a letter to America by air-**mail**.*

mail
to send a letter or parcel by post; to post: *Joe **mailed** the parcel three days ago.*

main
most important: *The **main** thing is to be happy and healthy. Meet me at the **main** entrance to the school.*

mainly
most of the time; usually; nearly all: *Dad works **mainly** in Singapore, but sometimes has to go to Europe on business. Your work is **mainly** very good, but you sometimes make mistakes.*

maize
small round yellow seeds that are eaten as a vegetable: ***Maize** is also called 'sweet corn', because it tastes rather sweet.*

Also called **corn**.

make

1 to produce; to prepare; to get something ready: *My mum* ***makes*** *all her own clothes. My dad* ***made*** *this toy train for me out of a piece of wood. Please could you* ***make*** *the tea? Jenny always* ***makes*** *her own bed.* **2** to force someone to do something; to cause someone to do something: *The teacher* ***makes*** *us do extra homework if we talk to each other during the lesson. The monkeys in the zoo* ***made*** *me laugh. The loud music* ***made*** *the dog howl.* **3** to cause someone to be something: *The children's bad behaviour* ***made*** *the teacher angry. I've got some news that is sure to* ***make*** *you happy. Sally is going to be* ***made*** *head girl of the school next term.* **4** to earn; to gain: *Mr Brown* ***makes*** *$300 a day. You will* ***make*** *a profit if you sell your house now.* **5** to perform certain actions: *We* ***made*** *a long journey. The explosion* ***made*** *a loud noise. We are not allowed to* ***make*** *a mess in the sitting-room. The headmaster* ***made*** *a short speech. Mum* ***made*** *a long telephone call. I've* ***made*** *a mistake.* **6** you can use **make** when you are talking about addition: *Two and two* ***makes*** *four.*

> made, making, has made

made from or **made out of** produced from something else: *Paper is* ***made from*** *wood. Mum* ***made*** *me a blouse* ***out of*** *one of her old dresses.*

made of produced from a certain material: *This wall is* ***made of*** *brick. This table is* ***made of*** *wood. This blouse is* ***made of*** *cotton.*

make up **1** to invent; to think up: *The teacher asked all the children to* ***make up*** *a poem. George* ***made up*** *an excuse to explain why he was late.* **2** to become friends again after a quarrel: *Ken and Robert had a quarrel, but they soon* ***made it up*** *again.* **3** to form something: *You need eleven players to* ***make up*** *a football team.*

make-up

lipstick, powder and other things that women or actors put on their faces: *My mum hardly ever wears* ***make-up****.*

male

a man or a boy; an animal that does not have babies or lay eggs: *A female horse is called a mare — what is the* ***male*** *called? A* ***male*** *bird is called a cock. Your father, uncle, brother and grandfather are* ***male*** *relations.*

> The opposite is **female**.

mammal

any animal whose female gives birth to babies alive and feeds her babies with her own milk: *Mice, dogs, elephants, whales, monkeys and human beings are all* ***mammals****.*

man

an adult male human being: *When a* ***man*** *marries a woman, he becomes her husband.* ***Men*** *can grow beards, but women and children can't.*

> Two **men**

manage

1 to be able to do something: *Will you* ***manage*** *to repair my bicycle? Can you* ***manage*** *to eat some more cake? Tim* ***managed*** *to get me a ticket for the match.* **2** to be in charge of something; to be the manager of something: *Mr Jones* ***manages*** *the export department. John* ***manages*** *the school football team.*

> managed, managing, has managed

manager

a person who is in charge of something such as a shop, a business or a sports team: *My dad complained to the* ***manager*** *of the restaurant because the food was very bad. Mr Johnson is the* ***manager*** *of the local football club.*

mane

the long hair on the back of the neck of a horse or a male lion: *A lion's* ***mane*** *is very thick.*

mango

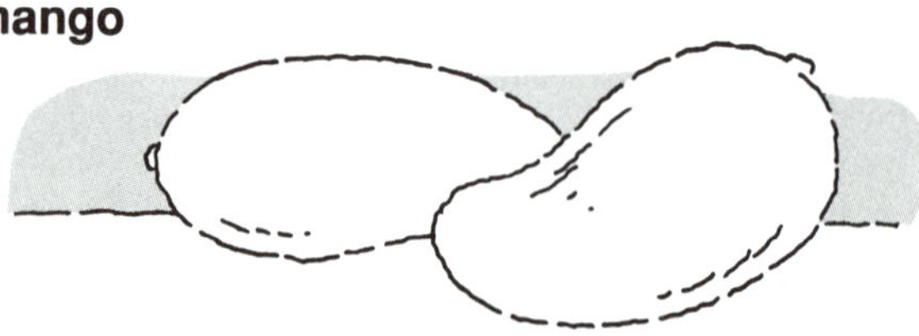

a large sweet yellow fruit that grows in hot countries: *We went to the market to buy* ***mangoes*** *and other fresh fruits.*

> Two **mangoes** or **mangos**

manner

1 the way you do something: *Mrs Lee shouted 'Hello!' in a friendly* ***manner****.* **2** the way a person usually speaks and behaves: *Chris always has a nice cheerful* ***manner****.*

manners
behaviour, especially polite behaviour: *Parents usually teach their children* ***manners****. Clare has very good* ***manners****. It is bad* ***manners*** *to spit on the ground.*

many
1 a large number of people or things: ***Many*** *children take the bus to school. You watch too* ***many*** *films on television.* **2** a certain number of people or things: *How* ***many*** *children are there in your class? How* ***many*** *records have you got?*

- Meaning 1: the opposite is **few**.
- Meaning 1: many, more, most

map

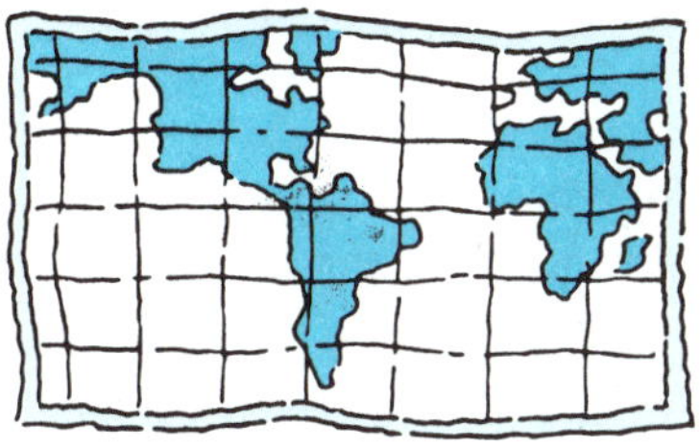

a drawing of a certain area such as a country or town as if seen from far above: *Could you show me on the* ***map*** *how to get to Victoria Street? My dad keeps a road* ***map*** *in the car. The teacher showed us India on a big* ***map*** *of the world.*

marbles
a children's game that is played with small coloured glass balls called 'marbles': *The boys were playing* ***marbles*** *in the playground.*

march
to walk with regular steps, in time with one another: *A troop of soldiers were* ***marching*** *along the street.*

March
the third month of the year.

mare
a female horse: *The parents of a foal are called a* ***mare*** *and a stallion.*

margarine
a soft yellow fat that is similar to butter and is made mainly from vegetable oil: *Do you prefer* ***margarine*** *or butter on your bread?*

margin
the blank edge round a written or printed page: *Always leave a* ***margin*** *on the left when you write a letter. The teacher crosses out the mistakes in our exercise books and writes the correct words in the* ***margin****.*

mark
1 a stain or a spot on something: *There's a dirty* ***mark*** *on your skirt. The coffee you spilt has left a* ***mark*** *on the carpet. My dog has a black* ***mark*** *on its nose.* **2** a point that a teacher gives to a pupil: *I got a good* ***mark*** *in my English exam. I got seven* ***marks*** *out of ten in my test. The teacher took off three* ***marks*** *for spelling mistakes. Susan got full* ***marks****.* **3** a sign: *I've made a* ***mark*** *on the street map to show you where our house is.*

mark
1 to put a stain on something: *That tea has* ***marked*** *the tablecloth.* **2** to give points for a piece of work and correct the mistakes in it: *The teacher* ***marked*** *our compositions.* **3** to put a label on something: *The pupils' coats must be* ***marked*** *with their names.* **4** to show: *I've put a cross on the map to* ***mark*** *the place where our house is.*

market
a place where goods are sold from stalls, usually in the open air: *Mum goes to the* ***market*** *once a week to buy fresh fruit and vegetables. There are clothes stalls and toy stalls at the* ***market*** *as well as food stalls.*

marmalade
a jam that is made from oranges, lemons or grapefruit: *I often have toast and* ***marmalade*** *for breakfast.*

marriage
1 the ceremony at which a man and woman become husband and wife; a wedding: *The* ***marriage*** *between John and Pauline will take place at St John's Church on 7 July.* **2** being married to someone: *My grandparents have had a long and happy* ***marriage****.*

marry
1 to become the husband or wife of someone: *My aunt* ***married*** *a lawyer. They* ***married*** *in church.* **2** to make two people husband and wife: *A priest* ***married*** *the couple.*

marries, married, marrying, has married

get married to become husband and wife: *My parents* ***got married*** *twelve years ago.*

When are Peter and Jenny ***getting married****?*

mask

a covering that you put over your face to disguise it, with holes for your eyes: *The bank robbers were wearing black* ***masks*** *so that nobody could recognize them. I've got a* ***mask*** *shaped like a gorilla's face.*

mast

a tall pole on a ship that the sails are fixed to: *The sailor climbed the* ***mast****.*

master

1 a man who has a servant or a slave: *Slaves were sometimes whipped by their* ***masters*** *for disobeying them.* **2** the owner of a dog: *A dog should learn to obey its* ***master*** *or mistress.* **3** a male teacher: *We've got a new mathematics* ***master****.*

> Meaning 1: the opposite is **servant**.

mat

1 a piece of cloth, or a flat piece of wood, cork or plastic, that you put under a plate on a table: *We have a set of six table* ***mats****.* **2** an object like a very small carpet: *Please wipe your shoes on the door****mat****. There is a bath* ***mat*** *beside the bath.*

match

1 a short thin stick of wood or cardboard with a tip that catches fire when you rub it against a rough surface: *David struck a* ***match*** *and lit the candle.* ***Matches*** *are sold in matchboxes.* **2** a game between two teams or players: *Dad is watching a football* ***match*** *on television. Which player won the last tennis* ***match****?*

> Two **matches**

match

to look similar to something else and go well with it: *The pattern on the curtains* ***matches*** *the pattern on the wallpaper. Michelle's blue shoes* ***match*** *her blue dress. Sue has a jacket with a skirt to* ***match****.*

material

1 any kind of stuff, especially stuff that things are made of: *Tables are made of solid* ***material*** *such as wood. Paper, wood, metal, glass, plastic and clay are all* ***materials****.* **2** cloth that is used to make clothes and other things: *Mum bought three metres of cotton* ***material*** *to make a dress for me.*

mathematics

a subject in which you study numbers: *Peter wants to study* ***mathematics*** *at university.*

> Called **maths** for short.

maths

short for **mathematics**: *My sister is very good at* ***maths****. Mr Simon is our* ***maths*** *teacher.*

matter

the thing that is wrong; a problem or difficulty that is upsetting you: *What's the* ***matter*** *— why are you crying? What's the* ***matter*** *with your bicycle? Is anything the* ***matter****? I'm OK — there's nothing the* ***matter****.*

matter

to be important: *'Does it* ***matter*** *where we sit?' 'No, it doesn't* ***matter****.' The only thing that* ***matters*** *is whether you are happy.*

mattress

the thick oblong object that is put on a bed for you to lie on: *I prefer a firm* ***mattress*** *to a soft one for sleeping on.*

may

1 to be allowed to do something: *'You* ***may*** *go home now,' said the teacher.* ***May*** *we come with you, please?* ***May*** *I have an ice-cream, please?* **2** you use **may** to say that something is possible: *Take your umbrella — it* ***may*** *rain later on. You* ***may*** *have left your exercise book on your desk. You* ***may*** *be late if you don't hurry.*

> may, might

May

the fifth month of the year.

maybe

perhaps: ***Maybe*** *we'll go to the zoo tomorrow,*

*if the weather is good. I can't find my pencil-case — **maybe** I left it at home.*

Write **maybe**, not **may be**.

me
a word I use when I am talking about myself: *Give that book to **me**. Sue rang **me** up this afternoon. 'Who's there?' 'It's **me**.' Paul is coming with Jenny and **me**.*

meadow

a field of grass: *There were cows in the **meadow**. The farmer is mowing the **meadow**.*

Say **med**-oe.

meal
the food that you eat at a certain time: *We have three **meals** a day — breakfast, lunch and dinner. We have a big **meal** in the evening.*

mean
1 to be understood in a certain way: *Vacation **means** holiday. 'What does 'a while' **mean**?' 'It **means** a short time.'* **2** to be trying to say something: *What do you **mean** by a 'huge mouse'?* **3** to intend: *I **meant** to come and see you yesterday, but I had too much work to do, so I couldn't. I'm sorry — I didn't **mean** to upset you. Your exercise book is **meant** for writing your homework in. The flowers are **meant** for Mum.*

meant, meaning, has meant

mean
1 not generous; not wanting to spend much money: *Don't be so **mean** — give some of the chocolate to your sister! Some people are very **mean** with their money.* **2** not kind; nasty: *It is **mean** to bully other children. It was **mean** of you not to help me.*

meaning
1 what a word means: *A lot of English words have several different **meanings**.* **2** an explanation: *What is the **meaning** of all this noise, children?*

meant
see **mean**: *I **meant** to come earlier but I missed the bus. I'm not telling you what you'll get for your birthday — it's **meant** to be a surprise.*

Rhymes with **sent**.

meanwhile
during this time: *I was walking home, and **meanwhile** my mum was looking for me in the playground. I'll make the coffee — would you lay the table **meanwhile**?*

measles
a children's disease that gives you little red spots all over your skin, and a high temperature: *Pauline got **measles** and a lot of other children caught it from her. You can only have **measles** once.*

Say **meez**-elz.

measure
1 to find the size or amount of something: *I **measured** the length of the line with my ruler. Dad **measured** the walls of the living-room.* **2** to show the size or amount of something: *A thermometer **measures** temperature.* **3** to be a certain size: *This table **measures** two metres by one metre.*

measured, measuring, has measured

meat
the flesh of animals used as food: *The **meat** of a sheep is called mutton, and the **meat** of a pig is called pork. Some people don't eat any **meat** at all.*

mechanic
a person whose job is to repair machines and vehicles: *Mr Higgs is a car **mechanic** and works in a large garage.*

Say mi-**kan**-ik.

medal
a piece of metal like a large coin that is given as a prize: *The winner of the race received a gold **medal**. The boy who saved his friend's life was given a **medal** for bravery.*

medicine
something that you swallow to cure an illness: *The doctor said I should take the **medicine** three times a day before meals. My mum gave me some **medicine** for my cough.*

Say **med**-sin.

meet

1 to come face to face with someone by chance: *I **met** Liz on my way to school this morning. My parents first **met** each other on a train.* **2** to join someone after arranging a time and place with them: *I'll **meet** you at the corner of our street at four o'clock. We arranged to **meet** at the entrance to the museum. The Scouts **meet** every Saturday afternoon.* **3** to be introduced to someone for the first time; to get to know someone: *Don't you know Mrs Lee? Do come and **meet** her. I'm so pleased to **meet** you! 'Goodbye, Mrs Lee — it's nice to have **met** you!'* **4** to collect someone: *We are going to the station to **meet** Granny.*

> met, meeting, has met

meeting

the coming together of a group of people to discuss something, or to listen to a talk by someone: *The next **meeting** of the swimming club will be on 20 January at 8 o'clock. I hope as many members as possible will attend the **meeting**. We shall discuss some new club rules at the **meeting**.*

melon

a large round juicy fruit with lots of seeds and a hard green or yellow skin: *Would you like a slice of **melon**?*

melt

to become soft or liquid in heat; to make something liquid: *The ice-cream will **melt** if you don't eat it soon. The snow is **melting** fast. Please put the butter in the fridge so that it won't **melt**. Mum **melted** the sugar in a pan.*

member

a person who belongs to a group or a club: *My parents are **members** of the tennis club.*

memory

1 the ability to remember things: *My dad has a good **memory** for numbers but a bad **memory** for people's names.* **2** something that you remember from the past: *The old woman told the children her **memories** of the time when she was a little girl.*

> A lot of **memories**

men

see **man**: *Which of these two **men** is Mr Lee?*

mend

to put something that is damaged right again; to repair something: *Tim **mended** the broken clock. My shoes need **mending**. My mum **mended** the tear in my trousers. An engineer came to **mend** the television.*

> Same as **repair**.

mention

to speak about something briefly: *Thomas **mentioned** his plan, but he didn't tell me much about it. Susan **mentioned** last night that she wasn't feeling very well.*

menu

a list of dishes to choose from in a restaurant: *Let's look at the **menu** and decide what we want to eat.*

> Say **men**-ew.

merry

an old word for happy and cheerful: *At Christmas people wish each other a '**Merry** Christmas'.*

merry-go-round

a round moving platform with toy horses, cars and other vehicles, that children can ride on: *There is a **merry-go-round** at the fair.*

mess

something that is untidy; dirt: *What a **mess**! Your room is in a terrible **mess** — tidy it up straight away. Tom spilt the food and it made a **mess** on the carpet.*

message

a piece of information that is passed from one person to another: *Bob isn't in — would you like to leave a **message** for him? I have a **message** for you from Mrs White. Mr Smith got a **message** telling him to ring his wife.*

messenger

a person who takes messages to people: *In the story, the king sent **messengers** to all the princes and princesses inviting them to a big feast. This letter was brought by **messenger**, not by post.*

met
see **meet**: *I **met** Paul on the bus. I've never **met** your sister.*

metal
hard stuff such as iron, steel, tin, or silver: *Coins are made of **metal**. Gold is a very precious **metal**. This knife has a **metal** blade and a wooden handle.*

meter
an instrument that measures how much electricity, gas or water has been used: *Every month a man comes to read the electricity **meter**.*

method
a certain way of doing something: *I can teach you a simple **method** of working out those sums. Mum uses a special **method** for making coffee.*

metre
a unit of length: *One **metre** is equal to 100 centimetres. The swimming-pool is about 30 **metres** long, 15 **metres** wide and two **metres** deep.*

- Say **mee**-ter.
- **m** is short for **metre**.

mew
to make the noise of a cat: *The kittens were **mewing** for their mother.*

mice
see **mouse**: *Joe keeps two white **mice** as pets.*

microphone
an instrument for picking up sounds that are made louder through a loudspeaker: *The pop singer sang into a **microphone** which he held close to his mouth.*

microscope
an instrument that makes very small objects look much larger so that you can study them: *I examined the leg of a dead fly under the **microscope**. Germs are so tiny that they can only be seen through a **microscope**.*

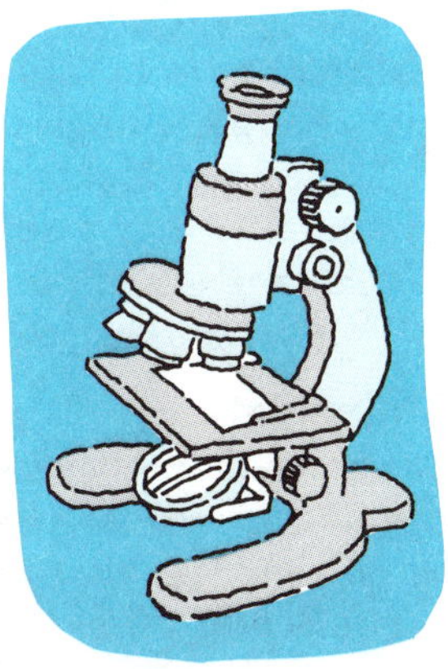

midday
twelve o'clock in the middle of the day: *I'll meet you in the café at **midday**.*

middle
the centre of something: *Your nose is in the **middle** of your face. We sat in the **middle** of the front row at the theatre.*

Same as **centre**.

midnight
twelve o'clock at night: *The last guests left the party after **midnight**.*

might
1 see **may**: *The path was so slippery that I thought I **might** fall. I **might** have caught the bus if I had hurried.* **2** you use **might** to say something is possible: *Jeffrey **might** win the prize if he works very hard. Sandra **might** come and see me this afternoon.*

mild
1 not cold; rather warm: *We had a **mild** winter last year. It's very **mild** today.* **2** not very bad: *Nicola has a **mild** cold.*

mile
a unit of length that is about the same as 1.6 kilometres: *We walked about three **miles** today. How many **miles** is it from your house to the city centre?*

milk
1 a white liquid that is produced by female animals as food for their babies: *It is good for babies to be fed on their mothers' **milk**.* **2** cows' milk: *People drink a lot of **milk**, and it is also used for making cheese, butter and yoghurt.*

milk

to get milk from a cow or a goat: *The farmer **milks** his cows twice a day.*

mill
1 a building where grain is ground into flour: *The farmer took his corn to the **mill**.* **2** a small machine for grinding coffee or peppercorns:

*We keep a pepper-**mill** on the dining-room table.* **3** a factory where steel, wool or cotton is produced: *Over 300 men work in this steel **mill**.*

million

1 the number 1 000 000: *A thousand times a thousand is one **million**.* **2** 1 000 000 in number: *Over twelve **million** people live in London. Are there more than a **million** hairs on your head? The sun is **millions** of miles away.*

millionaire

a person who is very rich and has at least a million dollars: *Mr Smith is a **millionaire** — he owns five houses, a yacht and seven fast cars.*

mind

your brain; the part of you that you think with: *Keep your **mind** on your work, Susan! Your **mind** is full of thoughts, ideas and memories. Sally can think of a way out of any difficulty — she has a very quick **mind**.*

bear in mind to remember; not to forget: *You had better do your homework carefully, **bearing in mind** that there will be an exam next week.*

change your mind to decide to do something different: *I waited at the bus stop for a few minutes, but then I **changed my mind** and walked all the way home.*

make up your mind to decide: *Now, **make up your mind** whether you want to come with us or not. Betty couldn't **make up her mind** which dress to buy.*

mind

1 to be upset by something: *'Do you **mind** if I open the window?' 'No, I don't **mind**.' Would you **mind** waiting a few minutes?* **2** to be careful of something: ***Mind** the step! **Mind** the iron — it's very hot! **Mind** that precious vase — don't drop it! **Mind** you don't trip over the cat.* **3** to look after someone or something for a certain time: *Would you **mind** the baby while I go shopping? Andrew was **minding** the luggage while his dad bought the tickets.*

never mind it's all right; don't worry: *'I'm sorry, I've broken a cup.' '**Never mind** — we can easily get another.'*

mine

use **mine** for something that belongs to me: *Are these crayons yours or **mine**? Here's your pencil — I've got **mine** in my pocket. Amy is a good friend of **mine**.*

mine

a place that is usually underground, from which things like gold, silver or diamonds are dug: *In a gold **mine** people have to dig deep holes and tunnels into the ground to get out the gold. A man who works in a **mine** is called a **miner**.*

mining

the taking of things such as gold, silver or diamonds from a mine: *A town is called a **mining** town when most people who live there earn their money from **mining**.*

minus

1 you use **minus** when you talk about subtraction: *Seven **minus** two is five (7 – 2 = 5).* **2** less than zero: ***Minus** three degrees (–3°) means three degrees colder than zero degrees (0°).*

> **Seven minus two** means the same as **subtract two from seven**.

minute

1 one of the sixty parts of an hour; sixty seconds: *It is five **minutes** past two. I'll be back in ten **minutes**.* **2** a very short time; a moment: *Could you wait a **minute**, please? Wait for me while I change my clothes — I won't be a **minute**.*

> Say **min**-it.

in a minute very soon: *I'll wash the dishes **in a minute**, but first I have to feed the dog.*

mirror

a flat piece of glass with a silver back, so that when you look at it you can see yourself: *My mum carries a little **mirror** in her handbag, so that she can look at herself when she puts on her make-up.*

mischief

behaviour that causes trouble to other people; naughty behaviour by children: *That boy is always up to some **mischief**. Keep out of **mischief** while I am out shopping.*

mischievous
naughty in a way that sometimes makes people laugh: *Some of the children played a **mischievous** trick on Mr Lee.*

miserable
very unhappy: *I felt very **miserable** when I lost my little cat.*

Miss
a title you use before the name of a girl or woman who is not married: *Our teacher is called **Miss** Walker. Good morning, **Miss** Lee!*

miss
1 to fail to hit something, or catch something, or score a goal: *Joe's first arrow **missed** the target. The man aimed his gun at the policeman, but he **missed**. Tim threw me the ball but I **missed** it. Pete kicked the ball hard but he **missed** the goal. That stone you threw only just **missed** my head!* **2** to arrive too late for something: *I **missed** the bus this morning. The film has already begun — you've **missed** the first ten minutes.* **3** not to hear or see something: *Sorry, I **missed** what you said. Our house is easy to find — you can't **miss** its yellow door.* **4** to feel sad because someone or something is no longer there: *You'll **miss** your friends when you move to Kuala Lumpur. I **missed** my dog when we went on holiday without him.* **5** not to go to something: *I'll have to **miss** my English lesson tomorrow as I'm going to the dentist.* **6** not to meet: *We **missed** you in the crowd.*

> Meaning 1: the opposite is **hit**.

missing
1 not able to be found: *Our cat has been **missing** for two days. I haven't found my **missing** earring yet.* **2** not attached anymore: *Your shirt has a button **missing**.*

mistake
something that is not correct: *I made a few spelling **mistakes** in my composition. There are no **mistakes** in your sums. Dad got on the wrong train by **mistake**. I took Colin's schoolbag by **mistake** — it looks so like mine.*

mistake
1 to be wrong about something: *My aunt **mistook** the date and arrived to stay with us a week too early.* **2** to think that one person or thing is another: *I often **mistake** Bob for his brother. Christina **mistook** my coat for hers because they look similar.*

> mistook, mistaking, has mistaken

mistaken
wrong: *You are **mistaken** if you think you can pass your exams without doing any work.*

mistook
see **mistake**: *I **mistook** your umbrella for mine because they look the same.*

mistress
1 a woman who has a servant: *The maid was frightened of her **mistress** at first.* **2** a woman who owns a dog: *This dog will obey no one but his **mistress**.* **3** a female teacher: *Our games **mistress** is very nice.*

mix
to stir or shake things together: *If you **mix** red paint with white paint you'll get pink paint. Mum **mixed** flour, salt, milk and eggs to make pancakes.*

model

a small copy of something: *The teacher showed us a **model** of an old sailing ship. Steven is making a **model** aeroplane.*

modern
belonging to the present time; new: *Many children are better than their parents at using **modern** machines such as computers.*

> The opposite is **ancient**.

moment
1 a very short time: *Wait a **moment**. I saw Tracy for a **moment** in the crowd, and then she disappeared.* **2** a certain point in time: *The **moment** Mum left, the telephone rang.*

at the moment now: *I'm very busy **at the moment**, but I'll help you with your homework later.*

in a moment very soon: *I'll be ready **in a moment**.*

Monday
the second day of the week; the day following Sunday: *I enjoyed the weekend so much that I didn't want to go back to school on **Monday**.*

money
coins or bank-notes that you use for paying for things: *How much **money** have you got left? Could you lend me some **money** for the bus?*

*Tim spends all his pocket **money** on sweets.*

monk
a man who serves God by praying, and lives together with other monks, away from other people: ***Monks** make a promise to God not to possess any wealth.*

monkey
an animal that looks quite like a small human being, with long arms and legs and a very long tail: *A **monkey** can climb trees very well and swing from branch to branch.*

monster
any great big ugly creature that you hear about in stories: *We watched a film about a sea-**monster** that came out of the sea and frightened everyone.*

month
one of the twelve divisions of the year: *January is the first **month** of the year. The summer holidays start in two **months'** time.*

monthly
happening once a month: *A **monthly** magazine is a magazine that is published once a month.*

mood
a person's feelings or temper at a certain time: *My dad is usually in a good **mood** at the weekends. Richard is in a bad **mood** today because his parents won't allow him to go to the football match.*

moon
the large shining object that you see in the sky at night, that moves round the Earth, and changes shape as the nights pass: *The **moon** hasn't got any light of its own — it looks bright because the sun is shining on it. Every four weeks there is a full **moon**, when the **moon** looks like a silver ball.*

mop
an object with a long handle and some soft material at the end, that you use for wiping floors: *Some **mops** have a sponge at the end, with a lever for squeezing it.*

mop
1 to wipe with a mop: *Mum **mopped** the kitchen floor.* **2** to wipe with a cloth or towel: *The boxer **mopped** the sweat from his face. Laura **mopped** up the spilt tea with her handkerchief.*

> mopped, mopping, has mopped

more
1 a greater number or amount of something: *Mike has **more** records than I have. Sarah drank **more** lemonade than I did. Take some of my ice-cream because I had **more** than you did. I've eaten **more** today than I usually do.* **2** an extra amount: *Take a few **more** biscuits. Would you like any **more** tea? There isn't enough paper — I'll need some **more**.* **3** you use **more** to compare people or things: *Paul is **more** hardworking than his brother. The sofa is **more** comfortable than the chair. These exams are **more** difficult than the exams last term. Give this heavy bag to Dad — he can carry it **more** easily than you can.* **4** again: *Let's listen to this record once **more**.*

> - Meaning 1: the opposite is **less** or **fewer**.
> - Meaning 3: the opposite is **less**.

morning
the part of the day before midday: *Jenny rang me at eight o'clock in the **morning**. We don't have to go to school tomorrow **morning** — it's Saturday.*

mosque

a building where people go to pray to God: *Many **mosques** have tall narrow towers, and roofs that are shaped like half a ball.*

> Say **mosk**.

mosquito

a small insect that bites people or animals and sucks their blood: ***Mosquitoes** often bite people at night when they are asleep.*

> - Say mos-**kee**-toe.
> - Many **mosquitoes** or **mosquitos**

most
1 nearly all: ***Most** of my friends live near me. I spent **most** of the evening doing my home-*

*work. **Most** children love going to the zoo.* **2** the greatest amount or number: *Which of you has read the **most** books? I ate lots of jelly, but Jim ate more and Joe ate the **most**. I like badminton and I like cycling, but I like swimming **most** of all.* **3** more than all the others: *Lucy is the **most** helpful girl in this class. This is the **most** interesting book that I've ever read.*

Meanings 2 and 3: the opposite is **least**.

moth
an insect with large grey or brown wings, that looks like a butterfly: *Some **moths** feed on wool, and eat holes in your clothes.*

mother
a female parent: *I call my **mother** 'Mum' or 'Mummy'.*

motor
the part of a machine or vehicle that makes it work; an engine: *The **motor** of a car needs petrol to make it work. A washing-machine has an electric **motor**.*

motorbike or **motorcycle**
a small motor vehicle with two wheels: *There are special spaces in the street for parking **motorcycles**. My brother is learning to ride a **motorbike**.*

motorboat
a boat that has a small engine: *We went to the island in a **motorboat**.*

motorist
a person who drives a car: ***Motorists** must look out for pedestrians who are crossing the road.*

motorway
a wide road with two or three lanes in each direction on which motor vehicles can travel from city to city: *Drivers are not allowed to turn on the **motorway**, because it is too dangerous.*

mountain
a very high hill: *Some **mountains** are very steep and difficult to climb. Mount Everest is the highest **mountain** in the world.*

mountaineer
a person who can climb the steep sides of mountains: *Edmund Hillary and Tenzing were the first **mountaineers** to reach the top of Mount Everest.*

mouse
a small animal with grey or white fur and a long tail: *A **mouse** eats all kinds of seeds and fruit. Some **mice** live in people's houses and some live in fields. A **mouse** squeaks when it is frightened.*

Lots of **mice**

moustache
the hair that grows on a man's upper lip: *Mr Watson has grown a **moustache**.*

Say mus-**tash**.

mouth
the opening below your nose, where your teeth and your tongue are: *What have you got in your **mouth**? Don't talk with your **mouth** full. The dog was carrying a bone in its **mouth**.*

move
1 to change the position of something; to change your position; to go from one place to another: *David was **moving** his arms. Don't **move** — stand still! The policeman said: 'You are not allowed to park here — please **move** your car.' The ship **moved** slowly out of the harbour.* **2** to go and live in a different home: *My granny **moved** into the flat next to ours when our neighbours **moved** out.*

moved, moving, has moved

move house to go and live in a different home: *The Smith family have **moved house** and now live in another part of the city.*

movement
moving; an action: *Waving is a **movement** you make with your hand.*

movie
a film: *Let's go to a **movie**. Have you seen any good **movies** lately? Who is your favourite **movie** star?*

mow
to cut grass: *The farmer was **mowing** the meadow.*

- Rhymes with **low**.
- mowed, mowing, has mown

Mr
a title used before a man's name: *Good morning, **Mr** Jones. We have a new teacher called **Mr** Walker.*

Mrs

a title used before a married woman's name: *Hello, **Mrs** Smith! Where is **Mrs** Stewart?*

much

1 a lot: *I don't like **much** sugar in my tea. I can't eat **much** because I'm not hungry. Michael didn't tell me **much** about his new school. I don't watch **much** television.* **2** far; a lot: *My new bicycle is **much** better than my old one. It's **much** too late to go to the zoo now — it's getting dark.* **3** a certain amount: *How **much** sugar do you take in your tea? How **much** does this bar of chocolate cost? How **much** is this bar of chocolate? That's far too **much**. I can't help you just now — I've too **much** work to do. Thank you very **much**.*

Meaning 1: much, more, most

mud

soft wet earth: *My shoes were covered in **mud**.*

muddy

covered in mud; containing mud: *Please take off your **muddy** boots. This pond is too **muddy** — you can't swim in there.*

mug

a large, deep cup: *You don't need a saucer with a **mug**. We usually drink coffee out of **mugs**.*

multiply

to add a number to itself a certain number of times: *4 **multiplied** by 3, or 4 × 3, equals 12: If you **multiply** four by three you get twelve.*

multiplies, multiplied, multiplying, has multiplied

mum or mummy

a name used by children for their mother: *Good morning, **Mum**! My **mum** is picking me up from school today. Where's **Mummy**?*

mumps

a disease that causes a painful swelling at each side of your face: *When Liz got **mumps**, a lot of the other children caught it from her.*

murder

to kill someone, not by accident: *The man who **murdered** his wife was sent to prison for fifty years.*

muscle

one of the pieces of flesh that are attached to the bones inside your body, and make your body move: *Boxers do special exercises to make their **muscles** strong.*

museum

a place where a lot of interesting and valuable things are put on show for people to look at: *On Sunday we went to a **museum** where we saw all kinds of old machines and vehicles.*

Say mew-**zee**-um.

mushroom

a special kind of plant that grows very quickly, with a short thick stem, and a top part like an umbrella: *You can eat some kinds of **mushroom**, but other kinds are poisonous. We had **mushroom** soup for lunch.*

music

sounds that are made by people playing instruments or singing: *I enjoy listening to pop **music**. We learn a lot of songs in our **music** lessons.*

musical

1 connected with music: *A piano is a **musical** instrument.* **2** good at music: *John is **musical** — he plays the violin in the school orchestra.*

musician

a person who plays an instrument well: *Many **musicians** teach music or play in an orchestra.*

must

1 you use **must** to say something is necessary: *You **must** hurry if you want to catch that bus. You **must** come home before six o'clock, or I'll be very angry with you.* **2** you use **must** to say something is probably happening: *You **must** be tired after your long journey. I **must** have left my keys at home.*

mutton

the meat of a sheep: *I don't like roast **mutton** or **mutton** stew.*

my

belonging to me: *I can make **my** own bed. This is **my** book, not yours. **My** leg is hurting.*

myself

1 I use **myself** when I do something to me or for me: *I looked at **myself** in the mirror. I hurt **myself** when I fell off my bike. I bought **myself** a big ice-cream.* **2** without help: *I can make my bed **myself**. I did this drawing **myself**.*

mystery

something that cannot be explained: *It's a **mystery** how the robbers got into the bank without being noticed.*

- Say **mis**-te-ri.
- A lot of **mysteries**

Nn

nail
1 a thin, pointed piece of metal that you can hit into wood or into a wall with a hammer: *Anna hammered a **nail** into the wall and hung a picture on it.* 2 the hard stuff that grows over the ends of your fingers and toes: *I can cut my finger**nails** myself. It's difficult to cut the **nails** on your right hand. Your toe**nails** need cutting.*

nail

to fasten something with nails: *Dad **nailed** a piece of wood across the door of the shed to keep it closed.*

naked
not wearing any clothes; bare: *There were some **naked** little children running about on the beach.*

name
a word by which a person, animal, place or thing is called: *What's your **name**? My **name** is Yvonne. What's the **name** of this street?*

name
1 to give a name to someone or something: *I **named** my dog Nicky. The baby is **named** Paul after his grandfather.* 2 to say the name of: ***Name** the capital city of Japan.*

named, naming, has named

nap
a short sleep: *My granny usually has a **nap** on the sofa in the afternoons.*

narrow
not wide; being only a small distance from side to side: *The lane is too **narrow** for two cars to pass each other. The children crept through a **narrow** passage into the cave.*

The opposite is **wide** or **broad**.

nasty
1 not pleasant; horrible: *What a **nasty** smell!* 2 unfriendly, mean: *Don't be so **nasty** to me!*

natural
1 not surprising; as you would expect: *It's quite **natural** to hate going to the dentist. It is **natural** for young children to copy older children.* 2 made by nature; not made by people: *Fruit and vegetables are **natural** foods.*

nature
1 everything in the world that was not made by people; all animals and plants: *We should protect **nature**, not damage it.* 2 the kind of person you are: *Mary is a nice girl — she has a kind **nature**.*

naughty
behaving badly; not obedient: *You **naughty** boy — stop hitting your little sister! Claire was punished for being **naughty**. The dog was very **naughty** — he ate all the sausages that were on the table.*

naughty, naughtier, naughtiest

near
at a short distance from somewhere; close to somewhere: *My desk is **near** the window. The railway station is quite **near** — you haven't got far to walk.*

The opposite is **far**.

nearly
almost; not quite: *It's **nearly** five o'clock. I'm **nearly** eight years old. We haven't got far to go now — we're **nearly** there.*

neat
very tidy: *Helen folded her clothes and put them in a **neat** pile. Simon has **neat** handwriting.*

The opposite is **untidy**.

necessary
needed; important: *It's **necessary** for you to learn English, so that you can speak it well when you are grown up. It is **necessary** to have a passport when you want to go abroad.*

neck
the part of you that joins your head to your

body: *Joanna is wearing a scarf round her **neck**. A giraffe has a very long **neck**.*

necklace

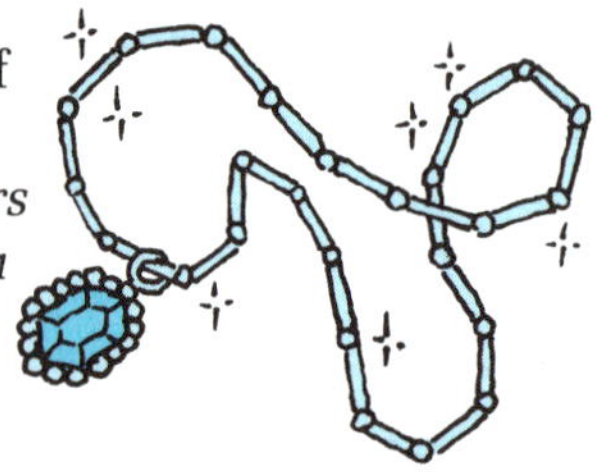

a chain or a string of beads that you wear round your neck: *Mrs Johnson is wearing a gold **necklace**.*

necktie

an American word for a tie: *Mr Walker is wearing a blue **necktie**.*

need

1 to want something; to be unable to do without something: *Plants **need** water and light to grow. I **need** a new ruler because my old one is broken. Do you **need** any help with your homework? Your hair is too long — it **needs** to be cut. Your bedroom **needs** tidying.* **2** to have to do something: *You **need** to work hard if you want to pass your exams. I don't **need** to get up early tomorrow.*

need not or **needn't** not to need to; not to have to: *You **needn't** worry about your exam — I'm sure you'll pass it easily.*

need

1 something necessary; something you must have: *Food is one of our main **needs**.* **2** reason: *There's no **need** to hurry — there's still plenty of time.*

needle

1 a small, very thin, sharp piece of steel, with a hole for thread, that is used for sewing: *I need a **needle** and thread to sew on the button.* **2** a thin stick, made of metal or plastic, that is used for knitting: *You knit with a pair of knitting-**needles**.* **3** a very thin, sharp, dark-green leaf like a needle, from a fir-tree or pine-tree: *The path through the forest was covered with pine-**needles**.*

neigh

to make the cry of a horse: *The foal **neighed** because it was frightened.*

Rhymes with **lay**.

neighbour

someone who lives next to you, or near you: *Our next-door **neighbours** are very friendly people.*

Say **nay**-ber.

neither

not the one, nor the other, of two people or things: ***Neither** of the twins was at school today. **Neither** Mary nor Molly was at school. 'Would you like tea or coffee?' '**Neither**, thank you.'*

nephew

the son of your brother or sister: *My cousin Joe is my parents' **nephew**, and his sister Jane is their niece. My brother and I are my uncle's **nephews**.*

nervous

worried; anxious; frightened: *Emma felt very **nervous** on her first day at the new school. I'm **nervous** about the maths exam. Peter was rather **nervous** about flying because he had never been in an aeroplane before.*

nest

1 a comfortable home made of twigs and grass that birds build to lay their eggs in: *A pair of swallows are building a **nest** under the edge of our roof.* **2** the home that a group of insects build to live in: *Wild bees, wasps and ants live in **nests**.*

net

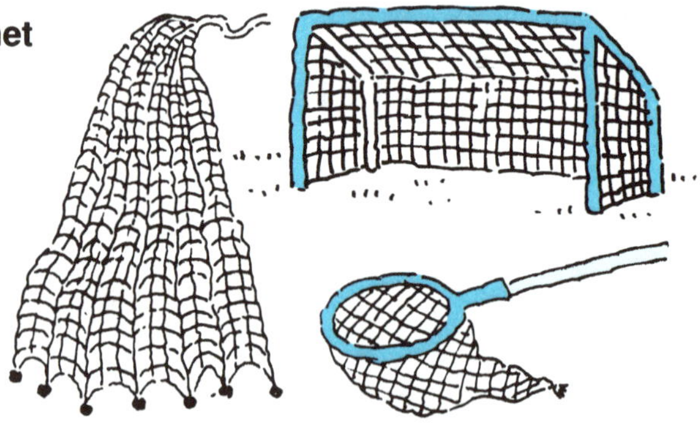

a material made of pieces of thread or string that are joined together with knots; a piece of this material for a special use: *Fishermen use large fishing-**nets** to catch fish. A tennis court is divided into two halves by a **net**. Steve kicked the football into the **net**.*

never

not ever; at no time: *I've **never** seen a real koala. David has **never** been to the cinema. I **never** go to bed without brushing my teeth. I'll **never** finish these sums.*

new

1 just made; just bought; not used or worn before: *We all admired Mum's **new** dress. Paul's **new** bicycle is faster than his old one.* **2** different: *Mr Jones has a **new** job. We have a **new** English teacher.* **3** just arrived: *You must look after the **new** pupils.*

The opposite is **old**.

news

1 a report about recent events: *We watched the 7 o'clock **news** on television. You can hear the **news** at 6 o'clock.* **2** recent information: *Is there any **news** from your friend in America? Have you heard the **news** about the bank robbery?*

newsagent

a person who has a shop that sells newspapers and magazines: *Please get me today's newspaper from the **newsagent's** at the corner.*

newspaper

a set of printed sheets containing news, that are folded, not fastened, together: ***Newspapers** that are published every day from Monday to Saturday are called 'daily **newspapers**'.*

Also called a **paper**.

newsvendor

a person who has a shop or a stall that sells newspapers: *Dad bought a copy of the Straits Times from the **newsvendor** at the station.*

next

1 following straight after this one: ***Next** Sunday we'll go to the zoo. This shop will be closed for the **next** two weeks. The doctor came out of his room and called '**Next** patient, please!'* **2** coming straight after: *Peter arrived first and Kenneth came **next**.* **3** nearest: *Turn left at the **next** junction. Please speak quietly — the baby is asleep in the **next** room.*

next door in the next flat or house: *Our granny lives **next door** to us.*

next to beside someone or something: *Linda sits **next to** me in the classroom. Linda's desk is **next to** mine. The playground is **next to** the school.*

nib

the pointed metal part of a fountain pen, from which the ink flows: *The **nib** of my pen broke when I dropped it.*

nice

1 pleasant: *Jenny is a very **nice** girl. Have a **nice** day! It's been **nice** meeting you.* **2** pretty; attractive: *What a **nice** dress! Your hair looks **nice**.* **3** good to eat: *These biscuits are **nice**.* **4** kind: *It was very **nice** of you to give me a birthday present.*

nice, nicer, nicest

nickname

a special short or funny name for someone: *Christopher's **nickname** is 'Toffee'. All his friends call him by his **nickname**.*

niece

the daughter of your brother or sister: *My cousin Rose is my parents' **niece**. My sister and I are our aunt's **nieces**.*

night

1 the period of time when it is dark: *Some animals sleep during the day and go out hunting at **night**. It rained all **night**.* **2** late evening: *My parents often go out on Saturday **nights**.*

Meaning 1: the opposite is **day**.

last night the night before today: *I didn't sleep well **last night**.*

You say **last night**, not **yesterday night**.

nightmare

a frightening dream: *Last night I had a terrible **nightmare** about a tiger attacking me.*

nine

1 the number 9: *Five and four is **nine**.* **2** 9 in number: *Paul is **nine** years old.*

nineteen

1 the number 19: *Ten and nine is nineteen.* **2** 19 in number: *My eldest sister is **nineteen** years old.*

ninety

1 the number 90: *Nine times ten is **ninety**.* **2** 90 in number: *One and a half hours are **ninety** minutes.*

no

1 the opposite of **yes**: *'Would you like some more tea?' '**No**, thank you.' 'Do you like football?' '**No**, I don't.' 'Can you come this afternoon?' '**No**, I can't — I'm very busy.' 'Have you done your homework?' '**No**, I haven't — have you done yours?' '**No**, not yet.'* **2** not any: *I have **no** money on me at present. There's **no** rice left. There were **no** pupils absent today.* **3** not; not at all: *Today's weather is **no** better than yesterday's — it's still raining.* **4** not allowed: *In the office there was a notice saying '**No** smoking'. '**No** running in the corridors!' shouted the teacher.*

no longer not any more: *Our dog is two years old — she's **no longer** a puppy.*

no-one

nobody: ***No-one** noticed that the cat had gone. **No-one** knows where the treasure is hidden.*

nobody

not anyone; no-one: *There is **nobody** in the classroom — where have all the children gone? **Nobody** likes going to the dentist.*

nod

to move your head quickly up and down to show that you agree: *You **nod** your head when you mean 'yes'. We asked the little boy if he'd like a piece of chocolate, and he **nodded**.*

> nodded, nodding, has nodded

noise

1 a sound: *I heard a strange **noise** outside. What was that funny **noise**?* **2** a loud sound that may annoy you or disturb you: *The baby can't sleep because you're making such a **noise**. Stop that **noise**! You can hear the **noise** of the traffic when the windows are open.*

noisy

making a loud noise: *Don't be so **noisy**, children!*

> - The opposite is **quiet**.
> - noisy, noisier, noisiest

none

not one; not any: *'How many biscuits have you eaten?' '**None**.' 'Is there some more tea?' 'No, there's **none** left.' **None** of the children knew the correct answer.*

> The opposite is **all**.

nonsense

foolish words or actions; something that is stupid; something that has no meaning: *Two and two doesn't make five — that's **nonsense**! You're talking **nonsense**. What **nonsense**!*

noodle

a long, thin strip made with flour, eggs and water: *We sometimes have fried **noodles** with chicken.*

noon

twelve o'clock in the middle of the day: *We have a break for lunch at **noon**.*

nor

and also not: *I'm not going, **nor** is Sarah. My sister likes neither tea **nor** coffee. Some people can neither read **nor** write.*

north

the direction to your left when you face the rising sun: *The wind is blowing from the **north**. A cold **north** wind is blowing. Mr Brown used to live in the **north** of England. Mr Kim comes from **North** Korea.*

nose

1 the part of your face that you use for breathing and smelling: *I had to hold my **nose** because of the nasty smell. A dog has a wet **nose**.* **2** the ability to smell: *Dogs have good **noses** — they can smell things from a long distance away.*

nostril

one of the two openings in your nose: *Gorillas have flat noses with large **nostrils**.*

not

a word that you use to say the opposite of something: *'Are you hungry?' 'No, I'm **not** hungry.' That's **not** true! Mum told me **not** to be late.*

note

1 a short letter; a few words written down: *Clare sent me a **note** to say she couldn't come to the party. Mum left a **note** saying she had gone shopping. Let me make a **note** of your address.* **2** a small piece of printed paper that is used as money: *Can you change a five-dollar **note** for single dollars? Coins and bank-*

***notes** are called cash.* **3** a sound in music that you play or sing: *When you play a scale, you play each **note** one after the other, going up or down.*

notebook

a small, blank book that you can write notes in: *I have a **notebook** in which I write down the things I have to do.*

nothing

no thing; not anything: *You get bored when you have **nothing** to do. Is there **nothing** else we can do to help you? **Nothing** is nicer than a quiet evening at home with a good book to read.*

notice

1 an announcement that gives information about something: *There was a **notice** on the door saying 'Private. Do not enter'. The head-master put a **notice** with the dates of the holidays on the **notice**board in the corridor.* **2** attention that you give to what is happening or what someone is saying or doing: *Take no **notice** of Jack — he's just showing off. The teacher asked Tom to stop talking, but he took no **notice** of her.*

notice

to see; to hear; to observe: *I suddenly **noticed** that Sarah had left. I didn't **notice** you coming in. Katie **noticed** a strange noise coming from the fridge.*

noticed, noticing, has noticed

November

the eleventh month of the year.

now

1 at present; at this moment: *We used to live in Thailand but we **now** live in Singapore. I can hear Dad coming **now**. Let's have lunch **now**.* **2** because of something: ***Now** that Michael has left school, he will have to find a job.* **3** you often use **now** when you tell people what to do: *Well **now**, I'll give you some advice. Stop talking, **now**. Be careful, **now**. There **now**, don't cry. **Now**, **now**, don't be rude.*

just now a moment ago: *'Where is Sue?' 'I saw her in the garden **just now**.'*

nowadays

at the present time: *It doesn't take very long to fly to Australia **nowadays**.*

nowhere

not anywhere: *The missing book was **nowhere** to be found. Some poor people have no money and **nowhere** to live. 'Where are you going tonight?' '**Nowhere** — I'm staying here.'*

number

1 a name of a figure: *Seven is my lucky **number**. Add up the following **numbers** — 3, 5, 8 and 14. What is your telephone **number**? I took a **number** 12 bus.* **2** a quantity of things or people: *Steve has a large **number** of records. There were a small **number** of children in the play-ground.*

numeral

a figure that you use to write a number: *1, 2, 3, 4, 5 are called 'Arabic' **numerals** and I, II, III, IV, V are called 'Roman' **numerals**.*

nun

a woman who serves God by praying and helping other people, and lives together with other nuns: ***Nuns** promise God not to possess any wealth and not to get married.*

nurse

a person whose job is to care for ill and injured people in hospital: *A **nurse** has to look after a lot of patients. **Nurse** Kelly works in the children's ward. Miss Kim is training to be a **nurse**.*

nursery

1 a place where very young children are looked after while their mothers are at work: *Mrs Kay takes little Peter to the **nursery** every morning before she goes to work.* **2** a play-room or bedroom for a very young child: *They painted the **nursery** a bright blue for their little son.*

Many **nurseries**

nursery rhyme short poem for young children: *'Jack and Jill went up the hill' is an old **nursery rhyme**.*

nut

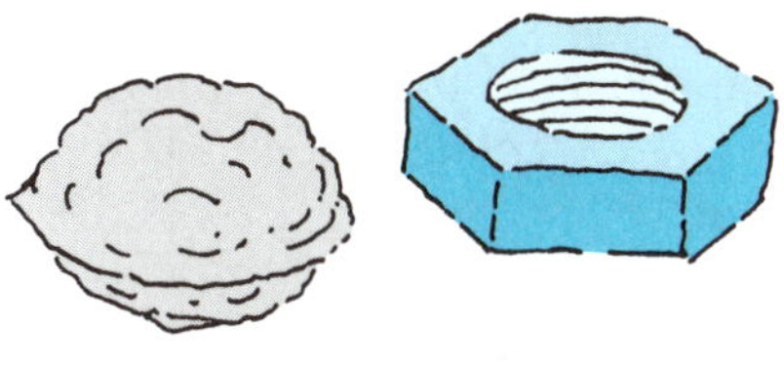

1 a hard fruit that grows in a very hard shell: *There are many kinds of **nuts**, such as walnuts and coconuts.* **2** a small round piece of metal with a hole through it that is screwed on to the end of a bolt: ***Nuts** and bolts are used to hold pieces of wood or metal together.*

oak
a large tree with hard wood: *The nut of an* ***oak*** *tree is oval in shape and is called an 'acorn'.* ***Oak*** *wood is used for making furniture.*

oar
a long piece of wood with a flat end, for rowing a boat with: *A rowing-boat has two* ***oars****, one fixed to each side.*

oats
a cereal plant: *Farmers in Britain grow wheat and* ***oats****. Horses eat* ***oats****.*

obedient
doing what you are told to do: *I hope you are all* ***obedient*** *children and always do what your parents tell you.*

obey
to do what you are told to do: *You must* ***obey*** *your teacher. The soldiers* ***obeyed*** *the order to shoot. Everybody who takes part in a game has to* ***obey*** *the rules.*

The opposite is **disobey**.

object
something that is not alive; a thing: *There were pencils, pens, rulers, rubbers, pins and many other small* ***objects*** *in the drawer.*

object
to dislike something; to disagree with something: *Bob* ***objected*** *to going to bed early.*

oblong
a shape that has two long sides and two short sides: *A chocolate bar and a ruler are both* ***oblong****.*

observe
1 to watch carefully: *Young children learn by* ***observing*** *older children. Have you ever* ***observed*** *an ant carrying a heavy load to its nest?* **2** to notice: *None of the children* ***observed*** *the teacher coming quietly into the room.*

observed, observing, has observed

obtain
to get: *More information about the accident can be* ***obtained*** *from the police.*

occupation
a job: *What is Mr Miller's* ***occupation****? Is he a doctor?*

occupy
1 to fill up space: *A large table is* ***occupying*** *the centre of the room.* **2** to use: *Is anyone* ***occupying*** *the seat next to you? All the toilets are* ***occupied****.* **3** to live in a place: *Our old flat is now* ***occupied*** *by a small family.* **4** to be busy doing something: *The children* ***occupied*** *themselves during the long journey by telling funny stories.*

occupies, occupied, occupying, has occupied

ocean
one of the five very large areas of sea that cover most of the earth's surface: *The five* ***oceans*** *are called the Atlantic, Pacific, Indian, Arctic and Antarctic.*

Say **o**-shen.

October
the tenth month of the year.

octopus

a sea creature with a round body and eight long, thin legs: ***Octopuses*** *live at the bottom of the sea. Have you ever eaten* ***octopus****?*

odd
1 unusual; strange: *That cloud is an* ***odd*** *shape — it looks like a kangaroo. It's* ***odd*** *that I never noticed that building before — I walk past it every day.* **2** various; different: *Michael earns some money by doing* ***odd*** *jobs for old people.* **3** not matching; not in a pair: *Peter is wearing* ***odd*** *socks — one brown and one black.*
odd number a number that is not able to be divided by 2: *1, 3, 5, 7 and 9 are* ***odd numbers****.*

The opposite is an **even number**.

of
1 belonging to someone or something; belonging to a group: *Amy is a friend* ***of*** *mine. Amy is one* ***of*** *my friends. The front door* ***of***

*our house is yellow. Two **of** the buttons are missing from this shirt.* **2** showing: *This is a picture **of** my parents.* **3** containing: *I gave my mum a box **of** chocolates for her birthday. Bob drank a whole bottle **of** lemonade. Would you like a cup **of** tea?* **4** you use **of** when you are talking about amounts or numbers: *Mum bought two kilos **of** rice. Sue has five pairs **of** shoes. Jeff has a large collection **of** stamps.* **5** you use **of** to describe actions: *The stealing **of** goods is called theft.* **6** you use **of** when you say the date: *Today is the first **of** April.* **7** you use of to show a cause: *The refugees died **of** hunger.* **8** about: *The teacher read us the story **of** Snow White.*

of course yes; certainly: *'Can you ride a bicycle?' '**Of course** I can!' 'Please would you open the door for me?' '**Of course**.'*

off

1 away from something: *Joe fell **off** his chair. Take your elbows **off** the table. The bus stopped and we got **off**. We got **off** the bus in the city centre. The bus drove **off** just before we reached the bus stop. Goodbye — I'm **off** to school now! Take your shoes **off**. I took the lid **off** the jar.* **2** not switched on: *Switch **off** the light. Have you turned **off** the fan? Is the television **off**?* **3** not at work: *Dad is taking tomorrow **off**. Mr Smith is **off** today.*

offer

to say that you are ready to give something or do something: *The boy **offered** the old lady his seat on the bus. Mum **offered** the guests tea and cakes. Pam **offered** to look after our cat while we were on holiday.*

office

1 a building or a set of rooms where a business is carried on: *The company's **offices** are in Hong Kong. My dad works in a newspaper **office**.* **2** a room where a certain person works: *Please take this note to the headmaster's **office**.*

officer

a person who has an important job in the army or the police: *Mike's father is a police **officer**.*

often

1 many times: *In summer we **often** go to the beach. You should take the dog for a walk more **often**.* **2** happening a certain number of times: *'How **often** do you go to the hair-dresser's?' 'I go once a month.'*

- Same as **frequently**.
- Meaning 1: the opposite is **seldom**.

oil

1 a liquid fat that comes from plants and is used for cooking: *Mum uses groundnut **oil** for frying food.* **2** a thick liquid that comes out of the ground and is used as a fuel, or to put on machines: *I put some **oil** on my bicycle to make it run better.*

oil palm a palm tree that has a fruit containing yellow palm oil: ***Oil palms** grow in hot countries.*

OK or okay

1 yes; all right: *'Will you come shopping with me?' '**OK**.'* **2** all right: *'Does this dress look **okay**?' 'No, it's a bit dirty.' 'Do you feel **okay**?' 'Yes, just a bit tired.' Is it **okay** if I come at five o'clock?*

old

1 having lived for many years: *You must always be polite to **old** people. When you grow **old**, your hair goes white. **Old** trees have thick trunks.* **2** having been made a long time ago: *This is a valuable **old** necklace — it belonged to my grand-mother.* **3** no longer useful: *I got a new watch because my **old** one didn't work any more. Mum threw away her **old** shoes.* **4** having a certain age: *'How **old** are you?' 'I am eight years **old**.'*

- Meaning 1: the opposite is **young**.
- Meanings 2 and 3: the opposite is **new**.
- Meaning 2: same as **ancient**.

on

1 touching something; covering something; sticking to something; supported by something: *Your pencil is lying **on** the desk. I am sitting **on** a chair. There's a fly **on** the wall. Put **on** your jacket. Leave your coat **on**. Remember to put the lid back **on** the jar. There's a dirty mark **on** your skirt.* **2** hanging from: *My jacket is hanging **on** a hook.* **3** in or into a vehicle: *There were a lot of people **on** the bus. Dad got **on** the wrong train.* **4** during a certain day: *We went to see my granny **on** Saturday. My aunt arrived **on** Sunday evening. I was born **on** 24th February.* **5** about: *Rachel has a book **on** horses. A policeman gave us a talk **on** road safety.* **6** you use **on** with **telephone**, **television** and **radio**: *I spoke to John **on** the telephone. We watched a good film **on** television last night.*

My father is listening to a concert ***on*** *the radio.* **7** being carried by someone: *I have no money* ***on*** *me at present.* **8** supported by a part of your body: *Jenny was standing* ***on*** *one leg. The patient lay* ***on*** *his back.* **9** in or into the working position: *Would you switch* ***on*** *the light, please? I switched* ***on*** *the television. Is the TV still* ***on****?* **10** continuing without stopping; continuing after a stop: *You mustn't go* ***on*** *talking after I've told you to stop. We'll go* ***on*** *with the game after lunch. The teacher stopped reading, but we all shouted "Please go* ***on****!"*

and so on and more of the same kind of thing: *When you have influenza, you have a headache, a cough, a cold, a sore throat* ***and so on****.*

on and on continuing for a long time: *The headmaster's talk went* ***on and on****.*

on fire burning: *The house is* ***on fire****!*

on time at the correct time: *Please try to arrive* ***on time****.*

once

1 one time: *I've been abroad only* ***once****. Mike has his hair cut* ***once*** *a month.* **2** at some time in the past: *Singapore was* ***once*** *ruled by Britain.* **3** as soon as; when: ***Once*** *you understand the rules, the game is very easy.*

at once **1** immediately: *My dog always comes* ***at once*** *when I call him.* **2** at the same time: *I can't hear any of you if you all talk* ***at once****.*

once upon a time used at the beginning of a fairy-tale, meaning a long time ago: ***Once upon a time****, in a far country, there lived a beautiful princess.*

one

1 the number 1: ***One*** *and* ***one*** *is two.* **2** 1 in number: *The baby is* ***one*** *year old today. There is only* ***one*** *biscuit left. A crowd is a large number of people all together in* ***one*** *place.* **3** a thing or person: *Here's my right shoe, but where's the left* ***one****? Do you like these red apples, or do you prefer the green* ***ones****? Mum is the tidy* ***one*** *in our family.* **4** a thing or person from a group: *Janet borrowed* ***one*** *of my crayons. Alan is* ***one*** *of my friends.*

one by one one after the other: ***One by one****, the children began to arrive at the party. The doctor examined the children* ***one by one****.*

one another each other: *We are not allowed to talk to* ***one another*** *during lessons.*

onion

a large round vegetable that grows underground: ***Onions*** *have a very strong smell, and when you cut them, tears come into your eyes.*

only

1 no more than: *There is* ***only*** *one piece of chocolate left. The walk to the station will* ***only*** *take five minutes. I've got two sisters but* ***only*** *one brother. It's* ***only*** *three o'clock — we've got plenty of time.* **2** without brothers or sisters: *Paul is an* ***only*** *child.* **3** no others: ***Only*** *the headmaster has a key to this cupboard. This is the* ***only*** *photograph I have of my aunt. Kate was the* ***only*** *one to get full marks in the test.* **4** just; and nothing else: *I* ***only*** *saw Jenny — I didn't talk to her. Tony is* ***only*** *interested in football and nothing else.*

open

1 not shut: *All the doors and windows were* ***open****. Don't leave the door* ***open****. A bee flew in through the* ***open*** *window.* **2** ready for business or use: *The shop is* ***open*** *until half past five. Is the museum* ***open*** *on Sundays?*

The opposite is **closed** or **shut**.

open-air

outside: *We went to an* ***open-air*** *concert in the park.*

open

1 to make open: *Please could you* ***open*** *the door? Who* ***opened*** *this packet of biscuits?* **2** to become ready for business or use: *The restaurant* ***opens*** *at six o'clock in the evening. When does the zoo* ***open****? A new shop is* ***opening*** *next week. The* ***opening*** *hours of the bank are from 9 o'clock in the morning till 6 o'clock in the evening.*

The opposite is **close** or **shut**.

opener

a tool that is used to open something: *I opened the tin of beans with a tin-****opener****. May I borrow your bottle-****opener****?*

operate

1 to work: *The washing-machine isn't* ***operating*** *properly. I don't know how to* ***operate*** *this machine.* **2** to cut open a person's body to mend a damaged part: *The doctors* ***operated*** *on the patient's heart.*

operated, operating, has operated

operator

1 a person whose job is to connect people by telephone: *Ask the* ***operator*** *to connect you to* *this number.* **2** a person whose job is to work a machine: *My brother is training to be a computer-**operator**.*

opposite
1 facing: *A large block of flats has been built **opposite** our school. Who lives in the house **opposite**? Richard's house is **opposite** to mine. Jack is sitting **opposite** Jean.* **2** across on the other side: *I saw Susan on the **opposite** side of the road.* **3** completely different: *The two boys walked off in **opposite** directions.*

opposite
something that is completely different: *Bad is the **opposite** of good.*

or
1 you use **or** to say what else is possible: *Shall we go to the zoo **or** to the museum? Is that your parcel **or** mine?* **2** because if you don't: *Hurry up, **or** you'll be late.*

orange
1 a round, juicy fruit with a thick skin that is between yellow and red in colour: *You have to peel an **orange** before you can eat it. **Orange** juice is made by squeezing **oranges**.* **2** the colour of an orange: ***Orange** is my favourite colour. Can you lend me your **orange** crayon?*

orang-utan

a large ape with brown fur: ***Orang-utans** live in the forests of Borneo and Sumatra.*

orbit
the circular journey that something makes round a star or planet: *The earth is in **orbit** round the sun. A satellite was put into **orbit** round the earth.*

orchard
a piece of land where fruit trees are grown: *The farmer lets us pick apples in his **orchard**.*

orchestra
a group of musicians who play various instruments together: *The **orchestra** played music by Mozart. John plays in the school **orchestra**.*

Say **or**-kes-tra.

orchid
a plant that has flowers of an unusual shape and beautiful colours: *Dad gave Mum a beautiful pink and white **orchid** for her birthday.*

Say **or**-kid.

order
1 a command telling someone to do something: *The general gave an **order** to his soldiers. Soldiers have to obey **orders**. The soldiers carried out the general's **orders**.* **2** a request for something to be served or to be sent: *A waiter came to our table to ask us for our **order**.* **3** an arrangement of things: *Put the numbers 5, 3, 1, 4, 2 in the right **order**.*

Meaning 1: same as **command**.

in order to or **in order that** words you use to say why you do something: *I had to run **in order to** catch the bus. I had to run **in order that** I shouldn't be late.*

out of order broken; damaged: *We had to climb the stairs because the lift was **out of order**. This telephone is **out of order**.*

order
1 to tell someone to do something: *The teacher **ordered** the children to stand up.* **2** to ask for something to be served or to be sent: *Dad called the waiter and **ordered** some food. Please **order** a taxi for 5 o'clock. I've **ordered** the new dictionary from the bookshop.*

Meaning 1: same as **command**.

orderly
in proper order; well-behaved: *There was an **orderly** queue of children at the bus stop.*

ordinary
usual; not special: *My brother has a racing bike, but my bike is just an **ordinary** one.*

organ
1 a part of your body: *If you eat good food, and take plenty of exercise, you will keep your heart and your lungs and all your other **organs** healthy.* **2** a large instrument similar to a piano: *When we go to church, Mr Jones plays the hymns on the **organ**.*

organization
1 a business; a company: *My uncle works for an **organization** that makes computers.* 2 a large group; a large club: *The Scout Movement is an **organization** for boys.*

organize
to arrange something; to prepare for something: *My parents are **organizing** a big party. Our music-teacher has **organized** a concert in the school hall.*

organized, organizing, has organized

orphan
a child whose parents have both died: *Maria is an **orphan** and lives with her aunt and uncle.*

ostrich
a large bird with large feathers, long legs, a long, thin neck and a small head: ***Ostriches** cannot fly but they can run fast.*

other
1 more; different: *Mike and five **other** boys were playing football in the playground. There are three books on the table and some **others** on the shelf. There are monkeys, tigers, giraffes, zebras and many **other** animals in the zoo.* 2 the second of two things or people: *Where is my **other** glove? One of the twins has fair hair, and the **other** one has dark hair.* 3 the rest: *Mum looks after the baby while the **other** children go to school. John has arrived, but where are all the **others**?*

otter
a small animal with short legs, a long tail and brown fur: *An **otter** can swim very well. **Otters** catch fish to eat.*

ought
you use **ought** to say what someone should do: *You really **ought** to help your mother. You **ought** to go to the dentist if you have toothache. We **ought** not to tell lies.*

Say **awt**.

ounce
a unit of weight that is about 28 grammes: *There are 16 **ounces** in one pound. I'd like six **ounces** of ham, please.*

Written **oz** for short.

our
belonging to us: *This is **our** house. **Our** neighbours are very nice people.*

ours
we use **ours** for something that belongs to us: *That yellow car is our neighbour's, not **ours** — **ours** is in the garage. Peter and Bob are friends of **ours**.*

ourselves
1 the word we use when we do something to or for us: *We looked at **ourselves** in the mirror.* 2 without help: *We built this hut **ourselves**.*

out
1 not in a house; away from home: *The children are **out** in the garden. We went **out** for a walk. My parents are **out**.* 2 from inside something: *I opened the drawer and took **out** a few sheets of paper.*

The opposite is **in**.

out of the way not blocking the way: *When an ambulance is going along the street, other vehicles have to get **out of the way**. Mum moved the table **out of the way** so that she could sweep the floor.*

outdoor
happening outside: *Football is an **outdoor** game.*

The opposite is **indoor**.

outdoors
outside: *Don't go **outdoors** if it's raining.*

The opposite is **indoors**.

outer
away from the centre; on the outside: *The **outer** wall of the prison is five metres high. The spaceship travelled away from the earth and the other planets and into **outer** space.*

outing
a short trip: *We went on an **outing** to the seaside. The teacher took us on an **outing** to the museum.*

outside
1 not inside a building: *Let's go **outside**. The children were playing **outside**. The newspaper has been left **outside** the door.* 2 on the outside:

*The house has been painted white both inside and **outside**.*

The opposite is **inside**.

outside
the outer surface of something: *The **outside** of the school is painted grey. A coconut is brown on the **outside** and white on the inside.*

The opposite is the **inside**.

oval
shaped like an O: *An egg is **oval**.*

oven
the inside of a cooker, where food is put to be cooked: *Cakes and biscuits are baked in an **oven**. Please close the **oven** door.*

over
1 higher than something: *We hung the clock on the wall **over** the fire-place.* **2** covering something; on top of something: *Mum spread a cloth **over** the table.* **3** from one side to the other: *The horse jumped **over** the fence.* **4** down from a high or upright position: *David looked **over** the edge of the high rock. Mum tripped **over** the cat. Be careful not to fall **over**. Tim knocked **over** his glass.* **5** more than: *That old man is **over** eighty years old. Children of the age of twelve and **over** have to pay the full price. We'll be on holiday for **over** three weeks. Mike's bicycle cost **over** $200.* **6** finished: *The game isn't **over** yet. We must go back to school when the holidays are **over**.* **7** remaining; not used: *There's nothing left **over**. There are two cakes for each of us, and two **over**.* **8** everywhere in a place: *The tourists come from all **over** the world. The toys were scattered **over** the floor.* **9** in a certain direction: *Come **over** here. Your book is **over** there.*

Meanings 1, 2 and 5: The opposite is **under**.

overflow
to flow over the sides: *The river has **overflowed** its banks. I forgot to turn off the bath-tap, and the water **overflowed** on to the floor.*

overhead
above; over your head: *A helicopter flew **overhead**. An electric train gets its power from an **overhead** cable.*

overseas
1 across the sea; abroad: *Mr Smith went **overseas**. The company has its headquarters **overseas**.* **2** belonging to foreign countries: *There are a lot of **overseas** students at this university.*

overtake
to go past someone or something that is travelling in front of you: *We **overtake** all the trucks when we drive on the motorway.*

overtook, overtaking, has overtaken

overtook
see **overtake**: *The police car **overtook** all the other cars.*

owe
to have to pay back money to someone: *'How much do I **owe** you?' 'You **owe** me $10.'*

- Rhymes with **no**.
- owed, owing, has owed

owl
a bird with a round head and flat face, a small, curved beak and large eyes: ***Owls** hunt small animals at night.*

own
1 belonging only to you: *I have my **own** bedroom. Michael has his **own** television.* **2** without help: *I can make my **own** bed.*
on your own **1** alone: *I don't want to go to the playground **on my own**. Don't leave small children **on their own** in the house.* **2** without help: *I can't carry this heavy box **on my own**.*

own
to have; to possess: *We used to rent a flat but now we **own** a house. Who **owns** that car?*

Same as **possess**.

owner
a person who owns something: *Are you the **owner** of that car?*

ox
a bull that is used for pulling carts or ploughs: *The plough was pulled by an **ox**.*

Two **oxen**

oxygen
a gas without colour or smell that is part of the air you breathe: *Nobody can live without **oxygen**.*

Say **ox**-i-jen.

oyster
a small creature that lives in the sea and has a large flat shell: *You can eat **oysters**. Some **oysters** produce pearls inside their shells.*

Pp

pack
1 to put clothes, shoes and other things into a bag, suitcase or trunk: *I've **packed** all I need and I'm ready to go. Have you **packed** your suitcase?* **2** to squeeze close together in one place: *Hundreds of people were **packed** into the hall. The bus was **packed** with people.*

pack
1 a bag that you carry on your back; a bag that is carried on the back of an animal: *The mountaineers were climbing up the mountain with their **packs** on their backs. The donkey carried two heavy **packs**.* **2** a set of playing cards: *There are 52 cards in a **pack**.*

package
things that are wrapped up and tied for posting or delivering; a parcel: *Could you please take this **package** to the post office?*

packet
a small container that is usually made of paper or thin cardboard: *Mum bought three **packets** of biscuits. This **packet** of cigarettes is empty.*

paddle
a short, light oar, with a flat part at one end or both ends, for making a small boat move through the water: *You must hold the **paddle** in both hands.*

paddle

1 to move a boat through the water with a paddle: *Steve **paddled** his little boat along the river.* **2** to walk about or play in shallow water: *The little children were **paddling** in the sea.*

paddled, paddling, has paddled

page
one side of a sheet of paper in a book, newspaper or magazine: *Please open your books at **page** 16. Now turn to **page** 18. The answers to the questions are on **page** 57. This magazine has 64 **pages**.*

paid
see **pay**: *Robert **paid** $2 for his hamburger. Have you **paid** the bill?*

pail
a bucket, especially one that is made of metal or wood: *Fill this **pail** with water.*

Same as **bucket**.

pain
a feeling that you have when you have been hurt or when you are ill: *I have a **pain** in my stomach. Show me where you feel the **pain**. The man was in terrible **pain**.*

painful
causing pain: *My foot was so **painful** that I could hardly walk.*

painless
causing no pain: *The injection will be quite **painless**.*

paint
1 a liquid for colouring objects: *Dad bought a tin of yellow **paint** for the front door. When he had finished, he put a notice beside the door saying 'Wet **Paint**'.* **2** a coloured material that you use with water to colour pictures with: *Use your **paints** to colour your drawing.*

paint
1 to put paint on walls, doors or other things: *Mum and I **painted** the kitchen walls white. Our front door is **painted** yellow.* **2** to make a picture of something using paint: *Liz **painted** a bunch of flowers.*

painter
1 a person whose job is to put paint on walls, doors and window frames: *My parents employed a **painter** to paint our living-room.* **2** an artist who paints pictures: *William Turner was a famous English **painter**.*

painting
a painted picture: *The teacher pinned our **paintings** up on the wall.*

pair
1 two things of the same kind that are used together: *Vicky has five **pairs** of shoes. There*

is a pair of gloves on the table. **2** a single thing that is made up of two parts: *That **pair** of trousers needs mending. This **pair** of scissors is very blunt.* **3** two people or animals; a couple: *The children walked along the pavement in **pairs**. We read a story about a **pair** of cats called Tom and Tim.*

palace
a very large house where a king, queen or president lives: *Queen Elizabeth lives in Buckingham **Palace** in London.*

pale
1 light in colour; not bright; not dark: *Carol is wearing a pale **blue** dress.* **2** having less colour in your face than usual: *You look **pale** — are you feeling sick? The boy went **pale** with fear when he saw a large snake in the grass in front of him.*

- pale, paler, palest
- The opposite is **dark**.

palm
1 a tall tree that grows in hot countries and has very long, pointed leaves growing from the top of its trunk: *Coconuts grow on coconut **palms**.* **2** the inside surface of your hand between your wrist and fingers: *Peter was holding the baby hamster in the **palm** of his hand.*

Say **pahm**.

pan
a round metal container with a handle, for cooking food in: *Please put the **pan** on the cooker. Where is the lid of this **pan**?*

pancake

a very thin, flat, round cake that is made of flour, milk and eggs and fried in a frying-pan: *Susie spread some strawberry jam on her **pancake**, then she rolled it up and ate it.*

panda
a very large, black and white animal that is similar to a bear and lives in the mountains of China: ***Pandas** feed on bamboo leaves. **Pandas** are very rare animals.*

pane
a flat piece of glass fitted into a window: *The burglar smashed a window-**pane** to get into the house.*

pansy

a small plant that has white, yellow or purple flowers, with large round petals: *We've got some **pansies** growing in our garden.*

Lots of **pansies**

pant
to breathe quickly: *The children were **panting** because they had been running up the stairs.*

panther
a leopard, especially a black one: *There are two large black **panthers** in the zoo.*

pants
1 a piece of clothing that you wear over your bottom, under your other clothes: *Here is a clean pair of **pants**. Here are your clean **pants**.* **2** an American word for trousers: *Where are my green **pants**?*

papaya
a large fruit that has a smooth yellow-green skin, sweet orange flesh and lots of black seeds in its centre: ***Papayas** grow on trees in hot countries.*

paper
1 a material that is used for writing on or wrapping things: *I need a pen and **paper** to write a letter. Could you give me another piece of **paper**, please? The children were making **paper** hats.* **2** a newspaper: *Dad is reading the **paper**.*

parachute

an object like an umbrella made of very light, strong material, that is attached to a person by strings, and opens out after the person has jumped from an aircraft: *A **parachute** is used for making you fall slowly from an aircraft to the ground. The soldiers were dropped by **parachute**.*

Say **par**-a-shoot.

parade
a procession of people or vehicles moving

along the street to celebrate some event: *There was a big **parade** to celebrate the start of the festival.*

parcel
something that is wrapped and tied so that it can be sent by post: *My granny sent me a **parcel** on my birthday. The postman brought a **parcel** for you this morning.*

pardon
a word you use when you have not heard properly what someone has just said: ***Pardon**? Could you repeat that last sentence?*
I beg your pardon I am sorry: ***I beg your pardon** — what did you say?*

pardon
to forgive: *The king **pardoned** the prisoners and set them free.*

parent
a mother or father: *'Where are your **parents**?' 'Mum is in the garden, and Dad has taken the baby for a walk.'*

park
a large, public piece of land with grass and trees, usually in a town: *The children were playing in the **park**.*

park
to stop a vehicle somewhere and leave it there: *Dad **parked** in front of the hotel. Don't **park** your motorbike on the pavement.*

parrot
a bird with a curved beak and brightly-coloured feathers, that can be taught to imitate what people say: *My uncle keeps a **parrot** in a big cage, and it always says 'Good morning' to him.*

part
something that is a bit of a whole thing; a piece: *Your head, arms, legs, hands and feet are all **parts** of your body. I missed the first **part** of the film. Mum divided the cake into eight equal **parts**.*

part
1 to divide: *Marianne has long brown hair that is **parted** in the middle.* **2** to go away or take away; to separate: *Some small children don't like being **parted** from their mothers. Sally and I walked together to the crossroads and then **parted**.*

partner
one of two people who do something together: *I need a tennis **partner** for the match tomorrow. Find a **partner** and join hands.*

party
a meeting of guests, often to celebrate something: *I invited all my friends to my birthday **party**. I went to three **parties** last week.*

Lots of **parties**

pass
1 a successful result in an examination: *Anna got a **pass** in English and arithmetic.* **2** a ticket that allows you to do something, for example to travel free or to get into a building: *You must show your **pass** when you get on the bus.*

pass
1 to go past: *I can post your letter when I **pass** the letter-box on my way to school. Please let me **pass** — I'm in a hurry. Mike **passed** me in the street but he didn't notice me.* **2** to overtake: *A green car **passed** me as I was cycling along the road.* **3** to move along; to go: *The procession **passed** along the street.* **4** to take something and give it to someone: *Could you please **pass** me the salt? Please **pass** the photographs round so that everyone can see them.* **5** to be successful in an examination or a test: *Andrew **passed** in English but failed in Chinese. My elder sister has **passed** her driving test.* **6** to spend time: *We played a game of cards to **pass** the time.*

passage
1 a long, narrow way; a corridor: *There was a long, dark **passage** leading from the hall to the kitchen. The headmaster's room is at the end of the **passage**.* **2** a short piece of writing, or a bit of music: *Read the following **passage** and fill in the missing words.*

passenger
a person who travels in a vehicle, boat or aeroplane: *This car holds four people — the driver and three **passengers**.*

passport
a card or a small, flat book with your name, description and photograph, which you need for travelling to foreign countries: *We had to show our **passports** when we got off the plane in Tokyo.*

past
1 after: *'What's the time, please?' 'It's five **past***

three.' The train leaves at half ***past*** *eight. Hurry — it's* ***past*** *eight o'clock!* **2** passing someone or something: *I noticed that the new shop was open when I walked* ***past*** *it this morning. Mum drove* ***past*** *me in the car without seeing me.*

past
the time before the present time: *In the* ***past****, people used candles to light their homes.*

The opposite is the **future**.

past
1 belonging to the time before the present: *In* ***past*** *times, people used horses for travelling, not cars.* **2** the one or ones just before now: *It has been raining for the* ***past*** *three hours.*

paste
soft wet stuff of various kinds: *You squeeze tooth****paste*** *from the tube on to your toothbrush. You can make a sticky* ***paste*** *from flour and water for sticking bits of paper together.*

paste

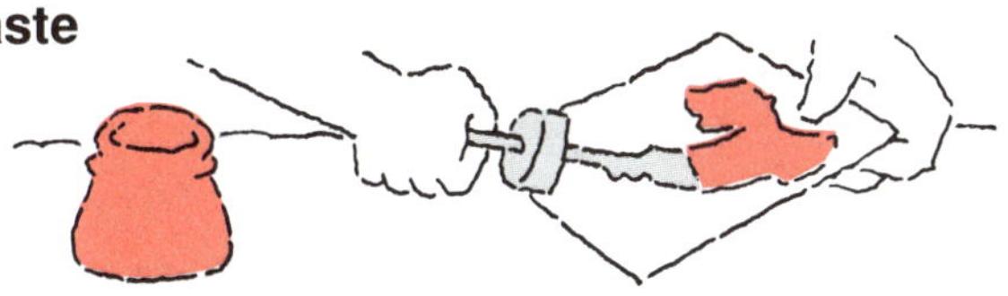

to stick; to glue: *Maria* ***pasted*** *the pictures into her book.*

pastime
a hobby: *Fishing is my dad's favourite* ***pastime****.*

pastry

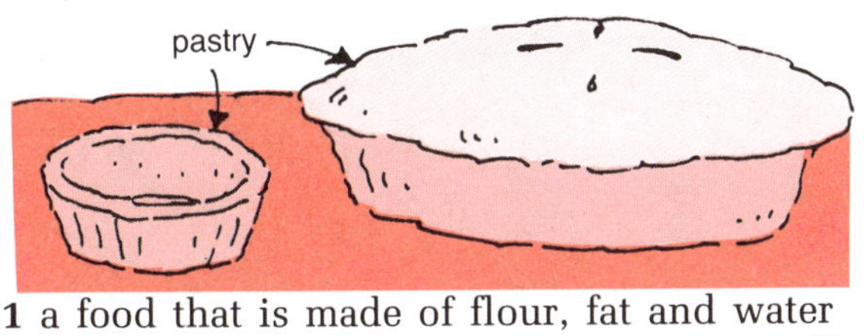

1 a food that is made of flour, fat and water and used for making pies and tarts: *You roll your* ***pastry*** *flat, put it in a special dish, fill it with fruit or some other food, and then bake it in an oven.* **2** a kind of small cake that is made with sweet pastry: *I ate three* ***pastries*** *filled with cream.*

Meaning 2: lots of **pastries**

pat
a light, gentle blow or touch with your hand: *When I passed my exam, my dad gave me a* ***pat*** *on the shoulder and said, 'Well done!'*

pat
to strike someone or something gently with your hand to show you are fond of them, or to comfort them: *Rachel* ***patted*** *the pony's neck. The doctor* ***patted*** *the patient's arm and told him not to worry.*

patted, patting, has patted

patch
1 a piece of material that is used to cover a hole in something: *My mum sewed two* ***patches*** *over the holes in my jeans.* **2** a small piece of ground: *A vegetable* ***patch*** *is a part of a garden where vegetables are grown.*

path
a narrow way for walking along: *There is a* ***path*** *that goes through the forest. We took a* ***path*** *across the fields.*

patient
being able to wait quietly, without complaining: *It will be your turn on the computer soon — just be* ***patient****!*

patient
a person who is being treated by a doctor or dentist: *The dentist asked the next* ***patient*** *to come in. The hospital had too many* ***patients*** *and not enough beds.*

pattern
1 a coloured design on cloth, paper or some other material: *Clare was wearing a dress with a* ***pattern*** *of little butterflies. I don't like the* ***pattern*** *on this wallpaper.* **2** something that you copy when you make something: *You need a dress-****pattern*** *for cutting out the material to make a dress.*

pavement
a path with a hard surface along the side of a road or a street: *You must walk on the* ***pavement****, not on the road.*

paw
the foot of a dog, cat, lion, bear or similar animal: *The dog was howling because it had a thorn in its* ***paw****.*

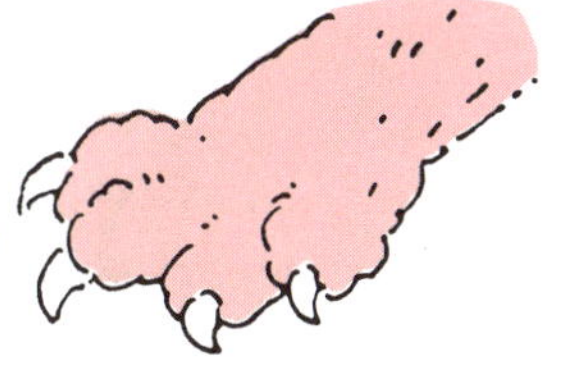

pay
1 to give money for something: *How much did you* ***pay*** *for that record? My dad* ***paid*** *the bill by cheque. Mr Lee* ***paid*** *the taxi-driver.* **2** to give: *You must* ***pay*** *attention to what the teacher says.*

paid, paying, has paid

payment
the amount of money that is paid: *The television can be paid for in twelve monthly **payments**.*

pea
a very small, round, green vegetable that grows in a pod: ***Peas** are soft and taste a bit sweet. We had fried fish, boiled potatoes and **peas** for dinner.*

peace
1 not being at war: *These two countries have always been at **peace**.* **2** a period of being quiet and not being disturbed: *Mum said she needed some **peace** and told us to play outside. Please leave me in **peace** — I want to read my book.*

> Meaning 1: the opposite is **war**.

peaceful
quiet; calm: *It's very **peaceful** in the country because there is no traffic noise.*

peach
a round, juicy fruit with a soft, yellow and red skin, sweet yellow flesh and a hard nut in the middle, called a stone: *We had **peaches** with cream for lunch.*

peacock

a large bird: *A male **peacock** has very long, beautiful coloured feathers that it can lift and spread out like a fan. A female **peacock** is called a peahen.*

peak
1 the pointed top of a mountain: *The **peaks** of the mountains were covered with snow.* **2** the part of a cap that sticks out in front: *The **peak** of a cap keeps the sun out of your eyes.*

peanut
a small brown nut that grows in a shell under the ground; a groundnut: *I bought a bag of roasted **peanuts**.*

pear
a sweet fruit that is similar to an apple but round at the bottom and narrow at the top: *This **pear** is still hard because it's not ripe yet.*

pearl

a small, round, shining white jewel that is formed by an oyster inside its shell: *Mrs Jones is wearing a **pearl** necklace.*

pebble
a small, smooth stone: *The children were throwing **pebbles** into the river. The beach is covered with **pebbles**.*

peck
to pick something up with the beak: *The birds **pecked** at the corn.*

pedal
a part that you press with your foot, on a bicycle or a piano, or some other machine or instrument: *When you ride a bicycle you push the two **pedals** with your feet.*

pedal

to ride a bicycle: *Bob **pedalled** down the road.*

> pedalled, pedalling, has pedalled

pedestrian
a person who is walking along a road or a street: *The **pedestrian** was knocked down by a car while he was crossing the road.*
pedestrian crossing a place where pedestrians can cross a road or a street: *Vehicles must stop at a **pedestrian crossing** to let pedestrians cross.*

peel
to take the skin off fruit or vegetables: *The chimpanzee **peeled** a banana and ate it. Please would you **peel** the potatoes for me?*

peel
the skin you remove from fruit and vegetables: *Please put the orange **peel** in the dustbin.*

peep

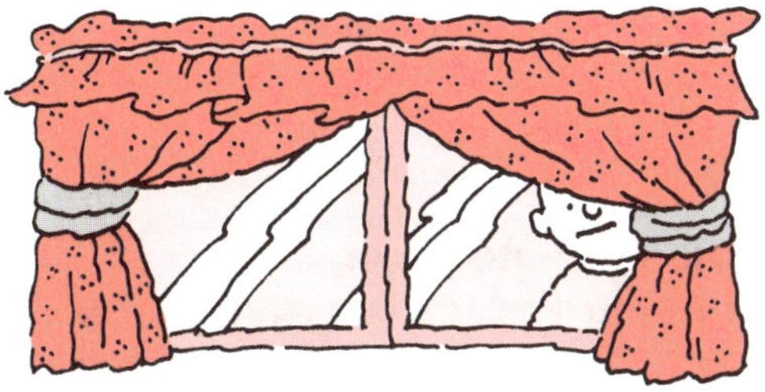

to look quickly, trying not to be noticed: *Joe **peeped** at the answers at the back of the book while the teacher wasn't looking. Sarah **peeped** round the corner to see if anyone was coming.*

peg

1 a short piece of wood or metal for fastening something to: *You fasten a tent to the ground with tent **pegs**.* 2 a hook on a wall or door: *Hang your coat on this **peg**.* 3 a wooden or plastic object that is used for fastening laundry to a line to dry: *I fastened my wet towel to the line with two clothes **pegs**.*

pelican

a large water-bird that has a huge beak with a kind of bag: *A **pelican** uses its beak for catching and carrying fish.*

pen

a long, thin object for writing in ink with: *My **pen** has a broken nib.*

pencil

a long, thin object made of wood with a long, black or coloured centre, for writing or drawing with: *This **pencil** is blunt — it needs sharpening. We have to write our homework in ink, not in **pencil**.*

penguin

a large black and white bird that cannot fly but can swim very well: ***Penguins** live in the Antarctic. **Penguins** feed on fish and other small sea creatures.*

people

men, women and children: *There were eight **people** in the room. A lot of **people** were waiting at the bus stop.*

pepper

1 the dried, hot-tasting berries of the pepper plant that are ground and used for seasoning food: *Please put the salt and **pepper** on the table.* 2 a shiny oval vegetable that is bright green, red or yellow in colour: *You can chop up **peppers** and put them in a salad.*

perfect

1 without any faults; excellent: *Mrs Lee speaks **perfect** Chinese. Nobody is **perfect** — we all make mistakes.* 2 just right: *It's a **perfect** day for going to the beach.*

perform

1 to act, dance, sing, play a musical instrument, or do something else to entertain an audience: *At the end of term, some of us are going to **perform** a play in the school hall to entertain the teachers and the other pupils.* 2 to do: *In this song, you have to **perform** actions as well as sing words.*

performance

the performing of something, especially for an audience: *There will be three **performances** of the school play.*

perfume

1 a liquid that smells pleasant; scent: *Mum put a few drops of **perfume** behind her ears.* 2 a pleasant smell: *I love the **perfume** of roses.*

perhaps

it is possible that; maybe: ***Perhaps** we'll go cycling tomorrow, but we haven't decided yet. Jenny is late — **perhaps** she missed the bus.*

period

1 a certain length of time: *Mr Jones had to stay in hospital for a **period** of seven weeks. We had a short **period** of cold weather.* 2 the time for a lesson: *We have six English **periods** a week. On Mondays we have a double **period** of English.*

permission

allowing someone to do something: *The teacher gave the children **permission** to go home early. Pupils must not leave the classroom during lessons without **permission**.*

permit

to allow someone to do something: *The headmaster does not **permit** pupils to ride their bicycles in the playground. Nicola's parents **permitted** her to go to the cinema on her own.*

- Same as **allow**.
- The opposite is **forbid**.
- permitted, permitting, has permitted

person

a man or woman: *I like lots of people, but*

*Sally is the nicest **person** I know.*

Lots of **people**

persuade
to make someone do something by arguing with them or advising them: *At first, David didn't want to come with us to the museum, but we **persuaded** him. You mustn't try to **persuade** me to tell you the secret.*

persuaded, persuading, has persuaded

pest

a creature, such as a rat, a mosquito or a cockroach, that is harmful to people, animals, plants and things: *Caterpillars are **pests** because they eat the leaves of cabbages and other plants.*

pet
a tame animal that you keep in your home: *Michael keeps a rabbit as a **pet**. My parents bought me a hamster from a **pet** shop.*

petal
one of the coloured parts of a flower: *This orchid has pink and red **petals**.*

petrol
a transparent liquid that is used as a fuel for cars and other vehicles: *There's hardly any **petrol** left in the **petrol** tank.*

petrol station a garage where petrol is sold: *We'll stop at the next **petrol station** to fill up the petrol tank.*

phone
a telephone: *I spoke to Mary on the **phone** this morning. The **phone** was ringing for a long time but nobody answered it. John picked up the **phone** and dialled a number. Please be quiet — Dad is making an important **phone** call.*

Say **fone**.

phone
to call someone on the telephone; to ring: *I'll **phone** you tomorrow. Mark **phoned** to tell me he couldn't come.*

- Say **fone**.
- phoned, phoning, has phoned

photo or photograph
a picture that is taken with a camera: *I took a lot of **photos** of animals in the zoo. This is a good **photograph** of you.*

Say **foe**-toe and **foe**-to-graf.

pianist

a person who plays the piano: *Mr Lee is the **pianist** for the school choir.*

piano
a large musical instrument with white keys and black keys that you press down with your fingers: *Laura is learning to play the **piano**. I have **piano** lessons twice a week.*

pick
1 to choose; to select: ***Pick** the record you like best.* **2** to take flowers or fruit from a plant; to gather: *I **picked** some daisies in the garden and put them in a vase. Don't **pick** the berries unless they are ripe.*

pick up **1** to lift: *I bent down to **pick up** my pencil from the floor. Mrs Smith **picked up** the baby.* **2** to collect someone or something from somewhere: *Mum **picked** me **up** from school today. I've ordered a loaf of bread from the baker — could you please **pick** it **up** on your way home?* **3** to learn something without being taught: *My granny never studied English at school — she just **picked** it **up** by listening to other people.* **4** to stand up: *The old man fell over and **picked** himself **up** again.*

picnic
a meal that you take with you and eat outside: *We'll go to the beach and have a **picnic** there. Let's go for a **picnic** tomorrow.*

picture
1 a painting or drawing: *Who painted this beautiful **picture**?* **2** a photograph: *I took a lot of **pictures** when I was on holiday.*

the pictures the cinema: *We went to the **pictures** yesterday but it wasn't a good film.*

pie

a kind of food that is made of pastry with meat, vegetables or fruit inside: *Would you like some cream on your apple* ***pie****? I had a steak* ***pie*** *and potatoes for lunch.*

piece

1 a part of something: *There are 500* ***pieces*** *in this jigsaw.* **2** a bit: *Would you like another* ***piece*** *of cake? Michael tore the newspaper into little* ***pieces****. Take a new* ***piece*** *of paper and start your drawing again. A glove is a* ***piece*** *of clothing.*

pier

a long platform of stone or wood built out into the water at a harbour: *The fisherman walked along the* ***pier*** *and went down some steps to his boat.*

Rhymes with **ear**.

pig

a pink-coloured farm animal with a fat body, short legs, a short curly tail, and a large round flat nose called a 'snout': *Pork, ham and bacon all come from* ***pigs****. The* ***pigs*** *grunted while they were eating in their sty.*

pigeon

a fat, grey or brown bird that usually lives in a town: *We fed the* ***pigeons*** *in the park with pieces of old bread.*

Say **pid**-jen.

piglet

a baby pig: *The mother of a* ***piglet*** *is called a sow, and the father is called a boar.*

pile

a number of things that are lying on top of one another; a heap: *There was a* ***pile*** *of books on the table. There were* ***piles*** *of stones and sand on the pavement where the road was being dug up.*

pile

to make a pile of something: *The shop-assistant* ***piled*** *the tins on the shelf. The table was* ***piled*** *with boxes.*

piled, piling, has piled

pill

a small, round object containing medicine: *You must swallow the* ***pill*** *without chewing it. The doctor told the patient to take two* ***pills*** *three times a day.*

pillow

a soft cushion for your head: *I have two* ***pillows*** *on my bed. A cover for a* ***pillow*** *is called a* ***pillowcase*** *or* ***pillowslip****.*

pilot

a person who flies an aircraft: *The* ***pilot*** *landed the plane at Singapore Changi Airport for fuel before flying on to Japan.*

pin

a short, thin, pointed piece of metal for holding pieces of cloth or paper together, or for fixing them to something: *The poster is fixed to the wall by four* ***pins****.*

pin

to fasten with pins: *Mum* ***pinned*** *up the hem of my dress. I* ***pinned*** *the picture to the wall.*

pinned, pinning, has pinned

pinch

1 to squeeze someone's flesh tightly between your thumb and first finger: *Stop* ***pinching*** *my arm!* **2** to steal: *Who* ***pinched*** *my bar of chocolate?*

pine

1 a tall tree that has cones and long needle-like leaves, called pine-needles, which do not fall off in winter. **2** the wood of this tree: *A lot of furniture is made of* ***pine****.*

pineapple

a large oval fruit with a brown skin and sweet juicy yellow flesh, that grows on a low plant, in hot countries: *Would you like another slice of* ***pineapple****?*

pink

a colour between red and white: *A flamingo has* ***pink*** *feathers. If you mix white paint with a little bit of red paint, you get* ***pink*** *paint.*

pint

a unit for measuring liquids, equal to about

half a litre: *Please get me three **pints** of milk.*

pipe

1 a long metal or plastic tube for water, oil or gas: *In modern houses, the water **pipes** cannot be seen because they are inside the walls.* **2** an object with a narrow tube leading into a little bowl, that men use for smoking tobacco: *Uncle Jack often smokes a **pipe**.*

pirate

a person who attacks and robs ships: *The **pirates** attacked the ship at night and stole all the valuable things that were on board. A **pirate** ship has a black flag with a white skull and two crossed bones on it.*

pistol

a small gun that is held in one hand: *The bank-robbers were carrying **pistols**, but they didn't fire them at anyone.*

pit

a large hole in the ground: *The men dug a **pit** and covered it with branches in the hope of trapping the tiger.*

pitcher

1 in baseball, the player who throws the ball: *The **pitcher** threw the ball to me, but I missed it.* **2** a large jug: *I filled the **pitcher** with hot water.*

pity

1 a feeling of sadness for another person's problems: *We were filled with **pity** for the people who had been injured in the train accident.* **2** a fact that makes you a little sad: *What a **pity** you can't come with us! It's a **pity** it's raining — we wanted to have a picnic today.*

place

1 a certain spot; a certain area; a certain town: *The children discovered the **place** where the treasure was hidden. I don't know this **place** as I've never been here before. It's useful to have a car for travelling from **place** to **place**. Singapore is a great **place** to live. Show me the **place** on your leg where the bee stung you. In many old towns there is a big open space called a market-**place**, where people bought and sold goods or cattle.* **2** a space where someone or something belongs: *Please put the books back in their right **places** on the book-shelf.* **3** a seat: *Michael went to his **place** and sat down.* **4** a position in a race or competition: *Vicky won second **place** in the drawing competition. Who was in first **place**?*

take place to happen: *The wedding will **take place** in August. The reading competition **took place** yesterday in the school hall.*

place

to put: *Kate **placed** the cups carefully on the table. Richard **placed** six chairs round the table.*

placed, placing, has placed

plain

a wide, flat area of land covered with grass but without many trees: *You will see buffalos on the **plains** of North America.*

plain

1 without any coloured pattern added: *Our school uniform is a **plain** white blouse or shirt, with a **plain** blue skirt or trousers.* **2** very simple in shape and design: *Mum's clothes are **plain** but smart.* **3** ordinary; not special: *The food we get at school is **plain** but good for us. **Plain** chocolate is chocolate without milk added to it.* **4** easy to see or understand: *It is quite **plain** why Julie doesn't want to come to the football match — she doesn't like football. She made it **plain** that she wasn't interested in football. It was **plain** to Joe's piano teacher that he had not been practising the piano.*

plan

1 an idea about how to do something: *The robbers worked out a **plan** for getting into the bank at night. We'll only succeed if everyone follows the **plan**.* **2** an arrangement to do something: *What are your **plans** for tomorrow? Peter had to change his **plans** for the morning because his mother asked him to go shopping.*

plan

1 to decide how something is to be done: *We spent a long time **planning** the party.* **2** to intend to do something: *What do you **plan** to do in the holidays? We are **planning** to go to Thailand this summer.*

planned, planning, has planned

plane
an aeroplane: *Mrs Liu went to Hong Kong by* ***plane****. There were 180 passengers on the* ***plane****.*

planet

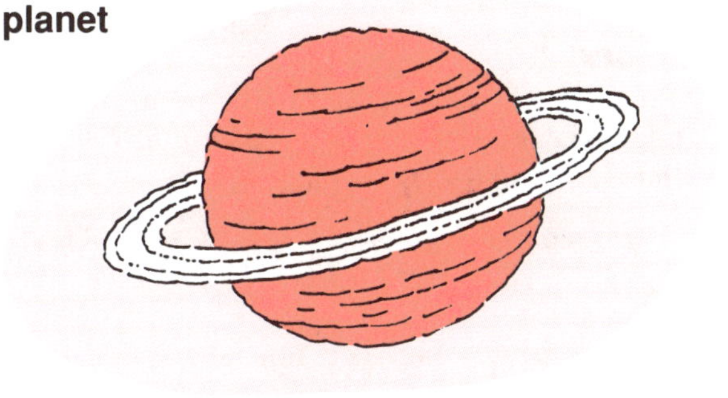

a huge round object in space that moves round the sun or another star: *Mercury, Venus and the Earth are the three* ***planets*** *that are closest to the sun. There are nine* ***planets*** *revolving round the sun.*

plank
a long, flat piece of wood: *The floor of the hut was made of* ***planks****.*

plant
anything that grows from the ground and has roots, a stem and leaves: *All* ***plants*** *need water and light to grow.*

plant
to put a seed or plant into the ground so that it will grow: *The gardeners* ***planted*** *young trees and bushes in the park. The garden was* ***planted*** *with shrubs.*

plaster
1 a powder mixed with water that is put on walls and ceilings, and dries to form a hard, smooth surface: *The man mixed some* ***plaster*** *to repair the wall.* **2** similar white stuff that is used to make a hard covering round a broken arm or leg to support it: *Christine has her arm in* ***plaster****.* **3** a piece of sticky tape for covering a small cut or wound: *Mum put a* ***plaster*** *over the cut on my knee.*

plastic
a light but solid material that is made from oil and used for making many different objects: ***Plastic*** *does not break easily but it melts when heated. These cups and bowls are made of* ***plastic****.*

plate
a flat dish for holding food: *Tom put four* ***plates****, cups and saucers on the table. Don't put too much food on your* ***plate*** *or you won't be able to eat it all.*

platform
1 a stage in a hall, for people to stand on to make a speech or perform something: *The members of the orchestra arranged themselves on the* ***platform****.* **2** the raised area beside the railway line in a railway station: *The train to Kuala Lumpur will leave from* ***Platform*** *1. A lot of people were waiting on the* ***platform*** *for the train to arrive.*

play
1 to amuse yourself: *My little sister is* ***playing*** *with her toys. The children are* ***playing*** *on the beach.* **2** to take part in a game: *The boys are* ***playing*** *football. Do you* ***play*** *tennis?* **3** to make music on an instrument: *Andrew* ***plays*** *the piano very well. Carol* ***played*** *us a tune on the violin.* **4** to put on a record or tape: *Shall I* ***play*** *another record?* **5** to act a part: *Jack is going to* ***play*** *the part of the prince in the school play.*

play
a story that is written for acting, and is performed in a theatre or on television or the radio: *We went to the theatre to see a* ***play*** *by Shakespeare. I listened to a funny* ***play*** *on the radio.*

player
a person who takes part in a game: *There are eleven* ***players*** *in a football team. We need four* ***players*** *for this card-game.*

playful
liking to play and have fun: *Kittens and puppies are very* ***playful****.*

playground
a large open space for children to play in: *There is a big* ***playground*** *in front of the school, where we play after lunch. We have a* ***playground*** *near our house, with swings in it.*

pleasant
nice: *The weather is very* ***pleasant*** *today — not too hot and not too cold. A cool breeze is* ***pleasant*** *on a hot day. The headmistress has a very* ***pleasant****, friendly face.*

The opposite is **nasty**.

please
1 you use **please** when you are politely asking for something, or asking someone to do something, or asking to be allowed to do something yourself: ***Please*** *could I have an ice-cream? Would you* ***please*** *open the door for me?* ***Please*** *come in. Could I speak to*

*Helen, **please**?* **2** you use **please** when you are accepting something: *'Would you like some more tea?' 'Yes, **please**.'*

please

1 to do what someone wants you to; to satisfy someone: *You can't **please** everyone all the time.* **2** to like; to want: *Paul is very selfish — he does just what he **pleases** without thinking of other people.*

pleased, pleasing, has pleased

pleased

happy; satisfied: *I am very **pleased** with my new watch. The teacher was **pleased** with me for working so hard. I'm **pleased** to tell you that you have all passed the exam.*

pleasure

a happy feeling: *Granny says that our letters to her always give her a lot of **pleasure**.*

plenty

a large amount of something; enough: *We've got **plenty** of time to get to the station. 'Do you need any more paper?' 'No, I've still got **plenty**, thank you.'*

plough

a large farming tool that is pulled through the soil to break it up: *In the past, oxen or horses were used for pulling a **plough**, but nowadays most people use tractors.*

Rhymes with **cow**.

plough

to break up soil with a plough: *The farmer was **ploughing** the field ready for planting his seeds.*

Rhymes with **cow**.

plug

1 a small plastic object on the end of a wire, with two or three metal legs called 'pins' that fit into a socket in the wall: *You have to put the **plug** into the socket before you can switch on the television.* **2** a small round piece of rubber or metal that you put into the hole in a wash-basin, sink or bath, to stop the water running out: *This **plug** doesn't fit tightly enough.*

plum

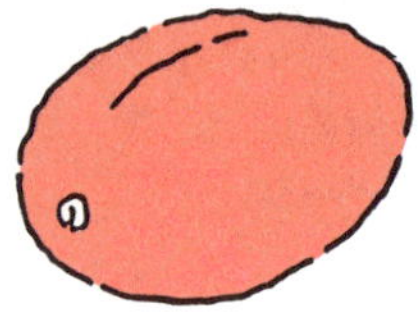

a small, oval fruit with red skin, and a stone in the middle: ***Plums** are soft and sweet.*

plumber

a person whose job is to fit and mend pipes in houses: *My mum sent for a **plumber** because the water pipe was leaking.*

Say **plum**-er.

plus

you use **plus** when you talk about addition: *Seven **plus** two equals nine (7 + 2 = 9).*

pocket

an extra piece sewn on to a piece of clothing, for putting things in: *I keep my keys, some money and a handkerchief in the **pocket** of my trousers. Mike stood with his hands in his **pockets**.*

pocket-money money that children get from their parents every week or month: *How much **pocket-money** do you get? I'm saving up my **pocket-money** to buy a bicycle.*

pod

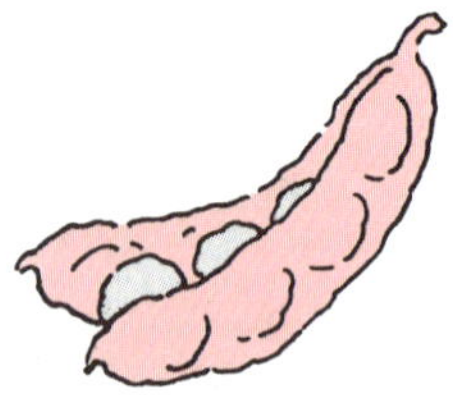

a long, hollow object that grows on some plants and contains the seeds: *Peas and beans grow inside **pods**.*

poem

a piece of writing arranged in lines, often with words that rhyme at the end of the lines: *At school we have to learn **poems** by heart and recite them to the rest of the class.*

point

1 the sharp end of something: *Pins and needles have very sharp **points**. I used the **point** of my knife to open the tin. I dropped my pencil, and the **point** broke.* **2** a place; a spot: *You can see the castle from this **point**.* **3** a time; a moment: *I was just going out of the house, but at that **point** the telephone rang.* **4** a mark you score in a game, test or competition: *Tim scored five **points** out of ten for his test. I beat Jenny in table-tennis by 21 **points** to 15.*

point

1 to show people what you want them to look at by stretching your first finger in that direction: ***Point** to the place on this map where your house is. John **pointed** at the bird sitting* *on the branch.* **2** to aim something in a certain direction: *The robber* ***pointed*** *his gun at the bank manager.*

point out to show: *When we visited the museum, the teacher* ***pointed out*** *some of the most interesting things. Which girl is Lucy — can you* ***point*** *her* ***out*** *to me?*

pointed

having a sharp end: *I don't like* ***pointed*** *shoes because they are not comfortable.*

poison

any stuff that can kill people or animals, or make them ill, if it gets into their bodies: *The farmer bought some* ***poison*** *to kill the rats on the farm.*

poison

1 to kill or harm with poison: *The farmer tried to* ***poison*** *the rats on the farm.* **2** to put poison into something: *In the play, the wine was* ***poisoned****, and everyone who drank it died.*

poisonous

containing poison; producing poison: *Don't pick those berries — they are very* ***poisonous****. The cobra has a very* ***poisonous*** *bite.*

pole

1 a long, thin piece of wood or metal: *The tent is supported by two metal* ***poles****. The man pushed the boat along the river with a* ***pole****.* **2** either of the points, one at the very north, and one at the very south of the earth, called the North **Pole** and the South **Pole**.

police

the men and women whose job is to make sure that people obey laws: *There has been a robbery — call the* ***police****! The* ***police*** *are investigating the murder. You must tell the* ***police*** *if your bicycle has been stolen. A* ***police*** *car chased the robbers' car along the motorway.*

police station the building where the police work: *The two policemen arrested the thief and took him to the* ***police station****.*

policeman or policewoman

a member of the police: *Two* ***policemen*** *and a* ***policewoman*** *came to investigate the robbery. If you get lost you can ask a* ***policeman*** *to show you the way home.*

> Two **policemen**, two **policewomen**

polish

stuff that you rub on to things that helps you to polish them better: *You need furniture* ***polish*** *to polish the table and shoe* ***polish*** *to polish your boots.*

polish

to make something shine by rubbing it with a cloth: *Mary* ***polished*** *her shoes. Mum is* ***polishing*** *the new car.*

polite

having good manners; not rude: *Carol is a very* ***polite*** *girl — she always says 'please' and 'thank you'. You should always be* ***polite*** *to older people. It's* ***polite*** *to open the door for other people.*

> - Same as **courteous**.
> - The opposite is **impolite** or **rude**.

pond

a small area of still water; a pool: *A lot of insects and frogs live by the* ***pond****. Robert fell into the* ***pond*** *and got very wet.*

pony

a small kind of horse: *Mr Martin has bought a* ***pony*** *for his children to learn to ride on.*

> - Lots of **ponies**
> - A pony is a small horse, not a baby horse. A baby horse is a **foal**.

pool

1 a small area of still water: *We watched some fish swimming about in a* ***pool*** *in the rocks.* **2** a small amount of liquid lying on a surface; a puddle: *There was a* ***pool*** *of oil on the floor of the garage.* **3** a swimming-pool: *Are you coming to the* ***pool*** *for a swim?*

poor

1 having too little money: *Some people are so* ***poor*** *that they haven't even got enough money to buy food for their families.* **2** needing pity: *The* ***poor*** *little dog was very thin and frightened.* ***Poor*** *little thing!* **3** not good: *Your handwriting is very* ***poor****, Martin — you must make it neater. Edward has to wear glasses because he has* ***poor*** *eyesight.*

> Meaning 1: the opposite is **rich** or **wealthy**.

pop

modern music that is liked by a lot of young

people: *I like listening to **pop** music, but I have never been to a **pop** concert.*

popcorn
grains of maize that have been heated until they burst open: *Would you like a bag of **popcorn**?*

popular
liked by a lot of people: *The zoo is a **popular** place to visit at weekends. The headmistress is very **popular** with the children.*

porch
a covered entrance to a building: *We waited in the **porch** until it stopped raining.*

porcupine

an animal that is covered with very stiff, sharp hairs like needles: *Other animals are afraid of attacking a **porcupine** because of its sharp needles.*

pork
the meat of a pig: *We had roast **pork** with potatoes for dinner.*

porridge
a thick, hot mixture made by boiling oats or rice in water: *Some people like **porridge** for breakfast.*

port
a place on a coast that ships go to, to have goods loaded on to them or taken off, where passengers can get on and off: *The ship sailed into **port**. Singapore is a very busy **port**.*

Same as **harbour**.

porter
1 a person who is in charge of the entrance to a building: *When you get to the hospital, ask the **porter** at the gate how to get to Ward 3.* **2** a person whose job is to look after a building, especially a block of flats: *Ask the **porter** to mend the broken tap.* **3** a person whose job is to carry bags and cases for people at a railway station or airport: *The old lady could not find a **porter** to carry her suitcase.*

position
1 the place where something is: *The house was in a beautiful **position** on top of a hill, with a view of the sea. Put the book back in its right **position** on the shelf.* **2** the way you put your body: *When you go to bed, do you lie straight, or do you lie in a bent **position**?*

possess
to own; to have something that belongs to you: *Bill is fond of reading and **possesses** a large number of books.*

Same as **own**.

possible
1 able to be done: *Is it **possible** to put toothpaste back into the tube? Will it be **possible** for you to come to the swimming practice tomorrow?* **2** able to happen; perhaps going to happen: *It's **possible** that we shall play football this afternoon, so don't forget to bring your boots.*

post
1 the collecting, transporting and delivering of letters and parcels; the letters and parcels that are sent: *Mr Brown sent the books by **post**. Has the **post** arrived yet? Is there any **post** for me?* **2** a pole fixed into the ground: *The car collided with a lamp-**post**.*
post office a building where you can buy stamps and send letters and parcels: *There was a long queue of people waiting at the **post office**.*

post
to send a letter or parcel by post: *Please could you **post** this letter for me? The parcel was **posted** two weeks ago and still hasn't arrived.*

postage
the money that you pay for sending a letter or parcel by post: *What is the **postage** for a letter to China?*

postcard

a card with a picture on one side that you send by post: *You don't need an envelope for a **postcard**. I sent all my friends **postcards** from Hong Kong.*

poster
a large notice for sticking on a wall: *Have you seen the **poster** advertising the play?*

postman
a person whose job is to deliver letters and parcels: *Has the* ***postman*** *been this morning?*

postpone
to put off to a later time: *The flight has been* ***postponed*** *till this afternoon because of fog.*

> postponed, postponing, has postponed

pot
1 a large pan or a deep dish for cooking things in: *Mum made the soup in a large* ***pot****.* **2** a container with a handle and a lid, for holding coffee or tea: *I picked up the coffee-****pot*** *and poured out three cups of coffee. The waiter brought us a large* ***pot*** *of tea.* **3** a container that is used for growing plants in: *This plant needs a larger* ***pot****.*

potato
a round or oval vegetable with a thin brown skin and hard white flesh: ***Potatoes*** *grow underground.* ***Potatoes*** *can be roasted, boiled or fried. Please peel these* ***potatoes*** *for me.*

> A kilo of **potatoes**

potato crisps potatoes that have been sliced very thin and then fried until they are crunchy: *You can buy bags of* ***potato crisps*** *with different flavours.*

poultry

1 birds that are kept on farms: *Chickens, ducks, geese and turkeys are called* ***poultry****.* **2** the meat of these birds: *The supermarket sells fresh and frozen* ***poultry****.*

pound
a unit of weight that is equal to 0.454 of a kilogramme: *I'd like half a* ***pound*** *of bacon, please. There are two* ***pounds*** *of rice in this bag.*

> Pound is often written **lb**.

pound
to keep hitting something with your fists: *The prisoner* ***pounded*** *on the door. Stop* ***pounding*** *the table!*

pour
1 to make a liquid flow out of a container: *Janet* ***poured*** *the tea out into cups.* **2** to flow in a stream: *Water was* ***pouring*** *down the wall from the hole in the pipe.* **3** to rain heavily: *It was* ***pouring*** *this morning. We looked out of the window at the* ***pouring*** *rain.*

powder
stuff that is very fine, like dust: *You can get* ***powder*** *with a nice smell to rub on your body after your shower.*

power
1 strength: *Athletes need a lot of* ***power*** *in their muscles.* **2** the ability to do something: *A little baby does not have the* ***power*** *to sit up.* **3** the thing that makes a machine or engine work: *A washing-machine works by electric* ***power****.* **4** control over people: *The police have* ***power*** *to arrest someone who is breaking the law.*

practice
1 doing something regularly so that you get better at it: *You need a lot of* ***practice*** *if you want to play the piano well.* **2** a period of exercise or trying something out, before a match or performance: *The team had a short* ***practice*** *before the match.*

practise
to do something regularly to improve your skill: *Laura* ***practises*** *the piano every day. You must* ***practise*** *your tennis more if you want to win the competition. The choir is* ***practising*** *a new song.*

> practised, practising, has practised

praise
to say that you admire a person or thing; to say you are pleased with someone or something: The teacher ***praised*** *the children for their good behaviour in the museum. The general* ***praised*** *the courage of his soldiers.*

> - The opposite is **blame**.
> - praised, praising, has praised

pram
a little vehicle that you push, for taking a baby from place to place: *Mum let Emma push the baby in her* ***pram****, when they went for a walk in the park.*

prawn

a small sea creature with a shell, a long tail and lots of legs, which you can cook and eat: *Mum made a sauce with **prawns** in it.*

pray
to speak to God; to ask God for something: *The people in the church knelt down and **prayed** to God. Everybody in the village **prayed** for rain.*

prayer
the words that you say when you pray: *The children said their **prayers** before they went to bed.*

precious
1 very valuable; worth a lot of money: *Diamonds are very **precious**. Gold and silver are **precious** metals.* **2** loved very much: *Children are very **precious** to their parents.*

prefer
to like better: *Which do you **prefer** — lemonade or orange juice? I **prefer** going by bus to walking. Katie **preferred** to stay at home rather than go for a walk.*

preferred, preferring, has preferred

prepare
to make something ready; to get ready: *Dad is in the kitchen **preparing** dinner. We **prepared** to go down to the beach for a swim. Have you **prepared** properly for your English exam?*

prepared, preparing, has prepared

presence
being present: *You must stop talking in the headmaster's **presence**.*

present
1 being here; being in a place: *Now that the whole class is **present** we can begin the lesson. Who was **present** in the bank when the robbers arrived?* **2** belonging to the time that we are living in now: *The **present** school choir is very good.*
at present at the moment: *The doctor is away **at present** but she will be back in half an hour.*

present
something that is given to you; a gift: *Do you want to see my birthday **presents**? The children got a lot of **presents** for Christmas. This doll was a **present** from my granny.*

president
1 a title used for the leader of some countries: *Who is the **president** of the United States of America?* **2** the leader of a club: *The football club has a new **president**.*

press

1 to push: *You **press** this button to switch on the television. **Press** the doorbell three times. I don't like being in a crowd with people **pressing** against me.* **2** to iron: *Your shirt needs **pressing**.*

pretend
1 to make yourself look as if you are doing something that you are not doing: *David **pretended** to be asleep. Dad is only **pretending** to be angry.* **2** to make up something and act as if it is true: *Let's **pretend** this room is a spaceship.*

pretty
1 attractive; nice to look at: *Jenny is looking very **pretty** in her new dress. The blue dress is **prettier** than the red one. My granny lives in a **pretty** little house by the sea.* **2** rather; very: *The film was **pretty** good, wasn't it? **Pretty** soon you will be speaking English well.*

Meaning 1: pretty, prettier, prettiest

prevent
to stop someone doing something; to stop something happening: *The rain **prevented** the children from playing outside. The bus driver had to stop suddenly to **prevent** an accident. Jack's dad tried to **prevent** him from leaving home.*

price
the amount of money that you have to pay to buy something: *What is the **price** of a litre of milk?*

prick
to make a tiny hole with a sharp point: *When I was sewing I **pricked** my finger on the needle, and it bled a bit.*

pride
the feeling of being pleased with what you have done or with things that belong to you: *Helen takes **pride** in being a good pupil. Paul looked with **pride** at his new bicycle.*

priest
a man who works in a church or temple: *Mr and Mrs Johnson were married by a **priest** in a church.*

prince
a son or grandson of a king or queen: *In the fairy-tale the frog turned into a **prince**. **Prince** William is the son of **Prince** Charles and the grandson of Queen Elizabeth.*

princess
1 a daughter or granddaughter of a king or queen: ***Princess** Anne is the only daughter of Queen Elizabeth.* 2 the wife of a prince: ***Princess** Diana is the wife of Prince Charles.*

principal
a headmaster or headmistress: *Mrs Peters is the **principal** of the dancing school.*

print
1 to put the words on to books, newspapers and magazines by machine: *The teacher took us to the newspaper office to watch the newspaper being **printed**.* 2 to write each letter of a word separately, not joining it to the next one: *Please **print** your name in this space.*

printer
1 a person whose job is printing books and papers: *We went to the **printer's** to watch the newspaper being printed.* 2 a machine that prints: *Has your computer got a **printer**?*

prison
a building where people are kept locked in small rooms, to punish them for breaking the law, and to protect other people from them: *The man was found guilty of murdering his uncle and was sent to **prison** for thirty years. The bank robbers are now in **prison**.*

prisoner
1 a person who is kept in prison: *Two **prisoners** have escaped from the jail.* 2 a person who has been captured by an enemy: *Thousands of soldiers have been taken **prisoner** by our enemies. A **prisoner** of war is a soldier who has been captured during a war.*

private
only for one person or a small group of people; not public: *This is a **private** park — that's why the gates are kept locked. You shouldn't listen to **private** conversations.*

The opposite is **public**.

prize
something you win in a game or competition; a reward for good work: *Mike won first **prize** in the swimming competition. The headmaster gave out the **prizes** to the best pupil.*

probable
expected to happen; very possible: *It's quite **probable** that Jenny will win the art prize — her drawing is very good.*

probably
a word you use when you think something will happen, or has happened, or that something is true: *I shall finish my work at 4 o'clock, so I'll **probably** come and see you at 4.30. Susan is late — she has **probably** missed the bus. Your sum is **probably** right, but you had better ask the teacher to make sure.*

problem
a difficulty: *I've got enough money for the bus, but my **problem** is that I don't know which bus to get on. If you are poor you have a lot of **problems**, such as how to pay for food and clothes.*

procession

a line of people and vehicles moving along the street to celebrate something; a parade: *Lots of people were waiting on the pavement to watch the **procession** go by. A band led the **procession**.*

produce
1 to make something in large numbers or amounts: *This factory **produces** cars and lorries. Rice is **produced** by many of the farmers in this area for the people in the city.* 2 to bring out: *The magician **produced** a rabbit from his hat.*

produced, producing, has produced

product
something that is produced in large numbers or amounts: *Rubber is one of the **products** of Malaysia. Japan exports radios, television sets, cameras and other similar **products** to Britain.*

professor
a university teacher: *Amy's father is a **professor** of English at the National University of Singapore.*

profit
the money that you gain when you sell something for more money than you paid for it: *If you buy a bicycle for $300 and sell it for $350, you have made a **profit** of $50.*

The opposite is **loss**.

programme
1 something that lasts a certain time, that you watch on television or listen to on the radio: *I sometimes watch children's **programmes** in the afternoons. Did you watch the **programme** on pandas yesterday? Mum is listening to a music **programme** on the radio.* **2** a printed piece of paper that gives you information about a play, concert, match or other event that you are attending: *Shall we buy a **programme**? May I look at your **programme**?*

promise
1 to say that you will, or will not, do something: *I **promise** that I won't be late. I **promise** not to be late. I won't be late, I **promise**.* **2** to say that you will give something to someone: *My parents have **promised** me a puppy for my birthday.*

promised, promising, has promised

promise
something you promise: *I made my parents a **promise** that I would practise the piano more often. I'll cook the dinner tomorrow — that's a **promise**!*

pronounce
to speak words or sounds: *How do you **pronounce** the word 'chauffeur'? A lot of people **pronounce** 'medicine' wrongly. The 'b' in 'lamb' and the 'k' in 'know' are not **pronounced**.*

pronounced, pronouncing, has pronounced

pronunciation
the pronouncing of words and sounds: *The teacher has to help us with the spelling and **pronunciation** of English words.*

proof
information that shows that something is really true: *The police have **proof** that the man stole the money from the desk, because they found his fingerprints on the drawer.*

proper
right; correct: *Please put the book back in its **proper** place. Let me show you the **proper** way to clean your teeth.*

properly
in the right way: *This sum is wrong — start again and do it **properly**. You must eat **properly** if you want to stay healthy.*

protect
to keep someone or something safe: *The mother bear **protected** her cubs from other wild animals. In winter people wear thick coats to **protect** themselves against the cold.*

Same as **guard**.

proud
1 being pleased with what you have done; being pleased with people or things that belong to you: *Margaret was **proud** of her good marks in the exam. Her parents were very **proud** of her too. Paul is **proud** of his new bicycle.* **2** thinking that you are better or more important than other people: *In the story, the rich princess was too **proud** to talk to the other children.*

prove
to show that something is true: *People thought that the earth was flat until scientists **proved** that it was round. The man has been **proved** guilty of theft because his fingerprints were found on the stolen goods.*

proved, proving, has proved

provide
to give something to someone: *When children are small, their parents **provide** them with everything they need. The school will **provide** textbooks for the pupils, but they have to **provide** their own pencils and pens.*

provided, providing, has provided

public
belonging to all the people of a town or country: *Parks are usually **public**. This is a **public** library, and everybody who lives in this town*

can borrow books from it. There are some ***public*** *telephones at the railway station.*

The opposite is **private**.

in public in front of other people, especially strangers: *You mustn't spit in* ***public****.*

publish
to prepare and print a book, magazine or newspaper: *This dictionary was* ***published*** *last year. A daily newspaper is* ***published*** *every day except Sundays.*

pudding
1 a sweet food that is eaten hot: *Christmas* ***pudding*** *is made with flour, eggs, raisins and other fruit, and boiled inside a bowl.* **2** a sweet dish at the end of a meal: *What's for* ***pudding****? We're having fruit salad for* ***pudding****.*

puddle

a small pool of water: *It has been raining and there are lots of* ***puddles*** *in the road.*

pull
to move something by holding on to it and leaning away from it; to drag: *Joe* ***pulled*** *the sofa over to the side of the room. Please* ***pull*** *off my boots for me. The cart was* ***pulled*** *by two oxen. Jenny* ***pulled*** *at the handle, but the door wouldn't open. Stop* ***pulling*** *my hair!*

The opposite is **push**.

pull
the action of pulling: *Robert gave the rope a strong* ***pull****.*

The opposite is **push**.

pump
a machine that forces air or a liquid into something or out of something: *A water* ***pump*** *makes water rise from under the ground. Motorists can get petrol from a* ***pump*** *at a petrol station. You use a bicycle* ***pump*** *to put air into the tyres of a bicycle.*

pump
to force air or a liquid into something or out of something with a pump: *Tim* ***pumped*** *up the tyres of his bicycle. Oil is being* ***pumped*** *out of the ground.*

pumpkin
a very large round yellow fruit with a thick skin and lots of seeds inside: *You make* ***pumpkin*** *pie from the soft flesh of a* ***pumpkin****.*

punch
a blow with your fist: *The thief gave the man a* ***punch*** *in the stomach.*

punch
to hit someone with your fist: *The thief* ***punched*** *the man on the nose and stole his wallet.*

punctual
arriving at the proper time; not late: *You were very late getting to school today, Lucy — please try to be more* ***punctual*** *in future.*

punish
to make someone suffer because they have done something wrong: *Dad* ***punished*** *me for breaking the window by stopping my pocket-money for a week. You deserve to be* ***punished*** *if you tell lies.*

punishment
a way of punishing someone: *The teacher gave the children some extra homework to do as a* ***punishment*** *for talking in class.*

The opposite is **reward**.

pupil
a child who goes to school: *This school has 800* ***pupils****.*

puppet

a doll that can be moved by strings that are attached to its arms and legs; another kind of doll that you can put over your hand and move with your fingers: *The children went to see a play that was performed by* ***puppets*** *on strings.*

puppy
a baby dog: *Our dog has had three* ***puppies****.*

Three **puppies**

pure

1 not mixed with anything else: *The king's crown was made of* ***pure*** *gold. My mum has a long dress of* ***pure*** *silk.* **2** clean: *The water that comes from a mountain spring is very* ***pure****.*

purple

a dark colour between blue and red: *There are* ***purple*** *and white pansies in the park.*

purpose

the reason for doing something; what you are trying to do; what something is used for: *The* ***purpose*** *of this meeting is to discuss the new rules. What is the* ***purpose*** *of this tool?*

purr

to make the low sound of a cat when it is pleased: *The cat* ***purred*** *when we stroked it.*

purse

a small bag for holding your money: *I looked in my* ***purse*** *for some change.*

push

to lean against something in order to move it: *Bill* ***pushed*** *the door open. After the accident two men* ***pushed*** *the car to the side of the road. The people behind me were* ***pushing*** *me. Stop* ***pushing****!*

The opposite is **pull**.

put

1 to place something: *Laura* ***put*** *the glasses on the table. Don't* ***put*** *any sugar in my tea. Where did you* ***put*** *the newspaper? John* ***put*** *his hands in his pockets. I'm going to* ***put*** *a new lock on the door. Dad's* ***putting*** *the baby to bed.* **2** to make someone be in a certain mood: *The children brought the teacher some flowers to* ***put*** *her in a good mood.* **3** to suggest or ask: *I've got a question to* ***put*** *to you, children.*

put, putting, has put

put aside to lay something down: *Amy was getting tired of reading, so she* ***put aside*** *her book.*

put away to put something back in its proper place: *George always* ***puts*** *his toys* ***away*** *when he's finished playing with them.*

put down **1** to set down something that you are holding: *I* ***put down*** *the box.* **2** to write: ***Put down*** *these sentences in your exercise books.* **3** to lower: *You can* ***put*** *your hands* ***down*** *now.* ***Put down*** *your umbrella — it has stopped raining.*

put in to fit something in a home: *We're having a new shower* ***put in****.*

put off **1** to delay doing something; to postpone: *Do your homework now — don't* ***put*** *it* ***off*** *till later.* **2** to switch something off: *Please* ***put off*** *the radio.*

Meaning 2: the opposite is **put on**, **switch on**.

put on **1** to dress yourself in a piece of clothing: *I* ***put on*** *my coat and gloves. Why don't you* ***put on*** *your new shoes?* **2** to switch on: *Please* ***put on*** *the light. Mike* ***put on*** *the heater.*

- Meaning 1: the opposite is **take off**.
- Meaning 2: the opposite is **put off** or **switch off**.

put out to stop a fire burning: *The fire brigade will soon* ***put out*** *the fire. The man* ***put out*** *his cigarette.*

put up **1** to raise: ***Put up*** *your hand if you know the answer.* **2** to fasten something on to a wall: *I* ***put up*** *two posters in my bedroom.* **3** to increase: *The landlord has* ***put up*** *the rent.*

put up with to bear: *I can't* ***put up with*** *this noise any longer.*

puzzle

a game where you have to think carefully to answer questions; a game where you need skill to put pieces together correctly: *My mum enjoys crossword* ***puzzles****. The pieces of a jigsaw* ***puzzle*** *fit together to form a picture.*

puzzle

to be very difficult for someone to understand: *The teacher's strange question* ***puzzled*** *the children. They were* ***puzzled*** *by the hard words in the book.*

puzzled, puzzling, has puzzled

pyjamas

a light, loose shirt and trousers that you wear in bed: *Where are my* ***pyjamas****? I have three pairs of* ***pyjamas****.*

Say pa-**jah**-mas.

python

a very large snake that kills animals by twisting its body round them tightly: *Some* ***pythons*** *are more than six metres long.*

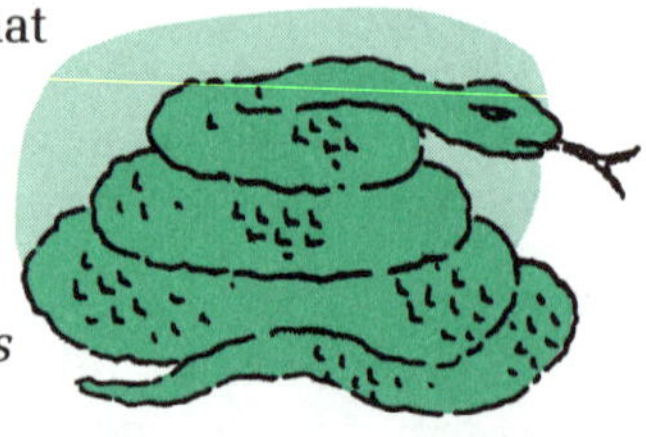

quack
to make the noise of a duck: *The ducks **quacked** as they swam across the pond.*

quality
1 how good or bad something is: *If you are going to walk a lot you must wear shoes that are of good **quality**. The **quality** of the food in this restaurant is very poor.* **2** something you notice in a person's behaviour: *Kindness and honesty are important **qualities** for a person to have.*

Different **qualities**

quantity
an amount or number: *What is the right **quantity** of rice to cook for six people? There's a small **quantity** of coffee left in the jar. Japan exports television sets in large **quantities**.*

- Same as **amount**.
- Large **quantities**

quarrel
an angry argument: *Richard is having a **quarrel** with his brother. Jill and I had a **quarrel** about whose bicycle was better.*

quarrel
to have an angry argument with someone: *My two brothers are always **quarrelling** over their toys. Have you **quarrelled** with Susan again? Stop quarrelling, children!*

quarrelled, quarrelling, has quarrelled

quarter

one of four equal parts of something: *The four children divided the bar of chocolate among them, so that each of them got a **quarter**. Mum cut the apples into **quarters**. The film lasts an hour and three **quarters**.*
quarter past fifteen minutes past a certain hour: *It's a **quarter past** two. The film begins at a **quarter past** five.*
quarter to fifteen minutes before a certain hour: *It's a **quarter to** three. The news is at a **quarter to** six.*

quay

a platform of stone at a harbour, where boats are loaded or unloaded: *The boats are tied up at the **quay**.*

Sounds like **key**.

queen

1 a woman who rules a country: ***Queen** Elizabeth lives in Buckingham Palace in London. A **queen** wears a crown at special events.* **2** the wife of a king: *The king and his **queen** welcomed the guests.*

queer
strange; odd: *There's a **queer** smell coming from the kitchen — what is Dad cooking? You see some **queer** animals at the zoo. Don't you think it's **queer** that there are some birds that can't fly?*

question
1 something you say or write, that you want an answer to: *Granny asked me a lot of **questions** about my school. The teacher asked what the capital of France was, but we couldn't answer her **question**.* **2** something in a school exercise or exam that you have to solve: *In the maths exam, the children had to answer five*

questions *in one hour. I couldn't answer* ***Question*** *Three.*

The opposite is **answer**.

queue

a line of people who are waiting for something: *There is a long* ***queue*** *at the post office. We joined the bus* ***queue****.*

Say **kew**.

queue

to stand in a queue: *We had to* ***queue*** *for half an hour to get into the cinema. A lot of people were* ***queuing*** *at the entrance for tickets.*

- Say **kew**.
- queued, queuing, has queued

quick

1 moving fast: *I tried to catch the cat, but she was too* ***quick*** *for me.* ***Quick*** *— get hold of the baby before he falls into the pond!* **2** taking only a short time: *Be* ***quick*** *if you want to come with me — I can't wait all day for you. We went for a* ***quick*** *trip into town. I had a* ***quick*** *look at the magazine. Which is the* ***quickest*** *way to the station?*

- Same as **rapid**.
- The opposite is **slow**.

quickly

fast; without delay: *Wait for me — you're walking too* ***quickly****. I* ***quickly*** *changed into my jeans.*

quiet

making very little noise; without noise: *Be* ***quiet*** *in case you wake the baby. It's very* ***quiet*** *in the house at night.*

- Same as **calm**.
- The opposite is **noisy**.

quilt

a thick, soft, light cover for a bed: *My* ***quilt*** *is filled with goose feathers.*

quite

1 rather; a certain amount: *It's* ***quite*** *cold today, isn't it? The film was* ***quite*** *good — I enjoyed it. Andrew is* ***quite*** *a good pupil. I* ***quite*** *like going to school.* **2** completely: *My purse is* ***quite*** *empty. 'Have you finished your homework?' 'No, not* ***quite****.' You were* ***quite*** *right to take the rotten apple back to the shop. I* ***quite*** *agree with you.*

quiz

a game in which you are asked questions that test your knowledge: *In the* ***quiz****, we were asked to spell 'Christmas', 'receipt' and 'dwarf'. Do you like watching television* ***quizzes****?*

Lots of **quizzes**

rabbit
a small animal with soft fur and long ears, that people keep as a pet: *Daniel has a white **rabbit** with pink eyes. People keep **rabbits** in hutches.*

race
1 a competition to see who or which is the fastest: *Joe came third in the **race**. Which runner won the **race**? I enjoy watching horse-**races** on television.* **2** a type of people who come from a certain part of the world: *In Singapore there are people of many different **races** — Malays, Indians, Chinese, Eurasians, Europeans and others.*

race
to compete with someone in a race; to see who is the fastest: *Jim **raced** against Joe in the swimming contest. Let's **race** to the end of the street. The two children were **racing** each other along the beach. I'll **race** you to school.*

raced, racing, has raced

rack

a shelf, or a set of shelves, or some other kind of object made for holding things: *Put these tools back in the **rack**. In a coach, train or plane, there is a **rack** above your seat for you to put your coat or bag on.*

racket

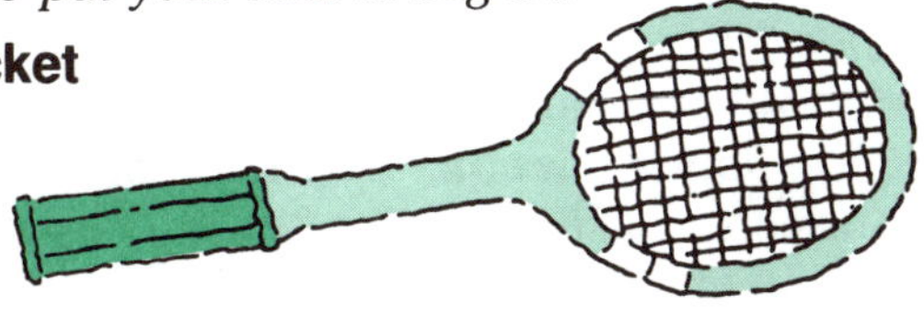

a kind of bat for hitting the ball in tennis, or the shuttlecock in badminton: *A badminton **racket** is lighter to hold than a tennis **racket**, and its handle is narrower.*

radio
an instrument with various switches and knobs that you turn, to listen to programmes that are being broadcast: *Dad is listening to the news on the **radio**. Please turn down the **radio** — it's far too loud.*

radish
a small red or white root with a strong, hot taste, that you can eat raw: *I chopped up some **radishes** to put in the salad.*

raft

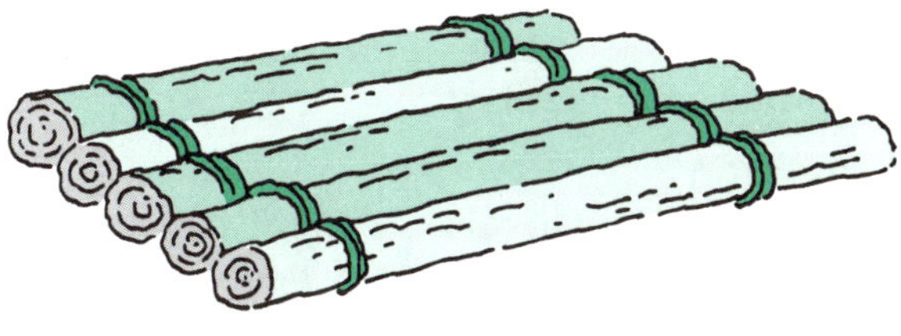

a number of large pieces of wood tied together, for using as a boat: *In the story, the children made a **raft** out of planks and used it to float along the river.*

rag
1 a piece of old cloth: *Thomas cleaned his bicycle with a **rag**.* **2** a torn piece of clothing: *The beggar was dressed in **rags**.*

rail
1 one of the metal bars in a fence; a metal bar to hold on to: *Hold on to the **rail** as you come down the steps.* **2** a bar to hang things on: *Hang the towel over the towel-**rail** to dry.* **3** one of the two long steel bars for trains to run on: *Never walk on the **rails**.* **4** transport by train: *The goods were sent by **rail**.*

railings
a fence made of metal or wooden bars: *There are **railings** all around the park.*

railway
1 the business of running trains, and transporting passengers and goods by train: *My father has a job on the **railway**.* **2** a track with two steel bars for trains to run on: *A new **railway** to London is being built. Trains run along **railway** lines.*
railway station a building beside a railway, where trains stop for passengers to get on or off: *The **railway station** has a ticket office, a waiting room, toilets, a few shops and a restaurant.*

rain
water that falls from the clouds in drops: *Plants need **rain** to grow. You'll get wet if you go out*

*in the **rain**. We've had a lot of heavy **rain** this week.*

rain
to fall as drops of water from the clouds: *It **rained** all day yesterday. Is it **raining**?*

rainbow
the coloured half-circle that can sometimes be seen in the sky opposite the sun when it is raining: *A **rainbow** has many different colours.*

raincoat
a coat that you wear to keep your clothes dry when it is raining: ***Raincoats** are made of waterproof material.*

raindrop
a single drop of rain: *I think it's going to rain — I felt a **raindrop** on my nose.*

raise
1 to move something upwards; to lift: ***Raise** your right hand. In the theatre, the curtain is **raised** just before the play begins.* **2** to make something higher: *The wall will have to be **raised** by about a metre.* **3** to increase: *The bus fares have been **raised** again.*

raised, raising, has raised

raisin
a sweet dried grape: *Mum baked a cake with **raisins** and nuts in it.*

rake
a garden tool that looks like a large comb with a long handle: *A **rake** is used to make the soil smooth and level or to gather leaves and grass into a heap.*

rake

to make the soil smooth with a rake; to gather up leaves and grass with a rake: *Michael was **raking** the dead leaves off the grass. Mum is **raking** the soil.*

raked, raking, has raked

ran
see **run**: *Paul **ran** home. The children **ran** along the beach.*

rang
see **ring**: *Susan **rang** the doorbell. The telephone **rang** but nobody answered it.*

rapid
quick; very fast: *The movements that insects make with their wings are so **rapid** that you can't see them.*

- Same as **quick**.
- The opposite is **slow**.

rare
not found very often; unusual: *There are some **rare** animals in the zoo, such as pandas and gorillas. This kind of orchid is very **rare**.*

- The opposite is **common**.
- rare, rarer, rarest

raspberry

a small, soft, red berry made of lots of little round sections containing seeds: ***Raspberries** are hollow inside. We filled the tarts with **raspberry** jam.*

A kilo of **raspberries**

rat
a small animal with a long tail and sharp front teeth that is similar to a mouse, but larger: *The **rats** have bitten a big hole in this sack and eaten some of the grain inside it.*

rather
1 quite; a bit: *I'm **rather** tired after digging in the garden. This is **rather** a difficult sum. Having a shower with your clothes on is a **rather** silly thing to do.* **2** you use **rather** to say you would prefer something: *I would **rather** watch television than go for a walk. Wouldn't you **rather** come to the movies with us than stay at home? I'd **rather** have a dog than a cat.* **3** instead of: *I chose a bar of chocolate **rather** than an ice-cream.*

rattle
a toy for a baby, that makes a rattling noise: *The baby was lying in his cot, playing with his **rattle**.*

rattle
to make a sound of things knocking together: *The cups* ***rattled*** *on the tray as the waiter carried it.*

rattled, rattling, has rattled

raw
not cooked: *You can eat most vegetables* ***raw****. Dogs like* ***raw*** *meat.*

The opposite is **cooked**.

ray
a line of light: *A* ***ray*** *of sunlight shone through the curtains and lit up the dust that was floating about.*

razor
a tool with a sharp blade for shaving hair off: *My dad shaves with an electric* ***razor****.*

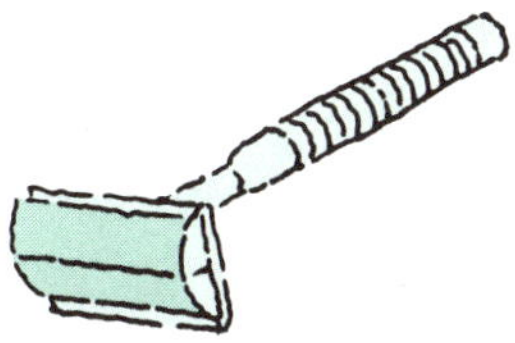

reach
1 to arrive at a place; to get somewhere: *We* ***reached*** *Melaka in the afternoon. You have to go through the house to* ***reach*** *the back garden.* **2** to touch; to get hold of something: *Put the meat away in the fridge, where the dog can't* ***reach*** *it. Dad can just* ***reach*** *the ceiling with the tips of his fingers. Can you* ***reach*** *the books on the top shelf?* **3** to stretch out your arm to get hold of something: *Lisa* ***reached*** *across the table for another biscuit.*

Meaning 1: same as **arrive**.

read
1 to look at words and understand them: *The children are learning to* ***read*** *and write English. I like* ***reading*** *adventure stories. Have you* ***read*** *this book? I* ***read*** *about the football match in the paper.* **2** to read aloud: *My mum often* ***reads*** *a story to me before I go to bed. Will you* ***read*** *to me tonight?*

read, reading, has read

reader
1 a person who reads a lot: *Jim is a keen* ***reader****.* **2** a book for reading at school: *There are a lot of stories in our English* ***reader****.*

ready
1 prepared; able to be used straight away: *Is dinner* ***ready*** *yet? Your bed is* ***ready*** *for you. Are these peaches* ***ready*** *to eat?* **2** able to go somewhere or do something straight away: *I'm* ***ready*** *to leave. I'll be* ***ready*** *in five minutes — I'm just going to have a shower.* **3** willing: *David is always* ***ready*** *to help.*

real
1 not imaginary; actually there: *Is there a* ***real*** *monster in that cave?* **2** natural; not imitated: *This bag is made of* ***real*** *leather. The jewels in the crown are* ***real****. Is this bracelet* ***real*** *gold?* **3** actual; true: *The pop star calls himself Dangerous Dan, but what is his* ***real*** *name?*

Meaning 1: the opposite is **imaginary**.

realize
to understand; to notice: *I* ***realize*** *that I can't have everything I want. I hadn't* ***realized*** *how late it was.*

realized, realizing, has realized

really
1 very: *That's a* ***really*** *nice dress! I'm pleased with you, children — you've worked* ***really*** *hard!* **2** very much: *I* ***really*** *enjoyed the concert.* **3** actually; in fact: *The police asked the people who saw the accident what* ***really*** *happened. My brother sometimes asks stupid questions but he's* ***really*** *very clever.* **4** you use **really** when you are surprised, and also when you are scolding someone: *'Danny drew this picture.' '****Really****? I didn't know he could draw so well.'* ***Really****, Andy! You mustn't be so rude to your father!*

rear
1 to feed and care for children or young animals while they grow up: *My grandmother had ten children to* ***rear****. The farmer* ***rears*** *chickens.* **2** to rise up on the back legs: *The horse* ***reared*** *in fright. The horse* ***reared*** *up.*

reason
a fact that explains why something happens, or why you do something; a cause: *The* ***reason*** *why Mike is afraid of dogs is that he was once bitten by a bulldog. We've finished our work, so there's no* ***reason*** *why we shouldn't go home. What is the* ***reason*** *for all this noise, children? The teacher had a good* ***reason*** *for punishing Johnny.*

reason
1 to be able to think and understand: *Human beings have the ability to* ***reason****.* **2** to work out something: *Mum* ***reasoned*** *that if Dad had taken the train at five o'clock, he would be home by six o'clock.*

reasonable

1 sensible; not silly or crazy: *You can't expect me to know everything — be* ***reasonable****! It's quite* ***reasonable*** *for parents to ask children to help with the housework.* **2** enough to satisfy yourself or someone else: *You should do a* ***reasonable*** *amount of schoolwork in the holidays.* **3** OK, but not good: *The weather is* ***reasonable****.*

receipt

a piece of paper saying that something has been paid for: *Dad paid the waiter for the meal, and asked for a* ***receipt****.*

Say re-**seet**.

receive

to get; to be given: *Kevin's parents* ***received*** *a letter from the headmaster yesterday. Who* ***received*** *the first prize?*

received, receiving, has received

recent

belonging to a time not long ago: *This is a* ***recent*** *picture of my parents. Newspapers tell you about* ***recent*** *events.*

recently

not long ago: *Have you seen Christine* ***recently****? This photo of my parents was taken quite* ***recently****.*

recess

a period of free time between lessons: *Julie and Jenny played with each other during* ***recess****.*

Say **ree**-sess.

recipe

a list of things you have to do to prepare and cook a certain dish: *There are some good* ***recipes*** *in this cookery book.*

Say **res**-i-pi.

recite

to repeat something aloud from memory: *We each had to learn a poem and then* ***recite*** *it to the rest of the class.*

recited, reciting, has recited

recognize

to know someone or something when you see or hear them because you have seen or heard them before: *You've grown so much that I hardly* ***recognize*** *you. I* ***recognized*** *Granny's handwriting on the envelope.*

recognized, recognizing, has recognized

record

1 a round, flat piece of black plastic that has sound, especially music, recorded on it: *My brother plays pop* ***records*** *all the time.* **2** a score or success, especially in a sport, that no-one has beaten so far: *Which athlete holds the world* ***record*** *for running 100 metres? If you beat a* ***record****, you can say that you have 'broken the* ***record****'.*

record

to put sound or a film on special tape, so that you can listen to it or watch it again in future: *My dad* ***recorded*** *a concert from the radio. There's a good film on television tonight — let's* ***record*** *it on the video-recorder.*

record-player

a machine for playing records on: *My brother played my new record for me on his* ***record-player****.*

rectangle

a flat shape with four sides; a square or an oblong: *Each side of a* ***rectangle*** *is the same length as the side opposite to it.*

red

the colour of blood: *Strawberries, raspberries and tomatoes are* ***red****. A robin has a* ***red*** *breast.*

referee

a person who is in charge of a game or match and makes sure that the rules are obeyed: *The* ***referee*** *sent two of the football-players off the field. The* ***referee*** *blew his whistle to stop the game.*

refresh
to cool someone down, or make them feel less tired: *I drank a **refreshing** glass of orange juice when I came back from my long walk. I'll go and have a shower to **refresh** myself.*

refreshments
food and drink for refreshing you; a snack: ***Refreshments** will be served after the meeting. There is a stall on the beach selling **refreshments** such as lemonade and ice-cream.*

refrigerator

a large container for keeping food cold, so that it stays fresh: *Meat should be kept in the **refrigerator**.*

Also called a **fridge**.

refuse
1 to say you will not do what someone has asked you to do: *I told my sister to tidy her bedroom, but she **refused**. My brother **refused** to help me.* **2** not to accept an invitation; not to accept something that is offered to you: *We shall have to **refuse** the invitation to the wedding because we shall be away on holiday then.*

- Meaning 2: the opposite is **accept**.
- refused, refusing, has refused

regular
1 usual: *Thursday is our **regular** day for shopping at the supermarket.* **2** coming at the same time each day: *You need **regular** meals if you want to stay healthy.* **3** even; with equal spaces: *You walk with **regular** steps. The tick of a clock is **regular**.* **4** done often; done every day: ***Regular** exercise will keep you strong and healthy.* **5** coming often: *Granny is a **regular** visitor to our house.* **6** shaped so that the parts or sides match: *A square is a **regular** shape.* **7** ordinary: *I haven't got enough money to buy the large bar of chocolate — I'll just get the **regular** size.*

regularly
1 always at the same time: *Eat **regularly**. We go to the swimming-pool **regularly** every Thursday.* **2** often: *Dad goes fishing **regularly**.* **3** in an even way: *Your heart beats **regularly**.*

reindeer
a large deer that lives in Northern Europe, Asia and America: *Both male and female **reindeer** have large horns called antlers.*

Lots of **reindeer**

rejoice
to be very happy about something: *The people **rejoiced** when they heard that their king was better after his illness.*

- The opposite is **grieve**.
- rejoiced, rejoicing, has rejoiced

relate
to tell a story: *Peter **related** everything that had happened to him on his voyage to Australia.*

related, relating, has related

related
belonging to the same family as someone: *Mike is **related** to Bob — they are cousins. Mike and Bob are **related**.*

relation
someone who belongs to your family; a relative: *Your mother, father, grandmother, grandfather, aunts, uncles, brothers, sisters and cousins are all your **relations**.*

relative
a relation: *Susan is going to stay with her **relatives** in Hong Kong for the holidays.*

relax
to rest: *The doctor told the patient to lie down and **relax**. My parents like to **relax** in the evening after working all day.*

remain
1 to stay; not to leave a place: *Pupils are not allowed to **remain** in the classroom during the lunch-break.* **2** to stay; to go on being: *The teacher asked the children a question but they **remained** silent.* **3** to be left: *Only a little bit of cake **remained** after we had all had a piece.*

remark
something that you say: *My brother made a*

remark *about my clothes that made everyone laugh except me.*

remark

to say: *'It's very late,' Peter* ***remarked****. He* ***remarked*** *that it was very late.*

remember

to keep something in your mind; to bring something back into your mind: *Can you* ***remember*** *what the teacher told us last week? I* ***remember*** *your face but I can't* ***remember*** *your name.* ***Remember*** *to switch off the lights before you go to bed.* ***Remember*** *to ring me tomorrow.* ***Remember*** *that you still haven't written to Granny.*

The opposite is **forget**.

remind

1 to make you remember something: ***Remind*** *me to ring Alice tomorrow. Mum* ***reminded*** *me that I still hadn't written to Granny.* **2** to make you think of someone or something: *Miss Smith always* ***reminds*** *me of my aunt because she looks very like her.*

remove

to take away; to get rid of something: *The doctor* ***removed*** *the bandage from John's leg to look at the cut on his knee. Please* ***remove*** *all this rubbish!*

removed, removing, has removed

rent

the money that someone pays every month or every week for using a house, flat or shop that is owned by someone else: *We pay $800* ***rent*** *a month for this flat.*

rent

1 to pay rent to the owner of a house, flat or shop: *We don't own this flat — we* ***rent*** *it.* **2** to let people use a place that belongs to you, in return for a rent: *Mr Wang* ***rents*** *this house to us.*

repair

to make something all right again; to mend: *The mechanic* ***repaired*** *the car. Could you* ***repair*** *these torn trousers for me?*

Same as **mend**.

repeat

to say something again: *Could you* ***repeat*** *the last sentence, please? The children had to* ***repeat*** *the new English words after the teacher.*

replace

1 to provide something new to take the place of something that is old, broken or lost: *I bought a new cup to* ***replace*** *the one I broke. We're going to* ***replace*** *our old car with a bigger one.* **2** to put something back in its proper place: *Please* ***replace*** *the books on the shelves when you have finished reading them.*

replaced, replacing, has replaced

reply

to say something to someone who asks you something or tells you something: *'How many players are there in a hockey team?' 'Eleven,'* ***replied*** *Peter. I must* ***reply*** *to my aunt's letter.*

- Same as **answer**.
- replies, replied, replying, has replied

reply

an answer: *The teacher asked John a question, but she couldn't hear his* ***reply****.*

report

1 a description of what has happened: *The man gave the police a* ***report*** *of the accident.* **2** a piece of paper that says how well a pupil has done during a term at school: *At the end of term each pupil gets a school* ***report****. Susan got a very good* ***report****.*

report

1 to give a description of what has happened: *The accident was* ***reported*** *in the newspaper.* **2** to tell someone about a person or thing: *Alan was* ***reported*** *to the headmaster for being rude to his teacher. Mr Brown* ***reported*** *the theft of his car to the police.*

reporter

a person whose job is to write reports for a newspaper or for television or radio: *The* ***reporter*** *tried to find out as much as possible about the bank robbery.*

reptile

any animal that has a skin covered with scales,

and lays eggs: *Alligators, snakes, lizards and tortoises are **reptiles**.*

request
to ask politely: *A notice in the hospital says 'Visitors are **requested** not to smoke'.*

rescue

to save someone: *The lifeboat was sent out to **rescue** the sailors from the sinking ship. The firemen **rescued** four people from the burning house.*

rescued, rescuing, has rescued

rescue
the saving of someone: *The people were taken to hospital after their **rescue** from the burning house. A man came to the **rescue** of the little boy who had fallen into the river.*

reserve
to ask for something to be kept for someone; to book: *My father phoned the restaurant and **reserved** a table for us. These two seats are **reserved** for the headmaster and his wife.*

reserved, reserving, has reserved

reservoir
a lake where water for drinking is stored: *The water for all the people in the city comes from a **reservoir** in the mountains.*

Say **rez**-erv-war.

respect
a feeling of liking and admiring someone, and being willing to do what they tell you: *You ought to feel **respect** for your parents. The President is held in great **respect** by everyone.*

respect
to admire and like someone because of their good qualities: *All the teachers and pupils **respect** the headmistress because she is kind and fair to everyone.*

rest
1 what is left when part of something is taken away; all the other people or things: *Can all of you eat the **rest** of the pudding? Jenny and her sister went home but the **rest** of us went swimming. Our lessons finished at 3 o'clock today, so we spent the **rest** of the day on the beach.* **2** a period of time when you are not working, or not taking exercise: *We climbed up the hill and sat down at the top for a **rest**.* **3** a sleep: *Granny likes to have a **rest** in the afternoon.*

rest
1 to stop working and relax in order to get new strength: *Let's stop and **rest** for half an hour. The doctor told the patient to **rest** for a few days.* **2** to relax: *Granny was **resting** her legs after her long walk.* **3** to lean something on something else: *Peter **rested** his bicycle against the wall.*

Meaning 1: the opposite is **work**.

restaurant
a place where people can go to buy and eat meals: *We went to an Indian **restaurant** last night.*

Say **rest**-ront.

result
1 something that happens because of something else: *The old man was lame as a **result** of an accident.* **2** the marks you get in an exam or test: *Alice got very good **results** in her exams.* **3** the answer to a sum: *Add up all these numbers and tell me the **result**.* **4** the score: *My dad was listening to the football **results** on the radio.*

retire
to stop working when you get to a certain age: *Mr Walker **retired** at the age of 65. My grandad is **retired**.*

retired, retiring, has retired

return
1 to come back; to go back: *Mr Wang **returned** from Hong Kong yesterday. The children **returned** to the classroom after lunch.* **2** to give, send or put something back where it came from: *You have to **return** the books to the library within three weeks. Please **return** the book to its shelf. David borrowed my pen and he hasn't **returned** it yet.*
return ticket a ticket that allows you to

travel to a place and come back again: *We bought **return tickets** to Kuala Lumpur.*

revenge
harm you do to someone who has hurt or harmed you: *Martin took his **revenge** on Susanna for laughing at him by throwing her bag out of the window.*

reward
1 something that you are given because you have worked hard, or behaved well, or helped someone: *Julie's mother bought her a new dress as a **reward** for cleaning the house so well.* **2** a sum of money that is given or promised for finding someone or something: *A **reward** of $5,000 has been promised to anyone who can help the police find the bank-robbers.*

Meaning 1: the opposite is **punishment**.

reward
to give someone a reward: *Mrs Lee **rewarded** Tom for finding her brooch for her.*

rhinoceros
a large, very heavy animal that has a thick skin and one or two horns on its nose: ***Rhinoceroses** live in Africa and Asia, and feed on plants.*

rhyme
to sound the same as another word, except for the first letter: *'Day' **rhymes** with 'say'. 'Niece' **rhymes** with 'peace'. Can you think of any words that **rhyme** with 'time'? 'Bee' and 'tree' **rhyme**.*

- Say **rime**.
- rhymed, rhyming, has rhymed

rib
one of the bones that go round your chest from your backbone: *Your heart and lungs are protected by your **ribs**.*

ribbon
a long strip of coloured material: *Kate tied her hair back with a blue **ribbon**.*

rice
white or brown grains that have to be boiled in water to make them soft enough to eat: *We have **rice** every day.*

rice-cooker
a special kind of electric pot for boiling rice in: *The rice takes ten minutes to cook in the **rice-cooker**.*

rich
having a lot of money: *If I was very **rich**, I would buy an aeroplane and travel all over the world. **Rich** people can afford to buy a lot of expensive things.*

- Same as **wealthy**.
- The opposite is **poor**.

rid
to remove something bad; to make something go away: *I'm trying to get **rid** of all this rubbish. What is the best way to get **rid** of flies?*

ridden
see **ride**: *I've never **ridden** a horse.*

riddle
a strange question that has a funny or clever answer: *The answer to the **riddle** 'What goes up when the rain comes down?' is 'an umbrella'.*

ride
a trip on a horse or bicycle; a trip in a car, bus or train: *The children went for a **ride** on their ponies. May I have a **ride** on your bicycle? We enjoyed our **ride** in the new car. It's only a five-minute bus-**ride** to the school.*

ride
1 to travel on a horse or another animal: *Bob is learning to **ride** a horse. Helen enjoys **riding** too. We **rode** our ponies round the field. Have you ever **ridden** on an elephant?* **2** to travel on a bicycle or motorbike: *Can you **ride** a bicycle yet? I **rode** 12 kilometres on my bike yesterday. I'll **ride** over to Jack's house this afternoon. You have to wear a helmet when you **ride** a motorbike.* **3** to travel in a car, bus or train: *It is more comfortable to **ride** in a car than on a bus.*

rode, riding, has ridden

rider

a person who rides a horse, bicycle or motorcycle: *The **rider** fell off his horse. The **rider** of the motorcycle was hurt in the accident.*

rifle

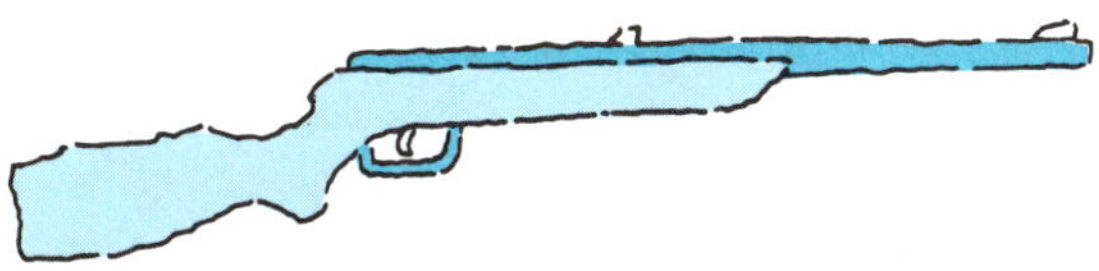

a long gun for shooting things that are far away: *The farmer shot a hare with his **rifle**.*

right

1 the same side as the hand that you use more: *When I write, I hold the pen in my **right** hand. Turn **right** at the next corner and you'll see the railway station on your **right**. In most countries people drive on the **right**.* **2** correct: *The teacher asked us a question, but nobody knew the **right** answer. You got most of your sums **right**, but you got three wrong. Put the book back in its **right** place.* **3** OK; all right: *The television stopped working, so a man came to put it **right** again.* **4** close: *Susan is standing **right** beside me.* **5** completely: *Go **right** to the end of the street and turn left.*

- Meaning 1: the opposite is **left**.
- Meaning 2: the opposite is **wrong**.

right away, right now immediately: *You can start **right away**. I can't come **right now** but I'll be ready in about half an hour.*

ring

1 a small circle of metal that you wear on your finger: *My parents both wear gold wedding **rings** on the **ring** fingers of their left hands.* **2** a circle: *The children sat in a **ring** round the teacher.* **3** the sound of an electric bell: *There was a **ring** at the door.* **4** a telephone call: *I'll give you a **ring** tomorrow afternoon.*

ring

1 to make a sound with a bell: *Michael **rang** the doorbell. The doorbell **rang**. The church bells were **ringing**. The telephone was **ringing** for a long time before someone answered it.* **2** to call someone on the telephone; to phone: *I'll **ring** you tonight. Sue **rang** this morning.*

rang, ringing, has rung

ring up to phone someone: *I must **ring up** my mum and tell her that I'll be late for dinner. Don't forget to **ring** me **up** when you come back from your holiday.*

ripe

ready to be gathered in; ready to be eaten: *The corn is **ripe**. The bananas are still green — they aren't **ripe** yet.*

rise

1 to move upwards: *Smoke was **rising** from the chimney. The birds **rose** into the air.* **2** to stand up: *The children all **rose** when the headmaster came in.* **3** to get out of bed in the morning: *Mr Miller **rises** every morning at six o'clock.* **4** to appear above the horizon: *The sun **rises** in the east and sets in the west.* **5** to become greater or higher; to increase: *The price of food is always **rising**. The patient's temperature **rose**. There will be a flood if the river **rises** much more.*

- Meaning 5: the opposite is **fall**.
- rose, rising, has risen

risen

see **rise**: *The sun has **risen**.*

river

a large stream of water that flows across the land: *The Amazon in South America is the largest **river** in the world. London is on the **River** Thames. We went across the **river** in a small boat.*

road

a way with a hard surface for vehicles to travel on: *We took the **road** that led to the station. Be careful when you cross the **road**. 'Are we on the right **road** for Kuala Lumpur?' 'No, this is the **road** to Melaka.'*

roam

to walk about without trying to go anywhere: *The beggar **roamed** the streets because he had no home. There are dangerous animals **roaming** about the jungle.*

Same as **wander**.

roar

a loud, deep noise: *The lion's **roars** frightened the children. The **roar** of the traffic sometimes keeps me awake at night.*

roar

to make a very loud, deep noise: *We heard the lions **roaring** at the zoo. The thunder **roared** and the lightning flashed. The audience **roared** with laughter at the man's jokes.*

roast

to cook meat in an oven or over a fire: *Mum **roasted** the chicken in the oven. We had **roast** beef and potatoes for dinner.*

rob

to steal money or valuable things from a person

or place: *Help! I've been* ***robbed*** *— my wallet has been stolen!*

robbed, robbing, has robbed

robber
a person who steals money or valuable things from a person or place: *The* ***robbers*** *forced the bank-manager to give them two million dollars.*

robbery
the stealing of money or valuable things from a person or place: *The police are investigating the bank* ***robbery***.

Many **robberies**

robin
a small bird with red feathers on the front of its body: ***Robins*** *are common birds in Britain.*

robot
a machine that works like a human being: *In factories, a lot of jobs are done by* ***robots*** *nowadays.*

Say **roe**-bot.

rock
the very hard stuff under the grass and soil, that the earth is made of: *You find bare* ***rock*** *at the top of mountains and round the coast. We had fun climbing on the* ***rocks*** *on the beach.*

rock
to swing gently backwards and forwards or from side to side: *Mum* ***rocked*** *the baby in her arms. She* ***rocked*** *the cradle. The boat was* ***rocked*** *by the waves.*

rocket

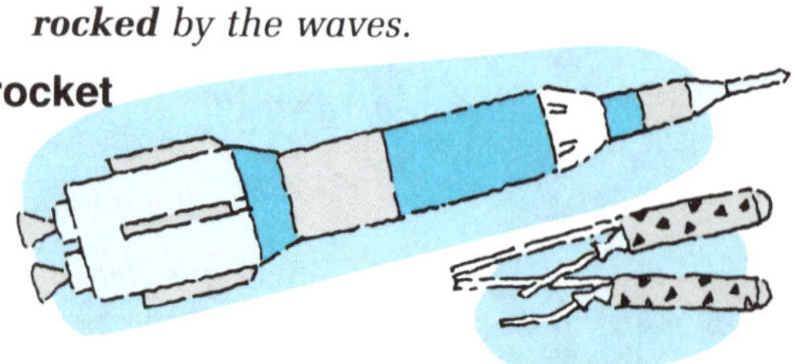

1 a vehicle for travelling into space: ***Rockets*** *are used for exploring the moon and the planets.* **2** a firework that is attached to a stick: *A* ***rocket*** *shoots high into the air and produces thousands of brightly coloured sparks.*

rod
a long, thin stick: *A fishing-****rod*** *is used for catching fish.*

rode
see **ride**: *Bob* ***rode*** *his bicycle very fast down the hill.*

roll
1 a long piece of material such as paper or cloth, that is wound round a tube: *A* ***roll*** *of toilet paper is called a toilet* ***roll***. **2** a bit of bread made in a round shape, that can be cut in half and filled with some food: *I had a cheese* ***roll*** *and a ham* ***roll*** *for lunch. Rosie spread butter and honey on her* ***roll***.

roll
1 to move by turning over and over: *The ball* ***rolled*** *down the street. Laura* ***rolled*** *the little ball towards the cat.* **2** to turn over: *The dog* ***rolled*** *on to its back. Dad* ***rolled*** *up his sleeves before washing the car.*

roller
1 a heavy wheel for making ground flat: *Dad rolled the grass with the garden* ***roller***. **2** a big wave: *The* ***rollers*** *came towards the shore.* **3** a small plastic tube for winding your hair round, to make it curly: *Liz puts her hair into* ***rollers*** *every night.*
roller-skate a kind of shoe with four small wheels fixed to it: *Mary got a pair of* ***roller-skates*** *for her birthday.*
roller-skate to move on roller-skates: *The children* ***roller-skated*** *along the pavement.*

roller-skated, roller-skating, has roller-skated

rolling-pin
a long heavy wooden object with a handle at each end, that you roll on top of pastry to make it flat: *If a burglar got into our house, I would hit him on the head with a* ***rolling-pin***.

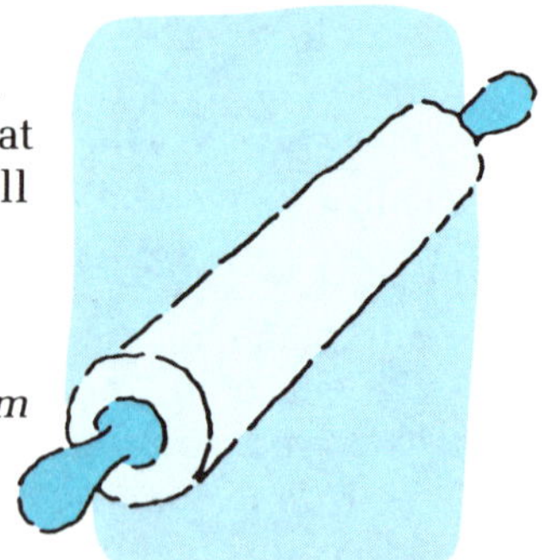

roof
1 the part that goes across the top of a building: *Has your house got a flat* ***roof*** *or a sloping* ***roof***? **2** some other object that is similar to this: *The* ***roof*** *of the car was damaged by a tree falling on it. I've burnt the* ***roof*** *of my mouth.*

room
1 one of the separate sections of a flat or house: *This flat has six* ***rooms*** *including a kitchen and bath****room***. *My bed****room*** *is next to the living-****room***. **2** a bedroom in a hotel: *My parents*

*took a double **room** and I got a single **room**. All the **rooms** in the hotel are booked.* **3** space: *There isn't enough **room** for a large table in our kitchen. We'll move the cupboard to make **room** for the television. There is **room** for over five hundred people in the hall.*

root

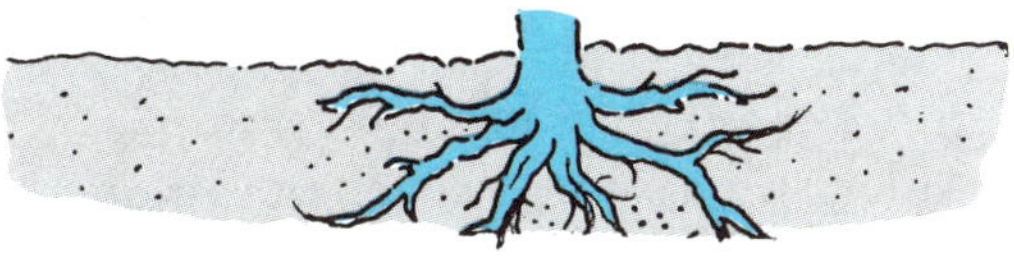

the part of a plant that grows under the ground: *Trees have very strong **roots**. The gardener pulled out the weeds by the **roots**.*

root beer a kind of lemonade that is made from various roots: ***Root beer** is an American drink.*

rope
a very strong, thick string made by winding strong materials together: *Mountaineers tie nylon **ropes** round themselves when they climb dangerous rocks. Mike tied his boat to the quay with a **rope**.*

rose
a flower with a sweet smell and thorns on its stem: *Dad bought Mum a bunch of red **roses** for her birthday.*

rose
see **rise**: *Everybody **rose** to their feet when the President came into the room.*

rot
to become bad; to go soft: *Apples **rot** if you don't use them. Wood **rots** in water.*

> rotted, rotting, has rotted

rotate
to turn like a wheel: *The blades of a helicopter **rotate** very fast and lift it into the air.*

> rotated, rotating, has rotated

rotten
1 gone bad; not good to eat: *We had to throw away the **rotten** strawberries.* **2** rotted: *The old tree trunk was **rotten**.*

rough
1 uneven; not feeling smooth and soft: *A cat's tongue is very **rough**.* **2** full of lumps and holes: *Driving on **rough** roads is bad for your car.* **3** full of waves; not smooth: *I felt sick on the boat because the sea was **rough**.*

> - Say **ruf**.
> - The opposite is **smooth**.

round
1 shaped like a circle: *Most coins are **round**. Plates are usually **round** too.* **2** shaped like a ball: *We know the world is **round**, but in the past people thought it was flat.* **3** in a circle: *A wheel goes **round**. The children ran **round** the tree.* **4** on all sides of something: *There is a fence **round** the playground.* **5** all over: *Peter looked **round** the room.* **6** in the opposite direction: *Vicky looked **round** and saw that a cat was following her. Dad turned the car **round** and drove back home.* **7** from one person to another: *Please pass the photos **round**. The news went **round** the village.* **8** to a certain place, usually your home or someone else's home: *Are you coming **round** this afternoon? Let's go **round** to Amy's.*

> Meaning 1: same as **circular**.

round
a part of a competition or match: *The winners of the first **round** will go through to the next **round**.*

row
1 a line: *The children were sitting in a **row** facing the teacher. The desks in the classroom are arranged in **rows**. The gardener planted the bushes in a **row**.* **2** a line of seats: *We sat in the front **row** of the theatre.*

row
to move a boat by using oars: *Can you **row** a boat? David **rowed** up the river.*

royal
connected with a king or queen: *The king and queen of a country and the members of their family are called the '**royal** family'.*

rub
to move one thing against another: *The cat **rubbed** its head against my leg. The back of my shoe is **rubbing** against my heel. Sometimes when people wake up they **rub** their eyes.*

> rubbed, rubbing, has rubbed

rub away to remove something by rubbing with a cloth: *Dad **rubbed away** the raindrops from his glasses.*
rub out to remove pencil marks with a rubber: *I **rubbed out** the whole sentence and started again.*

rubber
1 a strong material that can be squeezed and stretched: *Tyres are made of black **rubber**. Mum wears **rubber** gloves when she does the*

*washing-up. I put on my **rubber** boots when I go out in the rain.* **2** a small piece of rubber for rubbing out something written or drawn in pencil: *Please bring your pencil, **rubber** and ruler.*

rubbish
1 things that you throw away: *Our **rubbish** is taken away once a week. Please put the **rubbish** in the dustbin.* **2** nonsense: *Don't talk **rubbish**!*

rude
not polite; showing bad manners: *It's **rude** to stare at people. Jack was sent to the headmaster for being **rude** to his teacher.*

The opposite is **polite** or **courteous**.

rug
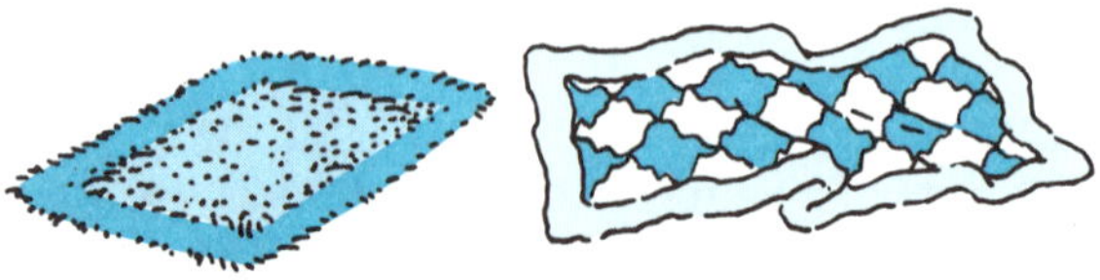

1 a mat or small carpet: *There is a **rug** beside my bed.* **2** a blanket, especially a coloured one with a pattern: *Jenny lay on the sofa and covered herself with a **rug**.*

rule
a law at school or in a game, that tells you that you must do something or that you must not do it: *I don't know the **rules** of this game. In football it's against the **rules** to touch the ball with your hand. Everybody must play by the **rules**. You must not break the school **rules**.*

as a rule usually: *I get up early **as a rule**.*

rule
to control a country: *In the fairy-tale the king **ruled** over a large kingdom.*

ruled, ruling, has ruled

ruler
1 a person who rules a country: *In the story, the king was killed in a battle, so the people had to choose another **ruler**.* **2** a long, narrow piece of plastic or wood for helping you to draw straight lines: *You can also use a **ruler** to measure things.*

run
1 to move fast with leaping steps, not walking steps: *This morning I had to **run** to school because I was late. My dog came **running** towards me.* **2** to move along: *Trains and trams **run** on rails.* **3** to flow: *Tears were **running** down the little boy's cheeks. Don't leave the tap **running**.* **4** to organize; to manage: *My uncle **runs** a paper-making business.* **5** to go regularly: *The buses **run** every twenty minutes. This train doesn't **run** on Sundays.*

ran, running, has run

run after to try to catch someone or something; to chase: *My sister **ran after** me with my keys, because I had forgotten to take them with me. Our dog is always **running after** cats.*

run along to go away: ***Run along** now, children!*

run away to escape: *The boy **ran away** from home because he thought his parents didn't love him.*

run down to knock down: *The girl was almost **run down** by a car when she ran across the road.*

run into **1** to meet someone by chance: *Today I **ran into** Jennifer and we had a long chat.* **2** to crash into something: *The car **ran into** a wall.*

run out **1** to have no more of something: *We've **run out** of lemonade — would you like orange juice instead? Hurry up — we're **running out** of time.* **2** to come to an end: *The lemonade has **run out**.*

run over to knock down: *The bus almost **ran over** a cat.*

runner
a person who runs: *There are five **runners** in this race. Jan is a fast **runner**.*

rung
see **ring**: *Have you **rung** Emma yet?*

rush
a hurry: *There's no **rush** — we still have plenty of time.*

rush
to hurry; to go quickly: *It's late — you must **rush** if you want to catch the bus. Andrew **rushed** into the classroom to tell us the news.*

rust
rough, red-brown stuff that spreads over iron and steel: *The old car was covered with **rust**. There's no **rust** on my bicycle.*

rusty
covered with rust: *Be careful not to hurt yourself on those **rusty** old nails. Your bicycle will get **rusty** if you leave it outside in the rain.*

sack

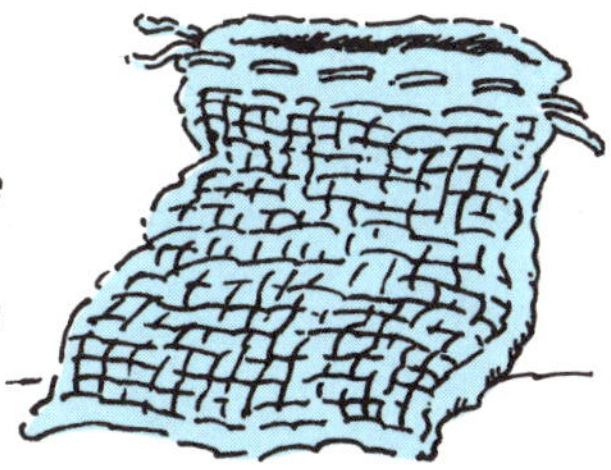

a large bag made of rough cloth, strong paper or plastic: *The rice was stored in **sacks**. The lorry was carrying **sacks** of grain.*

sack

to tell someone that you don't want them to work for you any longer: *Two of the labourers were **sacked** because they didn't work hard enough.*

sad

unhappy: *Nicola was **sad** because her dog had disappeared. You look very **sad** — what's wrong? The **sad** story made me cry. It was the **saddest** story that I had ever heard.*

- The opposite is **happy**.
- sad, sadder, saddest

saddle

a seat for a rider on a horse, bicycle or motor-cycle: *The bicycle **saddle** is too high for me.*

safe

1 not causing harm; not dangerous: *Is it **safe** to swim in this river? This old car isn't **safe** to drive. My brother is a **safe** driver. The dog is **safe** with children — it won't bite.* **2** protected from harm; not in danger: *You should keep your money in a **safe** place. I hope you'll have a **safe** journey home. The missing child has been found **safe** and well.*

- Meaning 1: the opposite is **dangerous**.
- safe, safer, safest

safe

a strong metal box or cupboard where money and valuable things are kept: *There is a small **safe** hidden behind the picture on the wall. The robbers forced the bank manager to open the **safe** and give them the money.*

safety

being safe: *Mum always worries about our **safety** when we are walking or cycling on busy roads.*

The opposite is **danger**.

safety belt a belt fixed to a seat in a car or aircraft, which you fasten round yourself so that you won't be thrown out of your seat in a crash: *Don't forget to fasten your **safety belt**.*

said

see **say**: *Bill **said** he didn't know if he could come. Please could you repeat what you've just **said**?*

sail

1 a sheet of strong cloth that is attached to the mast of a boat: *The wind fills the **sails** with air and makes the boat go forward.* **2** a journey in a ship: *My uncle took us for a **sail** round the island in his yacht.*

sail

1 to move across water: *The ship **sailed** along the west coast of Sumatra.* **2** to steer a ship with sails across water: *We helped my uncle to **sail** his yacht to the little island.*

sailing

1 the sport of sailing a ship: *Shall we go **sailing** today? A boat with sails is called a '**sailing** boat'.* **2** a regular voyage made by a ship or ferry: *When is the next **sailing** for Hong Kong?*

sailor

a member of a ship's crew whose job is helping to sail a ship: *The captain of the ship told the **sailors** what to do.*

salad

any cold dish of mixed vegetables or fruit: *Mum made a **salad** with tomatoes, cucumber and lettuce.*

salary
the money that someone is paid for work each month: *Teachers' **salaries** are paid regularly every month.*

Workers' **salaries**

sale
1 the selling of something: ***Sales** of cars have increased. These pictures are not for **sale**. There was a sign saying 'For **sale**' in front of the house.* **2** the selling of goods at cheap prices in order to sell them quickly: *Some of the big shops have a **sale** twice a year. Mum bought a lot of clothes in the **sales**.*

salesman
1 a man whose job is to sell goods to shops: *Mr Lee works as a **salesman** for a firm that makes toys — he has to persuade shops to buy the toys that his firm makes.* **2** a male assistant in a shop: *The **salesman** helped me to choose a good bicycle.*

Two **salesmen**

salt
a white powder that you put into food to give it a stronger taste: *This soup needs more **salt**.*

salty
tasting of salt: *Sea water is **salty** and so are tears.*

same
not different: *Linda and I are the **same** age — we are both eight. My sister goes to the **same** school as I do. At school all the girls wear the **same** clothes — a white blouse and a blue skirt. The houses in this street all look the **same**. Do the **same** as I do — if I walk backwards, you walk backwards too.*

The opposite is **different**.

sand
the fine yellow stuff that beaches and deserts are covered with: ***Sand** is made of very tiny stones and bits of shells. We built a big **sand**-castle on the beach.*

sandal

a light kind of shoe made with straps to go over your foot: ***Sandals** are cooler for wearing in hot weather than ordinary shoes.*

sandwich
two slices of bread with food in between: *Dad had two ham **sandwiches** for lunch. I made myself an egg-and-tomato **sandwich**.*

sang
see **sing**: *The children **sang** a carol.*

sank
see **sink**: *The ship **sank** in deep water.*

sardine
a small sea fish: ***Sardines** are packed into small tins for selling. We opened a tin of **sardines**.*

sat
see **sit**: *Peter **sat** in a rocking-chair. I've been so busy that I haven't **sat** down all day!*

satellite

an object that is fired into space to travel round the earth: ***Satellites** are used for sending signals and live television programmes to different parts of the world.*

satisfy
to make someone pleased; to give someone what they want: *The teacher wasn't **satisfied** with my homework so I had to do it again. Some customers in shops are very difficult to **satisfy**.*

satisfies, satisfied, satisfying, has satisfied

Saturday
the seventh day of the week, the day after Friday: *In Britain, children don't go to school on **Saturdays**.*

sauce
a thick liquid with a certain flavour, that you pour over food to make it taste better: *We had spaghetti with tomato **sauce** for lunch.*

saucepan
a deep pan, usually with a long handle: *Mum cooked the potatoes in a **saucepan**. Put the lid back on the **saucepan**.*

saucer
a small dish for putting a cup on: *Angela put*

four cups and ***saucers*** *on the table for tea.*

sausage

chopped meat, fat and spices mixed together and made into a long shape like a finger, that you cook by frying or grilling: *We had* ***sausages*** *and chips at the cafe.*

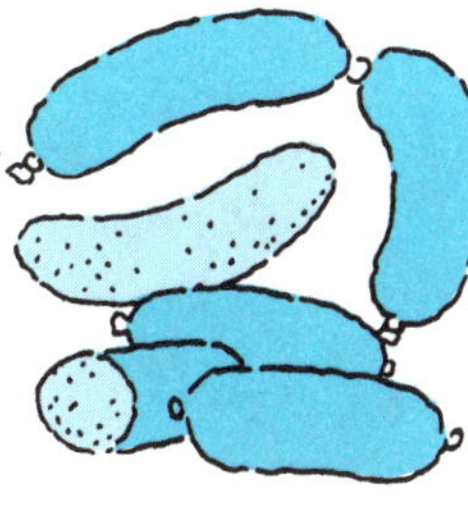

save

1 to bring someone out of danger; to rescue: *Would you be brave enough to jump into the sea to* ***save*** *someone from drowning? The doctors have* ***saved*** *the patient's life.* **2** to keep something instead of throwing it away: *My cousin collects stamps, so I always* ***save*** *stamps from envelopes to send to him.* **3** to keep money instead of spending it, so that you can buy something later: *Mike is* ***saving*** *up for a bicycle. Sarah has been* ***saving*** *most of her pocket money to buy a watch.* **4** not to waste something: *You will* ***save*** *a lot of money if you stop buying sweets. We must* ***save*** *water.*

saved, saving, has saved

savings

the money that you have saved: *My brother keeps his* ***savings*** *in the bank.*

saw

see **see**: *I* ***saw*** *Liz in the park yesterday.*

saw

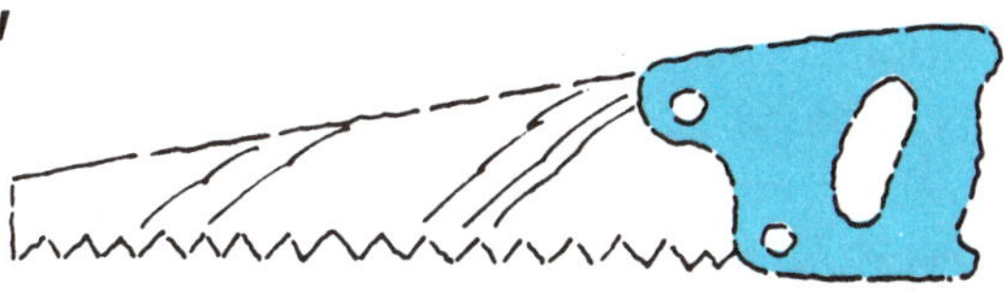

a tool for cutting wood that has a long blade with an edge like a row of sharp teeth: *The man used an electric* ***saw*** *to cut down the tree.*

saw

to cut with a **saw**: *The gardener* ***sawed*** *a few branches off the tree. The man was* ***sawing*** *the log in two. The log has been* ***sawn*** *up.*

sawed, sawing, has sawn

sawdust

the stuff like yellow powder, made of tiny bits of wood, that is produced when wood is being sawn: *There was* ***sawdust*** *all over the floor after the carpenter had finished sawing the plank.*

say

1 to speak words: *'What did you* ***say****?' I* ***said*** *'Wait for me'. The doctor* ***said*** *she would come as soon as possible. People* ***say*** *this temple is very old. This temple is* ***said*** *to be very old.* **2** to contain a written message or notice: *The sign on the door* ***said*** *'Private'. What does the notice* ***say****? It* ***says*** *'No smoking'.* **3** to repeat: *Can you* ***say*** *a poem for me?*

said, saying, has said

scald

to burn your skin with hot liquid: *The cook* ***scalded*** *her hand with boiling water.*

scale

1 in music, a group of notes going up or down in order: *Michael is practising his* ***scales*** *on the piano. The music teacher taught us the* ***scale*** *of C.* **2** one of the tiny, thin, flat pieces that cover the skins of fish and reptiles: *Mum removes the* ***scales*** *from the fish before cooking them.*

scales

a machine for weighing: *The greengrocer weighed the apples on the* ***scales****. We have* ***scales*** *in our bathroom for weighing ourselves.*

scar

a mark on the skin that is left by a cut: *There is still a small* ***scar*** *on my finger where I cut myself on some broken glass.*

scare

to frighten: *You'll* ***scare*** *the baby if you shout. The cat* ***scared*** *me by jumping on to my bed in the dark. I was too* ***scared*** *to move. My sister is* ***scared*** *of spiders. Tim was* ***scared*** *of telling his parents that he had broken the vase. The birds were* ***scared*** *away by the dog.*

scared, scaring, has scared

scarf

a long, narrow piece of clothing that you wear round your neck to keep yourself warm; a square piece of cloth that a woman wears round her shoulders or over her head: *Mum knitted me a long, blue **scarf** for the winter.*

Two **scarfs** or **scarves**

scatter

to drop a lot of things so that they lie all over the place: *The little boy **scattered** his toys all over the house. The load from the lorry was **scattered** over the road after the accident.*

scene

1 the view that you see in front of you: *From her bedroom window, Sally looked out on a **scene** of fields and mountains.* **2** the place where something happens: *The **scene** of the story is a village in England.* **3** a part of a play or film: *In the last **scene** of the play, the son was united with his parents again.*

scenery

1 the appearance of a place: *The tourists admired the beautiful mountain **scenery** in New Zealand.* **2** boards with things such as houses and trees painted on them, that you put on a stage to make a play seem more real to the audience: *We all helped the teacher to paint the **scenery** for the school play.*

scent

a pleasant smell: *This rose has a beautiful **scent**.*

Same as **smell**.

school

a place for teaching children: *My little sister doesn't go to **school** yet. What do you want to do when you leave **school**? My **school** is not far from our house. You go to **school** to learn to read and write and do sums. Which lessons do you like best at **school**? **School**children carry their books to **school** in **school**bags.*

science

a subject in which you study natural things, such as animals, plants, rocks, metals, water, air and heat: *I prefer **science** lessons to English lessons.*

scientist

a person who studies or investigates natural things; a person who invents machines and other things: *A group of **scientists** are designing a spaceship to visit the planet Mars.*

scissors

a tool with two crossed blades that you use for cutting paper, cloth or hair: *Where are the **scissors**? This pair of **scissors** isn't sharp enough for cutting cloth.*

scold

to speak angrily to someone because they have done something wrong: *My mum **scolded** me for coming home late.*

scooter

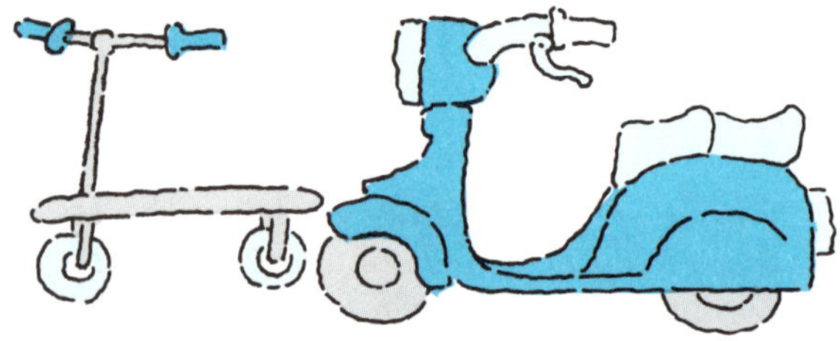

1 a child's vehicle made of a foot-board with two small wheels and a bar to hold on to: *You ride a **scooter** by putting one foot on the board and pushing the other against the ground.* **2** a small motorcycle: *My big brother rides a motor-**scooter**.*

scorch

to burn material just a little, leaving a brown mark on it: *Mum **scorched** my shirt with the hot iron.*

score

to get a point in a game: *Our best player **scored** five goals in the football match. In this quiz, each correct answer **scores** ten points.*

scored, scoring, has scored

score

the number of points scored by the teams or players in a game: *What's the **score**? The **score** is two goals to one.*

scorpion

a small animal of the spider family that has a large, curved tail with a poisonous sting: ***Scorpions** live in warm, dry parts of the world.*

scout

a member of a troop of boys, called the Scouts or Boy Scouts: ***Scouts** go camping, and learn how to do lots of useful jobs, and they also try to help other people.*

scrape

1 to damage something by rubbing it against something sharp or rough: *Dad drove too close* *to the wall and **scraped** his car. He **scraped** his car against the wall. Martin **scraped** his knees when he fell down in the playground.* **2** to clean something by rubbing it with a sharp object: *I **scraped** the potatoes clean. Bob is **scraping** the mud off his boots with a knife.*

scraped, scraping, has scraped

scratch
1 to injure skin by rubbing something sharp against it: *The cat **scratched** my hand with its claws. Sarah **scratched** herself on a thorny bush.* **2** to rub your skin with your fingernails to stop it itching: *Try not to **scratch** your spots.* **3** to make marks on something with a sharp object: *Tim **scratched** his name on the wall with a sharp stone.* **4** to make sounds by scratching: *When the dog wants to come in, he **scratches** at the door.*

scratch
a mark made by scratching: *My hand is covered with **scratches**. There's a long **scratch** on the side of the car.*

scream
to give a very loud cry: *The injured boy **screamed** with pain. 'Look out!' **screamed** the woman.*

screen
1 the blank place where pictures appear, on a television set or in a cinema: *Films are shown on a big **screen** in a cinema. A computer **screen** looks the same as a television **screen**.* **2** a flat, upright piece of furniture for dividing off part of a room: *There were **screens** between the hospital beds.*

screw
a kind of nail that you put into things by twisting it till it fits tightly: *One of the **screws** on my bicycle is loose.*

screw
1 to fix something with screws: *Dad **screwed** the sections of the chair together. I **screwed** the handle to the door.* **2** to fix something with a twisting movement: *Please **screw** the lid back on to the jam jar.*

screwdriver
a tool for turning screws: *I need a small **screwdriver** to undo the screws on my radio.*

scribble
to make untidy marks with a pencil or pen: *Don't **scribble** in your exercise book. My mum scolded my little brother for **scribbling** on his bedroom walls.*

scribbled, scribbling, has scribbled

scrub
to rub something hard in order to clean it, using soap and water; to remove dirt or stains by rubbing hard: *My mum was **scrubbing** the kitchen floor. Paul **scrubbed** the dirty marks off his jacket.*

scrubbed, scrubbing, has scrubbed

sea
the salt water that covers most of the earth's surface: *I enjoy swimming in the **sea**. The **sea** is very deep here.* **2** a certain piece of sea: *The Java **Sea** lies between Java and Borneo.*
by sea in a ship: *We went to America **by sea** and came back by air.*

seagull
a large white or grey sea-bird with a loud cry: *The **seagulls** were making a lot of noise.*

seahorse
a kind of small fish with a head like a horse's head, that swims in an upright position: *A **seahorse** has hard scales and a long, curved tail.*

seal
a large sea animal that swims about in the sea most of the time, but comes on shore to lie in the sun: *Grey **seals** have short, grey fur. **Seals** feed on fish.*

sea-lion

a large type of seal: ***Sea-lions** can be trained to perform tricks with balls.*

search
to look for something carefully: *We **searched** the whole house but couldn't find the hamster. I have been **searching** for my keys all afternoon.*

seashell
the shell of a sea creature: *The children were*

*looking for pretty **seashells** on the beach.*

seaside
a place beside the sea: *We are going on a trip to the **seaside** on Sunday. We enjoyed our holiday by the **seaside**.*

season
one of the four main divisions of the year: *The four **seasons** are spring, summer, autumn and winter.*

season
to add a flavour to food: *Mum **seasoned** the chicken with garlic.*

seasoning
something that is added to food to make it taste better: *Salt, pepper, spices, garlic and ginger are used as **seasoning**.*

seat
an object that you sit on: *Are there enough **seats** for everyone? I offered my **seat** on the bus to an old lady. Please take a **seat**.*

seaweed
the many kinds of plant that grow in the sea: *I swam under the water to look at the **seaweed**. You can cook and eat some kinds of **seaweed**.*

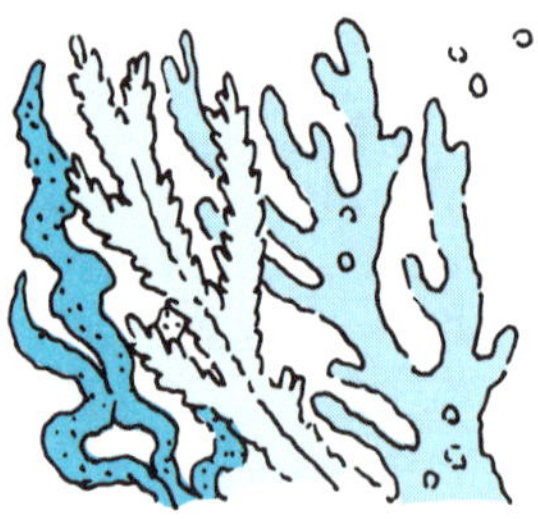

second
1 one of the sixty parts of a minute: *Joe ran the race in four minutes, eighteen **seconds**.* **2** a very short time: *I'll come in a **second**.*

second
next after the first: *February is the **second** month of the year. Michael finished the race in **second** place. He came **second** in the race.*

secret
not known to other people; hidden from other people: *There was a **secret** tunnel from the castle to the village. The spy used a false name and kept his real name **secret**.*

secret
something that is secret: *I'll tell you a **secret** if you promise not to tell anyone else. I won't tell you what I'm going to give you for your birthday — it's a **secret**.*

secretary
a person who is employed by someone to type letters, answer the telephone and make travelling arrangements for them: *The manager asked his **secretary** to book a seat on a plane to Tokyo for him.*

Two **secretaries**

section
a division of something; a part: *Each **section** of the model aeroplane has a number on it. Our mathematics course is divided into three **sections** — we study one **section** each term.*

see
1 to notice something with your eyes; to look at something: *Can you **see** that steeple in the distance? My dad can't **see** well without his glasses. I suddenly **saw** a mouse running across the floor. Let me **see** your drawing.* **2** to watch: *Did you **see** the television programme on horses yesterday afternoon? I've **seen** this film before. My parents went to the theatre to **see** a new play.* **3** to meet; to visit: *I'll be **seeing** Jenny this afternoon, so I'll give her book back to her then. Philip has toothache, so he's going to **see** a dentist tomorrow.* **4** to take someone somewhere; to go with someone: *I'll **see** you home.* **5** to understand: *I **see** what you mean. I don't **see** why I always have to go to bed so early.* **6** to find out: *I'll go to the shop and **see** if they have any bread left.*

saw, seeing, has seen

see someone off to go with someone to the place where they are starting their journey: *Are you coming to **see me off** at the airport? We **saw Granny off** at the station.*

seed
the small hard object in a plant, that a new plant grows from: *Plant the **seeds** in a row, a few centimetres apart. We feed our hamster on sunflower **seeds**. The **seeds** of a melon are flat and brown.*

seek
to try to find: *The police are **seeking** a man who was seen near the bank just before the time of the robbery. The woman **sought** in vain for her lost son.*

sought, seeking, has sought

seem
to appear to be something; to appear to do something; to look as if: *You **seem** to be surprised at the news. Thin people usually **seem** taller than they really are. The new headmistress **seems** a kind person. The exam is tomorrow, and I **seem** to have forgotten*

*everything. The little girl **seemed** to be upset about something.*

seen
see **see**: *Have you **seen** Jenny today?*

seesaw

a long, flat piece of wood or metal that is balanced on a support in the middle, so that when two people sit on it, one at each end, they go up and down in turn: *Two children were playing on the **seesaw** in the playground.*

seize
to take something suddenly; to grab: *Paul **seized** the ball from his little brother and ran away. Robert **seized** his sister by the arm, and pulled her back on to the pavement.*

- Say **seez**.
- seized, seizing, has seized

seldom
not often: *Lucy is **seldom** late for school. It's **seldom** as windy as it is today.*

The opposite is **often**.

select
to choose from a number of things or people: *Miss Pitt **selected** the children's best drawings to put up on the wall. I hope I'll be **selected** for the football team.*

Same as **choose**.

selfish
caring only for yourself and not for others: *A **selfish** person doesn't like sharing things with other people, or doing things to help other people. Don't be so **selfish** — let me have a little piece of your chocolate! It's very **selfish** of you not to let Jill use your bicycle.*

The opposite is **generous**.

self-service
serving yourself with goods or with food; not being served by a waiter or a shop assistant: *In a **self-service** restaurant, you buy food and drink at a counter, and take it to the table yourself. A supermarket is a **self-service** shop.*

sell
to give something to someone for money: *My dad **sold** our old car to our neighbour and bought a new one. Who **sold** you that bicycle? A greengrocer **sells** fruit and vegetables.*

- The opposite is **buy**.
- sold, selling, has sold

send
1 to post; to get something delivered to someone: *I **sent** postcards from Bangkok to all my friends. My aunt **sent** us a telegram saying that she was coming to see us the next day.* **2** to tell someone to go somewhere: *Dad **sent** me to the newsagent's to buy a newspaper. The teacher **sent** the naughty boy to the headmaster.* **3** to throw, push or kick: *Jack **sent** the ball into the goal with a splendid kick.*

sent, sending, has sent

send for **1** to ask someone to come: *My mum **sent for** a doctor because my sister had measles.* **2** to ask for something to be sent to you: *My dad **sent for** a taxi to take us to the station.*
send off to post: *I went to the post office and **sent off** the parcel.*
send out to send someone out of a room or house: *The teacher **sent out** the naughty boy. My dad **sent** me **out** to buy a newspaper.*

sense
1 one of the five powers that you notice things with — the powers of seeing, hearing, touching, tasting and smelling: *If you are completely deaf, you have no **sense** of hearing. A dog has a very good **sense** of smell.* **2** your ability to make good decisions about what to do: *You won't make mistakes if you use your **sense**.*
make sense to mean something; to be able to be understood: *This sentence doesn't **make sense** — I think you have left a word out.*

sensible
having plenty of sense; wise, not silly: *It was **sensible** of Jane to ring the police when she saw the man trying to break into the shop. She made a **sensible** decision.*

sent
see **send**: *My granny **sent** me a parcel. I was **sent** out to buy a newspaper.*

sentence
a group of words that you use to say something, or ask a question: *A **sentence** begins*

with a capital letter and ends with a full stop or some other mark. These are ***sentences****: 'John is late today.' 'Do you like my hat?'*

separate

1 apart; not joined up: *The garage is* ***separate*** *from the house. The house is divided into four* ***separate*** *flats.* 2 different: *Write each answer on a* ***separate*** *sheet of paper.*

separate

to move one thing away from another; to take apart or move apart: *A policeman tried to* ***separate*** *the men who were fighting. Mum broke the egg-shell and* ***separated*** *the yolk from the white. We all walked along together and then we* ***separated*** *at the crossroads.*

- The opposite is **join** or **unite**.
- separated, separating, has separated

September

the ninth month of the year.

serious

1 very bad; causing a lot of worry: *There was a* ***serious*** *accident on the motorway. Measles is a* ***serious*** *illness.* 2 not joking: *Paul is really* ***serious*** *about wanting to become a clown.* 3 quiet; working hard and not laughing a lot: *Tim is a* ***serious*** *boy — he would rather read than watch television or play with the other children. Why are you looking so* ***serious****?*

servant

a person who is employed to work in another person's house: *A long time ago, wealthy people employed lots of* ***servants*** *to clean their houses, cook their meals and look after their children.*

The opposite is **master** or **mistress**.

serve

1 to give people food and drink at table: *The hostess* ***served*** *the soup to the guests. Ask the waiter to* ***serve*** *the wine.* 2 to help customers in a shop: *Which shop assistant* ***served*** *you? Are you being* ***served****?* 3 to work for someone; to do your duty: *The old man had* ***served*** *his master for forty years. In Singapore, young men have to* ***serve*** *in the army for two years. They* ***serve*** *their country as soldiers for two years.* 4 in tennis and other games, to throw up the ball and hit it, in order to start the game: *It's your turn to* ***serve****.*

served, serving, has served

set

1 a group of things that belong together: *A tea* ***set*** *contains a teapot, jug, tea cups, saucers and small plates. The plumber carried his* ***set*** *of tools in a large bag.* 2 a television is sometimes called a television set: *We have a television* ***set*** *in the corner of the kitchen.*

set

1 to put; to place: *Anna* ***set*** *the jug down on the table.* 2 to put plates, knives, forks, glasses and other things on a table for a meal: *Would you please* ***set*** *the table for me?* 3 to make an alarm clock go off at a certain time: *Bill* ***set*** *his alarm clock for seven o'clock.* 4 to disappear below the horizon: *It gets cooler when the sun* ***sets****.* 5 to give someone a test or a task to do: *The teacher* ***set*** *a test for her pupils. In the fairy-tale the witch* ***set*** *the prince three tasks.*

set, setting, has set

all set ready: *We were* ***all set*** *to leave when the phone rang.*

set fire to something or **set something on fire** to make something start burning: *The burglars* ***set fire to the house*** *after they had stolen all the valuable things. A boy once tried to* ***set our school on fire****.*

set free to allow a person to leave prison; to let an animal or bird out of a cage: *The innocent man was* ***set free****. Peter felt sorry for his aunt's canary, so he* ***set*** *it* ***free****.*

set off or **set out** to start a journey: *We* ***set off*** *for the beach. The children* ***set out*** *to explore the cave.*

settle

1 to get into a comfortable place: *I* ***settled*** *down in the armchair to read my book.* 2 to be quiet and keep still: ***Settle*** *down, children!* 3 to go and live somewhere: *The refugees* ***settled*** *in America.*

settled, settling, has settled

seven

1 the number 7: *Three and four are* ***seven****.* 2 7 in number: *Sue is* ***seven*** *years old. There are* ***seven*** *days in a week.*

seventeen

1 the number 17: *Twenty minus three is* ***seventeen****.* 2 17 in number: *My elder sister is* ***seventeen*** *years old.*

seventy

1 the number 70: *Seven times ten is* ***seventy****.* 2 70 in number: *In Britain people are not*

*allowed to drive faster than **seventy** miles an hour.*

several
more than two, but not very many; some: *The bus is often **several** minutes late. We've visited the zoo **several** times. I've got **several** books about aeroplanes. **Several** of the pupils failed the exam.*

sew
to use a needle and thread, or a sewing machine, to make things, mend things or join things together; to stitch: *Mary cut out the pieces of cloth and **sewed** them together. Please could you **sew** this badge on to my jacket? I've **sewn** the buckle back on to your sandal. Are you good at **sewing**?*

- Rhymes with **go**.
- sewed, sewing, has sewn

sewn
see **sew**: *I've **sewn** your button on again.*

shabby
old and worn out: *Your jacket looks very **shabby** — you need a new one.*

shade
1 a place that is not in the sun: *Let's sit in the **shade** of this tree. It's cooler in the **shade**.* **2** a variety of a colour: *The young leaves of a plant are usually a brighter **shade** of green than the old ones.*

shadow

a dark shape on the ground or on a wall, caused by an object blocking the light: *Have you noticed that your **shadow** gets longer in the evenings? The children made funny **shadows** on the wall with their hands.*

shady
giving shade from heat and light: *We sat in a **shady** place during the midday heat. We had our picnic under a large, **shady** tree.*

shake
to move quickly from side to side: *The children tried to **shake** the apple tree so that the apples would fall down. When you **shake** your head, you mean 'no'.*

shook, shaking, has shaken

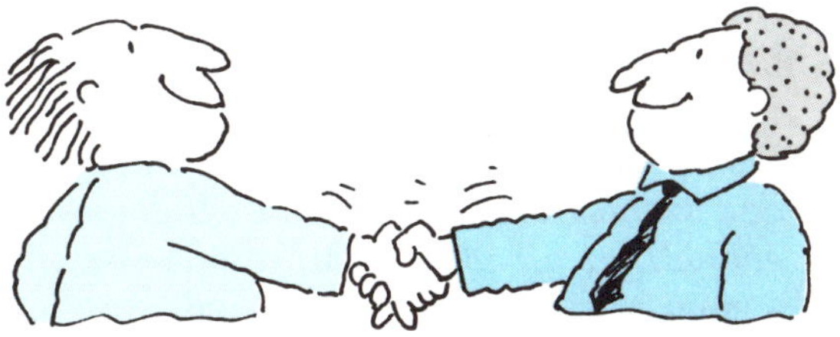

shake hands to greet someone by gripping their right hand with your right hand: *People usually **shake hands** when they are introduced to each other. Mr Smith **shook hands** with Mr Brown. The teacher **shook** Mum's **hand***

shall
1 you use **shall** with **I** and **we** to say what you are going to do: *We **shall** go shopping tomorrow morning. I **shall** not need any dinner tonight. I **shall** be leaving at nine o'clock. **Shall** I ever see you again?* **2** you use **shall** when you are suggesting something or asking for advice: ***Shall** we go to the beach today? How many tickets **shall** I buy? **Shall** I tell Mum about the broken vase, or **shan't** I?*

You can shorten:
- **I shall** to **I'll**
- **we shall** to **we'll**
- **shall not** to **shan't**

shallow
not deep: *The children were playing in the **shallow** end of the swimming-pool. You must stay in **shallow** water if you can't swim.*

The opposite is **deep**.

shame
1 an unpleasant feeling you get when you have behaved badly: *Philip was full of **shame** at his bad behaviour.* **2** a pity: *What a **shame** you are not allowed to come with us!*

shameful
very bad: *What **shameful** behaviour!*

shampoo
a liquid for washing your hair with: ***Shampoo** makes a lot of foam when you rub it into your hair.*

shan't
short for **shall not**: *We **shan't** wait for a bus — we'll walk.*

shape
the form that an object has: *What **shape** is a*

*peach? A peach is round in **shape**.*

shaped
having a certain shape: *The earth is **shaped** like a ball.*

share
1 to use something together with other people: *Emma **shares** her bedroom with her sister. We had to **share** textbooks because there were not enough for all of us.* **2** to divide something among a group or between two people: *Liz **shared** the ice-cream out among her guests. My sister and I **shared** the chocolate between us.*

shared, sharing, has shared

shark

a large, fierce fish that has sharp teeth: *Some types of **shark** attack people when they are swimming.*

sharp
1 having a very thin edge that cuts well: *This knife is very **sharp**. You need a **sharp** pair of scissors to cut cloth. Sharks have very **sharp** teeth.* **2** having a good point: *This pencil isn't very **sharp**. A needle has a **sharp** point.* **3** changing direction suddenly: *There are lots of **sharp** bends on this road. The car made a **sharp** left turn.* **4** seeing well; hearing well: *Eagles have **sharp** eyes. Dogs have **sharp** ears.*

Meanings 1 and 2: the opposite is **blunt**.

shave
to cut away hair with a razor: *My dad **shaves** every morning. Mr Walker has **shaved** off his beard. Many monks **shave** their heads.*

shaved, shaving, has shaved

she
you use **she** when you are talking about a girl or woman: *Mary realized that **she** had made a mistake. I don't know that woman — who is **she**?*

shed
a wooden hut, or a larger building, for storing things in: *We have a **shed** in our garden to keep our gardening tools in.*

she'd
short for **she had** or **she would**: *Rachel went outside to play after **she'd** finished her homework. Katie said **she'd** be back in half an hour.*

sheep
a farm animal that is kept for its wool and its meat: *A **sheep** bleats. A baby **sheep** is called a lamb. A shepherd looks after a flock of **sheep**. The meat of a **sheep** is called mutton. **Sheep** feed on grass.*

Lots of **sheep**

sheepdog

a dog that is trained to help a shepherd to guide a flock of sheep: *The shepherd tells his **sheepdogs** what to do by whistling to them.*

sheet
1 a large piece of cloth for putting on a bed, under the other covers: *Mum put clean **sheets** on our beds.* **2** a large, thin, flat piece of something: *The teacher gave each child two **sheets** of paper.*

shelf
a long flat piece of wood or metal for putting things on, fixed to a wall, or fixed inside a cupboard: *Put the books back on the right **shelves**. I can't reach the cups on the top **shelf** of the kitchen cupboard.*

Lots of **shelves**

shell
1 the hard outer part of an egg or nut: *Egg-**shells** break easily. A coconut **shell** is very hard.* **2** the hard back of a tortoise or snail; the hard outer part of small sea creatures: *A tortoise can pull its head and legs into its **shell**. The children collected **shells** on the beach.*

she'll
short for **she will**: *Angela doesn't know whether **she'll** be allowed to come to the party.*

shelter
a place where you are protected from something: *A harbour provides ships with **shelter***

from the wind. I went into the doorway of a shop to take ***shelter*** *from the rain.*

shelter
1 to find shelter: *It started to rain, so we* ***sheltered*** *under a tree.* **2** to give shelter: *An umbrella* ***shelters*** *you from the rain.*

shepherd
a person whose job is to look after sheep: *The* ***shepherd*** *and his two dogs gathered in the sheep.*

Say **shep**-erd.

she's
short for **she is** or **she has**: *This is Ann —* ***she's*** *a friend of mine. Elizabeth is coming to see me when* ***she's*** *finished her homework.*

shield
a broad piece of metal or wood that soldiers used to carry to protect themselves from their enemies' swords and arrows: *The soldiers marched into battle with their swords and* ***shields****.*

shield
to protect: *I put my hand up to* ***shield*** *my eyes from the sun.*

shine
1 to give out light; to point a light towards something: *The sun is* ***shining****. The policeman* ***shone*** *his torch on the burglar's face.* **2** to be bright: *Jennifer polished her shoes until they* ***shone****.*

shone, shining, has shone

ship
a large boat: *The cargo of rice was transported to Hong Kong by* ***ship****. There were over five hundred passengers on board the* ***ship****.*

shipwreck
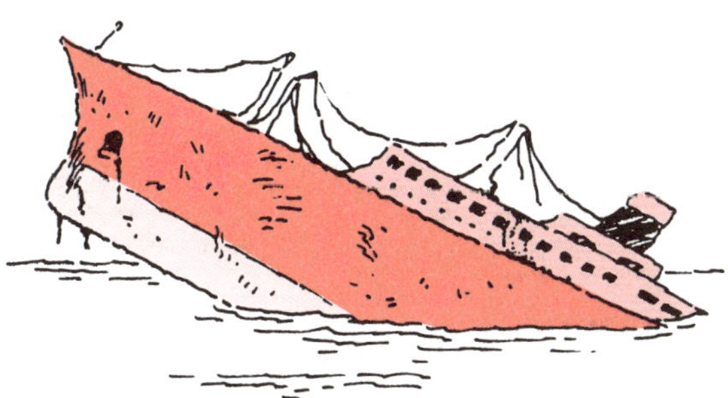

the sinking of a ship in an accident at sea: *The whole cargo was lost in the* ***shipwreck****. All the passengers were rescued from the* ***shipwreck****.*

shirt
a light piece of clothing that a man or boy wears on the upper part of his body: *A* ***shirt*** *has sleeves, a collar and buttons down the front. Mr Jones is wearing a grey suit, a white* ***shirt*** *and a blue tie.*

shiver
to tremble because you are cold or frightened: *I was* ***shivering*** *with cold after walking home in the wind and rain. The horrible noise made us* ***shiver*** *with fright.*

shock
1 an unpleasant surprise: *The news of the accident gave us all a* ***shock****.* **2** a sudden pain that you get when you touch an electric wire: *Richard got an electric* ***shock*** *when he touched the plug.*

shock
to make people very upset: *Everyone was* ***shocked*** *by the horrible accident. I'm* ***shocked*** *at you for telling lies.*

shoe
a piece of clothing for your foot, made of leather or some other strong material: *I've got a new pair of running* ***shoes****. Lucy is wearing blue* ***shoes*** *today.*

shoelace
a string for fastening a shoe: *I showed my little sister how to tie her* ***shoelaces****. Your* ***shoelace*** *has come undone.*

shone
see **shine**: *The sun* ***shone*** *all day. The sun hasn't* ***shone*** *for the last three days.*

shook
see **shake**: *I asked the little girl if she'd like a sweet, but she* ***shook*** *her head.*

shoot
1 to fire a bullet from a gun; to fire an arrow from a bow: *The bank-robbers were* ***shooting*** *at the policemen. Peter* ***shot*** *an arrow at the target.* **2** to injure or kill with a bullet or arrow: *The policeman* ***shot*** *the robber in the leg. One of the robbers was* ***shot*** *dead. The hunter went out to* ***shoot*** *hares.* **3** to move very fast: *Simon suddenly* ***shot*** *out of the room. A police-car* ***shot*** *past us.* **4** to kick a ball at a goal: ***'Shoot!'*** *shouted the spectators.*

shot, shooting, has shot

shoot

a plant that is just beginning to grow from a seed; any new part that is growing from a plant: *The first* ***shoots*** *appeared two weeks after my mum had sown the seeds. The deer was eating the young* ***shoots*** *on the fir trees.*

shop

a place where you can buy things: *You can buy bread and cakes at a baker's* ***shop****. This* ***shop*** *is open on Saturdays but it's closed on Sundays.*

shop

to go to shops and buy things: *We always* ***shop*** *on Saturdays.*

> shopped, shopping, has shopped

shopkeeper

a person who owns a shop: *I asked the* ***shop-keeper*** *for two bars of soap.*

shopping

1 the buying of things in shops: *We go* ***shopping*** *twice a week. Do you have a lot of* ***shopping*** *to do today?* **2** the things that you have bought: *I helped mum carry home the* ***shopping****.*

shopping centre a part of a town, or a very large building, where there are a lot of shops: *You can buy almost anything in this new* ***shopping centre****.*

shore

the land along the edge of the sea or a lake: *We walked along the* ***shore*** *looking for seashells.*

short

1 not lasting long; brief: *John did his homework in a very* ***short*** *time, so that he could go out and play. The Queen made a* ***short*** *speech. Your composition is too* ***short****, Jane — you should have written more.* **2** not long: *Andrew has very* ***short*** *hair. Kate has had her hair cut* ***short****. Your skirt is far too* ***short****, Susan! Mrs Lee showed us the* ***shortest*** *way to the zoo.* **3** not tall; smaller than other people: *The cook was a* ***short****, fat man.*

> - Meanings 1 and 2: the opposite is **long**.
> - Meaning 3: the opposite is **tall**.

short cut a quick way of getting somewhere: *The children took a* ***short cut*** *through the park to get to school.*

short for a short way of saying: *'Phone' is* ***short for*** *'telephone'. 'Jenny' is* ***short for*** *'Jennifer'. 'Don't' is* ***short for*** *'do not'.*

short of not having enough of something: *I'm* ***short of*** *money — could you lend me some? We're* ***short of*** *rice. The country is* ***short of*** *water.*

shorten

to make shorter: *You can* ***shorten*** *'I have' to 'I've'. This skirt needs to be* ***shortened****.*

shorts

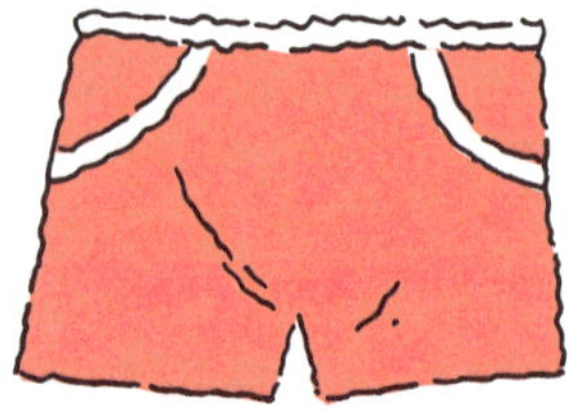

short trousers that don't cover your knees: *Where are my white* ***shorts****? Here is a clean pair of football* ***shorts****.*

shot

1 the firing of a bullet from a gun: *The soldier fired a* ***shot*** *into the air.* **2** the action of kicking or hitting a ball: *That was a good* ***shot****! Take a* ***shot*** *at goal!*

shot

see **shoot**: *The hunter* ***shot*** *a deer. The robber was* ***shot*** *in the leg.*

should

1 you use **should** when you are saying that something is the right thing to do: *You* ***should*** *brush your teeth twice a day. You* ***should*** *not tell lies. We* ***shouldn't*** *waste food,* ***should*** *we? We're going the wrong way — we* ***should*** *have turned right, not left.* **2** you use **should** with **I** and **we** to say that you want to do something: *I* ***should*** *like to come with you. We* ***should*** *like to go to Australia next year for our holidays.* ***I'd*** *love to see the new film at the cinema.*

> You can shorten
> - **I should** to **I'd**
> - **we should** to **we'd**
> - **should not** to **shouldn't**

shoulder

the part of your body between your neck and the upper part of your arm: *The man was carrying his little daughter on his* ***shoulders****. A* ***shoulder****-bag has a long strap so that you can carry it over your* ***shoulder****.*

shouldn't
short for **should not**: *You **shouldn't** put off your homework till late at night. We should always tell the truth, **shouldn't** we?*

shout
1 to talk very loudly; to say something very loudly: *We had to **shout** because of the loud music. There's no need to **shout** — I'm not deaf. 'Watch out!' Peter **shouted**.* 2 to talk to someone in an angry voice: *Stop **shouting** at each other! Don't **shout** at me!*

shout
a loud cry: *We heard a **shout** coming from the window.*

shovel

a tool for lifting and moving earth, sand or other things: *A **shovel** has a round metal blade and a long handle.*

show
1 to let someone see something: *Please **show** me your photos. You must **show** the conductor your bus pass.* 2 to point to someone or something: ***Show** me the boy who hit you. A lady **showed** me the way to the museum.* 3 to guide: *The waiter **showed** us to our table in the restaurant.* 4 to teach someone how to do something: *My brother **showed** me how to tie a bow.*

showed, showing, has shown

show off 1 to do things that you think other people will admire: *Keith is always **showing off** to the girls. Don't **show off**!* 2 to show something to other people so that they can admire it: *Richard brought his new bike to school so that he could **show** it **off** to everyone.*

show
1 a play or something else that is performed in a theatre or on television: *Did you watch the acrobats in the television **show** last night? Mum and Dad are going to a **show** at the theatre tonight.* 2 an exhibition: *We went to the motor **show** to look at all the new cars.*

shower
1 a spray of water that you stand under to wash; the place where the spray is fitted: *We have a bath and a **shower** in our bathroom. Jenny is in the **shower**.* 2 the action of washing yourself by standing under a spray of water: *My dad takes a cold **shower** every morning. I always have a **shower** after swimming in the sea.* 3 a short period of rain: *Let's wait inside till the **shower** is over.*

shown
see **show**: *You haven't **shown** me your new bicycle yet.*

shrank
see **shrink**: *This sweater **shrank** when it was washed.*

shriek
to scream suddenly: *Sue always **shrieks** with fright when she sees a spider. The children were **shrieking** with laughter.*

shrink
to become smaller: *Jeans **shrink** when they are washed in hot water for the first time.*

shrank, shrinking, has shrunk

shrub

a small bush: *There are some rose-bushes and other **shrubs** in the garden.*

shrunk
see **shrink**: *This pullover seems to have **shrunk** — it's too small for me.*

shut
1 to move a door, window, drawer or book so that it is no longer open; to close: ***Shut** the door, please! The door **shut** with a loud bang. **Shut** your books, children.* 2 to close and lock a shop; to be closed: *Shops in Britain usually **shut** at half-past five. Mr Lee **shut** up his shop and went home.*

- Same as **close**.
- shut, shutting, has shut

shut off to stop something working; to stop something flowing: *Dad **shut off** the engine by turning the car-key. The plumber **shut off** the water before he repaired the pipe.*
shut up to stop talking: *My brother told me to **shut up**. It's rude to say '**shut up**!'*

shut
closed; not open: *Is the window **shut**? Most shops are **shut** on Sundays.*

shuttlecock

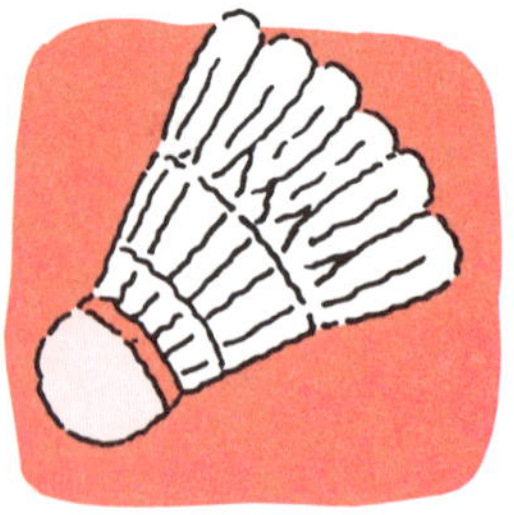

a very light object made of cork and feathers, for hitting in badminton: *You have to hit the **shuttlecock** very hard with your racket to make it go over the net.*

shy

1 feeling nervous when other people are around, especially people you don't know: *Tim was too **shy** to talk to the guests. My little sister is **shy** of strangers.* **2** getting frightened easily: *Deer are very **shy** animals.*

> The opposite is **bold**.

sick

1 ill: *Martin was very **sick** and had to stay in bed.* **2** bringing up food out of your mouth from your stomach: *I think I'm going to be **sick**. I was **sick** three times on the boat.*

side

1 the left or right of something or someone: *Jane lives on the same **side** of the street as I do. Susan is sitting on my left **side**.* **2** the left, right, top, bottom, back or front of something: *A brick has six **sides**. A square has four equal **sides**.* **3** the front or the back of something thin and flat: *Write on both **sides** of the paper.*

sideways

towards one side; not forward or backward: *A crab walks **sideways**.*

sigh

to take a long, deep breath and breathe out noisily: *Andrew **sighed** when he saw how much homework he had to do.*

sight

1 the ability to see: *The blind man had lost his **sight** when his eyes were hurt in an accident.* **2** the distance within which you can see something: *We went on to the deck of the ship to see if the land was in **sight**.* **3** something that you see: *The yachts sailing in the bay were a lovely **sight**.* **4** something that is worth visiting: *The guide showed the tourists the **sights** of Singapore.*

sight-seeing

visiting the famous and interesting places in a city: *The tourists went **sight-seeing** in Singapore.*

sign

1 a mark that means something: *+ is the **sign** for addition.* **2** a movement you make to tell someone something: *My brother made a **sign** to me to keep still.* **3** a written notice or small picture telling you something: *The **sign** said 'Swimming pool', with an arrow telling us which way to go. Do you know the meanings of all the road **signs**?* **4** something that shows what is going to happen: *Clouds are sometimes a **sign** of rain. Wind is sometimes a **sign** that the weather is going to change.*

sign

to write your name: *The headmaster **signed** the letters after his secretary had typed them. Please **sign** your name here.*

signal

1 a sign, such as a movement of the hand, a light, or a sound, which gives a certain message: *The referee blew his whistle as a **signal** for the match to start. Tom flashed a **signal** to Peter with his torch.* **2** a set of coloured lights telling drivers when to stop and when to go: *You must stop when the traffic **signal** is red, and you can go when it is green.*

signature

your own name written by you: *My dad's **signature** is difficult to read.*

signpost

a pole with a sign that shows the direction and distance of places: *There is a **signpost** at the crossroads. The **signpost** said 'London 45 miles'.*

silence

a time when there is no sound: *The teacher asked us a difficult question, and there was a long **silence** before anyone answered. The children listened in **silence** to the story.*

silent

1 not speaking: *The children stayed **silent** while the teacher read to them.* **2** without any sound: *The house was empty and **silent**.*

> Same as **quiet**.

silk

1 very fine soft threads that are produced by a kind of caterpillar called a 'silkworm': ***Silk** is made into cloth.* **2** cloth made from these threads: *Mum's white blouse is made of **silk**. Mrs Jones is wearing a blue **silk** scarf.*

silly
not sensible; stupid: *It's very **silly** to run across the road without looking to see if any cars are coming. I'm tired of my little sister's **silly** questions.*

> Same as **foolish**.

silver
a brightly shining metal that is used for making jewellery and other things: *These teaspoons are made of **silver**. Nicola is wearing **silver** earrings.*

similar
like something else; alike: *A rat is **similar** to a mouse, but much bigger. Tim and his brother look very **similar**.*

> Same as **like** or **alike**.

simple
1 not difficult: *These sums are very **simple**. I'm sure you all know the answer to such a **simple** question.* **2** not special; plain: *The food we get at school is **simple** but healthy.*

> - Meaning 1: same as **easy**.
> - simple, simpler, simplest

since
1 from that time till now: *I've been waiting for you **since** three o'clock. I haven't seen Joan **since** last Sunday. Mr Smith broke his leg last year and he has been limping ever **since**.* **2** because: ***Since** it was raining, we played indoors. Let's walk home, **since** we've missed the bus.*

sing
to make tunes with your voice: *Katie **sings** very well. We **sing** the words of the songs while Mum plays the piano. The birds start **singing** early in the morning.*

> sang, singing, has sung

singer
a person who sings: *The music teacher is going to choose the best **singers** out of each class to sing in the school choir. Who is your favourite pop **singer**?*

single
1 only one: *The spider hung from the ceiling on a **single** thread.* **2** even one: *This book is written in a foreign language — I can't understand a **single** word of it.* **3** for one person only: *There are **single** rooms and double rooms in most hotels.* **4** not married: ***Single** men are called bachelors. You put 'Miss' before the surname of a **single** lady.* **5** for going to a place only, not coming back from it: *Shall I get a **single** ticket or a return ticket to Kuala Lumpur?*

sink
1 to go down in water; not to float: *If you throw a stone into water, it will **sink**. Help — the boat is **sinking**! The ship struck a rock and **sank**.* **2** to go down deep into something: *Our feet **sank** into the sand as we walked along the beach.*

> - Meaning 1: the opposite is **float**.
> - sank, sinking, has sunk

sink
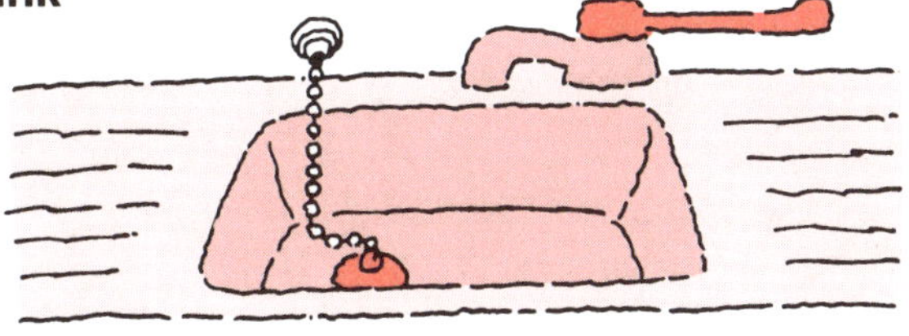

a basin in a kitchen where you wash the dishes: *Put the dirty pan in the **sink**.*

sip
to drink something very slowly by taking just a small amount each time: *This tea is very hot — **sip** it slowly. I **sipped** a little of Dad's wine but I didn't like the taste.*

> sipped, sipping, has sipped

sir
a polite word that you use when you talk to a man: *We say '**Sir**' to the masters at school. Please, **sir**, may I open the window? Thank you, **sir**! 'Can I help you, **sir**?' asked the shop assistant.*

siren
an instrument that makes a long, loud noise as a warning: *Police cars, fire engines and ambulances have **sirens**. Three fire engines drove past us with their **sirens** screaming.*

sister
a girl or woman who has the same parents as you do: *I have two **sisters** and one brother. Aunt Mary is my father's youngest **sister**.*

sit
1 to rest on your bottom; to take a seat: *The children **sat** on the floor round the teacher.*

*Mum was **sitting** in the armchair. I was **sitting** at my desk doing my homework. Can you find a chair to **sit** on?* **2** to take a seat; to sit down: *Come and **sit** next to me.*

sat, sitting, has sat

sit back to lean back in a chair: *Dad **sat back** in an armchair and read the paper.*

sit down to take a seat; to get into a sitting position: ***Sit down**, children! We **sat down** on a bench to eat our sandwiches.*

sit up to get into a sitting position after you have been lying down or leaning back: *Little babies aren't strong enough to **sit up** by themselves. **Sit up** straight, children!*

sitting-room
a room in a house where you can sit comfortably; a living-room: *In the evenings, we often watch television in the **sitting-room**. When the guests arrived, Mum took them into the **sitting-room**.*

six
1 the number 6: *Three and three are **six**.* **2** 6 in number: *David is **six** years old.*

sixteen
1 the number 16: *Four times four is **sixteen**.* **2** 16 in number: *David's elder brother is **sixteen** years old.*

sixty
1 the number 60: *Six times ten is **sixty**.* **2** 60 in number: *An hour has **sixty** minutes.*

size
1 how big or small something is: *We measured the playground to see what **size** it was. The playground is about half the **size** of a football field. Is a hamster the same **size** as a mouse?* **2** a certain size in clothes or shoes: *'What size shoes do you take?' 'I take **size** 34.' The first dress that I tried on in the shop was too big for me, so I tried on a smaller **size**.*

skate
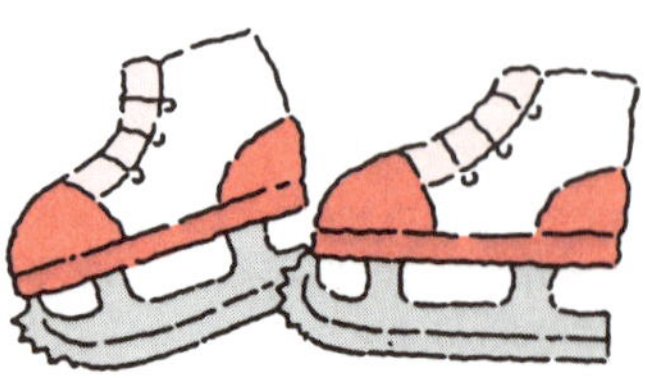

a boot with a steel blade fixed underneath it, that you wear for moving about on ice: *These **skates** are getting too small for me — I need a new pair of **skates**.*

skate
to move on skates: *Can you **skate**? I'm learning to **skate**. The children went **skating** on the frozen pond.*

skated, skating, has skated

skeleton
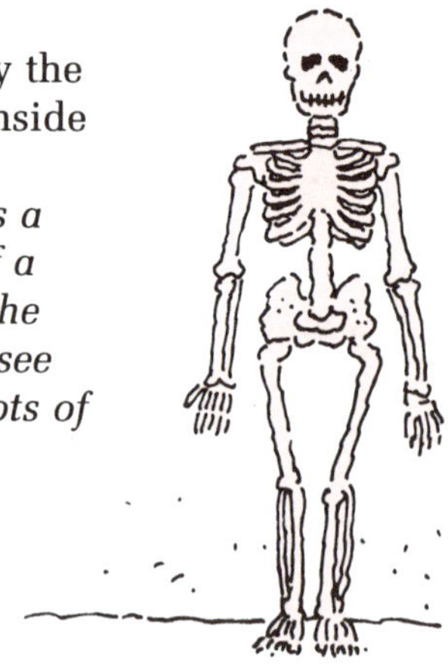

the shape made by the joined-up bones inside your body: *The teacher showed us a model **skeleton** of a human being. In the museum you can see the **skeletons** of lots of different animals, birds and fish.*

skid
to slide sideways: *The back wheel of John's bicycle **skidded** on the wet road and he fell off.*

skidded, skidding, has skidded

skill
the ability to do something that is difficult: *Everyone admired Jenny's **skill** at drawing. You go to school to learn the **skills** of reading and writing.*

skin
1 the stuff that covers your body: *After the baby has his bath, Mum rubs cream on his **skin** to keep it soft. Some people have pale **skins** and some people have dark **skins**.* **2** the stuff that covers a fruit or vegetable: *Please put the banana **skin** in the dustbin. Mum put the tomatoes in hot water to get the **skins** off.*

skip
1 to go along, hopping on each foot in turn: *The children **skipped** round the room in time to the music.* **2** to jump over a rope that you turn under your feet and over your head: *Mary and Julie turned the **skipping** rope while Jenny **skipped** in the middle.*

skipped, skipping, has skipped

skirt
a piece of clothing that is worn by girls and women, which hangs down from the waist: *Susan is wearing a blue **skirt** and a pink blouse.*

skull
the round, hollow bone of your head, containing your brain: *People who ride on motor-*

cycles have to wear helmets so that they don't damage their ***skulls*** *when they have a crash.*

sky
the space above the earth, where you can see the sun, the moon and the stars: *Today the* ***sky*** *is blue and there are no clouds in it. Can you see that flock of geese flying across the* ***sky****?*

skyscraper
a very high building that has a lot of floors: *Have you ever been on the top floor of a* ***skyscraper****?*

slam

to shut a door or window with a loud bang: *Don't* ***slam*** *the door! The sudden wind made the window* ***slam*** *shut.*

slammed, slamming, has slammed

slap
to give someone a blow with the palm of your hand: *Judy* ***slapped*** *her brother in the face because he had been rude to her.*

slapped, slapping, has slapped

slave
a servant who is owned by his master and is not free to leave him: *A long time ago, masters used to whip their* ***slaves*** *if they tried to escape.*

sleep
to rest your body, especially at night, by lying down and closing your eyes, so that you don't feel anything for a time: *Good night —* ***sleep*** *well! I can't* ***sleep*** *because I'm not tired.*

slept, sleeping, has slept

sleep
the time when you are asleep; a period of sleeping: *Children need a lot of* ***sleep****. Now, children, switch off the light and go to* ***sleep****. Granny has a short* ***sleep*** *in the afternoons.*

sleepy
wanting to go to sleep: *Peter was so* ***sleepy*** *that he couldn't keep his eyes open.*

sleeve
the part of a piece of clothing that covers your arm: *Paul is wearing a shirt with short* ***sleeves****.*

slept
see **sleep**: *I* ***slept*** *well last night. Have you ever* ***slept*** *on the floor?*

slice
a thin, flat piece cut from something; a section cut out of something: *I cut two* ***slices*** *of bread to make myself a sandwich. I got a big* ***slice*** *of Susan's birthday cake.*

slice

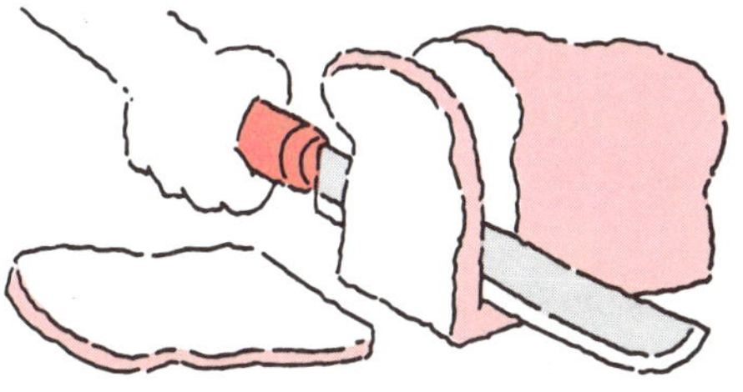

to cut food into slices: *Mum* ***sliced*** *the cucumber. Buy me a* ***sliced*** *loaf at the baker's.*

sliced, slicing, has sliced

slid
see **slide**: *Jim* ***slid*** *down the rail instead of walking down the steps. I couldn't find the book because it had* ***slid*** *under the sofa.*

slide
to move smoothly over something: *You must not* ***slide*** *in the school corridors. Joe grabbed a little fish out of the river, but it* ***slid*** *out of his hand again.*

slid, sliding, has slid

slide
a long, smooth, sloping piece of metal, set up in a playground, for children to slide down: *We've got a* ***slide*** *and a seesaw in our playground.*

slim
not fat; rather thin: *Mrs Jones is tall and* ***slim****. Taking exercise is a good way of keeping* ***slim****.*

slim, slimmer, slimmest

slip
1 to slide by mistake and lose your balance: *Joe* ***slipped*** *and fell on the ice.* **2** to slide out of the right position: *The knife* ***slipped*** *and cut my finger. The plate* ***slipped*** *out of my hand and fell on the floor.* **3** to move quietly, especially without being noticed: *I think I'll* ***slip*** *out of the house and buy some sweets.*

slipped, slipping, has slipped

slipper
a loose, comfortable shoe that you wear indoors, especially with your pyjamas: *I took off my robe and my* ***slippers*** *and got into bed.*

slippery
so smooth that you may slip: *Be careful — this mud on the path is very* ***slippery****.*

slope
1 a part of a road that goes upwards or downwards: *You can ride your bike very fast down a steep* ***slope****.* **2** the side of a hill: *Several houses have been built on the* ***slopes*** *above the village.*

slope
to go upwards or downwards: *The land* ***sloped*** *downwards to the sea. The house is built on* ***sloping*** *ground.*

> sloped, sloping, has sloped

slow
1 not fast; taking a long time: *The bus was very* ***slow*** *today because there was a lot of traffic. Why were you so* ***slow*** *to answer the telephone?* **2** showing a time earlier than the real time: *My watch is five minutes* ***slow****.*

> - Meaning 1: the opposite is **fast** or **quick**.
> - Meaning 2: the opposite is **fast**.

slow down to become slower; to make slower: *The police have warned drivers to* ***slow down*** *because of the fog.*

sly
clever at tricking people: *In the story, the* ***sly*** *fox invited the silly duck to his home, so that he could eat her up.*

> Same as **cunning**.

smack
to hit someone hard with your hand; to slap: *My mum* ***smacked*** *my little brother for being naughty. She* ***smacked*** *his hand.*

small
not large: *A mouse is a* ***small*** *animal. Helen is* ***smaller*** *than me. There's only a* ***small*** *amount of rice left. James is spelt with a capital J, and jug is spelt with a* ***small*** *j.*

> - Same as **little** or **tiny**.
> - The opposite is **big**.

smart
1 neat and attractive; fashionable: *You're looking very* ***smart*** *in your new dress. What a* ***smart*** *hat! Mr Johnson is wearing a* ***smart*** *blue suit.* **2** clever; able to understand things quickly: *Most of the children are pretty* ***smart*** *at using the computer.*

> Meaning 2: the opposite is **stupid** or **foolish**.

smash
1 to break into lots of pieces: *The vase dropped on the floor and* ***smashed*** *into little pieces. The burglars* ***smashed*** *a window to get into the house.* **2** to crash very hard into something: *The truck* ***smashed*** *into a lamp-post.*

smell
1 something that you notice through your nose: *Garlic has a strong* ***smell****. Roses have a* ***sweet*** *smell. That rotten fish has made a horrible* ***smell****. I like the* ***smell*** *of fresh bread. What's that* ***smell*** *coming from the kitchen? There's a* ***smell*** *of burning.* **2** the ability to notice things through your nose: *Dogs have a very good sense of* ***smell****.*

> Meaning 1: same as **scent**.

smell
1 to notice something through your nose: *Dogs can* ***smell*** *things that are a long way away. I can* ***smell*** *burning.* ***Smell*** *these roses!* **2** to give off a smell: *The dinner* ***smells*** *very good. My hands* ***smell*** *of soap.*

> smelt, smelling, has smelt

smelt
see **smell**: *Bob said he* ***smelt*** *gas. Have you* ***smelt*** *these roses?*

smile
to turn up the corners of your mouth in a friendly way, or because you are happy or amused: *The girl from the house next door* ***smiled*** *at me and said 'hello'. We all* ***smiled*** *at the teacher's joke.*

> smiled, smiling, has smiled

smile
the action of smiling: *'How are you?' Paul asked with a friendly* ***smile****. The teacher gave me a* ***smile*** *when she met me in the street.*

smoke
the clouds of gas and bits of soot that go up into the air from something that is burning: *Clouds of* ***smoke*** *were coming out of the chimney. The kitchen was full of* ***smoke*** *after*

I burnt the toast. I hate the smell of cigarette ***smoke****.*

smoke

1 to have a burning cigarette, cigar or pipe in the mouth, and suck in the smoke from it: *My parents don't* ***smoke****. Mr Brown is* ***smoking*** *a pipe.* **2** to give off lots of smoke: *The factory chimney is* ***smoking****.*

smoked, smoking, has smoked

smoky
filled with smoke: *The room was very* ***smoky*** *after the party.*

smooth
even, not rough: *Babies have soft,* ***smooth*** *skins. The sea was nice and* ***smooth*** *when we went sailing yesterday.*

The opposite is **rough**.

smuggler
a person who does wrong by secretly taking expensive goods into a country, or out of a country: *The gang of* ***smugglers*** *used a cave to hide the goods in.*

snack
a small, quick meal: *'Shall we have a* ***snack*** *while we wait for the train?' 'Yes, let's — I'll have a sandwich and a cup of tea.'*

snail
a small creature with a soft body covered by a shell, which crawls slowly along the ground: *A* ***snail*** *can hide inside its shell.*

snake
an animal with a long, narrow body and no legs, that moves along the ground by twisting: *A* ***snake*** *was gliding through the grass.* ***Snakes*** *and alligators are reptiles.*

snap
1 to make a sudden sharp noise: *You* ***snap*** *your fingers by moving your middle finger quickly across your thumb. The lid of the box* ***snapped*** *shut.* **2** to break something suddenly with a loud noise: *Bob* ***snapped*** *the stick in half.* **3** to bite at something: *The dog is* ***snapping*** *at the cat. The dog* ***snapped*** *up the meat and ran away.*

snapped, snapping, has snapped

snatch
to grab something suddenly: *My little brother* ***snatched*** *the piece of chocolate out of my hand and ate it.*

sneeze
to blow air out of your nose with a sudden noise: *You* ***sneeze*** *a lot when you are getting a cold. The pepper made me* ***sneeze****.*

sneezed, sneezing, has sneezed

sniff

to take a short breath through your nose when you are trying to smell something: *Laura* ***sniffed*** *the flowers. A dog recognizes people by* ***sniffing*** *at them.*

snore
to make a loud noise at the back of your throat when you are asleep: *Dad fell asleep on the sofa and began to* ***snore****.*

snored, snoring, has snored

snow
tiny, white pieces of frozen water, called **snowflakes**, that fall from the sky in very cold weather: *The ground was covered with a thick layer of* ***snow****. A lot of* ***snow*** *had fallen during the night. Lots of children were playing in the* ***snow****, throwing* ***snowballs*** *and building* ***snowmen****.*

snow
to fall as snowflakes from the sky: *Look, it's* ***snowing****! It hardly ever* ***snows*** *in warmer countries.*

so
1 therefore: *Katie is ill* ***so*** *she can't go to school*

today. It was getting dark, ***so*** *I switched on the light.* **2** very: *Thank you* ***so*** *much! I'm* ***so*** *glad that the exam is over.* **3** enough to make something happen: *It was* ***so*** *hot that the chocolate melted. It was* ***so*** *cold that the pond froze.* **4** also: *'I like swimming.' '****So*** *do I.'* **5** Here are some other ways of using **so**: *'Are you getting a camera for your birthday?' 'Yes, I hope* ***so****.' If you haven't handed your work to the teacher, please do* ***so*** *now.*

so long goodbye: ***So long****, Vicky!*

soak

to make something very wet: *The heavy rain has completely* ***soaked*** *my clothes. I'm* ***soaked****!*

soap

stuff that you use with water for washing yourself: *We need a new bar of* ***soap*** *in the bathroom.*

sob

to cry noisily: *The little boy was* ***sobbing*** *because he had lost his mother in the supermarket.*

> sobbed, sobbing, has sobbed

soccer

another word for football: *The boys were playing* ***soccer*** *in the park. Who is your favourite* ***soccer*** *player?*

sock

a piece of clothing that covers your foot and ankle: *I need a new pair of* ***socks****. There's a hole in the heel of this* ***sock****.*

socket

an object fixed to a wall with specially shaped holes for fitting a plug into: *You must put the plug into the wall* ***socket*** *before you can switch on the television.*

sofa

a long, soft seat with a back and arms: *The four children were sitting side by side on the* ***sofa*** *watching television.*

soft

1 not hard; not firm: *Cotton wool is very* ***soft****. Clay is* ***soft*** *when it's still wet. It's nice to sleep on a* ***soft*** *pillow.* **2** smooth and pleasant to touch: *What lovely* ***soft*** *fur this little kitten has!* **3** not loud: *I can't hear what you're saying when you speak in such a* ***soft*** *voice.*

> - Meaning 1: the opposite is **hard**.
> - Meaning 3: the opposite is **loud**.

soil

the dark brown stuff that plants grow in: The gardener *raked the* ***soil*** *before he sowed the seeds.*

sold

see **sell**: *Mr Smith* ***sold*** *his old car and bought a new one. The old car was* ***sold*** *for $5000.*

soldier

a man who is in the army: *A troop of* ***soldiers*** *was marching along the road. Thousands of* ***soldiers*** *were killed in the battle.*

solid

hard; not a liquid: *Water becomes* ***solid*** *when it freezes.*

> The opposite is **liquid**.

solve

to find the answer to a problem: *The detectives have* ***solved*** *the mystery of the stolen jewels.*

> solved, solving, has solved

some

1 an amount of something; a number of something: *Would you like* ***some*** *ice-cream?* ***Some*** *of the tea was spilt on the carpet.* ***Some*** *of us helped the teacher to tidy the classroom and the rest went home. I ate* ***some*** *of the biscuits, but not all of them.* **2** certain: ***Some*** *birds, such as penguins, cannot fly.* ***Some*** *people can do things better with their left hands than their right hands.* **3** you use **some** when you can't say the exact thing or the exact time: *Draw a picture of a dog or* ***some*** *other animal. I'll be a famous actress* ***some*** *day.*

somebody

a certain person; someone: *I know* ***somebody*** *who keeps a monkey as a pet. I heard* ***somebody*** *shouting outside.*

somehow

in some way, though you don't know how: *I'm sure we'll be able to solve this problem* ***somehow****.* ***Somehow****, the prisoner got out of the locked room.*

someone

a certain person; somebody: *There is* ***someone*** *at the door — would you please go and see who it is? If you get lost, ask* ***someone*** *the way.*

somersault

an action that you perform by putting your head on the ground and rolling your body over it: *We all did **somersaults** on the grass.*

Say **sum**-er-sawlt.

something

1 anything: *Are you hungry — would you like **something** to eat?* 2 a certain thing: *I can see **something** strange in the sky — is it a bird or a helicopter?*

sometimes

at certain times; not always: *On Sundays we **sometimes** go sailing, and **sometimes** we visit Granny. **Sometimes** I walk to school but usually I take the bus.*

somewhere

in some place: *Tim lives **somewhere** in the north of Singapore but I don't know where exactly. 'Where are the scissors?' 'They are **somewhere** in my desk.'*

son

a male child: *Mr and Mrs Lee have two **sons** and one daughter. Dad is Granny's youngest **son**.*

song

a piece of music with words for singing: *We sang some Chinese **songs** in the singing class today.*

soon

1 in a short time from now: *I'll be back **soon**. It will **soon** be summer.* 2 early: *It's too **soon** to go to the cinema — the film doesn't start for another hour.*

as soon as immediately after; when: ***As soon as** it stops raining, we'll go to the shops. You'll get something to drink **as soon as** we get home. I'll mend your bicycle **as soon as** possible.*

sore

painful: *David can't swallow his food today, because he has a **sore** throat. Is that cut on your knee still **sore**? Is your knee still **sore**? My wrist feels **sore** — I must have hurt it when I fell over.*

sorrow

the feeling that you have when you are very sad: *The news of the king's death filled everyone with **sorrow**.*

The opposite is **joy**.

sorry

1 you use **sorry** when you apologize: *I'm **sorry** I'm so late. I'm **sorry** that I was so rude to you. I'm very **sorry** for being naughty.* 2 you use **sorry** when you ask people to repeat what they have just said: ***Sorry**, what did you say?* 3 sad: *I was **sorry** not to see you when you were in England. We were **sorry** for Mary when she broke her leg.*

sort

a type; a kind: *What **sort** of dog have you got? A mug is a **sort** of cup. There are books of many different **sorts** in our school library. I like all **sorts** of sweets.*

sort

to separate things into groups: *We **sorted** the shells into small ones and large ones.*

sort out to arrange things; to put things in order: *Computers are used for **sorting out** information. **Sort out** which clothes you want to take on holiday.*

sought

see **seek**: *The prince **sought** in vain for a way out of the witch's castle. At last the king found the wife he had **sought** so long.*

sound

something that you can hear: *I can hear strange banging **sounds** coming from upstairs. Quiet — don't make a **sound**! I love the **sound** of the wind in the trees.*

sound

to make a sound: *The bell **sounded** at the end of the lesson. A car-driver **sounds** his horn to warn pedestrians he is coming. The noise **sounded** like thunder.*

soundly

well: *I was sleeping so **soundly** that I didn't hear the alarm clock.*

soup

a hot liquid that you eat with a spoon at the beginning of a meal: *Mum is making chicken **soup** with noodles.*

sour

1 not sweet in taste: *Apples taste **sour** if you eat them before they are ripe. Lemon juice has*

*a **sour** taste. Vinegar is **sour** too.* **2** bad: *The milk will go **sour** quickly if you don't put it in the fridge.*

south
the direction to your right when you face the rising sun: *The wind is blowing from the **south**. There is a **south** wind today. The land round the **South** Pole is called Antarctica. Bangkok is in the **south** of Thailand.*

sow
a female pig: *The **sow** has had eight piglets.*

Rhymes with **how**.

sow
to put seeds on to soil so that they will grow into plants: *The gardener **sowed** grass seeds, but the birds ate most of them.*

- Rhymes with **toe**.
- sowed, sowing, has sown

sown
see **sow**: *This field has been **sown** with wheat.*

space
1 a place that you can put something into; an empty place: *Is there enough **space** for two more people in your car? This big table takes up too much **space**. Mum couldn't find a **space** to park the car in.* **2** the sky round the earth, and further away, where all the stars and planets are: *It is only 30 years since people on earth began to travel into **space**.*

spaceman
someone who travels in space: *In 1969, three **spacemen** travelled to the moon.*

Three **spacemen**

spaceship
a vehicle that carries people through space: *The **spaceship** took the spacemen to the moon and back to earth again.*

spade
a tool with a broad, flat, metal blade and a long handle, that is used for digging: *The gardener dug a hole with his **spade** and planted a young tree.*

spaghetti
long, thin, dried pieces of a food made from flour and water, which you cook in boiling water until it is soft: *I'd like some **spaghetti** with tomato sauce.*

spare
1 extra; not being used: *When Granny comes to stay, she sleeps in the **spare** room. Have you got a **spare** pair of football shorts that you could lend me?* **2** free for doing what you want: *What do you do in your **spare** time?*

spark
1 a tiny burning piece from a fire: ***Sparks** leapt out of the fire.* **2** a tiny flash caused by electricity: *I was scared when I saw **sparks** coming from the electric plug.*

sparkle
to shine with bright flashes of light: *A diamond **sparkles** with lots of different colours. The sea **sparkled** in the sun.*

sparkled, sparkling, has sparkled

sparrow
a small brown bird: *There are a lot of **sparrows** sitting in a row on the telephone wire.*

spat
see **spit**: *Joe **spat** out the cherry stone.*

speak
1 to say words; to talk: *David's throat was so sore that he could hardly **speak**. **Speak** in a loud, clear voice so that we can all hear — it's no good **speaking** in a whisper. The headmaster **spoke** to us at assembly about the new school rules. Hello — could I **speak** to Pat, please?* **2** to be able to talk in a certain language: *Do you **speak** English? Peter **speaks** English and Chinese. I can only **speak** a few words of French.*

spoke, speaking, has spoken

spear

a weapon with a long handle and a sharp point: *The hunters attacked the elephant with **spears**.*

special
1 not ordinary; unusual: *Your birthday is a **special** day — since it's your birthday you may choose something **special** for dinner. Nothing **special** happened to me today.* **2** different from others: *All the children have their own **special** jobs to do. A video camera is a **special** kind of camera for taking moving pictures.*

spectacles
glasses: *Mr Jones can't see very well without his* ***spectacles****. 'Where are my* ***spectacles****?' 'There's a pair of* ***spectacles*** *on your nose already.'*

spectator
someone who watches an event: *Thirty thousand* ***spectators*** *came to the football match.*

speech
a talk that someone gives to an audience: *The headmaster made a long* ***speech*** *before the prizes were given out to the best pupils.*

speed
how fast something moves: *The car was travelling along the motorway at a* ***speed*** *of 110 kilometres an hour. Joe dashed along to the ice-cream shop at high* ***speed****.*

spell
to say or write the letters of a word in the correct order: *How do you* ***spell*** *'tongue'? Please* ***spell*** *your name for me.*

spelt, spelling, has spelt

spell
a magic trick: *The wicked witch put a* ***spell*** *on the prince and turned him into a mouse.*

spelling
the ability to spell words in the correct way; the way that words are spelt: *Joe's* ***spelling*** *is terrible. Sarah is very good at* ***spelling****. The teacher gave us a* ***spelling*** *test.*

spelt
see **spell**: *Bob* ***spelt*** *my name correctly. Coffee is* ***spelt*** *C, O, F, F, E, E.*

spend
1 to use up money: *Richard* ***spends*** *all his pocket-money on sweets.* **2** to pass time: *We* ***spent*** *all day on the beach. We are* ***spending*** *our holidays in Australia next year.*

spent, spending, has spent

spent
see **spend**: *Miss Lee* ***spent*** *$200 on a new watch. My grandfather has* ***spent*** *all his life in India.*

spice
a kind of powder with a strong taste that is used to give a flavour to food: *Mum added a lot of* ***spices*** *to the dish. Pepper is a common kind of* ***spice****.*

spider
a tiny animal with eight legs and no wings, that spins a web: ***Spiders*** *catch insects in their webs, and then eat them up. My sister is afraid of* ***spiders****.*

spill

to pour out by mistake: *Mum was cross with Laura for* ***spilling*** *some milk on the tablecloth. I knocked over my glass of lemonade and it* ***spilt*** *all over the table.*

spilt, spilling, has spilt

spilt
see **spill**: *David* ***spilt*** *coffee down his shirt. Fetch a cloth — some water has been* ***spilt*** *in the passage.*

spin
1 to twist round fast: *A top is a toy that* ***spins*** *round on its point. John held the coin between his thumb and fingers and* ***spun*** *it on the table.* **2** to pull cotton or sheep's wool into a long, thin piece and twist it to make yarn: *In the past, women used to* ***spin*** *wool on little machines called* ***spinning*** *wheels.* **3** to make a web: *We watched a spider* ***spinning*** *its web in a corner of the classroom.*

spun, spinning, has spun

spinach

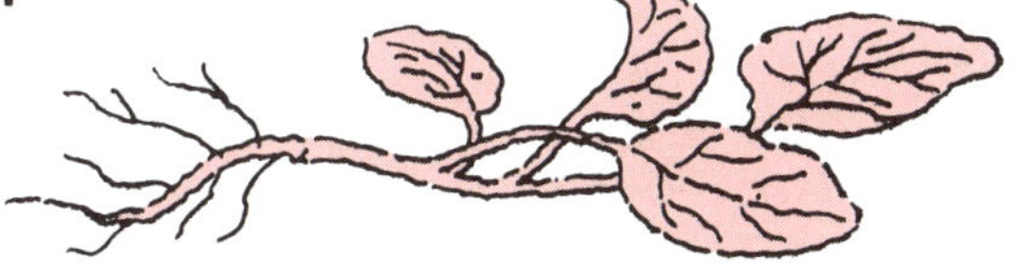

large, dark green leaves that you cook and eat as a vegetable: ***Spinach*** *contains lots of things that are good for your health.*

spine
the joined-up line of bones down the middle of your back; your backbone: *Your ribs are joined to your* ***spine****.*

spire
a tall, pointed tower: *Some churches have* ***spires*** *on top of their steeples.*

spit
1 to throw out some of the liquid that is made in your mouth: *It isn't polite to* ***spit*** *in public.* ***Spitting*** *on the floor is forbidden.* **2** to throw something out of your mouth: *When you brush your teeth, you* ***spit*** *out the toothpaste. The baby* ***spat*** *out the spinach because she didn't like it.*

spat, spitting, has spat

splash
1 to make something wet with drops of liquid: *A car went through a puddle just beside me and* ***splashed*** *my dress with dirty water. The baby likes* ***splashing*** *us with his bath-water.* **2** to make water fly about by jumping around in it, or pushing it about: *The children were* ***splashing*** *in the sea. We* ***splashed*** *through all the puddles as we walked home in the rain.*

splendid
excellent; very good; grand: *Well done, Susan — this is a* ***splendid*** *composition! What a* ***splendid*** *idea! That's* ***splendid****! New Zealand has some* ***splendid*** *mountains.*

split
1 to tear apart; to break apart: *I filled my schoolbag so full that it* ***split*** *down the side. I've* ***split*** *my trousers. The dish fell on the floor and* ***split*** *into two pieces.* **2** to divide: *We'll* ***split*** *the sweets up between us.*

split, splitting, has split

split
a tear; a long narrow hole: *There's a* ***split*** *in your trousers.*

spoil
1 to damage something; to make something less nice: *Stop bending the cover of that book — you'll* ***spoil*** *it. The rain* ***spoilt*** *our picnic.* **2** to give children everything they want: *Dad says that Granny* ***spoils*** *us when we stay with her. Don't give Katie so many presents — you mustn't* ***spoil*** *her.*

spoilt, spoiling, has spoilt

spoilt
see **spoil**: *Dad* ***spoilt*** *the dinner by burning it. The baby has scribbled all over my drawing and* ***spoilt*** *it.*

spoke
see **speak**: *I* ***spoke*** *to my granny on the phone yesterday.*

spoken
see **speak**: *I haven't* ***spoken*** *to Paul since last Monday.*

sponge
1 a piece of soft, light stuff full of holes, which you use for washing: *I've got a pink* ***sponge*** *for washing myself. Squeeze the* ***sponge*** *out well.* **2** a light kind of cake made of eggs and flour: *I'm going to make a jam* ***sponge*** *for tea.*

Say **spunj**.

spoon
a tool for eating, made of a little bowl fixed to a long handle: *You use a* ***spoon*** *for serving and eating liquids, such as soup. Get the* ***spoons****, knives and forks out of the drawer, and lay the table.*

sport
something you do to give you exercise, especially a game: *I enjoy cycling, running, football, table tennis, badminton and lots of other kinds of* ***sport****. I'm quite good at most* ***sports****.*

sportsman or sportswoman
a person who is good at sport: *Our games master is a very good* ***sportsman*** *— he's a fast runner, and he's a badminton champion too. Hundreds of* ***sportsmen*** *and* ***sportswomen*** *take part in the Olympic Games.*

Two **sportsmen**, two **sportswomen**

spot
1 a small, round mark; a dot: *Carol is wearing a dress with blue* ***spots*** *on it.* **2** a small stain; a mark: *Your shirt is covered with* ***spots*** *of paint.* **3** a little red lump on your skin: *Peter was covered in red* ***spots*** *when he had measles.* **4** a place: *The children showed the policeman the* ***spot*** *where they had found the gun.*

sprang
see **spring**: *The cat* ***sprang*** *at the mouse.*

spray

to cover with a lot of tiny drops: *Mum* ***sprayed*** *some perfume behind her ears. The sea water was* ***spraying*** *all over us while we stood on the rocks watching the waves.*

spread

1 to cover with something soft and sticky, such as jam: *Linda is **spreading** honey on her bread. **Spread** the glue evenly over the cardboard.* **2** to move outwards, covering a wide area: *The fire **spread** quickly through the forest. The teacher told the children to **spread** out round the hall.* **3** to lay something out: *Sam **spread** the map out on the table.*

spread, spreading, has spread

spring

1 the season of the year between winter and summer: *In the **spring** plants start to grow again.* **2** a piece of metal wire twisted round and round so tightly that it jumps back into shape if you squeeze it and then let it go: *Some mattresses and armchairs contain metal **springs**.* **3** a small stream that comes up through the ground: *Water from a **spring** tastes nice and fresh.*

spring

to jump; to move very suddenly: *The cat **sprang** off the chair when Dad sat down on it. The lid of the box **springs** open when you press this button.*

sprang, springing, has sprung

sprung

see **spring**: *If you grow fast, people say to you, 'You've **sprung** up a lot since I last saw you.'*

spun

see **spin**: *The spider **spun** a web across a corner of the doorway. In the story, the straw was **spun** into gold by a dwarf.*

spy

a person who is employed to find out secret information about another country: ***Spies** have special radios for sending secret messages to their own country.*

Two **spies**

spy

to watch someone secretly: *In the story, two children hid up a tree and **spied** on the robbers.*

spies, spied, spying, has spied

square

1 a flat shape with four equal sides: *In our maths lesson today we practised drawing **squares**, circles and triangles. Dad bought a **square** piece of glass to mend the window with.* **2** you use **square** when you measure a floor or some other flat surface: *The bedroom floor is 120 **square** metres.*

squeak

to make a short, high sound: *This door **squeaks** when you open it. The mouse **squeaked** with fright when the cat chased it.*

squeeze

1 to press hard: *You **squeeze** a sponge to get the water out of it. You **squeeze** an orange to get the juice out of it. **Squeeze** out this wet cloth for me.* **2** to force something to go into a narrow space: *The dog **squeezed** through a hole in the fence. How are we going to **squeeze** seven children into the back seat of the car?*

squeezed, squeezing, has squeezed

squirrel

a small animal with grey or brown fur and a long, thick tail, that can sit on its back legs and feed itself with its front paws: *We sat in the park watching the **squirrels** eating nuts and climbing trees.*

stable

a building where horses are kept: *The rider took his horse back to the **stable**.*

staff

a group of people who work for a school or a business: *This school has a **staff** of twenty teachers. Two members of the **staff** are leaving at the end of the term.*

stag

an adult male deer: *A **stag** has horns that spread out like branches.*

stage

a platform for people to perform on, to entertain an audience: *The singer walked on to the **stage** and everyone clapped.*

stain
a dirty mark made by a liquid: *The spilt wine left a **stain** on the carpet.*

stairs
steps inside a building that go from one floor to another: *Susan fell down the **stairs** and hurt her arm. Granny gets very tired when she climbs **stairs**.*

staircase
a set of steps inside a building: *There was a dark, narrow **staircase** leading to the top floor of the house.*

stale
not fresh; too old to eat: *We took some **stale** bread to the park to give to the ducks. The orange juice will go **stale** if you don't keep it in the fridge.*

The opposite is **fresh**.

stalk
1 the stem of a plant: *Daisies have short, thin **stalks**.* **2** the stem on which a fruit hangs from a tree: *You don't eat apple **stalks** or cherry **stalks**.*

stall
1 a place in a shed for one cow; a place in a stable for one horse: *The shed is divided into twelve **stalls**.* **2** a counter for selling things, especially in the street and at airports and railway stations: *I got this sweater at a clothes **stall** in the market. I'll go along to the book**stall** and buy a magazine to read on the journey.*

stallion
an adult male horse: *A **stallion** and a mare are the parents of a foal.*

stamp
a small piece of paper with a picture and a price printed on it, that you have to stick on envelopes and parcels before you post them: *Mum sent me to the post office to buy some **stamps**. Paul collects foreign **stamps**.*

stamp
to put your foot down very hard: *People sometimes **stamp** their feet when they are angry. Richard saw an ant crawling across the path and **stamped** on it.*

stand
1 to be upright, not sitting or lying; to be on your feet: *Simon's leg was so sore that he could hardly **stand**. All the seats on the bus were taken, so we had to **stand**. We **stood** in a circle round the teacher. Sarah screamed when Joe **stood** on her toe.* **2** to be in a certain place: *There is now a supermarket where the old school once **stood**.* **3** to put something upright: *Sarah picked up the fallen chair and **stood** it beside the desk.* **4** to stay in a position: *The door was **standing** open.* **5** to bear: *I can't **stand** this heat.*

stood, standing, has stood

stand aside to move to one side: *The policemen ordered everyone to **stand aside** and let the ambulance pass.*
stand back to move back: *A crowd gathered round the injured man, but a doctor told everyone to **stand back**.*
stand out to be seen very clearly; to be easily noticed: *The white tower **stands out** against the blue sky. Christine **stands out** among the other pupils — she's very clever.*
stand up to rise to your feet; to get up: *I pushed back my chair and **stood up**. You must **stand up** when a teacher comes into the classroom. **Stand up**, children!*

standard
the good or bad quality of something: *The **standard** of your work has been very good this term, children — I'm pleased with you. Your English and arithmetic have reached a high **standard**.*

star
1 one of the twinkling lights you see in the sky at night: *On a clear night, you can see hundreds of **stars** in the sky. The sun is a **star**.* **2** a flat shape with five or six points: *At Christmas, we decorated the classroom wall with silver **stars**.*
film star a very famous movie actor or actress: *Which famous **film star** would you most like to meet?*
pop star a very famous pop singer: *Who is your favourite **pop star**?*

stare
to look hard at something for a long time: *It's rude to **stare** at people. Tom stood **staring** at the snake, not daring to move.*

- Same as **gaze**.
- stared, staring, has stared

start
to begin: *Dad **starts** work at eight o'clock every*

morning. The baby ***started*** *to cry, so Mum picked her up. It's* ***starting*** *to rain again. Please* ***start*** *eating — don't wait for me. What time does the film* ***start****?*

Meaning 1: the opposite is **finish**.

start out or **start off** to begin a journey; to set off: *We* ***started out*** *very early in order to reach the ferry in good time. It's time we* ***started off****.*

start
the beginning of something; the place where something begins, such as a race: *The runners are all waiting at the* ***start****.*

startle
to give someone a fright: *The thunder* ***startled*** *the children. You* ***startled*** *me — I didn't see you come in.*

startled, startling, has startled

starve
1 to go on being hungry for a long time; to die of hunger: *Lots of children* ***starved*** *to death because their parents had no food to give them.* **2** not to give someone enough food: *The soldiers* ***starved*** *their prisoners.* **3** to be very hungry: *Can't we have dinner now? I'm* ***starving****!*

starved, starving, has starved

state
to say something in a clear way: *Please* ***state*** *your name, address and telephone number.*

stated, stating, has stated

state
the way something looks; the way something is: *This room is in a very untidy* ***state****. We got into an excited* ***state*** *as the holidays came nearer.*

station
a place where trains or buses stop to let passengers get on or off: *Could you tell me the way to the railway* ***station****? We got off the train at Victoria* ***Station****.*

statue
a large figure of a person or animal, made of stone or metal: *There is a* ***statue*** *of Queen Victoria in front of Buckingham Palace.*

stay
1 to visit a person or a place for a while: *Aunt Mary is coming to* ***stay*** *with us next week. How long is she* ***staying*** *for? She'll be* ***staying*** *in Singapore for a fortnight, then she'll* ***stay*** *two nights in a hotel in Kuala Lumpur.* **2** to remain in a place: *I'm* ***staying*** *at home today because I don't feel well. Would you like to* ***stay*** *for lunch? The doctor told the patient to* ***stay*** *in bed for a few days.* ***Stay*** *where you are and don't move! Can't you* ***stay*** *still while I comb your hair?*

stay up not to go to bed: *I wanted to* ***stay up*** *and watch television but my dad sent me to bed.*

steady
firm; not shaking: *This table isn't* ***steady*** *enough for writing on. You need a* ***steady*** *hand to draw straight lines without a ruler.*

steak
a thick slice of meat, especially beef, for grilling or frying: *We grilled* ***steaks*** *on the barbecue. Have a piece of* ***steak****.*

steal
to take something from someone without permission: *Burglars broke into the shop and* ***stole*** *the computers. The thief was sent to prison for* ***stealing*** *cars.*

stole, stealing, has stolen

steam
a cloud of tiny drops that rises from hot liquids and hot food: *Clouds of* ***steam*** *rose from the pan when I lifted the lid. The bathroom always gets full of* ***steam*** *when anyone takes a hot shower.*

steel
a very hard metal made from iron, that is used for making tools, vehicles, bridges and lots of other things: *These knives, forks and spoons are made of* ***steel****.*

steep
sloping up or down suddenly; rising or falling suddenly: *I had to push my bike up the hill because it was too* ***steep*** *for me to ride up. Be careful not to fall down these stairs — they're very* ***steep****.*

steeple
a high tower on a church: *There is a cross on top of the church* ***steeple****.*

steer
to move a vehicle to the left or right by turning the steering wheel: *The driver* ***steered*** *to the left to avoid the hole in the road.*

stem
the long, straight, narrow part of a plant that the leaves and flowers grow from; a stalk: *Roses have thorny* ***stems****.*

step
1 the action of moving your foot when you walk, run or dance: *Take two* ***steps*** *forward and one* ***step*** *back. Mum hurried along the road with quick* ***steps****. There are lots of difficult* ***steps*** *to learn in this dance.* **2** the sound that you make when you walk: *I can hear foot****steps*** *in the passage.* **3** the flat part of a stair you put your foot on, when you go up or down: *You have to climb two hundred* ***steps*** *to get to the top of the tower. The cat lay on the door****step*** *in the sun.*

step
to take a step; to walk: *The policemen asked everyone to* ***step*** *back so that the procession could pass. Look both ways before you* ***step*** *off the pavement. I* ***stepped*** *on the cat's tail by mistake.*

stepped, stepping, has stepped

stern
very firm with people you are in charge of, never letting them behave badly: ***Stern*** *parents expect their children to obey them. Our new teacher looks very* ***stern****. 'Stop that noise,' said the headmaster in a* ***stern*** *voice.*

Same as **strict**.

stethoscope

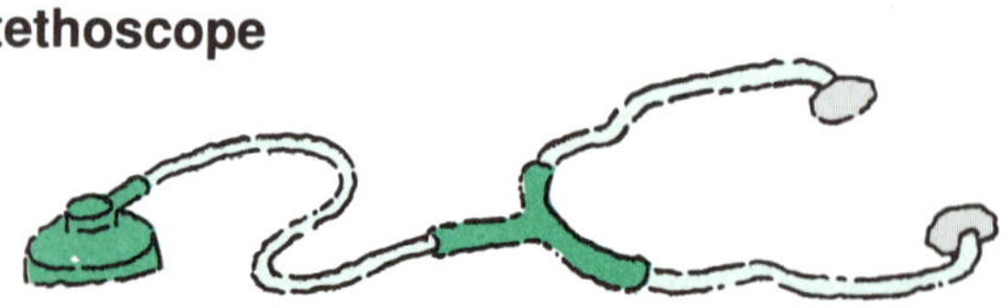

an instrument that a doctor uses to listen to your heart and lungs: *Peter took off his shirt so that the doctor could place the* ***stethoscope*** *on his chest.*

stew
a dish that is made by boiling meat and vegetables slowly together: *Mum made a beef* ***stew*** *with onions and carrots in it.*

stick
1 a dead branch; a dead twig: *The scouts were sent to collect dry* ***sticks*** *for firewood.* **2** a long, thin piece of wood for helping to support your weight when you walk: *Mrs White is very lame, but she can walk with the help of a walking* ***stick****.* **3** a long piece of wood shaped in a special way for playing a game with: *You hit a hockey ball with the curved end of the hockey* ***stick****.* **4** a long piece: *The teacher uses a* ***stick*** *of chalk to write on the blackboard.*

stick
1 to fix something with glue, or with some other sticky stuff: *I'll try to* ***stick*** *the broken cup together again. You* ***stick*** *a stamp on the top right-hand corner of an envelope. This stamp won't* ***stick*** *to the envelope. Mum* ***stuck*** *a plaster over the cut on my finger.* **2** to be unable to go on; to prevent someone or something from moving: *The car got* ***stuck*** *in the mud. This drawer has* ***stuck****. Please help me with my arithmetic — I'm* ***stuck****!* **3** to push something sharp into something: *Granny has a tiny little cushion for* ***sticking*** *her pins into. Stop* ***sticking*** *your elbow into me!*
stick out **1** to come out further than the rest of something: *Your nose* ***sticks out*** *of your face.* **2** to stretch out: *It's rude to* ***stick*** *your tongue* ***out****.*

stuck, sticking, has stuck

sticky
covered with stuff that sticks: *You lick the* ***sticky*** *side of a stamp. The baby's hands are all* ***sticky*** *with jam — they need wiping.*

stiff
1 difficult to bend; firm and hard: *You need some* ***stiff*** *cardboard and a pair of scissors for making this model.* **2** difficult to move: *I can't turn the key because the lock is so* ***stiff****.* **3** sore to move: *I've got a* ***stiff*** *neck. My legs are* ***stiff*** *after my long bicycle ride.*

still
1 not moving: *Please keep* ***still*** *while I brush your hair. Stand* ***still****, children! Sit* ***still*** *and get on with your work. The water in the lake was so* ***still*** *that it looked like glass.* **2** going on till now, and not stopping: *I am* ***still*** *doing my homework so I can't come out with you. It's six o'clock already and Pat* ***still*** *hasn't done his homework. Are you* ***still*** *up, children? It's time you were in bed.* **3** although it's difficult:

This knife has a broken blade, but I can ***still*** *use it. My puppy is very naughty —* ***still****, I love him.* **4** even more than that: *A hippo is a very big animal, but an elephant is* ***still*** *bigger.*

sting

1 to injure skin by pricking it and putting poison into it: *Do those insects* ***sting****? The wasp* ***stung*** *me on the arm.* **2** to be painful: *The shampoo made my eyes* ***sting****. My eyes are still* ***stinging****.*

stung, stinging, has stung

stir

to mix, especially with a spoon: *Mr Brown put milk and sugar in his coffee and* ***stirred*** *it. The cook is* ***stirring*** *the vegetables in the pan.*

stirred, stirring, has stirred

stitch

to sew: *Mum* ***stitched*** *the button back on to my coat. When I cut my head, I had to go to the hospital to get it* ***stitched****.*

stole

see **steal**: *A thief* ***stole*** *Mum's camera out of the car.*

stolen

see **steal**: *You must tell the police that your bicycle has been* ***stolen****.*

stomach

1 the part inside your body that food goes into after you have swallowed it: *Your* ***stomach*** *is at the left side of your body, just below your ribs.* **2** the front part of your body, just below your waist: *I've got a pain in my* ***stomach****.*

stomach-ache

a pain in your stomach: *Joe got a* ***stomach-ache*** *from eating too much chocolate.*

stone

1 the very hard stuff that rocks are made of: ***Stone*** *is used for building. The museum is a large* ***stone*** *building.* **2** a piece of this stuff: *The small* ***stones*** *on the beach are called pebbles. Never throw* ***stones*** *at anyone.* **3** the hard, round object in the middle of some fruits: *Peaches, apricots and cherries have* ***stones*** *inside. Mind you don't swallow the* ***stone****!*

stood

see **stand**: *We all* ***stood*** *up when the head-mistress came into the classroom. This church has* ***stood*** *here for over a hundred years.*

stool

a seat with legs but no back: *You sit on a piano* ***stool*** *to play the piano. We've got two chairs and three* ***stools*** *round our kitchen table.*

stop

1 not to do something any longer; to finish: *It has* ***stopped*** *raining. The rain has* ***stopped****.* ***Stop*** *shouting!* ***Stop*** *that noise!* **2** not to move any longer; to make something stand still: *The bus* ***stopped*** *to let passengers get off. This train doesn't* ***stop*** *at Melaka. Mrs Smith* ***stopped*** *the car and got out. We* ***stopped*** *to buy chips on the way home. We'll* ***stop*** *for lunch in five minutes. Dad raised his hand to* ***stop*** *a taxi.* **3** to stay somewhere for a while when you are on your way to somewhere else: *Dad* ***stopped*** *a few nights in Hong Kong on his way back from America.* **4** to prevent: *You really must* ***stop*** *your dog lying on our sofa. The rain didn't* ***stop*** *us from playing outside.*

- Meaning 1: the opposite is **start**.
- stopped, stopping, has stopped

stop

1 the action of stopping: *The ball rolled across the street and came to a* ***stop*** *at the kerb.* **2** a break during a journey: *We made two* ***stops*** *for meals on our way to Kuala Lumpur.* **3** a place where buses stop regularly: *We must get off at the next* ***stop****.*

bus stop a place where buses stop to let passengers get on or off: *There's a long queue at the* ***bus stop****.*

full stop a mark (.) at the end of a sentence: *After a* ***full stop*** *you have to start a new sentence with a capital letter.*

store

1 a shop selling food and other things you need: *The village* ***store*** *is the only shop in the village. A department* ***store*** *is a very large shop that sells lots of different kinds of goods.* **2** things that you keep so that you can use them: *We took a* ***store*** *of canned food with us* *when we went camping. We keep tins of food in the* ***store*** *cupboard in our kitchen.*

store

to put something into a place for keeping: *These biscuits will stay fresh if they are* ***stored*** *in a tin. We* ***store*** *logs for the fire in the wood-shed. Squirrels* ***store*** *away nuts for the winter. Our teacher is* ***storing*** *up all her old magazines for us to cut pictures out of. Television programmes can be recorded and* ***stored*** *on videotape.*

stored, storing, has stored

stork

a large bird with a long, pointed beak, a long neck and very long legs: ***Storks*** *build enormous nests on top of chimneys and church spires.*

storm

a period of very bad weather, with strong winds, thunder and lightning, and heavy rain: *A lot of trees were blown down in the* ***storm****. The ship sank during a terrible* ***storm*** *at sea.*

story

the description of a real or imaginary event; the tale of something: *My mother usually reads us a* ***story*** *before we go to sleep. I like adventure* ***stories*** *best. Would you like me to tell you a* ***story****? Is it a true* ***story****? Have you heard the* ***story*** *about the fox and the duck? We begged Granny to tell us the* ***story*** *of her life.*

Lots of **stories**

stove

a cooker: *My mother cooks with a gas* ***stove****. Fill this pan with water and put it on the* ***stove****.*

straight

1 not bent; not crooked: *Can you draw a* ***straight*** *line without a ruler? Some people have* ***straight*** *hair and some people have curly hair. Sit up* ***straight****, please!* **2** in a straight line; not turning in different directions: *This road goes* ***straight*** *to the city centre. Go* ***straight*** *on till you get to the crossroads, then turn left.* **3** immediately: *I always go* ***straight*** *home after school.*

Meaning 1: the opposite is **crooked**, **curved**, **bent** or **curly**.

straight away at once; immediately: *Dinner is ready — please come* ***straight away****! You must do your homework* ***straight away*** *after tea.*

strain

to separate something solid from something liquid: *What is the easiest way to* ***strain*** *noodles after boiling them? You* ***strain*** *tea so that you don't get tea-leaves in your cup.*

strange

1 unusual; odd: *What is that* ***strange*** *noise coming from the classroom next door? It would be very* ***strange*** *if you didn't know your own name.* **2** not seen before; not familiar to you: *There is a* ***strange*** *man at the door. This part of the country is* ***strange*** *to me.*

Meaning 2: the opposite is **familiar**.

stranger

1 a person whom you have never met before: *The teacher warned us never to talk to* ***strangers*** *in the street.* **2** someone who is in a place for the first time and does not know it well: *I can't tell you where the post office is — I'm a* ***stranger*** *here myself.*

strap

a narrow piece of material, especially leather, for fastening things and holding things: *The* ***strap*** *of my sandal is broken. I need a new watch-****strap****. Dad put a leather* ***strap*** *round his suitcase to keep it closed.*

straw

1 the dry yellow stalks of corn: *The floor of the stable is covered with* ***straw****.* **2** a thin plastic tube for sucking up a drink into your mouth: *We found David in the cafe, drinking orange juice through a* ***straw****.*

strawberry

a small red juicy fruit that grows close to the

ground: *We're having **strawberries** and cream for tea. Have some **strawberry** jam on your bread.*

Lots of **strawberries**

stream

1 a small river: *I can jump across the **stream**. The baby is paddling in the **stream**. **Streams** flow into rivers, and rivers flow into the sea.* 2 anything flowing in one direction: *A **stream** of cars was moving towards the seaside.*

street

a road in a town with buildings on both sides: *We are not allowed to play in our **street** because of the traffic. I met Mike in the **street** today. Joe lives at 219 High **Street**.*

strength

being strong: *Granny has been ill, but now she's getting her **strength** back. Tim pulled at the rope with all his **strength**.*

stretch

1 to make something longer or wider, especially by pulling: *You can **stretch** a piece of elastic. My swimming-costume looks very small, but it **stretches** when I put it on. The dog yawned and **stretched** itself.* 2 to reach for something with your arm stretched: *Joe **stretched** across the table for a chocolate biscuit. I **stretched** out my hand to turn off the radio.*

strict

making rules for people which you expect them to obey: *Our new teacher is **strict**, but we like her. John's parents are very **strict** with him — they won't let him watch television except at weekends. **Strict** rules are rules that you must never disobey.*

Same as **stern**.

strike

1 to hit: *Some parents never **strike** their children, even when they're naughty. The hockey ball **struck** me on the knee. Dad got very angry and **struck** his fist on the table. The man **struck** his head against the wall as he fell. One of the trees in the park was **struck** by lightning.* 2 to come into your head; to give you a certain feeling: *A good idea suddenly **struck** me. How does this idea **strike** you?* 3 to make a strong, clear sound: *The clock **struck** twelve. The teacher **struck** a note on the piano for us to sing.* 4 to rub a match on something rough to produce a flame: *Mum **struck** a match to light the candles with.*

struck, striking, has struck

string

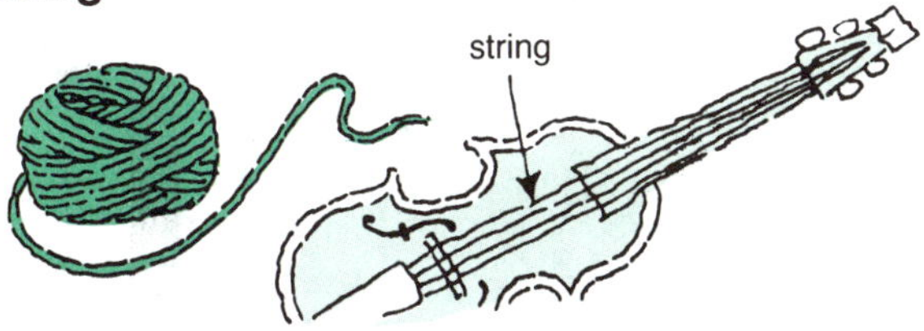

1 a thick thread made of thin threads twisted together, for tying and fastening things: *I need a long piece of **string** for tying this parcel up.* 2 one of the pieces of wire stretched across an instrument such as a violin, that you play with your fingers or with a bow: *There are four **strings** on a violin.*

stringed instrument an instrument that has strings, such as a violin or a guitar: *There are lots of **stringed instruments** in an orchestra.*

strip

a long, narrow piece of something: *A belt is a **strip** of material for wearing round your waist. We'll cut the newspaper into **strips**. There is a **strip** of grass in front of our house.*

strip

1 to remove something: *We had to **strip** off the old wallpaper before putting on the new wallpaper.* 2 to take off your clothes; to undress: *I **stripped** and had a shower. **Strip** off all your dirty clothes and put on clean ones.*

stripped, stripping, has stripped

stripe

a coloured line: *Peter is wearing a white shirt with blue **stripes**.*

stroke

to rub something gently in one direction: *Dogs and cats like being **stroked**.*

stroked, stroking, has stroked

stroke

1 the action of striking something; the action of hitting something with a bat or racket: *I must practise my badminton **strokes**.* 2 an action in swimming: *Keep your **strokes** slow and regular. Can you do back**stroke**?* 3 something that happens quickly and suddenly: *The man was killed by a **stroke** of lightning.*

stroll

to walk without hurrying: *We **strolled** along the path by the river.*

strong
1 not weak; having a lot of power: *I am **strong** enough to carry this suitcase on my own. Michael has **strong** arms. The wind was so **strong** that it blew the lady's hat off.* 2 easy to notice: *This cheese has a **strong** smell. Radishes have a **strong** taste.*

Meaning 1: the opposite is **weak**.

struck
see **strike**: *I **struck** the big bully in the face with my fist. The tower has been **struck** by lightning.*

struggle
1 to twist about, trying to escape: *The thief **struggled** to escape, but the policeman kept hold of him. The cat **struggled** out of my arms.* 2 to fight: *Jack and Tom were **struggling** together on the floor.* 3 to move with difficulty: *I **struggled** up the steep rock. The dog **struggled** through a hole in the fence.*

struggled, struggling, has struggled

struggle
the action of struggling; a fight: *After a short **struggle**, the man was arrested and taken to the police station.*

stubborn
not wanting to obey: *The **stubborn** donkey sat down in the road and wouldn't move. Why won't you do as I tell you? You're so **stubborn**!*

stuck
see **stick**: *Mum **stuck** the broken vase together again with glue. The car is **stuck** in the mud.*

student
1 a person who is studying at a university: *My eldest sister left school last year and she is now a **student** at the university.* 2 a pupil in a school: *Joe is a smart **student**.*

study
to spend time learning a subject: *We have been **studying** English for three years. You must all **study** hard for your exams.*

studies, studied, studying, has studied

study
the studying of something: *The **study** of numbers is called Mathematics.*

stuff
1 a word you use for something when you don't know what else to call it: *There's lots of white **stuff** on the ground — is it snow? What's that black **stuff** in the bucket?* 2 things: *We'll have to get rid of a lot of **stuff** when we move house.*

stuff
1 to fill very full: *The drawer was **stuffed** with clothes. Don't try to **stuff** too many things into your suitcase.* 2 to eat a lot of food: *The children have been **stuffing** themselves with ice-cream.*

stung
see **sting**: *A wasp **stung** me on the finger. Mike was **stung** by a bee.*

stupid
slow at understanding; doing and saying foolish things: *You must be really **stupid** if you still believe that babies are brought by storks. You've made a **stupid** mistake in your arithmetic. I've left my key inside the flat — how **stupid** of me!*

The opposite is **clever** or **smart**.

sty
a building where pigs are kept: *We went to the pig**sty** to watch the sow feeding her piglets.*

Two **sties**

subject
1 one of the things that you learn at school: *Drawing is my favourite **subject**. Peter's best **subject** is English. How many **subjects** do you study at school?* 2 the thing that a story or a composition is about: *Today I won't tell you what **subject** to write about — you can all choose your own **subjects**. I chose the **subject** 'Hippos'. Susan wrote three pages on the **subject** of 'roller-skates'.*

submarine

a ship that can travel under water: ***Submarines** can hide from enemy ships and attack them with special bombs.*

subtract
to take away a smaller number from a bigger

number: *If you **subtract** 3 from 7 you get 4. During your first year at school, you learn to add and **subtract**.*

- The opposite is **add**.
- 'Three minus two' means the same as 'subtract two from three'.

subtraction
the subtracting of a smaller number from a larger number: ***Subtraction** is harder than addition.*

succeed
to manage to do what you have been trying to do: *Tom **succeeded** in mending the old car and getting it to go again. I tried to persuade the teacher not to give us any homework, but I didn't **succeed**. Joe kept on trying to move the heavy stone, and at last he **succeeded**.*

success
doing something well; doing something that you have been trying to do: *I wish you **success** in your English exam. The police have been looking for the bank robbers, but so far without any **success**.*

The opposite is **failure**.

successful
having success: *I hope you'll be **successful** in finding your mother a nice present. Mrs Lee is a **successful** businesswoman — she owns lots of shops.*

such
1 of that kind: *I don't know why I put my key in the wrong drawer — I've never done **such** a thing before. Be quiet — you mustn't say **such** things!* **2** so great; so much: *This morning Dad was in **such** a hurry that he had no time for breakfast. It's **such** a pity that you can't play in the football match. It's **such** a hot day — let's go to the beach. You're **such** a fool sometimes! This room is in **such** a mess!*
such as for example: *Some animals, **such as** sheep and cows, only eat grass.*

suck
1 to draw liquid into your mouth from something: *Babies learn to **suck** milk from their mothers as soon as they are born. A lollipop gets smaller and smaller as you **suck** it. Lots of children **suck** their thumbs. You can **suck** up drinks through a straw.* **2** to draw in: *A vacuum-cleaner **sucks** up dirt from the carpet. A plant **sucks** up water from the soil.*

sudden
happening quickly, without being expected: *The balloon burst with a **sudden** loud bang. The tiger made a **sudden** leap at the deer.*

suddenly
happening quickly, without being expected: *I **suddenly** remembered that I hadn't switched off the radio. **Suddenly**, the door opened and a man walked in. The car in front **suddenly** turned right.*

suffer
1 to feel pain: *The patient **suffered** a lot of pain from his injuries.* **2** to have something wrong with you: *Dad went to bed early, **suffering** from a bad headache.*

sugar
the sweet white or brown stuff that you add to drinks and food to make them sweeter: *Do you take **sugar** in your tea? How much **sugar** shall I put in the cake?*

suggest
to mention an idea: *I **suggest** we take a picnic to the beach. What do you **suggest**, Bill? He **suggested** a different plan.*

suit
1 a jacket and trousers for wearing together, made of the same cloth; a matching skirt and jacket: *Today Mr Johnson is wearing a grey **suit**, a white shirt and a blue tie. Mum wears a black **suit** for going to work.* **2** clothes for a special use: *I changed into my swim**suit** on the beach. A diver wears a diving-**suit**. A spaceman wears a space**suit** when he leaves the spaceship.*

suit
1 to be okay for you: *Does the time of the meeting **suit** you?* **2** to make someone look attractive: *Short hair **suits** you. Red **suits** me better than yellow does. Your new dress **suits** you very well.*

suitable
right for something; okay: *Bring **suitable** clothes for camping. Sandals are not **suitable** shoes for climbing mountains in. When will be the most **suitable** time to call on you?*

suitcase
a case with flat sides and a handle that you carry your clothes in when you are travelling: *I packed my own **suitcase**.*

*Dad put all the **suitcases** in the back of the car.*

sum
1 a problem in arithmetic: *Liz is very good at **sums**.* 2 the result that you get when you add numbers together: *The **sum** of two and three is five.* 3 an amount of money: *The yacht costs an enormous **sum** of money.*

summer
the warmest season of the year: *In **summer** the trees are covered with green leaves. When do the **summer** holidays start?*

sun
1 the huge, bright yellow ball in the sky that gives light and heat to the earth: *The earth takes a year to go round the **sun**.* 2 light and heat from the sun; sunshine: *I enjoy sitting in the **sun** when it isn't too hot. The **sun** was shining all day. The **sun** has faded the curtains.*

Sunday
the first day of the week; the day after Saturday: *We don't go to school on **Sundays**. **Sunday** is the day when people go to church.*

sunflower
a very tall plant that has a large yellow flower with a big brown centre: *The seeds of **sunflowers** are used for making oil for cooking.*

sung
see **sing**: *Have you **sung** this song before?*

sunglasses
dark-coloured glasses that you wear to protect your eyes from bright sunlight: *Mike is wearing **sunglasses**. I've got a new pair of **sunglasses**.*

sunk
see **sink**: *The ship had **sunk** before the lifeboat arrived.*

sunlight
the light of the sun: *A ray of **sunlight** was coming in through a gap in the curtains.*

sunny
having a lot of bright sunshine: *It's warm and **sunny** today. We had lovely **sunny** weather for our holiday.*

sunrise
the rising of the sun in the morning; the time when the sun rises: *A lot of birds start to sing at **sunrise**.*

sunset
the setting of the sun in the evening; the time when the sun sets: *There was a beautiful **sunset** this evening. I must be home before **sunset**.*

sunshine
the light and heat of the sun: *We looked for a shady place in the park because we didn't want to sit in the **sunshine**.*

supermarket
a large shop selling food and other goods, which you take off the shelves yourself, and pay for when you leave: *We go shopping at the **supermarket** twice a week.*

supper
a small meal that you eat at night: *My parents invited some friends for **supper**.*

support
to carry the weight of something; to hold upright: *The new bridge is **supported** by strong steel cables. Don't climb on the fence — it isn't strong enough to **support** your weight. The wounded soldier limped back to the camp, **supported** by two friends.*

support
something that supports something else: *The railway bridge rests on three huge stone **supports**.*

suppose
1 to believe; to guess: *I **suppose** you have all heard the good news? 'I **suppose** you'll be going to the party?' 'Yes, I **suppose** so.' Who do you **suppose** will win the race?* 2 imagine what will happen if: ***Suppose** we miss the last bus — what shall we do? Just **suppose** you had a million dollars to spend!*

supposed, supposing, has supposed

sure
1 having no doubt; certain: *I'm **sure** that I haven't lost the key — it must be in my bag. I'm not **sure** what Mr Smith's address is. Are you quite **sure** you don't want anything to drink? I'll win the race — you can be **sure** of that! It's **sure** to rain soon — look at those dark clouds.* 2 of course; certainly: *'Would you help me carry these books?' '**Sure**!'*

make sure to act so that something is certain; to find out whether something is certain: *We arrived early at the cinema to **make sure** of* *getting good seats. I think Linda is coming tomorrow afternoon but I'll ring her to **make sure**.*

surface
the outside of something; the part of something that you see: *Most of the earth's **surface** is covered with water. The **surface** of this road is full of holes.*

surname
a person's family name: *I don't know Jenny's **surname**. My first name is David and my **surname** is Miller.*

surprise
something that you don't expect: *What a **surprise** seeing you here! I got a **surprise** when I saw the teacher in our sitting-room. I bought a bunch of flowers for Mum as a **surprise** for her birthday.*

surprise
to give someone a feeling of surprise: *I'm **surprised** that Peter is so late. I wouldn't be **surprised** if Jim won the painting competition. You behaved badly — I'm **surprised** at you!*

surprised, surprising, has surprised

surrender
to give in: *The general refused to **surrender** to the enemy.*

surround
to be all around; to come all around: *An island is **surrounded** by water. The park is **surrounded** by a fence. The police **surrounded** the bank to catch the robbers.*

suspect
to think that someone is guilty: *The police have arrested a man whom they **suspect** of theft. He is **suspected** of stealing cars.*

suspicion
the feeling that you cannot trust someone: *The cat and the dog looked at each other with **suspicion**.*

suspicious
1 feeling that you cannot trust someone: *Be **suspicious** of strangers who try to talk to you in the street.* **2** not able to be trusted: *That man standing by the door of the bank looks a bit **suspicious**.*

swallow
to make food or drink go down your throat to your stomach: *You must chew food well before you **swallow** it. Laura's throat was so sore that she could hardly **swallow**.*

swallow
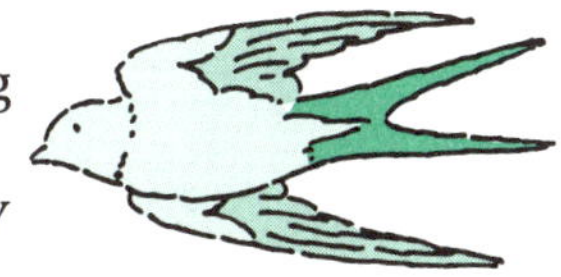
a small bird with long wings and a divided tail: ***Swallows** can fly very fast.*

swam
see **swim**: *The boy **swam** across the river.*

swan
a large white bird with a long curved neck, that swims and flies: *We see **swans** swimming about on rivers and lakes.*

swarm
a large group of insects flying together: *A **swarm** of bees is led by a queen bee. There are **swarms** of mosquitoes by the pond.*

swear
to promise something in a very serious way; to say you really are telling the truth about something: ***Swear** never to tell anyone our secret. I **swear** I'll never tell you a lie again. The man **swore** that he was innocent of the murder.*

swore, swearing, has sworn

sweat
to produce a liquid through your skin when you are hot: *Running fast makes you **sweat**.*

sweat
the liquid that comes through your skin when you are hot: *When you run, your clothes get wet with **sweat**.*

sweater
a jumper: *Mum is knitting me a woollen **sweater**. When I get home from school I change into my **sweater** and jeans.*

sweep
to clean a floor with a brush: *Would you please **sweep** the kitchen floor for me? Mum **swept** up the broken glass.*

swept, sweeping, has swept

sweet
1 containing sugar; tasting of sugar; not sour; not bitter: *Honey is **sweet**. I never eat **sweet** foods such as biscuits and cakes.* **2** attractive; lovely: *What a **sweet** little baby! The baby looks **sweet** in her pink dress.*

Meaning 1: the opposite is **bitter** or **sour**.

sweet
a small piece of something sweet, such as a chocolate or a toffee: *Have a **sweet**! Mum bought us each a packet of **sweets**.*

swell
to become thicker; to get bigger: *A wasp stung David on the finger, and his finger began to **swell**. The heavy rain has **swollen** the river.*

swelled, swelling, has swollen

swelling
a swollen bit on your body: *When you have mumps, you have a painful **swelling** on each side of your face. Rosemary has got a **swelling** on her arm where the wasp stung her.*

swept
see **sweep**: *Mum **swept** the floor. I've **swept** up all the rice that fell on the floor.*

swift
fast; quick: *The **swiftest** runner will win the race.*

swim
to keep yourself floating in water, and move along using your arms and legs; to move through water the way a fish does: *Can you **swim**? I'm going **swimming** this afternoon. We watched the fish **swimming** about in the aquarium.*

swam, swimming, has swum

swimming costume or **swimsuit** a tight-fitting piece of clothing that women and girls wear for swimming: *I changed into my **swimming costume** on the beach.*
swimming pool a very large kind of bath for swimming in: *There's a big **swimming pool** at the sports centre.*
swimming trunks short pants that men and boys wear for swimming: *Where are my **swimming trunks**? Mike has a new pair of **swimming trunks**.*

swim
a period of swimming: *I'm going down to the beach for a **swim**.*

swimsuit
see **swimming costume**: *Squeeze out your wet **swimsuit** and hang it up to dry.*

swing
to move from side to side; to move backwards and forwards: *You **swing** your arms when you walk. Tim was **swinging** on a rope that was hanging down from a tree. Suddenly the door **swung** open.*

swung, swinging, has swung

swing
a seat for swinging that hangs on ropes or chains: *We've got a seesaw and lots of **swings** in our playground.*

switch
a button for turning something electric on or off: *I couldn't find the light **switch** in the bathroom. You press this **switch** to turn on the television.*

switch
to change; to turn: *I don't like this television play — let's **switch** over to another programme.*
switch off to stop something electric working by pressing a switch: *Don't forget to **switch off** the light before you go to bed. Dad **switched off** the radio.*
switch on to start something electric working by pressing a switch: *Would you **switch on** the video recorder, please? Peter **switched on** his bedroom light.*

swollen
see **swell**: *David's finger has **swollen** up. Dad has got a **swollen** ankle after a fall.*

sword
a weapon with a long, sharp blade: *The prince drew his **sword** and killed the wicked dragon.*

Say **sord**.

swore
see **swear**: *The man **swore** that he was innocent. In the story, the children **swore** never to tell anybody the secret.*

sworn
see **swear**: *Remember that you have **sworn** not to tell anybody our secret.*

swum
see **swim**: *I've never **swum** in a river before — is it safe?*

swung
see **swing**: *The door **swung** open.*

syrup
a thick, sweet liquid made by cooking sugar with water or fruit juice: *There is usually plenty of **syrup** in a can of fruit.*

Say **si**-rup.

table
a piece of furniture with legs and a flat top: *Sally put the dishes on the **table**. Sally laid the **table**. We all sat down at the **table** and had our dinner.*

table-tennis
a game that is played by two people or four people on a large table, with small wooden bats and a small, light ball: *Shall we have a game of **table-tennis**? Jack and George are playing **table-tennis**.*

tablecloth
a cloth for covering a table: *Mum spread a white **tablecloth** over the table.*

tablespoon
a large spoon for serving food: *Here is a **tablespoon** for serving out the rice.*

tadpole
a very small animal with a round, black head and a long tail that grows into a frog or a toad: ***Tadpoles** live in ponds or lakes.*

tail
the part of an animal that sticks out from the end of its body: *A mouse has a long, thin **tail**. A fish swims by moving its **tail**.*

tailor
a person whose job is to make clothes for people: *Mr Jones had his suit made by a **tailor**.*

take
1 to reach out for something and hold it: *Linda **took** the glass that her mum gave her. The squirrel **took** the nut from me and ran away.* **2** to hold someone: *Sarah **took** her little sister by the hand.* **3** to carry something somewhere; to lead a person or animal somewhere: *I **took** the books back to the library. We **took** the dog out for a walk. Mum sometimes **takes** me to school in the car.* **4** to remove something: *Peter **took** the book down from the shelf. Have you **taken** my pencil? Jenny **took** the key out of her pocket. The dentist **took** out my bad tooth. If you **take** three away from five, you get two.* **5** to do some action: *I'm going to **take** a shower now. **Take** a look at this photo. Granny **takes** a short walk in the afternoons.* **6** to buy: *I'll **take** a kilo of carrots, please.* **7** to need: *'How long does it **take** you to walk to school?' 'It **takes** me twenty minutes.' The bus **takes** only five minutes to get there.* **8** to travel in a vehicle such as a bus, train or taxi: *I'm **taking** the next bus to the city centre. We **took** a taxi to the airport.* **9** to go along a road: *I **took** the wrong road, and got lost.* **10** to occupy: *This seat is **taken**. Please **take** a seat!* **11** to photograph: *I **took** a picture of my puppy. Let me **take** a photo of you.* **12** to eat; to drink: ***Take** one pill with some water. Do you **take** sugar in your tea?*

- Meaning 1: the opposite is **give**.
- took, taking, has taken

take away **1** to go away taking someone or something with you; to remove: *The police **took** the thief **away** in a police-van.* **2** to subtract: *If you **take** five **away** from seven, you get two.*

take down **1** to write down: *Please **take down** these questions to do for your homework.* **2** to remove something that is hanging up: *At the end of term the teacher **took down** all the pictures that she had put up on the wall.*

take off **1** to remove something that you are wearing: ***Take off** your shoes and put on your slippers. Dad **took** his gloves **off**.* **2** to leave the ground: *The plane **took off** for Hong Kong at half past five.*

take out **1** to remove something that is in or inside something else: *Anna opened the drawer and **took out** a handkerchief. Mum went over to the bookcase and **took** a book **out**.* **2** to invite someone out for a meal or a show: *Yesterday my uncle **took** us **out** to a restaurant for dinner.*

take part to be one of a group of people doing something: *Tim never **took part** in the other children's games.*

take place to happen: *The wedding will **take place** in June.*

take-away
1 cooked food that people buy at a restaurant and take home to eat: *Mum buys a **take-away** when she doesn't have time to cook a meal*

*herself. We'll have a **take-away** meal this evening.* **2** a restaurant that sells take-aways: *There's a Chinese **take-away** near our house.*

taken
see **take**: *Who has **taken** my ruler?*

tale
a story: *Do you know the **tale** of Jack and the Beanstalk? The old man told the children the **tale** of his voyage to India.*

talk
to speak; to have a conversation: *My little sister is only two years old but she can already **talk** very well. You must stop **talking** when the teacher comes into the classroom. Sally and Lucy **talked** to each other for a long time on the phone. What did you **talk** about?*

talk
1 a period of talking to someone; a conversation: *I had a long **talk** with Dad about computers. We had a long **talk**.* **2** a period of speaking to an audience: *A policeman came to our school to give a **talk** about safety on the roads.*

talkative
talking a lot: *Susan is a very **talkative** girl — she can't keep quiet for long.*

tall
1 big in height: *When you go along the street, you see people of all shapes and sizes — fat people, thin people, **tall** people and short people. A fir tree is **tall**, but a rose bush is small. There are a lot of **tall** buildings in the city centre.* **2** having a certain height: *How **tall** are you? Peter is much **taller** than George. Susan is the **tallest** of the three sisters.*

- The opposite is **short** or **small**.
- You can say 'a **tall** building' or 'a **high** building'.

tambourine
a circular instrument that you beat like a drum, with little pieces of metal round its sides that ring when you shake it: *Anna plays the **tambourine** in the school band.*

Say tam-bo-**reen**.

tame
used to living with people; not wild: *Mr Lee keeps a **tame** chimpanzee as a pet.*

The opposite is **wild**.

tank
1 a large container for liquids or gas: *There is a hot-water **tank** under the stairs. Mum drove to the petrol station and filled up the petrol **tank**.* **2** a heavy vehicle used by the army for going over very rough ground: ***Tanks** are covered with steel and have a big gun that can be turned in all directions.*

tanker
a ship for carrying oil: *Oil is exported from Brunei in huge **tankers**.*

tap
1 a handle that you turn to make water flow: *Basins, baths and sinks have **taps**. Please turn off the **tap**. Don't leave the **tap** running.* **2** a light knock; a quick touch: *I heard a **tap** at the door. David gave Sue a **tap** on the shoulder to attract her attention.*

tap
to hit something with a quick, light knock: *Mark **tapped** at the window. David **tapped** Sue on the shoulder.*

tapped, tapping, has tapped

tape
1 a long, narrow strip of plastic for recording sounds: *Dad recorded the concert on **tape**.* **2** a strip of material of various kinds, used for various jobs: *We need some sticky **tape** for mending this map.*

tape-recorder
a machine that records and plays music and other sounds on tape: *Dad recorded the concert on his **tape-recorder**.*

target
an object that you fire at, especially for practice: *The soldiers were shooting at a round wooden **target** marked with circles. Joe's shots hit the **target** every time.*

tart
a pie, especially one without a top, filled with fruit or jam: *Would you like another piece of apple **tart**? Have one of these jam **tarts**.*

task
a piece of work; a duty that must be done: *It's*

*usually my **task** to dry the dishes. The teacher gave each child a **task** to do, such as wiping the blackboard and putting away the books.*

taste

1 the flavour of something: *I don't like the **taste** of wine. Garlic has a strong **taste**. This bread has no **taste** at all.* 2 your ability to notice and recognize flavours with your tongue: *Your sense of **taste** is one of your five senses. Lemons are sour to the **taste**.*

taste

1 to notice and recognize the flavour of something: *I can **taste** ginger in this cake.* 2 to have a certain flavour: *This cake **tastes** of ginger. The milk **tastes** sour.* 3 to eat or drink a little bit of something in order to test its flavour: *Please **taste** the soup and tell me if it has enough salt in it.*

> tasted, tasting, has tasted

taught

see **teach**: *My elder sister **taught** me how to ride a bicycle. Mrs White has **taught** singing at this school for many years.*

taxi

a car that can be hired with its driver, especially for short journeys: *We took a **taxi** to the airport. Mum asked the hotel porter to call a **taxi** for her. Dad asked the **taxi**-driver to take us to the airport.*

> Same as **cab**.

taxi rank or **taxi stand** a place where taxis wait, ready to be hired: *There is a **taxi rank** at the railway station. We had to wait for a taxi at the **taxi stand**.*

tea

1 a drink that is made by adding boiling water to the dried leaves of a certain kind of bush: *Would you like **tea** or coffee? I had three cups of **tea**.* 2 a small meal in the afternoon: *We had cakes and sandwiches for **tea**. Our neighbour invited us to **tea** at four o'clock.*

teach

to help people to learn about a subject; to show someone how to do something: *Mrs White **teaches** English at our school. Miss Green **teaches** the piano. Mum **taught** me to swim. My brother is **teaching** me how to use the computer.*

> - The opposite is **learn**.
> - taught, teaching, has taught

teacher

a person who teaches, especially at a school: *Mrs White is our English **teacher**.*

team

a group of people who play together in a game: *You need two **teams** of eleven players for a football match. I hope I'll be chosen for the school swimming **team**.*

teapot

a pot for making and pouring tea: *Put the tea in the **teapot** before you pour in the boiling water.*

tear

a drop of liquid that comes from your eyes when you cry: ***Tears** ran down the little girl's cheeks. Lucy dried her **tears** with her handkerchief. The mother of the lost boy wept **tears** of joy when he was found again.*

> Rhymes with **near**.

in tears crying: *The little girl was **in tears** because she had lost her doll.*

tear

a hole that has been torn: *Mum mended the **tear** in my dress.*

> Rhymes with **hair**.

tear

1 to make a hole, especially in cloth: *Peter **tore** his trousers climbing over the fence. He **tore** his trousers on the fence. You've **torn** a hole in the sleeve of your jacket.* 2 to pull something apart: *I **tore** the letter into little pieces. Dad **tore** the cheque in half.*

> - Rhymes with **hair**.
> - tore, tearing, has torn

tear down to destroy: *The old factory was **torn down** to make room for a new shopping centre.*

tear out to remove something by pulling it out: *I **tore** this page **out** of an old magazine.*

tear up to tear something into pieces: *Susie didn't like her drawing, so she **tore** it **up**. The baby is **tearing up** the book.*

tease
1 to annoy an animal: *Stop **teasing** the dog or it will bite you.* **2** to laugh at a person: *Bob's friends sometimes **tease** him about his big nose.*

teased, teasing, has teased

teaspoon
a small spoon for stirring tea: *You put the **teaspoon** on the saucer beside the cup.*

teddy or teddy-bear
a soft toy bear: *Where is my **teddy**? My little brother always takes his **teddy-bear** to bed with him.*

Two **teddies**, two **teddy-bears**

teenager
someone who is between 13 and 19 years old: *When I'm a **teenager** I shall be allowed to buy my own clothes.*

teeth
see **tooth**: *I brush my **teeth** after every meal. Sweets are bad for your **teeth**.*

telegram
an urgent message that is sent from one post office to another by telephone, and then printed out and delivered: *Today the postman delivered a **telegram** from my uncle Bill in America.*

telephone
an object you use for speaking to someone from a distance: *The **telephone** rang for a long time before anyone answered it. Mrs Walker is talking to her son on the **telephone**. Please could I use your **telephone**? I'd like to make a **telephone** call.*

Called a **phone** for short.

telephone
to call someone on the telephone: *I'll **telephone** you tomorrow.*

- You say **phone** for short.
- telephoned, telephoning, has telephoned

telescope

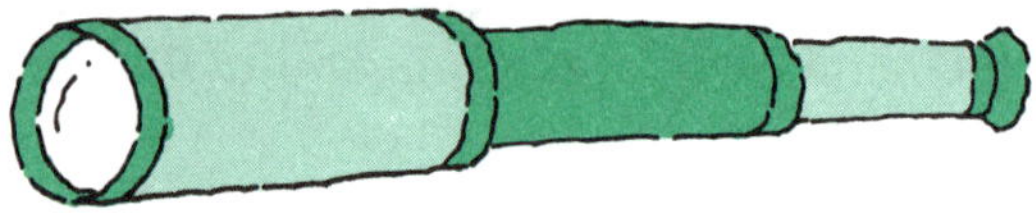

a kind of tube with lenses inside that makes distant objects appear larger and closer: *The captain looked through his **telescope** at the ship on the horizon.*

television
an object shaped like a box, with a screen for receiving broadcast pictures: *We've got a new colour **television**. I saw a good film on **television** last night. Do you often watch **television**?*

- Also called a **television set**.
- The short form is **TV**.

tell
1 to inform: *Please could you **tell** me how to get to the zoo? Sarah **told** me that it was your birthday today. Paul **told** us about his holiday.* **2** to say; to repeat: *My mum often **tells** me a story before I go to bed. You mustn't **tell** lies. I'll **tell** you a secret if you promise not to **tell** anybody else.* **3** to order someone; to advise someone: *Mum **told** me to come home before five o'clock. I **told** my dog to sit. My parents **told** me not to talk to strangers. The doctor **told** the patient to rest for a few days.* **4** to notice the difference; to know: *Can you **tell** the difference between a swallow and a swift? I can't **tell** one twin from the other. You can **tell** by the dark clouds that it's going to rain.*

told, telling, has told

temper
a mood, especially an angry mood: *Brian is in a bad **temper** today because he had to do extra homework instead of watching television.*

bad-tempered often getting angry without a good reason: ***Bad-tempered** people shout a lot.*

good-tempered cheerful and happy; not getting angry: *Mike is a **good-tempered**, helpful boy.*

lose your temper to show anger: *A man in the restaurant **lost his temper** and shouted at the waiter.*

temperature
1 heat that is measured in degrees: *Water boils at a **temperature** of 100 degrees. Fresh food must be kept at a low **temperature**.* **2** body

heat that is higher than usual because you are ill: *Mike must stay in bed because he has got a* ***temperature****. The patient has a* ***temperature*** *of 40 degrees.*

temple
a building where people pray to a god: *The monks were praying in the* ***temple****.*

ten
1 the number 10: *Two times five is* ***ten****.* **2** 10 in number: *My brother is* ***ten*** *years old. It's* ***ten*** *minutes to twelve.*

tender
1 soft; not tough: *This meat is nice and* ***tender****.* **2** sore; painful when touched: *Andrew's injured leg is still* ***tender****.*

Meaning 1: the opposite is **tough**.

tennis

a game for two or four players who use rackets to hit a ball to each other over a net: ***Tennis*** *is played on a* ***tennis court****. Do you play* ***tennis****?*

tent

a shelter made of strong cloth that is held up by poles and ropes: *The scouts put up their* ***tents*** *for the night. Have you ever slept in a* ***tent****?*

term
a part of the school year: *The year is divided into* ***terms*** *and holidays. We shall be starting the new computer course next* ***term****.*

terrible
very bad; unpleasant: *There has been a* ***terrible*** *accident on the motorway. Stop that* ***terrible*** *noise! The weather is* ***terrible*** *— it has been raining all day.*

terribly
very: *'Did I stand on your toe?' 'I'm* ***terribly*** *sorry!'*

terrific
1 wonderful: *We had a* ***terrific*** *holiday.* **2** great; large: *There was a* ***terrific*** *storm last night. The bomb exploded with a* ***terrific*** *noise.*

terrify
to frighten someone very much: *The noise of the explosion* ***terrified*** *the children. My sister is* ***terrified*** *of spiders. The little boy was* ***terrified*** *by the thunder.*

terrifies, terrified, terrifying, has terrified

terror
great fear: *In the story, the children screamed with* ***terror*** *when they saw a ghost coming through the closed door.*

test
a set of questions you are asked, to find out how much you know about a subject: *We had to do an arithmetic* ***test*** *this morning. We all passed the* ***test****.*

test
1 to ask people questions to find out how much they know about a subject: *The pupils were* ***tested*** *on their knowledge of English.* **2** to find out if something is all right before using it: *Mum* ***tested*** *the hot water with her finger before she put the baby in the bath.*

than
you use **than** when you are comparing things: *A van is smaller* ***than*** *a lorry. Peter is two years older* ***than*** *his sister. Mary can swim faster* ***than*** *I can. I like ice-cream better* ***than*** *chocolate. The test was easier* ***than*** *I thought it would be.*

thank
to say that you are grateful to someone for something: *John* ***thanked*** *me for the present. Tracy* ***thanked*** *me for helping her with her homework.*
thank you or **thanks** words you use to thank someone: ***Thank you*** *very much for your help.* ***Thanks*** *very much for your lovely present.* ***Thanks*** *a lot! Many* ***thanks*** *for the postcard from Tokyo. 'Would you like something to eat?' 'No,* ***thanks*** *— I'm not hungry.'*

that
1 you use **that** when you are talking about a person or thing that is a distance away from you: *'Who is* ***that*** *girl over there?'* ***'That'****s my sister.' Don't use this cup — use* ***that*** *one on the table. What is* ***that*** *you've got in your hand?* **2** you can use **that** when you describe something or someone or explain which person or thing you mean: *Milk is a liquid* ***that*** *comes*

*from cows. Where is the book **that** I left on the kitchen table? Who is the boy **that** you were talking to? Here are the pictures **that** I wanted to show you.* **3** you can use **that** after words such as **say**, **tell**, **know**, **think** and **hope**: *Bob told me **that** he had been to Australia. He said **that** his aunt lived in Sydney.* **4** you use **that** after so and such: *The children were so tired **that** they fell asleep in the car. It was such a hot day **that** we didn't want to play outside.*

Meaning 1: the opposite is **this**.

the
1 you use **the** when you mean special people or things, not just any people or things: *Where is **the** book I put on **the** table? Who is **the** boy sitting next to John? Our house is **the** one with **the** yellow front door. Please switch off **the** lights before you go to bed.* **2** here are some other words that usually have **the** before them: *Mum enjoys listening to **the** radio. Dad listened to **the** news on **the** radio. Andrew plays **the** piano very well. Shall we go to **the** cinema? Do you often go to **the** theatre?* **3** you use **the** before words such as **best**, **worst**, **largest**, **most**: *Who is **the** best pupil in your class? Who is **the** tallest in the class? Who can run **the** fastest? The last question in the test was **the** most difficult one.*

theatre
a building with a stage where plays and shows are performed: *We went to the **theatre** to see a play called 'Peter Pan'.*

Say **thee**-a-ter.

theft
stealing: *The man was sent to prison for **theft**. The judge said the man was guilty of **theft**.*

their
belonging to two or more people or things, or to an unknown person: *While our neighbours were on holiday we looked after **their** cat. Someone has left **their** coat behind.*

Sounds like **there**, rhymes with **hair**.

theirs
you use **theirs** for something that belongs to two or more people, or to an unknown person: *'Is this Mr and Mrs Lee's flat?' 'No, **theirs** is on the second floor.' We are friends of **theirs**. Don't take my pen — get someone else to lend you **theirs**.*

them
you use **them** when you are talking about two or more people or things, or an unknown person: *The children were talking in class, so the teacher told **them** to be quiet. If someone was drowning, could you save **them**?*

themselves
1 you use **themselves** in a sentence where people do something to or for themselves: *The girls looked at **themselves** in the mirror. Take bandages in case anyone hurts **themselves**.* **2** without help: *Clare and Helen made these cakes **themselves**.* **3** you sometimes use **themselves** to show whom you mean more clearly: *Tom and Dick couldn't go to the match **themselves**, so they gave their tickets to Jack and Harry.*

then
1 after that: *First put the tea in the teapot, **then** add the boiling water. When I got home I had my tea and **then** I did my homework. Get off that wall — you might break your leg, and **then** what would you do?* **2** at that time: *I tried to ring you at five o'clock yesterday — were you out **then**? I'll collect you at half past three, so please be ready by **then**.*

there
1 at that place; in that place; to that place: *Peter lives **there**. 'Where are the scissors?' '**There** they are, on your desk.' Don't go in **there**. I haven't been **there** for a long time.* **2** you use **there** when you give information or ask for information: ***There** are twenty children in my class. Is **there** any rice left? Weren't **there** any pencils in the drawer? **There**'s a good film on television tonight. Were **there** enough sweets for everybody? **There** are some more in the box.* **3** you use **there** to comfort and to scold people: ***There**, **there**, don't cry! **There**! I told you not to touch the hot iron, and now you've burnt yourself!*

Meaning 1: the opposite is **here**.

therefore
for that reason: *Mark is ill and **therefore** he has to stay in bed.*

thermometer
an instrument for measuring temperature, especially your body temperature: *Put the **thermometer** into your mouth — I want to take your temperature.*

these
you use **these** for things and people that are near you: *Do **these** books belong to you? **These***

*are my friends, Paul and Mike. I've seen **these** photos before but I haven't seen those.*

> The opposite is **those**.

they
you use **they** when you are talking about two or more people or things, or an unknown person: *Jenny and her brother didn't go to school today because **they** were both ill. I like bananas best when **they** are soft and sweet. Anyone can succeed if **they** try.*

they'd
short for **they had** or **they would**: ***They'd** left before us. They said **they'd** be back at five o'clock.*

they'll
short for **they will**: ***They'll** come and see us tomorrow.*

they're
short for **they are**: ***They're** having lunch.*

they've
short for **they have**: ***They've** been here before.*

thick
1 not thin; having a large distance between the two sides: *I had two **thick** slices of bread. A fortress has strong, **thick** walls.* **2** having a certain distance between the two sides: *The glass in the window is one centimetre **thick**.* **3** growing close together in a large amount: *There was a **thick** forest all round the witch's castle. Linda has **thick** black hair.* **4** not very liquid: *You can make **thick** soup with peas and potatoes.* **5** difficult to see through: *The airport was closed for several hours because of **thick** fog.*

> Meaning 1: the opposite is **thin**.

thief
a person who steals: *The **thief** stole the man's wallet. **Thieves** broke into the shop and stole all the precious jewellery.*

> - Same as **burglar**.
> - Two **thieves**

thigh
the part of your leg above your knee: *Your **thighs** are the fattest part of your legs.*

thin
1 not thick; having a short distance between the two sides: *This paper is very **thin**. The walls of this house are too **thin**.* **2** not fat; having not much flesh: *You'll get **thin** if you don't eat enough.*

> - Meaning 1: the opposite is **thick**.
> - Meaning 2: the opposite is **fat**.
> - thin, thinner, thinnest

thing
1 an object; something that is not living: *A pencil is a **thing** that you write with. A chair is a **thing** you sit on. What do you use this white **thing** for?* **2** a fact; an action; a quality; an idea: *It's difficult to remember **things** that happened when you were very young. I've got a few **things** to do before I go to bed. That was a stupid **thing** to do. The best **thing** about holidays is that you don't have to get up early in the mornings. We learnt about lots of different **things** today.*

think
1 to use your mind: ***Think** before you answer this question. I need time to **think**. Do animals **think**? What are you **thinking** about?* **2** to believe: *I **think** my dog is very clever. 'What do you **think** of Mike's plan?' 'I **think** it's very good.' Do you **think** it's going to rain soon?* **3** to care for others: *Mary is a good girl — she always **thinks** of other children.* **4** to remember: *I can't **think** of that girl's name.* **5** to plan: *My parents are **thinking** of moving to a larger flat.*

> thought, thinking, has thought

think out to plan: *Mike **thought out** the whole plan on his own.*
think up to invent: *I've **thought up** a new game for us to play.*

third
1 the next after the second: *Peter came first in the race and I came **third**. We live on the **third** floor.* **2** one of three equal parts: *There were three children, so each child got a **third** of the ice-cream.*

thirst
the feeling you have when you need something to drink: *People die of **thirst** if they have nothing to drink for a long time.*

thirsty
needing something to drink: *I need a drink — I'm very **thirsty**.*

thirteen
1 the number 13: *Seven and six are **thirteen**.*

2 13 in number: *My elder sister is* ***thirteen*** *years old.*

thirty
1 the number 30: *Three times ten is* ***thirty****.* **2** 30 in number: *'****Thirty*** *minutes' is the same as 'half an hour'. There are* ***thirty*** *days in April.*

this
1 you use **this** for a person or thing that is near you: ***This*** *is my friend Elizabeth. I like* ***this*** *picture much better than that one over there.* **2** you use **this** for a part of today, and for a period of time that belongs to the present: *What did you do* ***this*** *morning? We're going to the zoo* ***this*** *afternoon. It has been very hot* ***this*** *week.*

Meaning 1: the opposite is **that**.

thorn
a hard, sharp point that grows on the stem of certain plants: *Roses have* ***thorns****.*

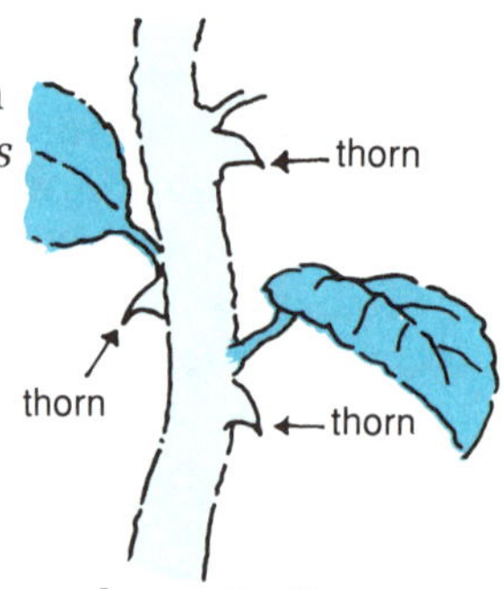

thorny
covered with thorns: *I tore my dress on a* ***thorny*** *bush.*

those
you use **those** for things and people that are a distance away from you: *'Do* ***those*** *pencils on the desk belong to you?' 'No, these are mine and* ***those*** *are Sheila's.'*

The opposite is **these**.

though
although: *We went for a walk even* ***though*** *it was raining.* ***Though*** *I enjoy school, I like the holidays better.*

thought
see **think**: *I* ***thought*** *you weren't coming. I've just* ***thought*** *of something — I forgot to lock the front door.*

thought
an idea: *I suddenly had a* ***thought****. A* ***thought*** *suddenly came into my head. Tim was thrilled at the* ***thought*** *of going to Australia for three weeks.*

thousand
1 the number 1 000: *Ten times one hundred is one* ***thousand****.* **2** 1 000 in number: *There were at least a* ***thousand*** *people in the theatre. The new car cost thirty* ***thousand*** *dollars. The moon is* ***thousands*** *of miles away.*

thread
a long, thin line of cotton for sewing with: *I need a needle and some* ***thread*** *to sew this button back on to my shirt.*

three
1 the number 3: *Two and one are* ***three****.* **2** 3 in number: *My younger sister is* ***three*** *years old. A tricycle has* ***three*** *wheels.*

threw
see **throw**: *Julie* ***threw*** *the ball to me.*

thrill
to make you very excited and pleased: *I was* ***thrilled*** *to hear that I'd won the competition. We were* ***thrilled*** *at the exciting news. Claire was* ***thrilled*** *with all her birthday presents.*

throat
the part at the back of your mouth: *I've got such a sore* ***throat*** *that I can hardly swallow. The doctor asked me to open my mouth wide so that he could look at my* ***throat****. Be careful not to eat the fish bones, because they might get stuck in your* ***throat****.*

throne
a splendid chair that is used by a king or queen during ceremonies: *The king wore his crown and sat on his golden* ***throne****.*

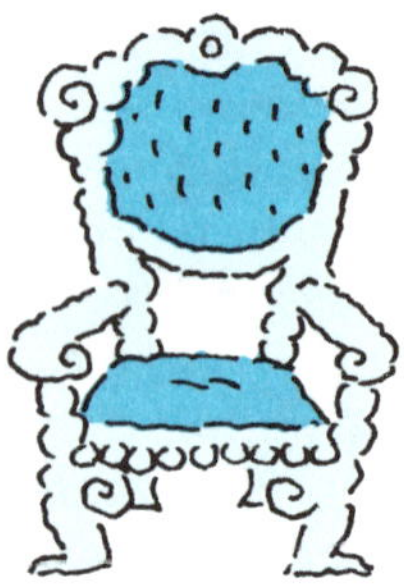

through
1 from one end to the other; from one side to the other: *The train is coming* ***through*** *the tunnel. There's a lot of water flowing* ***through*** *the pipe. You go into a room* ***through*** *the doorway. The cat got into the house* ***through*** *an open window. We drove* ***through*** *the town.* **2** from the beginning to the end: *I haven't read* ***through*** *the whole book yet.* **3** moving in the air or water: *A bird flies* ***through*** *the air and a fish swims* ***through*** *the water.*

Say **throo**.

throw
to make something go through the air: *In netball, the players try to* ***throw*** *the ball into a high net. Please* ***throw*** *me the ball. Some boys are* ***throwing*** *stones into the pond.*

threw, throwing, has thrown

throw away to get rid of something: *These old shoes can't be mended — you'll have to **throw** them **away**.*

thrown
see **throw**: *Somebody has **thrown** a stone through the window.*

thumb
the short, thick finger of your hand that is set apart from your other four fingers: *Lots of little children suck their **thumbs**.*

thunder
the loud noise that you hear after a flash of lightning: *A storm with **thunder** and lightning is called a **thunderstorm**.*

Thursday
the fifth day of the week; the day after Wednesday: *We'll go to the zoo on **Thursday**.*

tick
1 a mark (✓) for showing that something is correct: *The teacher put a red **tick** next to each right answer.* **2** the regular sound of a clock or watch: *The **tick** of the clock was the only sound in the room. My watch has a very quiet **tick**.*

tick
1 to put a tick next to something written: *The teacher **ticked** the names of the children who were present.* **2** to make a regular sound: *Our kitchen clock **ticks** very loudly.*

ticket
1 a small piece of paper that allows you to travel on a bus, train, or plane: *You buy your bus **ticket** when you get on the bus. You can buy your train **ticket** at the **ticket** office in the railway station. Dad bought four return **tickets** to Penang.* **2** a small piece of paper that allows you to go to a film, or a play, or a match: *Mum bought three **tickets** for the theatre. How much was your cinema **ticket**?*

tickle
to touch people in certain places that make them laugh: *Mum was **tickling** the baby's feet. I **tickled** my little brother under the arms.*

tickled, tickling, has tickled

tide
the regular moving of the sea in and out every day: *The **tide** is coming in. It's high **tide**. The **tide** is going out. At low **tide** you find lots of seaweed on the beach.*

tidy
1 kept in good order; neat: *My brother doesn't keep his bedroom **tidy**. Does my hair look **tidy**?* **2** liking everything to be neat: *My mum is a very **tidy** person.*

tidy
to make something neat by putting things away in their proper places: *Please **tidy** your room. Have you **tidied** your desk?*

tidies, tidied, tidying, has tidied

tidy up to tidy: *We must **tidy up** the classroom before the headmistress comes in.*

tie
1 to fasten something with a string or rope: *Jeff **tied** his pony to a tree. The parcel was **tied** with string.* **2** to make a bow or knot in something: *I can **tie** my own shoelaces. Sarah **tied** a ribbon round her hair.*

ties, tied, tying, has tied

tie up to fasten tightly with a string or rope: *The boy **tied up** the pony. The parcel was **tied up** with string. The burglar **tied up** the owner of the house.*

tie
a long, narrow piece of cloth that a man wears tied under his collar and hanging down the front of his shirt: *Mr Smith is wearing a white shirt and a red **tie**.*

tiger

a large wild animal of the cat family that has yellow fur with black stripes: ***Tigers** live in the jungles of Asia. A female **tiger** is called a **tigress**.*

tight
1 fitting closely; not loose: *Joe is wearing **tight** jeans. These shoes are too **tight** for me — my feet are hurting. I can't open this jar — the lid is too **tight**.* **2** firmly; not letting go: *Hold on **tight** to the rope so that you don't fall.*

Meaning 1: the opposite is **loose**.

till
up to a certain time; until: *I'll wait for you **till** five o'clock. Dad works from 8 o'clock **till** 6*

*o'clock. What have you been doing up **till** now?*

timber
wood, especially for building: *The house is built of **timber**.*

time
1 the hour and the minute at any point in the day: *What **time** is it? What's the **time**, please? The **time** on my watch is ten minutes past eleven. Have you learnt how to tell the **time** yet? I'll see you at the same **time** tomorrow. It's **time** for you to go to bed.* 2 a period that you do something in: *We've got plenty of **time** to catch the bus — we don't need to run. Did you enjoy the **time** you spent in Kuala Lumpur? I haven't seen George for a long **time**. We had a good **time** at the party.* 3 a point at which something happens: *We were living in America at the **time** of my sister's birth.* 4 the doing of something once: *How many **times** have you been to the zoo? This is the first **time** that Peter has been to the zoo. Please don't be late next **time**.* 5 the speed that you sing or play a tune at: *Keep in **time** with the piano when you sing.*
from time to time sometimes: ***From time to time** we go to the beach for a picnic.*
in time early enough: *I'll be home **in time** for dinner. I'll come home **in** good **time** to change before I go out.*
on time not late; punctual: *The train arrived **on time**. Please try to be **on time**.*

times
multiplied by: *Three **times** two is six.*

timetable
1 a list that shows when school classes are taught: *We'll get our new **timetable** at the beginning of term.* 2 a list that shows when trains, buses, boats or planes arrive and depart: *Mr Jones looked up the planes to Hong Kong in the **timetable**.*

timid
shy; frightened; not bold: *A mouse is a **timid** animal. The little boy was so **timid** that he tried to hide whenever he saw a stranger.*

The opposite is **brave** and **bold**.

tin
1 a silver-coloured metal: *You get **tin** from mines. We use **tin** mugs and **tin** plates when we go camping.* 2 a metal container that food is put into, to store for a long time; a can: *You open a **tin** with a **tin** opener. Mum bought three **tins** of pineapple.* 3 a metal box for biscuits, cake, tea or other things: *Mum keeps the biscuits in a **tin** so that they won't go stale.*

tiny
very little: *There's a **tiny** little insect walking up your arm. Some creatures are so **tiny** that you can see them only under a microscope.*

- Same as **small** and **little**.
- The opposite is **huge** or **big**.
- tiny, tinier, tiniest

tip
1 the narrow end of something long: *The **tips** of your fingers are called **fingertips**. A ball-point pen has a tiny ball at its **tip**.* 2 a small amount of extra money that you give to someone such as a waiter or taxi-driver: *Mum gave the waitress a **tip** because she was so friendly and helpful.*

tip
1 to roll over to one side; to lift up on one side: *The boat **tipped** over and we almost fell into the water. You have to **tip** up the jug to pour out the milk.* 2 to empty something from a container: *Lucy opened her purse and **tipped** the coins out on to her desk.* 3 to give some extra money to someone: *Mum **tipped** the waitress.*

tipped, tipping, has tipped

tiptoe
to walk on your toes, so that you make no noise: *We **tiptoed** out of the bedroom so that we wouldn't wake the baby.*
on tiptoe on your toes: *Paul stood **on tiptoe** to reach the shelf.*

tired
feeling that you need rest; wanting to sleep: *Sarah felt **tired** so she went to bed early. We were **tired** after the long walk.*
tired of no longer interested; bored: *I'm **tired of** this game — let's play another one. I'm **tired of** answering stupid questions.*

title

1 the name of something such as a book, film or song: *The **title** of the book is 'The Legend of the Monkey God'.* **2** a word that you use before someone's name, such as Mr, Mrs, Miss, Dr, Captain, Professor, Sir: *'Sir' is a **title** that is given to men who have served their country well, such as Sir Stamford Raffles.*

to

1 in the direction of something; towards: *I always walk **to** school. We drove from Singapore **to** Kuala Lumpur. We are going **to** Melaka for our holidays. We're going **to** a play this evening.* **2** you use **to** with words such as **give**, **send**, **listen**, **talk**, **write**: *Give this book **to** Alice. I'm sending these stamps **to** my cousin. Listen **to** me when I'm talking **to** you! I'll write **to** you from London. Have you replied **to** Sally's invitation yet?* **3** until; as far as: *Most people work from Monday **to** Friday. Susan is dressed in red from top **to** toe.* **4** before: *It's five minutes **to** three.* **5** here are some other ways of using **to**: *You must be kind **to** your little brother. Where's the key **to** this door? I tore the letter **to** pieces. Susan is junior **to** me at school. Stars are often compared **to** diamonds. We won the match by 5 goals **to** 2. Paul sang a song **to** his guitar. I couldn't do my sums, so the teacher came **to** my help.* **6** you often put **to** before a verb: *I don't want **to** go home yet. Elizabeth asked me **to** help her. We had **to** run **to** catch the bus. I was too tired **to** watch television. I ought **to** do my homework, but I don't want **to**.*

toad

an animal like a frog, but larger: *Can you hear the **toads** croaking by the pond?*

toast

a slice of bread that has been made brown and crunchy in a toaster or under a grill: *I had two pieces of **toast** with butter and marmalade. Would you like a fried egg on **toast** for lunch?*

toaster

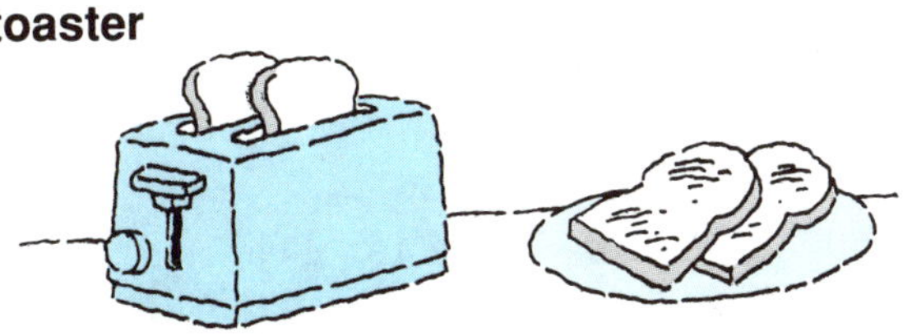

an electric machine for making slices of bread brown: *This **toaster** doesn't work properly — it sometimes burns the toast.*

tobacco

the cut and dried leaves of a certain plant, which are put into cigarettes and cigars, and also smoked in pipes: *Uncle Jack filled his pipe with **tobacco**.*

today

this day: *Helen isn't going to school **today** because she's ill. **Today** is Monday. What's **today**'s date?*

toe

one of the five parts that the end of your foot is divided into: *I've hurt the big **toe** on my left foot. The nails that grow on your **toes** are called **toenails***

toffee

a sticky sweet made of sugar and butter: *I don't like **toffee** because it sticks to my teeth when I chew it. I bought a bag of **toffees**.*

together

1 with someone; in a group: *My sister and I usually walk to school **together**. The children were playing **together** in the park.* **2** at the same time: *David and Steve arrived **together**.* **3** into one piece: *The carpenter nailed the two pieces of wood **together**. We'll try and stick this broken vase **together** again with glue.*

toilet

a place where you get rid of liquid and solid stuff from your body: *I want to go to the **toilet**. Where is the **toilet**, please?*

told

see **tell**: *Liz **told** me about her holidays. We were **told** that we must work harder.*

tomato

a soft round red vegetable that you put in salads, sauces and hot dishes: *Mum is making a salad with **tomatoes** and onions. We're having spaghetti with **tomato** sauce for dinner.*

Two **tomatoes**

tomorrow

the day after today: *We'll go to the zoo **tomorrow**. I'll finish my homework **tomorrow** morning before school.*

tongue

the soft red thing inside your mouth that you can move about: *You use your **tongue** for speaking, tasting and swallowing. The doctor asked me to put out my **tongue** so that he could examine it.*

Say **tung**.

tonight

this evening; the night of today: *Mum and Dad are going to the cinema **tonight**. You look tired — you must go to bed early **tonight**.*

too

1 more than you need; more than you want: *I've got **too** much rice — I can't eat it all. These jeans are **too** long for me. It's **too** hot today to sit in the sun.* **2** also; as well: *I've got a bicycle and my sister has one **too**. 'I'd like some ice-cream.' 'Me **too**!'*

took

see **take**: *Lucy **took** the books back to the library. I **took** a shower. Mr Smith **took** a taxi to the airport.*

tool

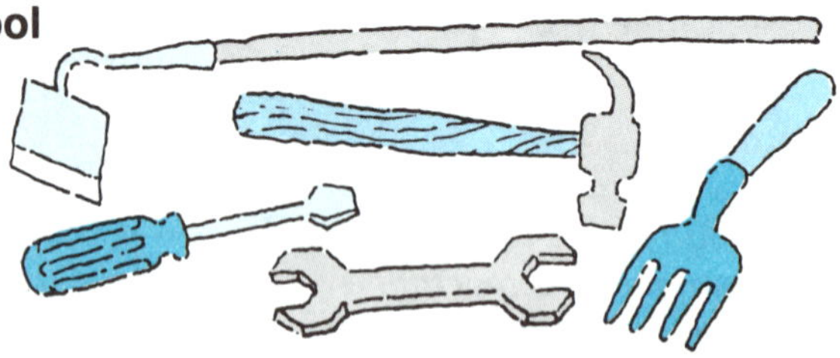

a thing that you use to help you do a job: *Dad has a screwdriver, a hammer, a saw and lots of other **tools** in his **tool** box. Spades, shovels, rakes and hoes are **tools** for the garden.*

tooth

1 one of the hard white objects growing in your mouth, that you use for biting and chewing food: *I lost another **tooth** today. You get your second **teeth** when you are about six. Your first **teeth** get loose and fall out. Don't forget to clean your **teeth** before you go to bed.* **2** one of the narrow points that a comb or a saw is divided into: *There are lots of **teeth** missing out of this old comb.*

A row of **teeth**

toothache

an ache in a tooth: *I've got terrible **toothache** — I must go to the dentist.*

toothbrush

a small brush for cleaning your teeth: *I've put too much toothpaste on my **toothbrush**.*

toothpaste

soft stuff that you put on your toothbrush to clean your teeth: *We need a new tube of **toothpaste**.*

top

1 the highest part of something: *We climbed to the **top** of the hill. Please do the exercise at the **top** of page 45. The book I want is on the **top** shelf. We took the lift to the **top** floor of the skyscraper.* **2** a cover; a lid: *The table is circular, with a glass **top**. I've lost the **top** of my pen. I can't get the **top** off this jar.* **3** the position of the person who gets the highest marks in a class: *Alice is **top** of the class again. She got **top** marks in all the exams.* **4** fastest: *The ambulance drove to the hospital at **top** speed.* **5** a small toy that spins on a pointed foot: *Joe spun his little wooden **top** on the table.*

Meanings 1 and 3: the opposite is **bottom**.

on top of resting on the top of something: *You've left your glasses **on top of** the fridge. We piled the books one **on top of** the other.*

torch

a small electric light that you can carry about with you: *Bob shone his **torch** along the path so that we could see our way.*

tore

see **tear**: *Peter **tore** his trousers on the fence. I **tore** the letter into little pieces.*

torn

see **tear**: *You've **torn** a hole in your dress.*

tortoise

a slow-moving animal with a hard shell: ***Tortoises** are reptiles. A **tortoise** pulls its head and legs inside its shell when it's frightened. Jim keeps a **tortoise** as a pet.*

Say **tor**-tus.

toss

1 to throw something upwards: *Vicky **tossed** the ball into the air.* **2** to move from side to side: *The boat **tossed** about in the storm. The ship was **tossed** by the waves.*

total

1 whole; complete: *What was the **total** cost of*

the holiday? **2** the amount that everything adds up to: *If you add up 5, 7, 9 and 11, the* ***total*** *is 32. The numbers come to a* ***total*** *of 32.*

touch

1 to put a part of your body, especially your hand, on to something; to feel with your fingers: *Don't* ***touch*** *the iron — it's very hot.* **2** to be so close to something that you press against it: *We had to sit so close together that our shoulders* ***touched****.*

touch

1 the feeling of being touched: *John felt a* ***touch*** *on his shoulder.* **2** the sense by which you feel things, especially through your fingers: *A kitten's fur is very soft to the* ***touch****.*

tough

1 strong; hard to break; hard to wear out: *Shoes have to be made of* ***tough*** *material such as leather.* **2** difficult to chew; not tender: *This meat is rather* ***tough****.*

- Say **tuf**.
- Meaning 2: the opposite is **tender**.

tour

1 a journey to several places; a trip: *We spent our holiday doing a* ***tour*** *of India.* **2** a short trip round a certain place: *The guide took the tourists on a* ***tour*** *of the palace.*

Rhymes with **poor**.

tour

to go on a tour around a place: *We* ***toured*** *Thailand last year. A party of visitors were* ***touring*** *the town of Melaka.*

tourists

people who are spending their holiday visiting places: *A guide showed a group of* ***tourists*** *the sights of Singapore.*

towards

in the direction of something: *My dog ran* ***towards*** *me when I came home. The teacher was standing with her back* ***towards*** *the class, writing something on the blackboard. Turn* ***towards*** *the audience when you speak, or they won't hear you. The ship was sailing* ***towards*** *Australia.*

towel

a large thick soft cloth for drying yourself: *Tom wrapped a big* ***towel*** *round himself when he came out of the shower.*

tower

a tall narrow part of a building higher than the rest of it; a tall narrow building standing by itself: *The castle is square, with a* ***tower*** *at each corner. In the story the princess was kept locked in a high* ***tower*** *on top of a mountain.*

town

1 a place where people live and work, larger than a village but smaller than a city: *Melaka is a* ***town*** *lying between the cities of Singapore and Kuala Lumpur.* **2** the centre of a city or a town, where most of the shops are: *Mum is taking me into* ***town*** *to buy a pair of shoes.*

toy

an object for a child to play with: *My little sister got a teddy-bear, a doll and lots of other* ***toys*** *for her birthday. Tim likes playing with his* ***toy*** *cars.*

trace

a faint mark left by something: *There were* ***traces*** *of egg on Peter's shirt. The detective found* ***traces*** *of blood on the floor. My dog disappeared without* ***trace****.*

track

1 a mark on the ground left by an animal, a person or a vehicle: *The men followed the elephant's* ***tracks****.* **2** a path; a rough road: *Donkeys can climb steep mountain* ***tracks****.* **3** a special hard wide path for athletes to run on: *The runners in the 1000 metres race have to go round the* ***track*** *four times.*

tractor

a motor vehicle with large back wheels that is

used on a farm for pulling a plough or other machines: *The farmer drove his* ***tractor*** *across the field.*

trade
the buying and selling of goods: *Japan does a lot of* ***trade*** *with Britain.*

traffic
cars, buses, lorries and other vehicles that are moving on the road: *There's a lot of* ***traffic*** *in the city centre. A policeman was directing the* ***traffic****.*
traffic jam a lot of vehicles all trying to go in different directions, but not able to move because there are so many of them: *There's a* ***traffic jam*** *at the crossroads.*
traffic lights a set of red, orange and green lights at places such as crossroads and pedestrian crossings, telling drivers when to stop and when to go: *You stop when the* ***traffic lights*** *are at red, and you go on when they are at green. Turn left at the next* ***traffic lights****.*

train

a long vehicle that is pulled by an engine along a railway: *We went to Kuala Lumpur by* ***train****. We took the 10 o'clock* ***train*** *to Kuala Lumpur. The* ***train*** *stopped at the station and all the passengers got off. A goods* ***train*** *is a* ***train*** *that transports goods, not people.*

train
1 to learn the skills that you need for a certain job; to teach someone skills: *I'd like to* ***train*** *as a teacher when I grow up. Sue's sister is* ***training*** *to be a dancer.* **2** to teach an animal some skills: *Dad has* ***trained*** *the dog to fetch his slippers. The police have well-****trained*** *dogs.* **3** to practise a sport; to do exercises for making you stronger and faster: *The athletes were* ***training*** *for the race. The football team* ***trains*** *every Saturday morning.*

translate
to change written words or spoken words into another language: *The teacher gave us some Malay sentences to* ***translate*** *into English. Mr Wang* ***translated*** *the tourist's question into Chinese.*

translated, translating, has translated

transparent
able to be seen through: *Glass and water are* ***transparent****. The box has a* ***transparent*** *lid, so you can see what is inside it.*

transport
to carry people or goods from one place to another: *A bus will be waiting at the airport to* ***transport*** *the passengers to the city centre. It is cheaper to* ***transport*** *goods by sea than by air.*

transport
the transporting of goods and people; vehicles for transporting goods and people: ***Transport*** *by air is more expensive than* ***transport*** *by sea. You have to buy a ticket to travel on any form of public* ***transport****, such as a bus or a train.*

trap
something arranged for catching an animal: *The hunters laid a* ***trap*** *for the tiger by digging a pit and covering it with branches.*

trap
1 to catch animals in traps: *The hunter* ***trapped*** *a rabbit and cooked it for his supper.* **2** to trick: *Joe* ***trapped*** *Susie into giving away her secret.* **3** to stop someone escaping: *The children were* ***trapped*** *in the cave when the tide came in.*

travel
to go from one place to another: *We* ***travelled*** *to Bangkok by train. We're going to spend a month* ***travelling*** *round Britain.*

travelled, travelling, has travelled

tray
a flat object made of wood, metal or plastic, for carrying things on, with a low edge to stop them falling off: *Mum put the glasses and cups on the* ***tray*** *and carried it into the sitting-room.*

treasure
a store of gold, jewels and other precious objects: *The pirates hid their* ***treasure*** *in a cave on an island. The place where the* ***treasure*** *was buried was marked on an old map.*

treat
1 to behave in a certain way to a person or animal: *You should* ***treat*** *your mother and father with respect. Always* ***treat*** *animals kindly. The donkeys have been badly* ***treated*** *by their owner — he used to beat them and*

starve them. **2** to try to cure: *The doctor is **treating** Sally's sore throat. Joe hurt his arm and had to get it **treated** at the hospital.*

treatment
1 the way you treat a person or animal: *These donkeys have had very cruel **treatment** from their owner.* **2** the way a doctor treats a patient: *This patient is very ill — he needs urgent **treatment**. What is the correct **treatment** for a bleeding nose?*

tree
the largest kind of plant, with a thick wooden trunk and branches: *Joe climbed up a **tree** and couldn't get down again. Some fruits, such as apples, pears and cherries, grow on **trees**.*

triangle

1 a flat shape with three sides: *In our maths lesson we practised drawing circles, squares and **triangles**.* **2** a metal bar shaped into a triangle, which you play by striking it with a short bar: *Jane and I play the **triangle** in the school band.*

trick
1 something you do to cheat someone; something mischievous you do to someone: *A man came to Mrs Brown's door and used a **trick** to steal her money — he asked her for a drink of water and when she was getting it, he stole her handbag. The teacher couldn't help laughing when we played a funny **trick** on her.* **2** a clever act that is done to amuse people: *The magician performed a **trick** with a pack of cards. The sea-lions at the circus are good at performing **tricks** with balls.*

trick
to cheat someone; to play a trick on someone: *We changed the time on the classroom clock and **tricked** the teacher into sending us home early.*

tricycle

a small vehicle with three wheels, for children to ride on until they're big enough to ride a bicycle: *My little brother enjoys riding his **tricycle** round the garden.*

trip
a journey to a place and back again: *We went on a **trip** to Fraser's Hill at the weekend. Mr Wang is away on a business **trip** to Hong Kong.*

trip
to knock your foot against something so that you fall, or nearly fall; to make someone do this: *Sarah **tripped** over a stone and fell. Tie your shoelaces — they may **trip** you if you leave them undone.*

tripped, tripping, has tripped

trip up to trip: *Alan tried to **trip** Lucy **up** by sticking his foot out in front of her.*

trishaw
a vehicle with three wheels that is pedalled along by the driver and has a seat for two passengers: *Tourists like to hire **trishaws** to take them round Singapore.*

troop
1 a group of soldiers: *The general commanded his **troops** to leave the camp. A **troop** of soldiers was marching along the road.* **2** a group of Boy Scouts: *Peter is going to join the Scout **troop** next year.*

trouble
1 problems; difficulties: *The librarian had a lot of **trouble** finding the book that Mike wanted. The man was in **trouble** for lying to the police.* **2** something that causes a problem: *The children are very well-behaved — they are no **trouble** at all.* **3** care: *Jane always takes a lot of **trouble** with her homework.*

troublesome
causing problems: *There are a few **troublesome** boys in the school who try to bully the younger children. Grandad has a **troublesome** cough, so he's going to the doctor.*

trousers
a piece of clothing that covers your bottom and the whole of each leg: *Paul is wearing blue **trousers** and a white shirt. Where are my black **trousers**? This pair of **trousers** is too small for me.*

truck
a lorry: *A **truck** was waiting at the quay to take the goods to the supermarket.*

true
correct, not false: *Is it **true** that Simon has*

measles? Tim says he can run faster than me, but it isn't ***true****. The teacher is reading us a* ***true*** *story about a cat and two dogs that walked across Canada.*

The opposite is **false**.

trumpet

a metal instrument with a high sound that you play by blowing hard into it: *The* ***trumpets*** *were blown to announce the arrival of the king.*

trunk

1 the main stem of a tree: *This old oak tree has a very thick* ***trunk****.* **2** the long nose of an elephant: *An elephant uses its* ***trunk*** *to pick things up and carry them.* **3** a large, strong box: *Mr Green packed his* ***trunk*** *and sent it to Australia by sea.*

trust

to know you can believe someone, or depend on them to do something: *You can't* ***trust*** *someone who keeps telling lies. You can* ***trust*** *Alice to look after the younger children.*

truth

the true facts: *You must always tell the* ***truth****. The judge wanted to know the whole* ***truth*** *about what had happened.*

The opposite is a **lie**.

try

an act of trying: *I can't do this crossword puzzle — why don't you have a* ***try****?*

try

1 to do your best to do something: *I* ***tried*** *to solve the puzzle, but I failed. Let's* ***try*** *and climb that wall. Go on,* ***try****! You won't know whether you can do it until you* ***try****.* ***Try*** *harder!* **2** to test; to find out if something is good: *Peter* ***tried*** *cleaning his teeth with soap. Have you* ***tried*** *this new ice-cream?*

tries, tried, trying, has tried

try on to put on a piece of clothing to see if it fits: *Mary* ***tried on*** *lots of dresses in the department store.*
try out to test something by using it: *Mike* ***tried out*** *his new bicycle on the pavement before riding it on the road.*

T-shirt or tee-shirt

a light cotton shirt, usually with short sleeves, that you pull on over your head: *Paul is wearing a* ***T-shirt*** *with red and white stripes.*

tube

1 a long, hollow object; a pipe: *The water flows through a plastic* ***tube*** *into the tank.* **2** a long narrow container made of soft metal or plastic, which you squeeze to get out the stuff that is inside: *We need a new* ***tube*** *of toothpaste.*

Tuesday

the third day of the week, the day after Monday: *We have a singing lesson on* ***Tuesday*** *afternoons.*

tumble

to fall: *Martin* ***tumbled*** *down the stairs.*

tumbled, tumbling, has tumbled

tune

a little piece of music: *John is whistling a* ***tune****. That song has a pretty* ***tune****. The teacher plays the* ***tune*** *on the piano.*

tunnel

an underground passage, especially one cut through a hill or under a river: *The train went through a* ***tunnel*** *in the mountains. Some prisoners dug a* ***tunnel*** *under the prison walls and escaped.*

turban

a long piece of cloth wound round a man's head: *Mr Singh is wearing a white* ***turban****.*

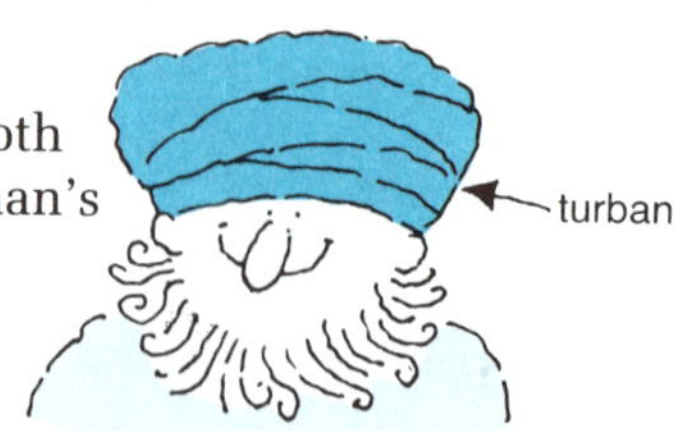

turkey

a large brown farm bird: ***Turkeys*** *are kept on farms for their meat. Some people eat* ***turkey*** *on Christmas Day.*

turn

your chance to do something; your duty to do something: *You must wait for your* ***turn*** *to use the swing. 'Whose* ***turn*** *is it to wash up?' 'It's*

*your **turn**'. We took **turns** to use the computer.*
in turn one by one: *Each of the pupils recited a poem **in turn**. When you walk, you put each leg forward **in turn**.*

turn
1 to move something round; to twist: *You have to **turn** the handle to open the door.* 2 to move something on to its other side: ***Turn** the meat over when it's cooked on one side. The dog **turned** over and went to sleep again. Linda was **turning** over the pages of a magazine. Please **turn** to page 16 in your textbook.* 3 to move so that you face in a new direction; to change direction: *Paul **turned** round and walked away. The teacher **turned** to me and asked me to read aloud. Dad **turned** the car round and drove back home. The path **turns** to the right. **Turn** left at the next crossroads. The car **turned** the corner.* 4 to change; to become: *At what temperature does water **turn** into ice? Grandad's hair has **turned** grey.*
turn down to make something less loud: *Please **turn down** the television — it's far too loud.*
turn off to stop electricity, water or gas flowing: *Michael **turned off** the light and went to sleep. Have you **turned off** the television? I **turned off** the tap. Has the oven been **turned off**?*
turn on to make electricity, water or gas start to flow: *Lisa **turned on** the radio. I **turned on** the tap and washed my hands. Mum **turned on** the gas cooker.*
turn up 1 to arrive: *A salesman **turned up** at our house wanting to sell a vacuum cleaner.* 2 to be found: *Don't worry — your watch will **turn up** again.* 3 to make something louder: *Please **turn up** the radio — I want to hear the news.*

turtle
a kind of large tortoise that lives in the sea most of the time: *A **turtle** has a shell and four limbs like flippers for swimming with.*

tusk
one of the two large curved teeth of an elephant, a walrus or wild boar: *An elephant can use its **tusks** to defend itself.*

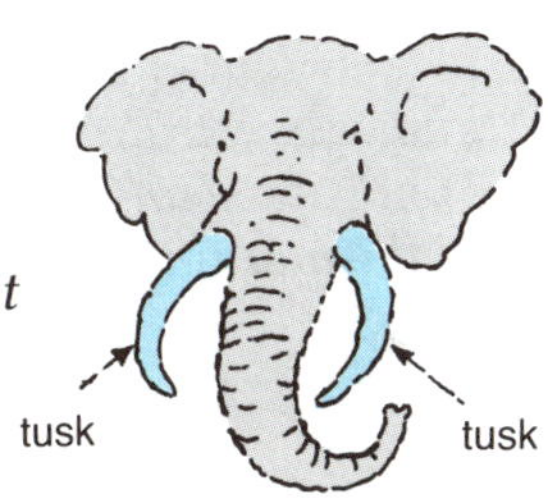

twelve
1 the number 12: *Three times four is **twelve**.* 2 12 in number: *Kate is **twelve** years old.*

twenty
1 the number 20: *Four times five is **twenty**.* 2 20 in number: *It's **twenty** minutes past three.*

twice
two times: *I've been to the zoo **twice**. My mum goes shopping **twice** a week. Liz had **twice** as much ice-cream as I had. My elder brother is **twice** as old as I am.*

twig
a small thin branch of a tree: *Dad cut a few dead **twigs** off the bushes.*

twin
one of two children who were born to the same mother at the same time: *Ruth and Jane are **twins**. Jane is Ruth's **twin** sister. Mrs Wang has given birth to **twins**.*

twinkle
to shine with tiny flashes of light: *The stars **twinkled** in the sky.*

twinkled, twinkling, has twinkled

twist
1 to turn: *I **twisted** round in my seat to see who was sitting behind me.* 2 to wind something round something else: *The dog's lead has got **twisted** round a lamp-post. Peter **twisted** the two bits of wire together.* 3 to bend this way and that way: *The road **twisted** through the mountains.* 4 to bend something into a wrong position: *Mrs Lee **twisted** her ankle when she tripped over a stone.*

two
1 the number 2: *One and one are **two**.* 2 2 in number: *My little sister is **two** years old.*
in two in half: *Tom broke the bar of chocolate **in two**.*

type
a kind; a sort: *What **type** of car do your parents have? There are lots of different **types** of instruments in an orchestra. A mug is a **type** of cup.*

type
to write something with a **typewriter**: *Dad's secretary is **typing** a letter. My elder sister is learning to **type**.*

typed, typing, has typed

tyre
a thick rubber ring that goes round a wheel and is filled with air: *My bicycle **tyres** need pumping up. Dad bought four new **tyres** for the car.*

ugly
unpleasant to look at; not attractive: *In the story, there was an* ***ugly*** *dwarf with a big head and small body, and a very long nose. The buildings that had been damaged by bombs were an* ***ugly*** *sight.*

- The opposite is **beautiful** or **pretty**.
- ugly, uglier, ugliest

umbrella
an object for protecting you from the rain, made of a circle of material stretched over rods, fixed to a long handle: *When you are not using an* ***umbrella****, you can fold it up into a small, narrow shape.*

umpire
a person who does the same job as a referee, in tennis or hockey: *An* ***umpire*** *has to make sure that the players don't break the rules of the game.*

unable
not able: *Mum was* ***unable*** *to lift the heavy table, so she got Dad to help her.*

uncle
the brother of your mother or father, or the husband of your aunt: *My aunt and* ***uncle*** *live in America.* ***Uncle*** *Jack is my father's elder brother.*

under
1 beneath something; covered by something: *You put a saucer* ***under*** *a cup. The mouse disappeared* ***under*** *the sofa.* **2** less than something: *Some children* ***under*** *five go to a nursery during the day. You will be able to do these sums in* ***under*** *half an hour.* **3** in someone's charge: *The headmaster has 24 members of staff* ***under*** *him.*

The opposite is **over**.

underground
below the surface of the ground: *The children explored an* ***underground*** *passage. Rabbits live* ***underground****.*

underground
an underground railway: *Dad travels to work on the* ***underground****.*

underneath
below; beneath; under: *There was a light hanging from the ceiling, with a table* ***underneath*** *it. 'I've lost my slippers.' 'Have you looked* ***underneath*** *the bed?'*

The opposite is **above**, **over**, or **on top of**.

understand
to know what something or someone means: *Do you* ***understand*** *this sentence? Make sure you* ***understand*** *the exam questions before you answer them. It's difficult to* ***understand*** *your parents when they use long words. We didn't* ***understand*** *what the teacher was saying.*

understood, understanding, has understood

understood
see **understand**: *At last I* ***understood*** *how to do the sum. Tell me if there are any words that you haven't* ***understood****.*

undid
see **undo**: *John* ***undid*** *his jacket and took it off.*

undo
to loosen; to separate; to unfasten; to untie: *Please could you* ***undo*** *the top button of my dress for me? I can't* ***undo*** *the knot in this string.*

undid, undoing, has undone

undone
see **undo**: *It's dangerous to walk about with your shoelaces* ***undone****, because you might trip over them. Your hair-ribbon has come* ***undone****.*

undress
to take your clothes off: *My little sister already knows how to dress herself and* ***undress*** *herself. I* ***undressed*** *and had a shower. You get dressed in the morning and you get* ***undressed*** *at night.*

uneven

not smooth and flat: *The surface of the road is* ***uneven*** *— it's full of holes.*

unfair
not fair: *There is one race for the younger children, and another race for the older children, because it would be **unfair** to the younger ones if they all ran in the same race.*

unfasten
to undo something that is fastened: *I ate so much at the party that I had to **unfasten** my belt. I **unfastened** Mum's necklace for her.*

unfriendly
not friendly: *Elizabeth didn't enjoy her first day at school because the other children were **unfriendly**, and wouldn't talk to her.*

unhappy
not happy: *Elizabeth was **unhappy** because the other children wouldn't play with her.*

uniform
a set of clothes that every member of a school or some other group has to wear: *Our school **uniform** is a white blouse or shirt, a blue tie, and a blue skirt or shorts. Every soldier has to keep his **uniform** clean and neat.*

unit
1 an amount that you use for counting money: *Dollars and cents are **units** of money. The main **unit** of money in Singapore and in America is the dollar.* **2** an amount that you use for measuring things: *We measure things in **units** called centimetres, metres and kilometres and we weigh things in **units** called grammes and kilogrammes.* **3** a section of something: *The mathematics course is divided into four **units** — you have to complete each **unit** before you start the next one.*

unite
to join things together: *Let's all **unite** and fight together against our enemies. The little boy who had been lost was glad to be **united** with his family again.*

The opposite is **separate**.

universe
the earth, the sun, the moon, and all the other planets and stars: *The earth is a very very tiny spot in the **universe**.*

university
a place that you go to when you leave school, where you can study your best subject: *My elder brother is going to study mathematics at **university**.*

Two **universities**

unkind
not kind; cruel: *It was very **unkind** of you to laugh at Mike for making a mistake. Never be **unkind** to animals.*

unless
if not: *I won't tell you my secret **unless** you tell me yours. **Unless** you work harder, Mary, you won't pass your exam.*

unload

to remove goods from a ship or vehicle: *The ship called at Hong Kong to **unload** its cargo of fruit.*

unpack
to take things out of a case: *I **unpacked** as soon as I arrived at the hotel. **Unpack** your clothes and put them away in the cupboard.*

untidy
not tidy; not neat: *Liz left her clothes in an **untidy** heap on the floor. Your writing is **untidy** — try to make it neater. What an **untidy** room! Tidy it at once! What an **untidy** mess! Clear it up at once!*

The opposite is **neat** or **tidy**.

untie
to undo something that is tied: *It's easier to **untie** your shoelaces than tie them. John **untied** the boat. Don't walk round with your shoelaces **untied**. I'm good at **untying** knots.*

unties, untied, untying, has untied

until
up to a certain time; till: *Dad is in his office from nine o'clock in the morning **until** six o'clock in the evening. Wait in the classroom **until** the bell rings.*

unusual
not usual; strange: *People with dark skin and blue eyes are very* ***unusual****. It's* ***unusual*** *for Philip to arrive so late — he's usually very punctual.*

unwrap
to take the wrapping off something; to open a parcel: *You mustn't* ***unwrap*** *your presents until your birthday.*

unwrapped, unwrapping, has unwrapped

up
1 to a higher position; in a higher position: *Is the lift going* ***up*** *or down? The little girl looked* ***up*** *at the teacher. I climbed* ***up*** *the ladder. The cat is* ***up*** *in the tree. We always stand* ***up*** *when the teacher comes in.* **2** out of bed: *What time do you get* ***up*** *in the morning? Dad's* ***up*** *already. Have you ever stayed* ***up*** *all night?* **3** towards someone or something; as far as something: *A stranger came* ***up*** *to me and asked what time it was. A taxi drove* ***up*** *and we got in. Count* ***up*** *to 100.* ***Up*** *to now, all our sums have been very easy.* **4** here are some other ways of using **up**: *Hurry* ***up*** *or we'll be late! Eat* ***up*** *all your food — don't leave any on your plate. Lock* ***up*** *the house before you leave. The baby has torn* ***up*** *the book.*

Meaning 1: the opposite is **down**.

uphill
moving up a hill or slope: *You get tired quickly when you cycle* ***uphill****.*

upper
higher; top: *A moustache is the hair that grows on a man's* ***upper*** *lip. The bedrooms are on the* ***upper*** *floors of the house.*

The opposite is **lower**.

upright
standing up: *When you are standing, you are in an* ***upright*** *position. Joe knocked over a chair, so he picked it up and put it* ***upright*** *again.*

upset
1 to make someone unhappy: *You have* ***upset*** *Mum by being so naughty.* **2** to knock something over: *The children were running round the classroom* ***upsetting*** *all the chairs.*

upset, upsetting, has upset

upset
unhappy: *You feel very* ***upset*** *when your mother or father is ill.*

upside down
with the top at the bottom and the bottom at the top: *You can't read your book if you hold it* ***upside down****.*

upstairs
1 to a higher floor: *Mum carried the baby* ***upstairs****.* **2** on a higher floor: *The baby is asleep* ***upstairs*** *in the bedroom.*

The opposite is **downstairs**.

up-to-date
recent; new: *A newspaper tells you all the* ***up-to-date*** *news. Mum gets a magazine every week to look at the pictures of the* ***up-to-date*** *fashions.*

upwards or **upward**
to a higher place: *A lift can move* ***upwards*** *or downwards. The road led* ***upward*** *into the hills.*

The opposite is **downwards**.

urgent
needing someone's attention immediately: *This man is very ill — he needs* ***urgent*** *treatment. Ring the doctor and tell him it's* ***urgent****.*

us
we use **us** when we are talking about ourselves: *When we have finished our work, the teacher lets* ***us*** *read our story-books. Molly and I are going for a walk — would you like to come with* ***us****?*

use
to do a job with something: *I* ***used*** *a knife to cut the string. What do you* ***use*** *a ruler for? We* ***use*** *water to wash with. This dictionary teaches you how to* ***use*** *English words. 'I've lost my pencil.' 'No, you haven't — it's on the desk. Why don't you* ***use*** *your eyes?'*

used, using, has used

used to **1** knowing something well; familiar with something: *Babies are so* ***used to*** *their own mothers that they sometimes cry if a stranger picks them up. We are all* ***used to*** *hard work in this school.* **2** you use **used to** when you say that someone once had a habit of doing something: *When I was on holiday by the sea, I* ***used to*** *go swimming every day. My mum* ***used to*** *wear glasses, but now she wears contact lenses.*

use up to use a lot of something; to use all of something: *A bath **uses up** more water than a shower does. **Use up** this drawing-paper before you buy any more.*

use

1 the using of something: *The teacher keeps a few story-books in her desk for the **use** of pupils. The **use** of computers in schools has increased a lot in the last ten years.* **2** the job that something is used for: *A penknife has a lot of **uses**.* **3** value; being useful: *These old shoes are no more **use** to me. You may have this blouse if it's any **use** to you. It's no **use** shouting for help when there's no-one to hear you. Always make good **use** of your time — don't waste it.* **4** the ability to use something: *The old man has lost the **use** of his legs, so he has to stay in bed.*

useful

giving you the help you need; doing a job well: *English is a **useful** language to learn because so many people speak it. A calculator is a very **useful** tool.*

useless

not useful; no use: *Let's throw away all this **useless** rubbish! It's **useless** trying to open a door with the wrong key.*

usual

happening in the way it always happens; happening in the way you expect; not strange or different: *Yesterday I got up at the **usual** time, but today I got up earlier than **usual** to do a job for Mum before going to school. We had our **usual** lessons this morning, but this afternoon we are going to do something different from **usual**.*

as usual as you expect; as always happens: *Dad arrived home this evening at 6 o'clock **as usual**. **As usual**, Alice is late for school.*

usually

most times: *I **usually** get home from school at half past three. We **usually** go swimming on Saturdays. The weather is **usually** cold in winter.*

utensil

a tool or container, especially one that you use in the kitchen: *Dad put away the pans and all the other **utensils** he had used to cook the meal.*

Vv

vacant

empty; not being used by anyone; not occupied: *The bathroom is **vacant** — you can go in.*

vacation

a holiday from school or work: *We're going to Japan in the **vacation**. Where are you going to spend your **vacation**?*

> Same as **holiday**.

vacuum

a space with no air in it: *When a spaceship moves out of the air that surrounds the earth, it travels through a **vacuum**.*

vacuum

to clean something with a vacuum-cleaner: *Dad is **vacuuming** the inside of the car.*

> Say **vak**-ewm.

vacuum-cleaner

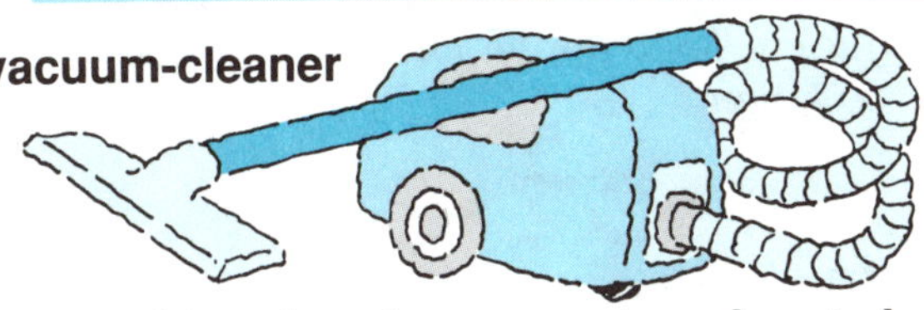

a machine that cleans carpets and seats by sucking dirt into itself: *A **vacuum-cleaner** has a bag that all the dirt goes into.*

vain

being too proud of the way you look: *Molly is very **vain** — she keeps admiring herself in the mirror.*

in vain with no success: *Jim tried **in vain** to lift the heavy box.*

valley

a low gap between hills: *Many **valleys** have a*

river running through them.

The opposite is a **hill** or **mountain**.

valuable
worth a lot of money; precious: *This necklace is made of gold, so it is very **valuable**.*

value
1 the amount of money that something is worth: *What is the **value** of this stamp? This broken vase is of no **value**.* **2** the quality of being useful: *If you learn to speak English well, it will be of great **value** to you when you grow up.*

van
a vehicle for carrying goods, smaller than a lorry: *The butcher delivers meat to people in his **van**. The **van**-driver parked his **van** in front of the shop.*

variety
1 a number of things of different kinds: *The ice-cream shop has a large **variety** of flavours to choose from — chocolate, coffee, strawberry, lemon, and lots of others.* **2** a sort; a type of something: *A raspberry plant is a **variety** of shrub.*

Meaning 2: many **varieties**

various
several; different: *We thought of **various** plans for our holidays, but at last we decided to go to Japan.*

Same as **different**.

vase
a container for putting flowers in: *The cat knocked over a **vase** of flowers.*

vegetable

a plant, or a part of a plant, that you can eat: *We grow potatoes, beans, carrots, radishes, cabbages and lots of other **vegetables** in our garden.*

vehicle
a car, bus, lorry, van, train, bicycle or anything e for carrying people or goods: ***Vehicles** with engines, such as cars, are called motor **vehicles**. A baby's pram is a kind of **vehicle**. A spaceship is a **vehicle** for carrying people into space.*

veil

a thin piece of material that you can see through, that a lady wears to cover her face: *A bride wears a white **veil** during the wedding ceremony.*

verb
the word in a sentence that tells you what happens: *Pick out the **verbs** in these sentences: 'The dog chased the cat.' 'Mum is putting on her coat.' 'Who are you?' 'I went for a walk.' The **verbs** are 'chased', 'is putting', 'are' and 'went'. Every sentence needs a **verb**.*

very
1 more than usual; especially: *Joe is **very** good at football — I expect he'll be chosen to play in the team. Mum was **very** cross with me for coming home late. Thank you **very** much for the present. An ant is a **very** small creature.* **2** exactly at a certain point: *Kate was trying to imitate the teacher's voice, and at that **very** moment, the teacher came into the room. Our house is at the **very** end of the street.*

vest
a light, thin piece of clothing for the top part of your body, that you wear under your other clothes: *You put your **vest** and pants on first, and then your other clothes.*

vet
a doctor for animals: *Susan had to take her puppy to the **vet** to have an injection.*

video
having to do with pictures on a television screen: *A **video** recorder records television programmes on to **video**tape. Films made by **video** cameras are stored on **video**tape too.*

view
the scene that you see from a certain position: *We have a good **view** of the harbour from our sitting-room window. We got out of the car and admired the beautiful **view** of the mountains and the lake.*

village
a group of houses and shops, smaller than a town: *There are about 300 people living in our **village**. Our **village** has a playground, a grocer's shop, a post office, a hotel, and about 50 houses.*

vinegar
a liquid with a strong, sour taste that you use for cooking, or to season food: *You can make a sauce out of oil and **vinegar** to pour on salad.*

violent
very strong: *Lots of trees were blown down by the **violent** winds. The man gave the dog a **violent** kick.*

violet
1 a very small purple flower: *Sally picked a little bunch of **violets** for her mother.* **2** a purple colour: *Susan is wearing a **violet** ribbon in her hair.*

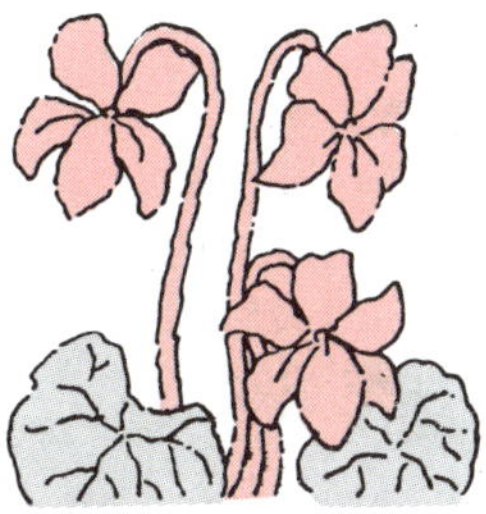

violin
an instrument with four strings, that you hold under your chin and play with a rod called a bow: *Philip plays the **violin** in the school orchestra.*

violinist

a person who plays the violin: *There are twelve **violinists** in the orchestra.*

visible
able to be seen: *The moon is not **visible** tonight, because it is covered by clouds. A ship was **visible** on the horizon.*

visit
1 to go to someone's house to see them: *My uncle **visited** us last night.* **2** to stay with someone for a few days or weeks: *My aunt comes over from America to **visit** us every July.* **3** to go and see a place: *We hope to **visit** the Tower of London when we are in England. I'd like to **visit** Sydney one day.*

visit
1 the action of going to visit a person or place: *We had a **visit** from my uncle last night. My uncle paid us a **visit** last night. Did you enjoy your **visit** to the museum?* **2** a few days or weeks that you spend staying with a person: *My aunt's **visit** lasted two weeks.*

voice
the sound that comes from your mouth when you speak or sing: *Peter recited the poem in a loud **voice**, so that the whole class could hear. Jennifer can sing very well — she has a nice **voice**. 'Stop talking,' said the teacher in a stern **voice**. We could hear angry **voices** in the corridor. Men have deep **voices** and children have high **voices**.*

volcano

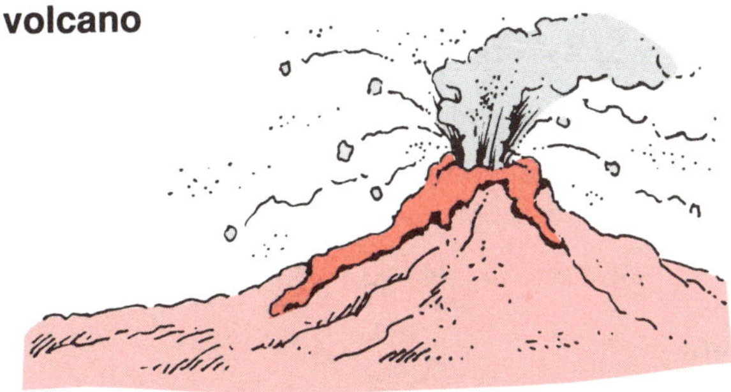

a mountain with a hole in the top, from which very hot, melted rocks sometimes pour out, from the middle of the earth: *Several houses in the village were damaged by the **volcano** last year.*

volume
1 a book: *The library contains more than ten thousand **volumes**. Mum's big dictionary has two **volumes**, marked **Volume** 1 and **Volume** 2.* **2** the amount of space inside a container: *What is the **volume** of the petrol tank?* **3** how loud or soft the sound is that comes from a radio or television: *Turn up the **volume** on the radio — I can't hear it.*

vowel
any of these letters — **a**, **e**, **i**, **o** or **u**: *There are three **vowels** in the word 'tiptoe' — **i**, **o** and **e**.*

voyage
a long journey: *A long time ago, the **voyage** from England to Australia in a sailing-ship used to take many months. I'd like to go on a **voyage** round the world.*

vulture
a large bird that feeds on dead animals: *The **vultures** were flying round the dead body of the elephant.*

Ww

wade
to walk through deep water: *Peter's ball fell into the river and he **waded** into the water to fetch it back.*

waded, wading, has waded

waddle
to walk like a duck: *Some ducks were **waddling** about beside the pond.*

waddled, waddling, has waddled

wag
to move from side to side: *Dogs **wag** their tails when they're happy.*

wage
the money that you earn by working: *Liz is a shop-assistant and her **wages** are $25 a day. She gets a daily **wage** of $25.*

waist
the narrow part of your body between your ribs and your hips: *You wear a belt round your **waist**.*

wait
1 to stay where you are, until someone or something comes: *I've been **waiting** half an hour already for the bus. Mum went into the shop and asked me to **wait** outside. Don't walk so fast — **wait** for me!* **2** to serve people with food and drink: *Mum and Dad had a big party, and my sister and I **waited** on the guests.*

waiter
a man who serves guests with food and drink in a restaurant: *The **waiter** led us to a table and took our order for dinner.*

waitress
a woman who serves guests with food and drink in a restaurant: *The **waitress** served us each with meat and vegetables.*

wake
to make someone stop sleeping; to disturb someone who is asleep: *Please be quiet — you'll **wake** the baby if you make so much noise!*

woke, waking, has woken

wake up **1** to stop sleeping; to open your eyes: *I didn't **wake up** till 8 o'clock this morning, so I was late for school.* **2** to stop someone sleeping: *Tomorrow my mother is going to **wake** me **up** early, to make sure I catch the bus.*

walk
to move along on foot: *If we miss the bus we shall have to **walk** to school. We were drawing silly pictures on the blackboard when in **walked** the teacher. We sometimes go **walking** in the mountains at the weekends.*

walk
a period of walking, especially to get exercise and fresh air: *We took the dog for a **walk** along the beach. I went for a **walk** in the park. Grandad takes a **walk** every afternoon. It's about five minutes' **walk** to school from my house.*

walkie-talkie

a radio that policemen or soldiers carry round with them, for sending and receiving messages: *A policeman in a car can use his **walkie-talkie** to talk to the policemen at headquarters.*

wall
a side of a building or room: *The **walls** of our house are made of brick. Jennifer's bedroom has one pink **wall** and three white **walls**. The teacher pinned our best drawings up on the **wall**.*

wallet

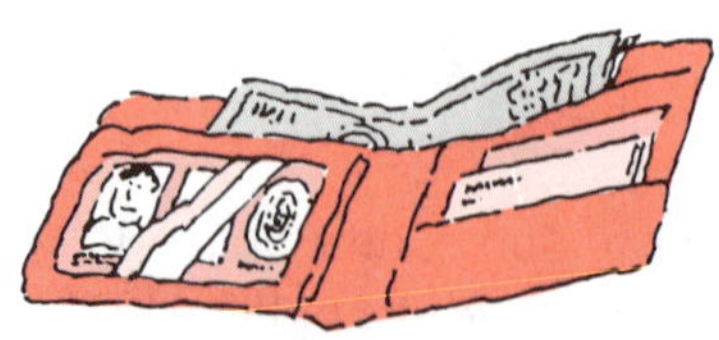

a flat purse for keeping paper money in: *Dad opened his **wallet** and took out a ten-dollar note to pay for the book.*

wallpaper
strips of strong paper for pasting on to walls to decorate them: *The **wallpaper** in my bedroom has a pattern of clowns on it.*

walnut

a nut that has a hard, oval shell in two halves: *You can make tiny little boats out of* ***walnut*** *shells. Mum chopped up some* ***walnuts*** *to put in the cake.*

walrus

a large sea animal like a seal, with a pair of tusks: *Some* ***walruses*** *were lying on the rocks in the sun.*

wand
a kind of stick, usually with a star at the end, filled with magic power, that a fairy uses in stories: *The fairy waved her magic* ***wand*** *and the wicked dwarf turned into a frog.*

wander
to go about from place to place, without planning to get anywhere: *The children spent the afternoon* ***wandering*** *in the woods and picking flowers.*

Same as **roam**.

want
1 to need something; to wish to have something: *I* ***want*** *a glass of water. Do you* ***want*** *a sweet? I don't* ***want*** *any more to eat, thank you.* **2** to wish to do something; to wish for someone else to do something: *I* ***want*** *to go home now. Do you* ***want*** *to come with me? The teacher doesn't* ***want*** *us to ask our parents for help with our homework.*

war
fighting between countries: *How long have these two countries been at* ***war****? Many soldiers were killed in the* ***war****.*

The opposite is **peace**.

ward
a big room in a hospital, with beds for patients: *The hospital has separate* ***wards*** *for men, women and children.*

warm
1 quite hot; not too hot; hot in a comfortable way: *We eat our meals in the garden when the weather is* ***warm****. Are you* ***warm*** *enough, or would you like me to turn on the heater? You need* ***warm*** *clothes in winter. This thick pullover will keep you* ***warm****.* **2** friendly: *My aunt gave us a* ***warm*** *welcome when we arrived at her house.*

The opposite is **cool**.

warm
to make something warm: *We* ***warmed*** *ourselves by the fire. I* ***warmed*** *my hands by the fire.*
warm up 1 to make something hot; to heat up: *The soup is cold — I'll* ***warm*** *it* ***up*** *for you.* **2** to make something more exciting and interesting: *We played a few games to* ***warm up*** *the party.*

warmth
pleasant heat: *After a cold winter, it's nice to feel the* ***warmth*** *of the sun again.*

warn
to tell someone that something bad is going to happen, or may happen: *There was an announcement on the radio* ***warning*** *us that a bad storm was coming. You'll be punished if you go on being naughty — I'm* ***warning*** *you! Mum* ***warned*** *us not to touch the hot iron.*

warning
1 something that someone says to warn you: *There was a* ***warning*** *on the radio about the storm.* **2** something that warns you: *Black clouds are a* ***warning*** *that rain is coming. The cyclist in front of us turned right without* ***warning****.*

was
you use **was** with **I**, **he**, **she** and **it** when you say what happened: *I* ***was*** *seven last week. The boy* ***was*** *knocked over by a car when he* ***was*** *crossing the street, but he* ***wasn't*** *hurt. The teacher said she* ***was*** *not pleased with our work.* ***Was*** *the film good, or* ***was*** *it boring? It* ***was*** *hot yesterday.*

You can shorten **was not** to **wasn't**.

wash
to make something clean with water and soap: *You should* ***wash*** *yourself in the morning and at night. Have you* ***washed*** *your hands? I had no time to* ***wash*** *because I was so late. Mum* ***washes*** *our clothes in the washing-machine. Whose turn is it to* ***wash*** *the dishes?*

wash
the action of washing: *When you have been*

*swimming, your hair usually needs a good **wash**.*

wash up to wash dishes: *Who is going to **wash up** after the meal?*

washing-machine

a machine for washing clothes: *Every evening Mum washes our dirty clothes in the **washing-machine**.*

wasn't

short for **was not**: *I **wasn't** allowed to paint my bedroom walls black. The exam was hard, **wasn't** it? It was hot yesterday, **wasn't** it?*

wasp

a stinging insect with a long striped yellow and black body, similar to a bee: ***Wasps** don't make honey. A **wasp** stung me on the neck.*

waste

1 to use up more of something than you need: *You mustn't **waste** water by leaving the tap running.* **2** not to make good use of something: *Don't **waste** time gazing out of the window, Jenny!*

wasted, wasting, has wasted

waste

the wasting of something: *Leaving taps running is a **waste** of water. It's a **waste** of time cleaning my shoes, because they'll soon get dirty again.*

watch

a kind of little clock that you wear on a strap round your wrist: *Jill looked at the time on her **watch**.*

watch

1 to look at someone or something: *The children **watched** the teacher doing the sum on the blackboard. **Watch** how I do this sum. I **watched** a good film on television last night. I don't **watch** television very much.* **2** to look after a person or animal: ***Watch** the baby for me while I go shopping. A shepherd **watches** over his sheep.*

watchman

a man whose job is to guard a building, especially at night: *The **watchman** at the bank telephoned the police when he heard the robbers trying to break in.*

Two **watchmen**

water

the clear, transparent liquid that is in rivers, lakes and the sea: *You can't drink sea **water** — you can only drink fresh **water** from a river or reservoir. Philip filled the jug with **water**. He poured out three glasses of **water**. Come for a swim — the **water** is lovely and warm.*

water

to give plants water: *If you don't **water** these flowers, they'll die.*

waterfall

a place on a river where the water is falling down from a high rock: *Water looks white when it is falling over a **waterfall**.*

watermelon

a large melon with a dark green skin and juicy pink flesh: *Would you like a slice of **water-melon**?*

wave

1 to raise your hand and move it backwards and forwards to greet someone or say good-bye to them: *Granny **waved** goodbye to us as she got on the plane. **Wave** your hand to Granny! I saw Tim **waving** to me on the opposite side of the street.* **2** to move backwards and forwards: *The children all **waved** their flags to greet the Queen when she visited their school.*

waved, waving, has waved

wave

1 the action of waving: *Mum gave me a **wave** from the doorway as I set off for school.* **2** one of the long, rolling, high bits in the sea, that come towards the shore: *The children enjoyed playing in the **waves** at the edge of the sea.* **3** a twisting or bending bit of hair; a curl: *Jane has long, dark hair with a lot of **waves** in it.*

wax

the stuff that candles are made of, which is hard when it is cool, and becomes liquid when it is heated: *The **wax** from the candles melted on to the birthday cake.*

way

1 the direction you go in to get somewhere; a road that you take: *I don't know the **way** to the* *post office. I asked a lady the **way** to the swimming pool. The children couldn't find the **way** out of the forest. There was a notice over the exit saying '**Way** Out'. I'll collect the newspaper from the newsagent's on my **way** home from school.* **2** a direction: *Look both **ways** before you cross the road.* **3** a distance: *It's a long **way** to school from my house. Peter beat the other runners by a long **way**.* **4** a position: *You're holding your book the wrong **way** up — turn it the right **way** up. You've written the letter **d** the wrong **way** round — it looks like a **b**.* **5** a method: *Which is the best **way** to do this sum? Do it the **way** I showed you. In the story, the children tried to think of a **way** of escaping from the giant's castle. The teacher has done her hair a different **way** today.* **6** how something looks: *Tidy the bathroom and leave it the **way** you found it.* **7** the manner you do something in: *The headmaster chatted to all the parents in a friendly **way**.*

in the way blocking the direction you are going in; stopping you getting on with something: *Dad couldn't drive along the lane because a big lorry was parked **in the way**. I can't do the housework if you children keep getting **in my way**.*

lose your way to stop knowing where you are: *Paul **lost his way** in the big city, but a policeman helped him to find his way home.*

make way to move out of the way: *The cars **made way** for the ambulance.*

out of the way not blocking the direction you are going; not in your way: *The car-driver got **out of the way** of the ambulance. Please keep **out of my way** while I'm carrying this pile of dishes.*

we

the word used for talking about ourselves: *I met Mary at the crossroads and **we** walked to school together. Miss Pitt told us **we** could go home early today.*

weak

not having much power in your body; not strong: *Babies are too **weak** to sit up by themselves. If you have nothing to eat or drink, you get **weaker** and **weaker**.*

> The opposite is **strong**.

wealth

lots of money and expensive things owned by someone: *Many people were jealous of the king's **wealth**, for he had a big palace and lots of money and jewels.*

wealthy

possessing a lot of money and expensive things: *My parents are not very **wealthy**, so they can't afford to buy me expensive toys.*

> - Same as **rich**.
> - The opposite is **poor**.
> - wealthy, wealthier, wealthiest

weapon

one of the many kinds of objects that people fight with: *Swords, bows and arrows, spears and bombs are all called **weapons**. I used a heavy stick as a **weapon** to hit the snake with.*

wear

to be dressed in something; to have something on your body: *Jenny is **wearing** a red blouse, a blue skirt, and white sandals. Susan **wore** her new dress for the party. Peter has **worn** glasses since he was five. Clowns **wear** funny big red noses.*

> wore, wearing, has worn

wear away, wear down to get damaged by being used: *My sweater is **wearing away** at the elbows. The steps have **worn down** in the middle, because so many people go up and down them.*

wear off to disappear: *I had a bad headache but it has **worn off** now.*

wear out to wear something or use something until it's no more use to you: *These shoes are **worn out** — I've had them for two years. Tony played his radio so much that he **wore out** the batteries in two weeks.*

weary

very tired: *Mum was so **weary** that she fell asleep in her chair.*

weather

the amount of heat, cold, wind, rain or sun that there is in a place: *Singapore has much hotter **weather** than Britain does. The **weather** has been cold and windy today. We had bad **weather** for our holiday — it rained all the time.*

weave

to make threads go over and under larger threads that are arranged in rows on a machine, until they make a big piece of cloth: *We went to a mill to watch people **weaving** cloth. Cloth is **woven**, but tights and sweaters are knitted.*

> wove, weaving, has woven

web
a very fine net that a spider makes: *A spider has spun a **web** in the corner of the window. Lots of flies and one wasp have been caught in the spider's **web**.*

we'd
short for **we would**, **we should**, or **we had**: *We told Mum **we'd** come home when **we'd** finished our football practice.*

wedding
the ceremony of getting married: *Miss Lee and Mr Wang are getting married — their **wedding** will take place in March. My parents have been invited to the **wedding**.*

Wednesday
the fourth day of the week, the day after Tuesday.

> Say **wenz**-day.

weed
a wild plant that is growing where you don't want it to grow, especially in your garden: *When you come back from a long holiday, you usually find that your garden is full of **weeds**.*

weed
to get rid of weeds from a garden by digging them up: *Jeff **weeded** the garden with a hoe.*

week
1 a period of seven days: *It took us a **week** to sail the yacht from Singapore to Sydney.* **2** the period from one Sunday to the next Saturday: *We have a singing lesson once a **week**, on a Wednesday. I'll see you next **week**.* **3** the five days that people work on, from Monday to Friday: *The school is used during the **week**, but not on Saturday and Sunday.*

weekend
Saturday and Sunday: *We don't go to school at the **weekend**. We are going to spend next **weekend** with my grandparents. Did you have a good **weekend**?*

weekly
1 happening once a week: *We have a **weekly** singing lesson with the music teacher.* **2** published once a week: *Mum buys a **weekly** fashion magazine.*

weep
to cry; to let tears come from your eyes: *The sad film made Mum **weep**. We **wept** when we heard the bad news.*

> - The opposite is **laugh**.
> - wept, weeping, has wept

weigh
to find out how heavy something is by placing it on the scales: *I **weighed** myself on the scales in the bathroom. You have to have your luggage **weighed** at the airport, before it is put on to the plane. John **weighs** 32 kilogrammes.*

weight
1 the amount that something weighs: *What is your **weight**? My **weight** is 35 kilos.* **2** the quality of being heavy: *The **weight** of the apples made the branch bend down to the ground.*

welcome
to greet guests in a friendly way: *The host and hostess **welcomed** their guests as they arrived.*

> welcomed, welcoming, has welcomed

welcome
the welcoming of someone: *Mum gave us a big **welcome** when we arrived home from our camping holiday.*

welcome
1 received and accepted with happiness: *You're **welcome** — please come in. My uncle is always a **welcome** visitor at our house. **Welcome** to Singapore! **Welcome** home! The extra money that my parents gave me was very **welcome**.* **2** allowed by someone to do something or to take something: *You're **welcome** to borrow any of my books. You're **welcome** to this pair of shoes if they fit you.*

we'll
short for **we shall** or **we will**: ***We'll** meet Granny off the plane tomorrow.*

well
a deep, round hole made down into the ground, that you can get water from: *The people of the village got water from a **well**. The cat fell into the **well**.*

well
1 healthy: *I don't feel very **well**. Granny was ill, but she's quite **well** again.* **2** okay; all right: *I thought I had failed my exam, but all was **well**.* **3** with success; in a good way: *Janet plays the piano **well**.* **4** fine: *Jeremy is doing **well** at school.* **5** properly: *Shake the bottle*

well. *Do you know Marie* ***well****?* **6** by a long way: *My brother has* ***well*** *over fifty records.* **7** here are some other ways of using **well**: ***Well****! What a surprise!* ***Well****, when the witch found her lost broom, she got on to it and flew away.*

- Meaning 1: well, better
- Meanings 3, 4, 5: well, better, best

as well as and; not only: *David is learning Chinese* ***as well as*** *English.*
well done! words you say to someone who has gained a success: *You've won the competition —* ***well done!***

went
see **go**: *We* ***went*** *to the zoo yesterday.*

wept
see **weep**: *Susan* ***wept*** *when her kitten was hurt. She had never* ***wept*** *so much in her life.*

were
you use **were** with **we**, **you** and **they** when you say what happened: *We* ***were*** *sitting at the table when the door opened. Liz and I* ***were*** *late for school yesterday.* ***Were*** *you frightened? There* ***were*** *two sweets left in the jar last night, but they* ***were*** *not there this morning.*

we're
short for **we are**: *Hurry up —* ***we're*** *late!*

weren't
short for **were not**: ***Weren't*** *you afraid? The questions were difficult,* ***weren't*** *they?*

west
the direction in which the sun sets: *The wind is blowing from the* ***west****. There is a strong* ***west*** *wind. The Indian Ocean lies to the* ***west*** *of Malaysia.*

wet
1 soaked with water or another liquid: *You will get* ***wet*** *if you go out in the rain. I've washed my hair and it's still* ***wet****. If you run hard, your clothes get* ***wet*** *with sweat. The car skidded on the* ***wet*** *road.* **2** raining: *It was* ***wet*** *yesterday. We had very* ***wet*** *weather last week.* **3** not dry; liquid: *Don't touch the* ***wet*** *paint.*

- The opposite is **dry**.
- wet, wetter, wettest

we've
short for **we have**: ***We've*** *finished the job at last!*

whale
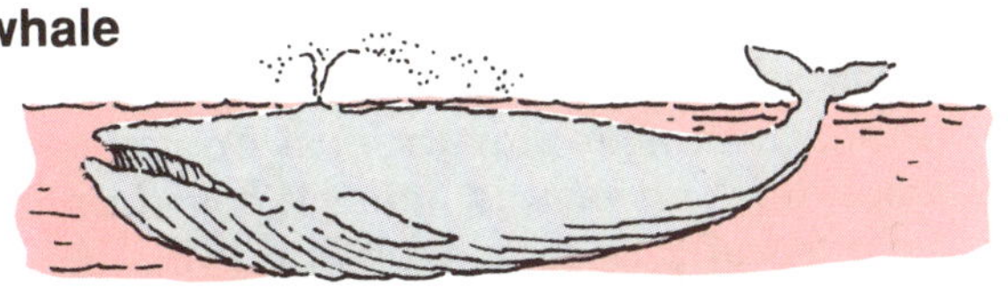

the biggest animal that lives in the sea, shaped like an enormous fish with a smooth skin: *Two* ***whales*** *were swimming along beside the ship.*

what
1 you use **what** when you ask questions, especially about things: ***What*** *time is it?* ***What****'s your name?* ***What*** *did you say?* ***What****'s happened?* ***What*** *does 'calculate' mean?* ***What*** *is a baby cat called? 'Do you know* ***what*** *you want to be when you grow up?'* **2** you use **what** when you are surprised, pleased or angry about something: ***What*** *a silly question!* ***What*** *a fool I am!* ***What*** *a beautiful day it is!* ***What*** *a rude thing to say!* **3** here are some other ways of using **what**: *Did you find* ***what*** *you wanted? This tool is just* ***what*** *I want for mending my bicycle.* ***What*** *I need is a cool drink! I don't understand* ***what*** *you mean.*

wheat
a kind of cereal plant: *The farmer has three fields of* ***wheat****. Bread is made from* ***wheat****-flour.*

wheel
a round, rolling object that is fixed to vehicles to make them able to move along the ground: *A bicycle has two* ***wheels****, a tricycle has three* ***wheels*** *and a car has four* ***wheels****. Our car has a flat tyre, so we'll have to change the* ***wheel****.*

wheel
to push a vehicle that has wheels: *Joe* ***wheeled*** *his bicycle into the shed.*

wheelbarrow
a small cart with only one wheel, that you push: *Dad put his garden tools into the* ***wheelbarrow*** *and wheeled it down the garden to the vegetable patch.*

wheelchair
a special chair with wheels for a person who cannot walk very well: *Granny can wheel herself round her flat in her* ***wheelchair****.*

when
1 you use **when** to ask about time: ***When** is Granny coming to stay with us? Do you know **when** this school was built? **When** does the train leave?* 2 as soon as: ***When** I've finished my homework, I'll come round to your house. **When** Jack got home, he went straight to bed.* 3 at a certain time; during a certain time: ***When** I was on holiday in Australia, I visited Tasmania. Mum takes my little brother to a nursery **when** she goes to work. **When** you see Jane, give her this book.*

whenever
every time: ***Whenever** I see Mrs Lee, she asks me if I'm working hard at school.*

where
1 what place?: ***Where** have you put my book? **Where** does this bus go? **Where** do zebras come from?* 2 the place that a certain thing happened in: *Singapore is the place **where** I was born. This is the shop **where** Mum bought my dress.*

wherever
in every place; to every place: *Sally takes her doll with her **wherever** she goes.*

whether
you use **whether** with words like **ask** and **know**; it means the same as if: *I asked the teacher **whether** I could go home early. I don't know **whether** Mum will let me go to the party or not. I can't decide **whether** to buy an ice-cream or a bar of chocolate.*

which
1 you use **which** when you ask someone to pick out a thing, or a person: *'**Which** colour do you like best?' 'I like red — **which** do you like best?' **Which** room is the television in? **Which** of the girls is the tallest? **Which** boys are going to play in the football team? **Which** is the biggest city in the world? 'Shall I buy a red pen or a black pen? I don't know **which** one to choose.'* 2 you can use **which** when you are describing a kind of animal or thing, or explaining which thing you mean; it means the same as **that**: *A tiger is a fierce wild animal **which** catches other animals and eats them up. Where is the book **which** I left on the table?*

while
1 during a certain time: *The classrooms were painted **while** we were on holiday. Mum likes to sing **while** she does the housework.* 2 a short time: *I'm going out to buy a newspaper — I'll be back in a little **while**.*

whimper
to cry in a quiet, soft way: *The puppy is **whimpering** because he has hurt his paw. The baby **whimpered** for a few minutes, and then fell asleep.*

whip
a long, thin strip of leather fixed to a handle, for striking a person or animal: *The **whip** made a long red mark on the prisoner's back.*

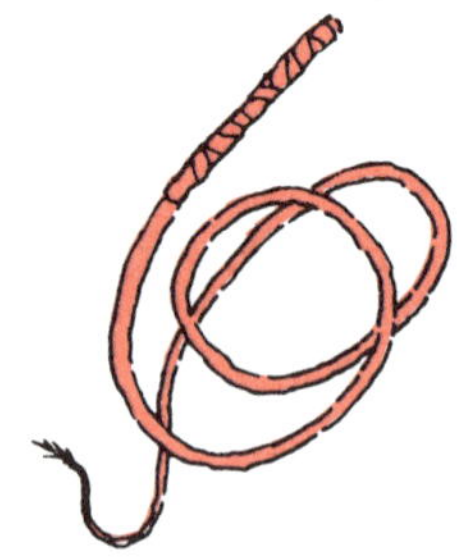

whip
1 to strike with a whip: *The farmer **whipped** his horse to make it go faster.* 2 to stir a liquid very fast to make it become thick: *Mum asked Sue to **whip** the cream.*

> whipped, whipping, has whipped

whiskers
the long, strong hairs growing above the mouth of an animal such as a cat or a rat: *The baby tried to pull the cat's **whiskers**, but the cat ran away.*

whisper

to speak in a very soft voice: *You **whisper** something in someone's ear when you don't want other people to hear. Miss Pitt told Sue and Sally to stop **whispering**.*

whisper
a very soft voice: *We spoke in **whispers**, so that we wouldn't wake the baby.*

whistle
1 to make a loud, high sound through your lips: *The gardener is **whistling** a tune while he works. Janet **whistled** to her dog to make him come back.* 2 to make a sound like someone whistling: *The wind **whistled** in the trees.*

> • Say **wis**-el.
> • whistled, whistling, has whistled

whistle
1 the sound of someone whistling: *The dog heard Janet's **whistle** and he came running*

back. **2** a small instrument that makes a whistling sound: *The referee blew his* ***whistle*** *at the end of the match.*

white

1 the colour of milk: *You must clean your teeth every day to keep them nice and* ***white****. There are some little* ***white*** *clouds in the blue sky. The* ***white*** *part of an egg is a transparent liquid before it is cooked.* **2** pale: *Some people have* ***white*** *skins and some people have dark skins.*

who

1 which person?: ***Who*** *drew this picture on the blackboard?* ***Who*** *is that girl in the red dress? Someone phoned you this morning, but I don't know* ***who*** *it was.* **2** you use **who** when you are describing a kind of person, or explaining which person you mean; it means the same as **that**: *A postman is a person* ***who*** *delivers letters. The man* ***who*** *telephoned said his name was Mr Brown.*

whole

complete, with nothing missing: *'Have you eaten the* ***whole*** *bar of chocolate already? I've only eaten half of mine.' The* ***whole*** *class is here today — no-one is absent. It would be nice to spend the* ***whole*** *of the day on the beach.*

> Say **hole**.

whom

1 you use whom when you ask to which person something is done: ***Whom*** *did you visit yesterday? To* ***whom*** *was the letter sent?* **2** you use **whom** to describe a kind of person, or explain which person you mean: *A patient is a person* ***whom*** *a doctor is treating. The teacher to* ***whom*** *I gave the note told me to wait till she had finished reading it.*

whose

1 of which person? belonging to which person?: ***Whose*** *umbrella did you borrow?* ***Whose*** *pencil is this?* **2** you use **whose** when you are describing a kind of person, or explaining whom you mean: *An orphan is a child* ***whose*** *parents have both died. All the children* ***whose*** *work is untidy will have to do it again.*

why

because of what? for what reason?: ***Why*** *is Sally crying? Do you know* ***why*** *the teacher is angry with Philip? The reason* ***why*** *she is angry is that he was very late.*

wicked

very bad in the way you behave; very naughty; very cruel: *Some* ***wicked*** *men knocked the old lady down and stole her purse. It is* ***wicked*** *to tell lies.*

> - Same as **bad** or **evil**.
> - The opposite is **good** or **kind**.

wide

1 being a big distance from side to side: *A motorway is a very* ***wide*** *kind of road. The river is too* ***wide*** *to swim across.* **2** being a certain distance from side to side: *The swimming pool is 50 metres long and 15 metres* ***wide****. We measured the doorway to see how* ***wide*** *it was.*

> - Same as **broad**.
> - The opposite is **narrow**.

width

the distance between the two sides of something: *The swimming pool is 15 metres in* ***width****.*

wife

the woman that a man is married to: *Some husbands are good at helping their* ***wives*** *to look after the children. A* ***wife*** *usually changes her surname to her husband's surname.*

> Two **wives**

wig

false hair that you wear over your own hair: *Jenny wore a grey* ***wig*** *when she was acting the part of an old lady in the play.*

wild

1 not used to living near people; not tame: *Pandas and many other kinds of* ***wild*** *animals are disappearing from the world.* **2** not growing in a garden: *Blackberries grow* ***wild*** *along the sides of fields.*

> Meaning 1: The opposite is **tame**.

will

you use **will** to say what people or things are going to do: *Tim says he* ***will*** *come and see me this evening. The concert* ***will*** *take place in June. Mum* ***will*** *not let me watch television until I've finished my homework.* ***Will*** *you please be quiet, children!* ***Will*** *you help me, or*

***won't** you? Dad has phoned to say **he'll** be late home.*

You can shorten:
- **I will** to **I'll**
- **you will** to **you'll**
- **he will** to **he'll**
- **she will** to **she'll**
- **we will** to **we'll**
- **they will** to **they'll**
- **will not** to **won't**

- will, would

willing
wanting to do something; glad to do something: *Are you **willing** to help me? I want some **willing** people to help me paint the scenery for the school play.*

win
to come first in a race or a competition: *Paul **won** the 100-metre race. Will Susan **win** the singing competition? Jenny has **won** second prize in the dancing contest. I **won** this doll at a fair.*

- The opposite is **lose**.
- won, winning, has won

wind
air that is moving very fast: *There is a cold **wind** blowing from the east today. It's very calm today — there's no **wind**. Philip ran like the **wind** to catch the bus.*

Rhymes with **pinned**.

wind
to twist round and round: *Granny is **winding** the wool into a ball. Liz **wound** a ribbon round her pigtail and tied it in a bow. The little road **winds** up the steep hill.*

- Rhymes with **find**.
- wound, winding, has wound

wind up to turn a little screw on a clock or watch, to keep it going: *I forgot to **wind up** my watch last night, and it has stopped.*

windmill
a tall building with four large wooden pieces called 'sails' fixed to it, which are pushed round by the wind: *As the sails of the **windmill** turn, they give power to the machines inside to grind the corn into flour.*

window
an opening in the wall of a building, with a pane of glass fitted into it: *Light comes into a room through the **windows**. I looked out of the **window** to see if it was raining.*

windy
with a lot of wind: *It was so **windy** that Mrs Wang's hat blew off. **Windy** weather is dangerous for ships.*

wing
the part of a bird's or insect's body that it flies with: *Birds have two **wings**. The eagle spreads its **wings** and flew into the sky. Penguins have **wings** but they can't fly. When an insect flies, it moves its **wings** so fast that you can't see them.*

wink
to shut one eye and then open it again quickly: *You **wink** at people to show that you don't really mean what you say. Dad **winked** at me, and asked my little sister if he could borrow her bicycle.*

winner
someone who wins a race or a competition: *Janet was the **winner** of the drawing competition. The other prize-**winners** were John and Kathy.*

winter
the season between autumn and spring: *In the cooler parts of the world, **winter** is the coldest season, with cold winds and snow.*

wipe
1 to clean something by rubbing it with a cloth: *Mum **wiped** the table clean with a wet cloth. Some milk was spilt on the floor, so we had to **wipe** it up.* **2** to dry: *Stop crying — here is a handkerchief to **wipe** your eyes with.*

wiped, wiping, has wiped

wire
a long, very thin piece of metal: *When you switch on the television, electricity goes along **wires** from the plug to the television and makes it work. The fence round the garden is made out of **wire**.*

wisdom
the quality of being wise; knowledge and good sense: *I often ask Granny for her advice because she is full of **wisdom**.*

wise
having a lot of good sense: *Granny is very **wise***

— *she often gives me good advice. It isn't* ***wise*** *to spend your money on toys that you don't need.*

The opposite is **foolish**.

wish

1 to be very eager for something to happen, especially something impossible: *I* ***wish*** *I could fly. Tom* ***wished*** *he could pass his exams without doing any work. I* ***wish*** *I hadn't told the teacher a lie.* **2** **wish** is a polite word for want: *Good morning — I* ***wish*** *to buy a jigsaw for my grandson.* **3** to say that you hope for something for someone else: *I* ***wish*** *you lots of happiness.*

wish

1 something that you are eager for: *In the story, the boy made a* ***wish*** *that he could fly to the moon and his* ***wish*** *came true.* **2** a hope for someone else to have happiness and success: *You send people best* ***wishes*** *on their birthdays.*

witch

a woman with magic powers, especially of an evil kind: *The wicked* ***witch*** *turned the prince into a frog.*

with

1 in someone's company; among other people; among other things: *I like going to football matches* ***with*** *my father. I've been playing badminton* ***with*** *Paul. Put this fork away in the drawer* ***with*** *the other forks.* **2** using something for a job: *Dad mended Jane's doll* ***with*** *some glue. Use this knife to chop the vegetables* ***with***. **3** you use **with** with **cover** and **fill**: *My shoes are covered* ***with*** *mud. Fill this jug* ***with*** *milk.* **4** you use **with** when you talk about fighting or competing: *Jeff has been fighting* ***with*** *Peter again. Susan and Jenny are competing* ***with*** *each other in the badminton contest.* **5** you use **with** to describe someone or something: *I've got a doll* ***with*** *blue eyes and golden hair. A man* ***with*** *a crooked back was going slowly along the road.* **6** you use **with** to say how you do something: *I want you to carry these cups* ***with*** *great care.* **7** because of something: *Liz was shivering* ***with*** *fright.* **8** in the care of someone: *Leave the baby* ***with*** *me — I'll look after him.* **9** here are other ways of using **with**: *Be careful* ***with*** *my camera! What shall I do* ***with*** *these books? Something is wrong* ***with*** *the television set.*

within

1 inside: *There were some funny sounds coming from* ***within*** *the dog's kennel.* **2** taking no longer than a certain time: *The painters said they would finish the job* ***within*** *a fortnight.*

without

1 with none of something; not having something: *We cannot live* ***without*** *air. Sam arrived at the swimming pool* ***without*** *his swimming trunks. I can't fix these screws* ***without*** *a screwdriver.* **2** not with someone: *My sister was feeling sick today, so I went to school* ***without*** *her. If we don't hurry, the bus will leave* ***without*** *us!* **3** not doing something: *Dad must be angry — he left home this morning* ***without*** *saying goodbye. You'll never learn to play the guitar* ***without*** *practising.*

do without not to have something: *There is no milk in the house — we shall have to* ***do without*** *it till tomorrow. You can* ***do without*** *water for three days, but you can't* ***do without*** *air for more than three minutes.*

wizard

a man with magic powers: ***Wizards*** *wear long black coats and tall pointed hats.*

woke

see **wake**: *The noise* ***woke*** *the baby. I* ***woke*** *up very early this morning.*

woken

see **wake**: *The baby was* ***woken*** *by the noise.*

wolf

a wild animal that looks like a large dog, with a pointed nose and pointed ears, and thick grey fur: *A baby* ***wolf*** *is called a cub.* ***Wolves*** *go about together, hunting animals such as deer.*

Several **wolves**

woman

an adult female human being: *When a* ***woman*** *marries a man, she becomes his wife.* ***Women*** *and children have high voices, but men have deep voices.*

Two **women**

won
see win: *Which horse **won** the race? Ray has **won** first prize in the singing contest.*

wonder
1 a feeling you have when you see something strange: *The children were filled with **wonder** when they saw the snow on the ground.* **2** something that a lot of people go and see, such as a splendid building, or a splendid waterfall: *I'd like to see the Great Wall of China and all the other **wonders** of the world.*

wonder
1 to be surprised about something; to be puzzled about something: *Have you ever **wondered** why most people can do things better with their right hands than with their left hands?* **2** to want to know: *I **wonder** what I'll get for my birthday.*

wonderful
very good; very beautiful: *We had a **wonderful** time at the fair. I saw some **wonderful** acrobats on television last night. In the story, the secret garden was full of **wonderful** flowers.*

won't
short for **will not**: *The television **won't** work — what is wrong with it?*

wood
1 the stuff that trees are made of, which is used for making furniture and floors, and is also used as a fuel for burning on a fire: *Pencils are made of **wood**. We need some more **wood** for the fire.* **2** a large group of trees: *The witch lived in the middle of a big, dark **wood**.*
woods a large group of trees: *When you walk through the **woods** you see lots of different kinds of trees.*

wooden
made of wood: *Mum used a **wooden** spoon to stir the stew with. In the park there are lots of **wooden** benches for people to sit on.*

woodpecker
a bird with a long, sharp beak that makes holes in the bark of trees to find insects to eat: *A **woodpecker** makes a loud tapping noise with its beak.*

wool
the thick, soft hair of sheep, which is made into yarn for knitting and weaving: *The **wool** is cut off the sheep and then it is washed and spun into yarn.*

woollen
made of wool: *If you visit Britain in the winter, you will need **woollen** clothes to keep you warm.*

word
a group of letters that mean something: *'He' is a short **word**, and 'headquarters' is a long **word**.*

wore
see **wear**: *Sheila **wore** her red dress for Jenny's party.*

work
1 something you do that needs a lot of energy or a lot of attention: *Today Dad did a lot of **work** in the garden — he dug the soil, weeded the vegetable patch and cut the grass. Your school**work** is improving, Jack. You should all spend at least an hour on your home**work**. At the end of the lesson we hand our **work** to the teacher and she marks it. Roger is doing his arithmetic — don't disturb him while he's at **work**.* **2** a job: *Lots of people come to the city to find **work**.* **3** the place where your job is: *My mother goes to **work** at 8 o'clock. Is she still at **work**? What time does she get home from **work**?*

Meaning 1: the opposite is **rest**.

work
1 to do work: *Mum is **working** in the garden. Dad **works** in a big office. You must **work** harder at your English, Tom — you are not **working** hard enough.* **2** to operate in an automatic way: *The television isn't **working** — it must be broken. The washing-machine won't **work**.*

Meaning 1: the opposite is **rest**.

work out to think out the right answer to something; to solve a problem: *I can't **work out** how to do this puzzle. Have you **worked** that sum **out** yet? **Work out** how many hours there are in a week.*

worker
someone who has a job, especially in a factory: *The nylon factory employs 700 **workers**.*

workman
a man who does jobs such as building and repairing roads and houses: *A **workman** came to repair our roof.*

Two **workmen**

world
1 the planet that we live on; the earth: *Nowadays it is easy to telephone people who live on the other side of the **world**. Which is the highest mountain in the **world**?* **2** another planet: *In the story, the children met some strange creatures from another **world**.*

worm
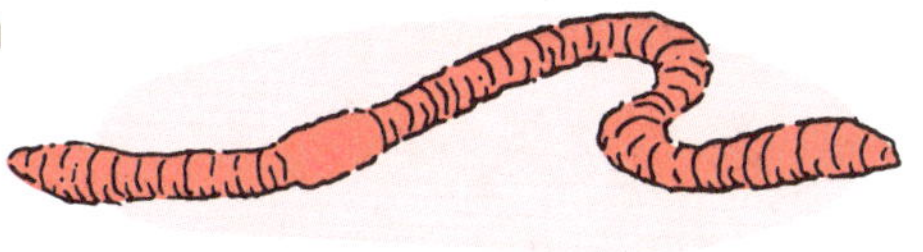

a small animal with a long, narrow body and no legs: *A long **worm** was crawling across the path. Birds eat **worms** and insects.*

worn
see **wear**: *Mike has **worn** glasses since he was four.*

worried
full of worry: *Mum is **worried** because the baby is ill. She is **worried** about the baby.*

worry
to feel unhappy and anxious about something: *Mum **worries** about me when I'm late coming home from school. Don't **worry** so much!* **2** to upset someone: *The bad news **worried** everybody.*

worries, worried, worrying, has worried

worry
worrying about something; something that worries you: *The thought of the exam fills me with **worry**.*

Lots of **worries**

worse
bad compared with something else: *The weather was bad yesterday, but it's **worse** today. The weather is **worse** than it was yesterday. 'Is your headache better now?' 'No, it's **worse**.' Which is **worse** — to be deaf or to be blind?*

The opposite is **better**.

worst
worse than all the others: *Can you remember the **worst** pain you ever had? To be lame is bad, to be deaf is **worse**, but to be blind is **worst** of all.*

The opposite is **best**.

worth
1 having a certain value: *Be careful with that vase — it's **worth** a lot of money! This ring is **worth** about $500. A broken watch is **worth** nothing.* **2** good enough for doing something: *What a silly film that was — it wasn't **worth** watching!*

worth
the amount you can sell something for; the value of something: *This old piano is of very little **worth**. Go to the post office and buy me ten dollars' **worth** of stamps.*

would
1 see **will**: *Andrew said he **would** come and see me this evening. Mum **would** not let me watch television until I had finished my homework. Dad telephoned to say **he'd** be late home.* **2** you use **would** to say something is possible: *David **would** get higher marks for his arithmetic if he worked harder. You **would** have caught the bus if you had hurried. She **would** have been late if she hadn't hurried. I **would** never tell my parents a lie. What **would** you do if you met a tiger?* **3** you often use **would** with **like** to say 'want' in a polite way: *I **would like** some more ice-cream, please. **Would** you **like** to come to my party? Anna says **she'd like** a doll for her birthday.*

You can shorten:
- **I would** to **I'd**
- **you would** to **you'd**
- **he would** to **he'd**
- **she would** to **she'd**
- **we would** to **we'd**
- **they would** to **they'd**

wouldn't
short for **would not**: *Mary **wouldn't** tell me her secret. You'd like to go to the circus, **wouldn't** you?*

wound
an injury, especially one that is made with a weapon: *The bullet made a bad **wound** in the soldier's leg. The **wound** left a scar on his leg.*

Say **woond**.

wound
to hurt a person or an animal with a weapon: *Many soldiers were **wounded** in the battle. The spear **wounded** the lioness but it didn't kill her.*

Say **woond**.

wound
see **wind**: *Mum **wound** the wool into a ball. Has the clock been **wound**?*

Say **wownd**.

wove
see **weave**: *The workers in the mill **wove** the woollen yarn into cloth.*

woven
see **weave**: *This silk cloth was **woven** in Japan.*

wrap
to put something round; to put a cover round something: *Peter **wrapped** a towel round himself after his shower. I need some pretty paper to **wrap** Mum's birthday present in.*

wrapped, wrapping, has wrapped

wrap up 1 to put a cover round something: *Jenny bought a book for her dad and **wrapped** it **up** in red paper.* **2** to put warm clothes on: *You must **wrap** the baby **up** well in cold weather.*

wrapping
the paper round a parcel: *Mum undid the string and took the **wrapping** off her present.*

wrestle
to fight someone, especially as a sport, using your hands, arms and legs, but not your fists: *In Sumo **wrestling**, one man tries to push the other one out of the ring. The two boys **wrestled** with each other in the playground.*

wrestled, wrestling, has wrestled

wriggle
to twist about: *The long worm **wriggled** through the grass. Please stop **wriggling** and stand still while I comb your hair.*

wriggled, wriggling, has wriggled

wring
to squeeze something by twisting it, especially to get rid of the water in it: ***Wring** the water out of the towel before you hang it up to dry. Mum washed the tablecloth and **wrung** it out.*

wrung, wringing, has wrung

wrist
the part of your arm just above your hand: *You wear a watch round your **wrist**.*

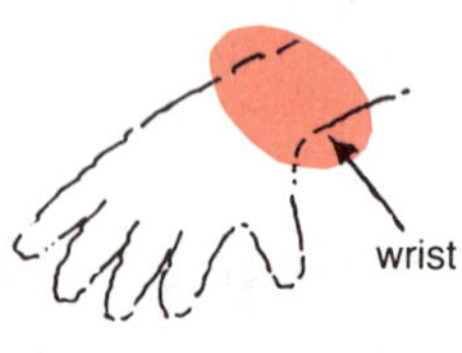

write
1 to make letters and words, especially on paper, with a pen or pencil: *You go to school to learn to read and **write**. The teacher gave the children some paper to **write** on. They all **wrote** their names at the top of the paper. John is **writing** his homework in his exercise book. The teacher **writes** out the difficult words on the blackboard.* **2** to make up a story, or a book, or a poem: *My uncle is **writing** a book about aeroplanes. Miss Pitt wants us to **write** some stories and poems for the school magazine.* **3** to write a letter to someone and send it: *I'll **write** to you from New Zealand when I get there. I **wrote** a long letter to Granny.*

wrote, writing, has written

write down to make a note about something: ***Write down** my address so that you won't forget it.*

writer
someone who writes books or stories; someone who writes things for magazines and newspapers: *Which **writer** wrote the book called 'Alice in Wonderland'?*

writing
the way you write: *Your **writing** is untidy — you must improve it.*

written
see write: *Have you **written** your composition yet?*

wrong
1 not correct: *That's the **wrong** way to do the sum. I got seven sums right and three sums **wrong**. You've spelt 'design' **wrong**. I've brought the **wrong** bag home — this is Janet's. I thought that baby foxes were called puppies, but I was **wrong**. You can't read a book if you hold it the **wrong** way up.* **2** bad; not right: *It is **wrong** to tell lies. Tom did **wrong** to steal Jenny's pen.* **3** not working properly; not going well: *What is **wrong** with the television? The computer has gone **wrong**. What's **wrong** — why are you crying?*

Meanings 1 and 2: the opposite is **right**.

wrote
see **write**: *The teacher **wrote** the word on the blackboard.*

wrung
see **wring**: *Mum **wrung** out the wet towel. Have you **wrung** the cloth out?*

X-ray
a special kind of photograph that shows people's bones inside their bodies: *The nurse at the hospital took an* ***X-ray*** *of Joe's ankle to see if it was broken.*

xylophone

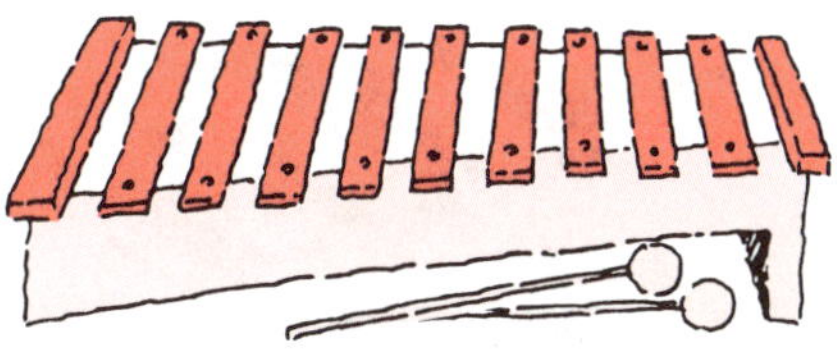

an instrument made of flat bars of different lengths arranged side by side, which you strike with a small hammer to play a tune: *I have just learnt to play a new tune on the* ***xylophone****.*

yacht
a small sailing ship: *My uncle has a* ***yacht*** *with red sails. Last week he sailed his* ***yacht*** *from Melaka to Singapore.*

Say **yot**.

yard
1 a unit of length that is almost as long as a metre: *The swimming pool is 30* ***yards*** *long and 10* ***yards*** *wide.* **2** a space near a building, with hard ground, not grass: *There is a* ***yard*** *behind our school for us to play in, with a big wall round it. Judy and Ginny were bouncing balls in the* ***yard****.*

yarn
thread: *The woollen* ***yarn*** *was woven into cloth at the mill.*

yawn
to take a big breath and stretch your mouth very wide, when you are tired: *You're* ***yawning****, Peter — it's time you went to bed!*

year
the time that the earth takes to go once round the sun: *There are 365 days in a* ***year****. There are 12 months in a* ***year****. I started school three* ***years*** *ago. 'How old are you?' 'I'm seven* ***years*** *old.' The first day of the* ***year*** *is 1 January and the last day is 31 December.*
all year round for the whole year: *In Singapore you can swim in the sea* ***all year round****, because the weather is always hot.*

yell
to cry very loudly: *My little sister* ***yelled*** *when she fell and hurt her knee.*

yellow
the colour of the sun; the colour of the yolk of an egg: *A daisy has a* ***yellow*** *centre.* ***Yellow*** *is a bright colour.*

yes
the opposite of **no**: *'Do you like English, Paul?'* ***'Yes****, I do.' 'Would you like a biscuit?'* ***'Yes****, please.' 'Can you see the yacht?'* ***'Yes****, I can.' 'Have you read this book?'* ***'Yes****, I have.' 'You aren't ten yet, are you?'* ***'Yes****, I am.' I asked Mum if I could go to Jim's party, and she said* ***yes****.*

yesterday
the day before today: ***Yesterday*** *it was raining, but today it is fine. I didn't have time to do my homework* ***yesterday*** *evening, so I'm doing it this morning instead.*

yet
in the time up till now; so far: *Has the mail arrived* ***yet****? 'Have you written to Granny* ***yet****, to thank her for the present?' 'No, not* ***yet****.' Don't come in — I'm not dressed* ***yet****.*

yoghurt
a food that is made from milk, and has a sour taste: *I like* ***yoghurt*** *with a strawberry flavour.*

yolk
the yellow middle part of an egg: *The* ***yolk*** *of an egg is liquid when it is raw, and solid when it is cooked.*

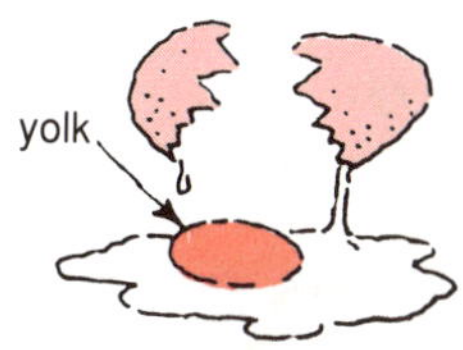

you
you use **you** for the person you are speaking to: *Do **you** want to come shopping with me? Shall I tell **you** a secret? Can I help **you**? David and I are going with Dad but **you** and Diana are going with Mum.*

you'd
short for **you would** and **you had**: ***You'd** have won if **you'd** run harder.*

you'll
short for **you will**: ***You'll** be late if you don't hurry.*

young
not old; little: ***Young** babies sleep most of the time. You're too **young** to go to the cinema alone. A **young** cow is called a calf. Kay is two years **younger** than I am. Who is the **youngest** in the class?*

The opposite is **old**.

your
belonging to you: *Is this **your** pen or Angela's? Don't forget to bring **your** camera with you. **Your** nose is above your mouth.*

you're
short for **you are**: ***You're** looking very smart today.*

yours
you use **yours** for something that belongs to the person you are speaking to: *This is Tom's book, not **yours**. **Yours** is on your desk. Is Steven a friend of **yours**?*

yourself
you use **yourself** or **yourselves** when the person or the people you are speaking to do something to or for themselves: *You spend too long looking at **yourself** in the mirror, Susan! You'll all make **yourselves** sick if you eat so much jelly and ice-cream.*

yourself, yourselves

youth
the time when you are young: *Dad spent his **youth** on a farm, but he came to the city when he was 20.*

you've
short for **you have**: ***You've** broken my pencil.*

yo-yo
a toy that rolls up and down a piece of string: *Sit still, Mary — you keep jumping up and down like a **yo-yo**.*

zebra
an animal like a small horse, that has a white body with black stripes: ***Zebras** live in Africa. Lions hunt **zebras**.*

zebra-crossing

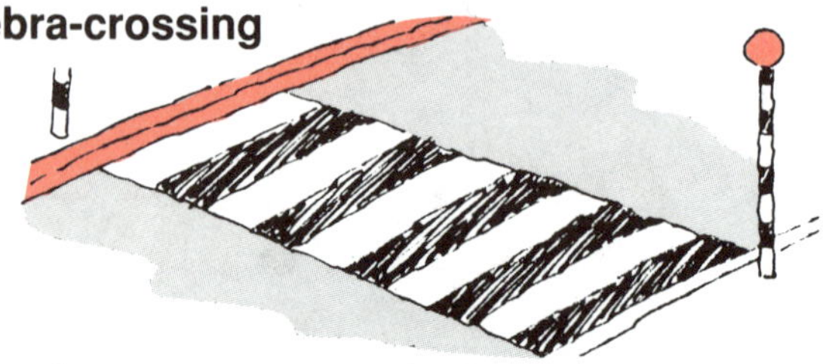

a place on a street marked with white stripes, where cars stop for pedestrians to cross: *You should always cross the street at the **zebra-crossing**.*

zero
1 the number 0: *The number 100 has a one and two **zeros**.* **2** the place on a thermometer that temperatures are measured from: *It is very cold today — the temperature is two degrees below **zero**.* **3** the time when something is going to happen, such as a spaceship taking off: *It is now five minutes to **zero**.*

zig-zag

full of sharp bends: *A **zig-zag** path led up the mountain. The letter Z is made of a **zig-zag** line.*

zip or **zipper**
a long, narrow metal part on a piece of clothing, for fastening it: *I can't wear this skirt because the **zip** is broken. Could you fasten the **zipper** on my dress for me?*

zoo
a large place where lots of wild animals are kept for people to go and see: *The monkeys are my favourite animals at the **zoo**.*